LABOUR LAW, WORK, AND FAMILY

LABOUR LAW, WORK, AND FAMILY

Critical and Comparative Perspectives

Edited by
JOANNE CONAGHAN
and
KERRY RITTICH

OXFORD
UNIVERSITY PRESS

OXFORD
UNIVERSITY PRESS

Great Clarendon Street, Oxford OX2 6DP

Oxford University Press is a department of the University of Oxford.
It furthers the University's objective of excellence in research, scholarship,
and education by publishing worldwide in

Oxford New York

Auckland Cape Town Dar es Salaam Hong Kong Karachi
Kuala Lumpur Madrid Melbourne Mexico City Nairobi
New Delhi Shanghai Taipei Toronto

With offices in

Argentina Austria Brazil Chile Czech Republic France Greece
Guatemala Hungary Italy Japan Poland Portugal Singapore
South Korea Switzerland Thailand Turkey Ukraine Vietnam

Oxford is a registered trade mark of Oxford University Press
in the UK and in certain other countries

Published in the United States
by Oxford University Press Inc., New York

British Library Cataloguing in Publication Data

Data available

Library of Congress Cataloging in Publication Data

Labour law, work, and family : critical and comparative perspectives / edited by
Joanne Conaghan and Kerry Rittich.
  p. cm.
Includes bibliographical references and index.
ISBN-13: 978–0–19–928703–1
ISBN-10: 0–19–928703–1
1. Labor laws and legislation. 2. Work and family. 3. Women—
Employment—Law and legislation I. Conaghan, Joanne. II. Rittich, Kerry.
K1820.L33 2005
344.01—dc22

2005018525

Typeset by Newgen Imaging Systems (P) Ltd., Chennai, India
Printed in Great Britain
on acid-free paper by
Biddles Ltd., King's Lynn

ISBN 0–19–928703–1   978–0–19–928703–1

1 3 5 7 9 10 8 6 4 2

Contents

Part III. 'Family-Friendly' Labour Law

Part IV. Conclusion: A Cautionary Tale

Notes on Contributors

Mutsuko Asakura is Professor of Law at Waseda University, Japan. She lectures and researches widely in the areas of labour law, employment law, social security law, and feminist jurisprudence and has published various articles and books in these fields.

Anna Chapman is a Senior Lecturer in Law and a member of the Centre for Employment and Labour Relations Law at the University of Melbourne. She teaches Australian labour law, anti-discrimination law, and contracts, and is a Director of Studies of the Labour Relations Law Graduate Teaching Programme. Her research focuses on law and sexual preference, gender, and race in labour markets.

Hugh Collins studied law at Oxford and Harvard Universities. He is currently Professor of English Law at the London School of Economics, and was formerly a Fellow of Brasenose College, Oxford. His publications include *Justice in Dismissal: The Law of Termination of Employment* (OUP, 1992) and *Employment Law* (Clarendon Press, 2003).

Joanne Conaghan is a Professor of Law at the University of Kent at Canterbury and former managing editor of *Feminist Legal Studies*. Her areas of research include labour law, tort, and feminist legal theory, and she has published widely in all three fields. She is a member of the Co-ordinating Committee of the International Network on Transformative Employment and Labour Law (INTELL) and co-editor (with Richard Michael Fischl and Karl Klare) of *Labour Law in an Era of Globalization: Transformative Practices and Possibilities* (OUP, 2002).

Richard Michael Fischl is Professor of Law at the University of Miami in Coral Gables, Florida. A former appellate lawyer with the National Labor Relations Board, he teaches various courses on labour and employment law. His articles on labour law and legal theory have appeared in various law journals, and he is co-editor (with Joanne Conaghan and Karl Klare) of *Labour Law in an Era of Globalization: Transformative Practices and Possibilities* (OUP, 2002). He is a member of the Co-ordinating Committee of the International Network on Transformative Employment and Labour Law (INTELL).

Judy Fudge is a Professor at Osgoode Hall Law School, York University in Toronto. She has published widely on labour and employment topics, with a special emphasis on the regulation of women's paid work, labour law history, and precarious employment. Her publications include *Labour before the Law* (OUP, 2001) and the forthcoming collection (co-edited with Rosemary Owens) *Precarious Work, Women, and the New Economy: The Challenge to Legal Norms* (Hart Publishing, 2005).

Hiroko Hayashi is Professor of Law at the Faculty of Law, Fukuoka University. She was a Fulbright scholar at Yale University, New York University, and Columbia University; an ACLS fellow at Cornell University and at Hastings College of Law, University of California, and a visiting scholar at the School of Management and Labor Relations, Rutgers University. In 1992 she submitted an expert opinion to the Fukuoka District Court, which established the legal elements of sexual harassment and led to the first successful sexual harassment suit in Japan. She is the author of many articles in the areas of employment discrimination, sexual harassment, and workers' compensation, and has lectured widely overseas as well as in Japan.

Csilla Kollonay Lehoczky is a Professor of Law and Chair of the Labour and Social Law Department at the Eötvös Loránd University, Budapest, Hungary. She also teaches at the Central European University in Budapest. She is a member of the European Committee of Social Rights supervising the implementation of the European Social Charter. Her field of interest and publications cover various areas of labour and employment law, social protection, and equal opportunities law.

Maria Rosaria Marella is Professor of Law at the Faculty of Law, University of Perugia, Italy and managing editor of the Italian legal journal, *Rivista critica del diritto privato*. Her areas of research include torts, family law, feminist legal theory, and European private law. She has published and lectured widely in all these fields.

Clare McGlynn is a Professor of Law at the University of Durham, UK. Her current research interests include anti-discrimination law and the emerging family law of the European Union. She is also the author of *The Woman Lawyer: Making the Difference* (Butterworths, 1998).

Guy Mundlak is a Professor of Law at the Faculty of Law and the Department of Labour Studies, Tel-Aviv University. He teaches and studies the role of law in the design of social policy, and its effects on labour market institutions. He is also writing and actively advocating the advancement of social human rights and equal treatment, primarily in the fields of work and social security.

Rosemary J. Owens is a Reader in the Law School at the University of Adelaide, where she researches and teaches labour and industrial relations law, constitutional law, and feminist legal theory. Her particular research interests are the construction of women and work in international and national legal systems and the legal regulation of contingent work. She is editor of the *Australian Journal of Labour Law*.

Kerry Rittich is Associate Professor in the Faculty of Law and the Women's Studies Programme at the University of Toronto. She researches in the areas of international law and institutions, labour law, human rights, feminist theory, and critical legal theories. She is the author of *Recharacterizing Restructuring: Law, Distribution, and Gender in Market Reform* (Kluwer Law International, 2002) and a member of the Co-ordinating Committee of the International Network on Transformative Employment and Labour Law (INTELL).

Lucy Williams is Professor of Law at Northeastern University, where she was the School of Law's 1994–5 Public Interest Distinguished Professor. She has written and lectured widely in the area of welfare and poverty law. Before entering academic life, Lucy practised poverty law at the Legal Assistance Foundation of Chicago and later at the Massachusetts Law Reform Institute. She is also a member of the Co-ordinating Committee of the International Network on Transformative Employment and Labour Law (INTELL).

Acknowledgements

This book has been a long time in gestation. Ever since it emerged as a critical issue in the first gathering of participants in the International Network on Transformative Employment and Labour Law (INTELL) in Andover in 1994, the work/family divide has been a key focus of discussion and debate both on and off the conference floor at subsequent INTELL gatherings. In this way, the book can truly be said to be the collective result of long engagement among a group of scholars who come from a range of diverse jurisdictions and disciplinary orientations but who share a common interest in the pursuit of a transformative labour law project. We would like therefore to thank all of our colleagues in INTELL, past and present, for the many ways in which they have contributed to bringing this project to its intellectual fruition.

A number of individuals have played a crucial role in ensuring that this book came about. These include, most importantly, our contributors; we are abundantly grateful for their insight, imagination, patience, and commitment. We are also grateful to our institutions, the Universities of Toronto and Kent, without whose financial support we would not have been able to meet and plan this project. The supportive role played by our co-members of the Co-ordinating Committee of INTELL, Michael Fischl, Karl Klare, and Lucy Williams, cannot be overstated. They have been wonderful advisers, mentors, friends, and colleagues and they have been there for us even through great personal tragedies of their own. Others colleagues associated with INTELL, such as Marley Weiss, have also given us assistance at critical points in the completion of this project.

At Kent, we would like to thank John Wightman, Head of Department, for his support throughout the project, and Cheryl Dolder, our enormously dedicated and wonderfully resourceful research assistant. We would also like to thank Mark Dean for his technical assistance and, in particular, for his infinite patience with stubborn and idiosyncratic documents. Joanne would also like to thank her colleagues from *Feminist Legal Studies* and from the AHRC Centre for Research on Law, Gender, and Sexuality, for the many opportunities they provided for exploring the themes and issues which have gone into the making of this book.

At the University of Toronto, the Wright Foundation for Legal Research provided economic support that enabled the recruitment of extremely dedicated and skilled research assistants, Sarah Davidson-Ladly and Ruth Chen. The Social Sciences and Humanities Research Council of Canada also provided crucial funding for research costs associated with this project.

Finally, and of course most importantly, our gratitude goes to those we love—to our families and particularly to our partners, Paddy and Robert. The times at which each of them stepped in to close up the breach between the demands of work and those of family and the wider communities of which we are a part, sometimes at marked personal cost, are simply too numerable to mention. They are both continual reminders of the arbitrary and unstable boundaries between the world of work and the rest of life, boundaries they negotiate with grace and ease; and they remind us daily why issues of work and family are of fundamental importance both to personal happiness and to human flourishing.

List of Abbreviations

ACTU	Australian Council of Trade Unions
AFL-CIO	American Federation of Labour-Congress of Industrial Organizations
AFDC	Aid to Families with Dependent Children
AJLL	*Australian Journal of Labour Law*
ALI	American Law Institute
AWA	Australian Workplace Agreement
BIG	Basic Income Grant
BJIR	*British Journal of Industrial Relations*
CEE	Central Eastern European
CEDAW	Committee on the Elimination of All Forms of Discrimination Against Women
CVWP	Countervailing Workers' Power
DfEE	Department for Education and Employment (UK) (now DfeS)
DfES	Department for Education and Skills (UK)
DTI	Department of Trade and Industry (UK)
EC	European Community
ECJ	European Court of Justice
EIRO	European Industrial Relations Observatory
EJIL	*European Journal of International Law*
EPWP	Expanded Public Works Programme
EU	European Union
FFW	Family Friendly Workplace
GDP	Gross Domestic Product
HREOC	Human Rights and Equal Opportunity Commission (Australia)
HRM	Human Resources Management
IFI	international financial institutions
ILJ	*Industrial Law Journal* (UK)
ILO	International Labour Organization
IMF	International Monetary Fund
INTELL	International Network on Transformative Employment and Labour Law
LQR	*Law Quarterly Review*
MLR	*Modern Law Review*
MNC	Multinational Corporation
MNE	Multinational Enterprise
OECD	Organization for Economic Cooperation and Development
OJLS	*Oxford Journal of Legal Studies*
OUP	Oxford University Press

TANF	Temporary Assistance to Needy Families
TUC	Trades Union Congress
UCC	Uniform Commercial Code
UK	United Kingdom
UN	United Nations
UNDP	United Nations Development Programme
USA	United States of America
WTO	World Trade Organization

1

Introduction: Interrogating the Work/ Family Divide

JOANNE CONAGHAN AND KERRY RITTICH

In recent years, gender has emerged as an increasingly important focus of attention in discourse in and around labour law, gradually moving from the margin to the mainstream of labour law debate. A number of reasons account for gender's increased prominence in legal and political discourse around work. As the labour force has been 'feminized' and women have ceased to be secondary/peripheral workers, the male norm around which labour law has been structured has become both less persuasive and more problematic. As a consequence, analyses of gender inequality have become progressively more sophisticated, implicating core aspects of traditional labour law frameworks (for example, employment protection provision or collective bargaining practices) in the creation of adverse distributional effects for women. Meanwhile, economic restructuring and the 'feminization' of labour have repositioned certain features of working life typically associated with women—low pay, flexible working practices, job insecurity—as central labour concerns, while the decline in developed economies of the family wage and the corresponding increase in the participation of women with young children in paid work has forced the issue of reconciling work and family obligations on to legal and policy agendas. Finally, against the background of these developments, the rhetoric and reality of globalization has brought into relief the ubiquity and extent of women's economic exploitation worldwide, compelling an examination of its particular manifestations in different contexts and the role of law and institutions in its production.

Inevitably, this application of a gender lens to the world of work has served simultaneously to highlight and problematize the structural and discursive boundaries between work and family, production and reproduction, paid and unpaid work. The rise in demand for contingent labour combined with legal and policy initiatives to promote 'family-friendly' working practices in developed economies have brought into focus the dependence of current workplace norms on a particular social paradigm which assumes the performance of considerable amounts of unpaid care work by women in a home and/or community context. This dependence is reflected in labour law and discourse. Indeed, virtually all of the conceptual and analytical tools which labour law deploys—concepts of work, worker, or workplace; notions of cost, benefit, and the allocation of value; models of justice and/or efficiency—presuppose a (gendered) division of labour in which 'reproductive' work is sharply distinguished from 'productive' work, and is largely consigned to the 'private' realm of non-market relations.

As a consequence, while work remains a deeply gendered activity with systemic adverse distributional outcomes for women, gender is assigned little analytical significance in conventional labour law discourse. Moreover, while virtually all labour regulation strategies are necessarily shaped and informed by encounters at the boundaries of the productive and reproductive realms, labour law fails to acknowledge or take account of this in large part because of a lack of any conceptual apparatus to identify and chart such encounters.

The object of this collection of essays is to consider the myriad implications for labour law—whether as a discipline, a mode of regulation, a repository of norms, or a site of political conflict—of reconceiving the terrain of work in terms which acknowledge the structural and discursive effects of the work/family boundary and reposition unpaid care work as integral to the performance and structure of productive activity. The aim is to demonstrate why and how attention to the intersection of the spheres of work and family, rather than a matter primarily of interest to women and feminist scholars, is central to the regulatory, policy, and institutional challenges which states and policymakers currently face. Here, we seek to launch this project by situating it, substantively and methodologically, within the broader context of contemporary debate around the world of work. We also provide a brief summary of the individual chapters and an account of the schematic structure within which they are located.

I WORK, FAMILY, AND 'THE HORIZONS OF TRANSFORMATIVE LABOUR LAW'[1]

All of the contributors to this volume are participants in the International Network on Transformative Employment and Labour Law (INTELL), an informal international network of scholars who, since 1994, have been engaging in transnational dialogue which seeks to identify, analyse, and respond to the conceptual, theoretical, and policy challenges posed for labour law by globalization. In 2002, a first collection of INTELL essays,

---

[1] See Klare, K., 'The Horizons of Transformative Labour Law', in J. Conaghan, R. M. Fischl, and K. Klare (eds.), *Labour Law in an Era of Globalization: Transformative Practices and Possibilities* (Oxford: OUP, 2002), 3.

Labour Law in an Era of Globalization, was published, bringing together key themes and contentions arising from such engagements. In particular, the book examined how transformations in the world of work, sometimes identified in terms of 'globalization'[2] or the 'new economy',[3] have changed the terrain upon which labour law operates and called into question the operative assumptions underpinning the rules and institutions regulating work, assumptions which have guided the activities and analyses of labour and employment lawyers and scholars for at least half a century. A central premise of many of the analyses in the collection was that the rules and institutions governing work and the concepts and assumptions underlying established approaches to the legal regulation of work might themselves contribute to the 'problem of work' in the new economy. Contributors probed the ways in which law creates and supports the evolution of workplace practices; how it tilts the playing field between workers and employers in the new economy; and how it creates advantages and disadvantages among workers in different sectors and regions.

The essays in this new collection pick up on the emerging significance of work and family issues in *Labour Law in an Era of Globalization* and take them to be of key importance in understanding, tracking, and evaluating current changes in the world of work. They consider how the terrain of 'work' is legally constituted and regulated through the creation and deployment of distinctions such as public and private, work and family, production and reproduction. In particular, they question how we classify 'workplace' issues and separate them from family, household, or 'private' concerns. They examine the ways in which these legal classifications have particular distributive outcomes, imposing differential costs, risks, and burdens on, inter alia, women and men. The essays also attempt to explain how and why the debates around the work/family divide have taken the form that they have in particular contexts and with what effects.

Work/family issues were once understood to be almost entirely concerned with women. However, increasingly, negotiating the work/family boundary is recognized as central to the regulatory challenges of the new economy. Changes in both labour markets and households have destabilized the operative assumptions of the rules and institutions governing work and social protection in fundamental rather than marginal ways. Workers are no longer presumptively male—in most industrialized states, the labour market participation of women

---

[2] For broader consideration of globalization in a labour law context, see essays in Conaghan et al., above, n. 1, esp., Klare, above, n. 1.

[3] For an account and analysis of 'new economy' discourse in a labour law context, see Conaghan, J., 'Labour Law and "New Economy" Discourse', *AJLL*, 16 (2003), 9.

approaches if not equals that of men. In addition, households are no longer necessarily organized around the 'nuclear family' norm: rather, they take a variety of different forms and are dynamic rather than stable over time. These transformations call into deep question both the needs and interests of workers and the capacities of households (specifically women) to provide support and labour for a broad range of essential, but 'non-market', social and economic services.

While changes in both the economy and the household have now brought them to the surface in salient ways, the issues raised at the intersection of the household and the labour market are not new. However, we think that there is now an unprecedented opportunity for critical intervention: the limits of conventional legal and social categories have created both an opportunity and a demand for the far-ranging analyses in which the authors of this collection are engaged.

II THE MANY DIMENSIONS OF THE WORK/FAMILY PROJECT

The regulatory debates around work and family encompass a broad set of issues and questions which can be approached in a variety of ways and to a range of different ends. Here we describe three different ways of thinking about work/family issues, all of which are reflected across the essays in the collection. First, analysis of work/family issues can be carried out in a variety of *modes*. Second, work/family issues can be explored across a range of *contexts*. Finally, work/family issues can be examined through the lens of the specific legal and social *issues* or *questions* that they raise.

Modes of analysis

Because legal rules and institutions help to constitute the work/family divide in multiple different ways, a variety of analytical approaches may be deployed to probe it in a labour law context. One prominent approach is *policy-driven* or *instrumental*, that is, concerned with the extent to which analysis of work and family issues can aid the development of particular policy prescriptions or help effect the realization of social, political, or economic goals. Here, a dominant policy concern is with the extent to which the organization of work can be adapted to take better account of family needs. An alternative or additional policy consideration may be the advancement of equality (particularly sex equality) goals and the extent to which current configurations of work and family thwart or inhibit equality-seeking strategies. Yet another emerging policy focus is on the extent to which legal rules and institutions are implicated in advancing or impeding women's labour market participation, something which may be linked to gender equality but may also derive from concerns about economic competitiveness, fiscal or welfare reform, or social inclusion. Such approaches may entail an assessment, on the basis of empirical and other context-based information, of the effectiveness of legal regulation, such as its distributional implications for women, and prescribe policies and reforms accordingly.[4]

An alternative or supplementary approach is to consider issues of work/family from a *normative* perspective, that is, from a perspective which seeks to identify the norms underpinning current conceptions of work and family[5] and subject them to critical scrutiny, often from a competing normative framework. While such analysis is most often centred around equality concerns, distributive justice, and autonomy, it may also engage with a broader set of values and ethical discourses such as social, constitutional, and human rights.[6] Scholars adopting this kind of approach typically draw upon feminist and other critical analyses of equality to problematize the current state of the public/private divide and to make arguments for a better reconciliation of work and family conflicts as a necessary step to women's equality and/or to all workers' self-realization. A particular virtue of explicit normative perspectives is that they can both serve as a strong counterpoint to more narrowly instrumental engagements, especially those which are efficiency-based[7] and bring to the surface the normative dimensions of approaches, such as those prioritizing efficiency over equality, which might otherwise remain submerged.

Yet another way of approaching the work/family divide is to consider it in terms of the *functions* it serves or purports to serve. The idea here is to situate work/family issues within an analysis of the roles which work and family as institutions play, whether separately or together, within the broader context of economic, social, and political imperatives, whether they are the interests of capital or capitalism, the tenets of neo-liberalism, the impact of globalization, or the requirements of social reproduction. Such work tends to include an historical dimension and to focus strongly on processes of social and economic change, as this provides a lens through which legal and political developments in a work/family context

---

[4] Almost all of the essays in this volume address policy and instrumental concerns to some extent. However, see in particular essays by Asakura, Hayashi, and Owens.

[5] See e.g. essay by Chapman, in this volume.

[6] As e.g. in ILO advocacy of a right to 'decent work'. See further Owens, R., 'Decent Work for the Contingent Workforce in the New Economy', *AJLL*, 15 (2002), 209, and Conaghan, in this volume.

[7] See e.g. essay by Rittich considering the tension between equity and efficiency approaches in an international regulatory context.

can be assessed.[8] A related approach is *ideological*. Here the focus is on how discourses around work and family operate to represent as natural and universal forms and practices which are in fact the product of particular economic and social conflicts and political and legal choices. Ideological critiques tend to focus on critical examination of the values and assumptions which underpin and inform legal arrangements around work and family, for example, assumptions about motherhood and/or about women's proper role.[9] They may also be *historical* in orientation, tracking and locating particular ideologies within the broader social and political conflicts and movements and the legal and political traditions that influenced their form and effects.[10] Or, where the purpose is directly to disrupt a prevailing ideological view, the critique may take the form of counter-narrative or even fantasy.[11]

Finally, legal scholarship on work and family may concern itself with the operation of the work/family dichotomy at a *conceptual* or *discursive* level, addressing, for example, the precise legal mechanics involved in the constitution of work and family as separate and conflicting spheres. Here, a main focus is doctrinal, entailing the examination of key legal concepts of labour law, such as the employment relationship, within the broader context of disciplinary norms and conventions. Conceptual or discursive critiques may also seek to bring to the foreground basic assumptions about the legal frame—for example, the belief that contract necessarily furthers autonomy or that private law rules and processes, in contrast to labour market institutions, are neutral in respect of distributive outcomes—in which work/family conflicts arise. A primary purpose of such work is to analyse the relationship between legal forms and concepts and concrete social arrangements, particularly in the broader context of social and economic change, and to highlight the ways in which different conceptual frameworks can themselves cause problems to alternatively materialize or disappear and render potential solutions available or invisible and, in so doing, inhibit, distort, or advance movements towards progressive change.[12]

Contexts of analysis

The analysis of work/family issues can be performed across a wide range of different contexts, as the essays in this collection demonstrate. For

---

[8] Fudge's analysis, in this volume, of working-time regulation in a Canadian context exemplifies this kind of approach.   [9] See e.g. McGlynn, in this volume.
[10] See e.g. Fudge and Kollonay, in this volume.
[11] See e.g. Fischl's account, in this volume, of a fantasy world where women's work counts.   [12] See e.g. essays in this volume by Collins, Conaghan, Marella, and Rittich.

example, the context may be *local*, that is, site-, industry-, region-, or country-specific.[13] It may be *comparative*, looking at work/family issues in different regional and institutional settings simultaneously.[14] It may be concerned with regulatory regimes governing work and family at a *transnational*, *international*, or *global* level.[15] In addition, work/family issues may be considered in an *intra-disciplinary* context, that is, within the confines of labour law rules, contexts, applications, and discourse[16] or the approach may be *cross-disciplinary*, that is, it may operate across disciplines of law encompassing, for example, private law,[17] welfare law,[18] family law,[19] and immigration law.[20] Finally such analysis may be *multi-regulatory*, encompassing modes of regulation other than law, including practice, tradition, agreement, cultural, and social norms,[21] approaches that have always been more common in labour law analysis than in the context of other legal disciplines.

The purpose of identifying the range of different contexts in which work/family issues may surface and be addressed is not only to signal the diversity of approaches in this collection but also to highlight the potential scope and extent of the work/family project in a labour regulation context.

Key issues and questions arising from work/family analysis

While it is an acknowledged tendency of labour law scholarship to equate considerations of work and family with the concerns of women workers, it has not yet fully been recognized how analysis of the work/family nexus may inform many of the wider issues relating to the regulation of work, such as what constitutes work and who is a worker. Nor is there a sophisticated and nuanced appreciation of the way in which these conceptions operate within other fields of law in relation to work, particularly welfare, tax, immigration, and citizenship law. Moreover, work/family issues are also intimately bound up with crucial debates around the transformation in state and economic forms and discourses and strategies of privatization, deregulation, and decentralization. They inform in particular debates concerning labour market flexibility, the regulation of working time, and broader work/life considerations. They are also of significance in the context of debates about different modes of

---

[13] See e.g. essays by Owens, Fudge, Kollonay, Asakura, and Hayashi, in this volume.
[14] See e.g. Mundlak and Marella, in this volume.
[15] See e.g. essays by McGlynn and Rittich, in this volume.
[16] See e.g. Chapman, Collins, and Conaghan, in this volume.
[17] See e.g. Rittich and Marella, in this volume.   [18] See e.g. Williams, in this volume.
[19] See e.g. Marella, in this volume.   [20] See e.g. Mundlak, in this volume.
[21] See e.g. Rittich, Williams, and Hayashi, in this volume, among others.

labour regulation, such as the viability and desirability of individual rights versus collective strategies for workers, the uses and limits of voluntary forms of regulation, the interaction of national or supra-national regulatory levels, and the merits of 'soft' versus 'hard' regulation in the context of work issues. Work/family considerations are also of crucial importance in the context of normative or distributive questions arising from the regulation of work. This is true not just (and most obviously) around sex equality concerns, but also with regard to strategies of social inclusion and debates around distributive justice between the north and the south in the context of global economic integration. Many of the essays in this volume endeavour to locate the work/family debate within these broader considerations, out of the belief that they are of crucial importance to the constitution and regulation of work and the distribution of work-generated benefits and opportunities in the contemporary economic world.

Emerging from these analyses, we think, are a number of key points. Specifically, the work/family nexus and the issues it engages are fundamental to the reconstitution of the sphere of work broadly understood and any failure fully to recognize this is destined to limit the value of analyses of the changes currently taking place in that sphere. Most importantly, because work remains deeply gendered, any aspiration towards a progressive, let alone transformative, labour law must confront and acknowledge the extent to which the work/family divide is implicated in currently inequitable distributive outcomes, both between men and women, among different social classes, and across different geographic and political regions.

Work and family versus the work/life 'balance'

In labour law literature in general, a focus on work and family is often aligned with, equated to, or, increasingly, subsumed by a preoccupation with 'work/life' considerations. Within a work/life frame, a concern with reconciling the conflicting demands of work and family is viewed as part of a broader problem of how to secure a better balance between 'work' and 'life' activities, contributing to the overall well-being of the individual.[22] So viewed, work/life concerns are best understood as expressive of a general aspiration to individual happiness and self-fulfilment, generating

[22] See further Collins, in this volume.

a desire to limit the time spent in paid work activities in order to pursue other, more worthwhile life goals (such as participating in the community or seeing the world).

While recognizing the importance of this broader normative focus and indeed endorsing efforts to relate contemporary labour debates with aspirational discourses about human needs and capacities, we are nevertheless cautious about the analytical deployment of a work/life balance frame in the context of work/family considerations. Moreover, our caution is intensified as the preoccupation shifts from a general concern with gender equality to a specific focus on increasing women's labour market participation, now a central objective in wider debates around labour market regulation and reforms to social security.

Our reasons for caution are as follows. First, concerns with securing a balance between work and life activities tend to reassert and entrench the work/life dichotomy rather than interrogate or destabilize it. Secondly, a work/life balance perspective may render the gendered nature of the work/life dichotomy invisible.[23] Thirdly, the issue of work/life balance becomes reformulated as a gender-neutral preoccupation with fulfilling individual desires or facilitating lifestyle choices. Women's need for access to working arrangements which accommodate their family responsibilities becomes represented in terms of individual 'choices' by particular women to pursue family and career simultaneously, and the role of the state, in the form of family-friendly policies, becomes the facilitation of that choice (among others). However, the structural context in which these choices are exercised—including a long-hours work culture, increasingly competitive labour markets, a new emphasis on performance-based pay, declining real wages, weakened bargaining power and greater overall economic insecurity for workers, and most importantly, labour markets that are still deeply stratified by gender and a gendered division of labour at home—remains relatively unprobed and hence undisturbed, despite the fact that it, too, is affected by the regulatory matrix governing work. This is one reason why family-friendly policies do not tend to impact significantly on the gender division of labour in the private sphere. The potential for ongoing, even increasing, disadvantage to women in such circumstances, despite the presence of policies that recalibrate the work/life balance, seems clear.

These possibilities are not displaced where attention to the work/life balance is linked to concerns about women's low levels of labour market participation and efforts to reduce excessive 'dependency' on the state.

---

[23] See e.g. a recent OECD report on the question which is entitled 'Balancing Work and Family Life: Helping Parents into Paid Employment': OECD, *Employment Outlook 2001* (Paris: OECD, 2001), ch. 4.

Women may benefit from policies that are designed primarily for the purposes of enhancing economic competitiveness and reducing fiscal strain. However, just as routinely they do not, often because of the failure to observe that such 'non-working', 'dependent' women are in fact performing crucial work and providing valuable services on an unpaid basis, work that they typically must continue to perform even as they enter the market. Thus, there is no guarantee that the attempt to 'accommodate' women's family obligations in the context of these objectives will be progressive rather than coercive and disadvantageous for women. The state's strong economic interest in the regulation of social reproduction and the potential for conflict between the demands of gender equality and other policy objectives tends not to surface in analyses conducted under the rubric of 'choice' and in the neutral language of 'balancing'.

Our point is not that labour scholars should eschew broader engagements with the relation between work and life—indeed, we would encourage such engagements—or confine their attention to family-focused concerns in which the gender dimension is more evident. However, it is important not to become, or remain, blind in the pursuit of 'life' to the extent to which 'work' remains expressive of a form of social and economic organization in which caregiving is positioned as a largely unpaid, gendered activity necessarily outside the core domain of labour. Rather, it is important to adhere to an analytical frame in which the very process of conceiving 'work' and 'life' as separate spheres is thoroughly interrogated. It is our contention that this requires, above all, attention to the relationship between gender and forms of work, both 'paid' and unpaid', and it is in the context of the work/family nexus, not work/life balance that this key relationship emerges as central.

Situating debate about work and family

The collection opens with two chapters, by Joanne Conaghan and Kerry Rittich, which locate work and family issues within the broader contours of contemporary labour law and market reform debates. Conaghan's essay engages with the disciplinary tradition of labour law. Her concern is to highlight the extent to which the current parameters of labour law constrain the development of effective new ways of thinking about work and family, particularly in the context of radical changes in the material world of work. She argues that for labour law scholars to fulfil their progressive aspirations they must rethink the categories through which those aspirations are articulated as well as the contexts in which they are deployed. Conaghan's critique of labour law as a discipline is followed by Rittich's engagement with current approaches to market reform and governance within the international financial institutions. Rittich's analysis shows how, while reform proposals in this context often advocate attention to gender equality, largely because of the potential overlap between improved equality and greater efficiency and economic growth, nonetheless analyses of market processes and outcomes are often blind to the economic costs and contributions of unpaid work. Moreover, an enduring scepticism about labour market regulation and state 'intervention' in the economy works to discourage the use of institutional mechanisms that might redistribute the costs and risks of care in more equitable ways. The result, Rittich contends, are efforts to encourage greater market participation by women under increasingly competitive conditions, something which seems destined to exacerbate gender inequality even as gender equality as a concept becomes normalized.

Together these opening chapters set the scene for a closer look at particular aspects of the work/family debate throughout the rest of the collection.

Reimagining the worker

One of the most powerful and pervasive themes emerging from scholarly scrutiny of the intersection of work and family is the presence and operative effects of an idealized worker whose experience in the labour market and encounters with paid work are unencumbered by considerations derived from their caregiving responsibilities in a family context. A related concern is the reliance upon a particular conception of paid work and the privileging of the paid work relationship as synonymous with 'work' for purposes of debate about labour regulation and policy-making. The chapters in this section engage with these images of work and worker with a view to problematizing them and reimagining the terrain they now occupy within the field of labour law. As their authors indicate in various ways, the legal rules and institutions, both existing and proposed, which govern work and labour markets not only reflect deeply problematic ideas about work and workers, they help to constitute or reinforce some of the very problems scholars and policymakers are now attempting to address.

Chapman's essay draws upon Sandra Berns' model of the 'unencumbered citizen'[24] and applies it to particular areas of Australian labour law such as the arbitration awards system and the provisions of sex discrimination law. Chapman contends that a close scrutiny of Australian labour regulation supports Berns' thesis that although the male breadwinner model of worker is in decline, both in fact and in labour policy and

---

[24] Berns, S., *Women Going Backwards: Law and Change in a Family-Unfriendly Society* (Aldershot: Ashgate Publishing, 2002).

lawmaking, the paradigmatic model of worker remains unencumbered, that is, without concrete responsibility for anyone other than oneself. The implications of this model in terms of limiting women's opportunities to participate in paid work are then considered. This is followed by a rather different perspective adopted by Hugh Collins. Collins explores the way in which demands for greater worker flexibility are changing the very basis of the employment relationship. Focusing in particular on legal initiatives to enhance worker access to flexible working arrangements, Collins argues that despite limitations in form and content, the legal enshrining of a 'right to flexibility' has the potential fundamentally to alter the traditional power dynamics between workers and employers, particularly with regard to matters of working time.

Guy Mundlak takes up the theme of working time in his study of the regulation of 'live-in' domestic workers across a number of jurisdictions. Mundlak argues that difficulties encountered by states in regulating the working hours of live-ins are illustrative of the way in which traditional labour law mechanisms depend upon clear boundaries between work and life, workplace and home, working time and non-working time, boundaries which dissolve in the context of the concrete experience of domestic live-ins. Mundlak contends that the solution to the problem of working time regulation in a live-in context cannot be found in either traditional labour law or mainstream feminist discourse, and that a key to understanding (and therefore going some way to solving) the problem of live-in labour regulation requires confronting the class and alienage dimensions to the issue. Maria Rosaria Marella approaches the question of how to conceptualize and attribute value to domestic work from the perspective of private law, contrasting the value of solidarity normally associated with the family with the idea of exchange which lies at the heart of contract law. Surveying the case law and the accompanying literature in both European and North American jurisdictions, Marella demonstrates the incoherent stance adopted by the courts in relation to the economic valuation of women's care work and considers the merits and demerits, from a gender equity perspective, of 'marketizing' the family, that is, of introducing market norms of promise and exchange into the sphere of 'solidaristic', intimate relations.

The final two essays in this section focus on notions of work. Mutsuko Asakura highlights the gendered character of work in a Japanese context and shows how this has been intensified by greater diversification in the forms of work, to the detriment of women workers. She goes on to assess the effectiveness of legal steps to address the problems of women workers in the context of the proliferation of 'atypical' work. Asakura's concern with the problems in particular of low-waged, precarious workers presages Lucy Williams' focus on what she calls 'gaps in the work-family discussion'. As Williams points out, the distinction between 'work' and 'family' does not adequately reflect the way in which work is carried out or experienced either by poor women in the industrialized world or by the majority of women in developing countries; they are better understood to be engaged in 'family provisioning' aimed at family survival through a fluid combination of paid work, unpaid family work, 'grey' market and subsistence work. Williams' chapter is an indictment of the preoccupation by both middle-class feminists and economic reformers with paid work as the primary emancipatory solution to the problem of women's disadvantage. It is also a call to progressive labour scholars to take seriously the position of poor women who occupy the fringes of traditional labour terrain or fall outside its margins altogether, by rethinking the distinctions between work and family.

Family-friendly labour law

When issues of work and family surface in labour law discourse it is almost invariably in the context of 'family-friendly' policies or the 'work/life balance'. However, the primary concern is usually to increase the labour market participation of women and the primary focus has become the development of mechanisms, both legal and extra-legal, which allow women workers to effect a better reconciliation of their competing market and family demands. In many ways, developments in labour law have simply mirrored wider reform proposals to increase the number of women workers in order to relieve the wage pressure on employers and reduce the fiscal burden that 'non-productive', 'dependent' citizens impose on states. In view of the underlying concerns, it is not surprising that the resulting reforms typically still compel women to pay a price in terms of leisure time, income, and/or work opportunities. The failure to move beyond the goal of reconciliation and consider reforms that would challenge and subvert either the gender division of labour at home or the presumption of the unencumbered worker at work raises serious questions about whether 'family-friendly' equates with 'women-friendly' and whether there is anything of substance to be gained—for women and for workers generally—from family-friendly initiatives. These themes inform the chapters in this section of the collection.

Clare McGlynn sets the scene by presenting a critical overview of EU law and policy in a family-friendly context. She argues that although European policy rhetoric is strongly imbued with gender equality aspirations, the legal reality, reflected in particular in decisions of the European Court of Justice, is the reinscribing of gendered norms of parenting into the evolving jurisprudence which do little to challenge the gendered division of labour in a family-based, caregiving context.

Rosemary Owens takes up these themes in an Australian context, considering recent initiatives to introduce paid maternity leave. Owens locates the debate about paid leave within the context of a broader set of changes in Australia, including changing workplace demographics, pressures on businesses to adapt to the demands of a 'new', global economy, and concerns about the declining fertility rate and the ageing of the Australian population. She argues that the focus on paid leave, with its institutional acceptance of the separation of work and family and its denial of the economic importance of reproductive labour, is not only an inadequate response to the serious problems of social reproduction which Australia currently faces, but is also an ineffective route to women's equality because it fails to challenge the sexual division of labour.

The scene then shifts to Canada where, courtesy of Judy Fudge, we encounter efforts to effect a better work/life balance through the reform of working time regulation. Fudge focuses on the recent experience of Ontario where, under the guise of work/life policies, the government has introduced working time reforms more concerned to deliver managerial flexibility than to reduce working hours. Fudge argues that Ontario's adoption of a new working time regime exemplifies the emergence of a new 'dual-earner gender contract', which is expressive of attempts by the state to manage social reproduction in the context of women's increased labour force participation. Fudge contends that, not only is the model unsustainable in terms of the demands of social reproduction, it condemns both men and women, in distinct and gendered ways, to a much poorer work/life balance.

This bleak picture of work/life initiatives is not displaced by Csilla Kollonay Lehoczky's account of the experience of women in the context of economic transition in Hungary. Kollonay Lehoczky begins by reflecting on the singular failure of 'family-friendly policies' in the former communist regimes of Central and Eastern Europe to deliver equality for women, largely because the mechanisms ensuring women's full participation in the public sphere of work had no effect on the gendered allocation of labour in the private sphere of family life. However, the experience of Hungarian women in the context of the transition to a market economy is arguably worse, as much of the state support for child-care has been withdrawn and women have found themselves subject to the disciplinary power of market imperatives which consign them to a precarious world of low pay and job insecurity in a labour context in which a male norm of the unencumbered worker has vigorously reasserted itself. Kollonay Lehoczky argues strongly for the gender-neutral refashioning of norms of work to ensure that gender equality is finally realized.

Hiroko Hayashi concludes this section considering the circumstances of women workers in Japan, framing her discussion in the twilight world of the *sozai* factories where work and family sometimes fuse in sinister and gender-disadvantaging ways. As she describes, women workers now find themselves caught between employers who increasingly seek to avoid accommodating women's family obligations and current efforts by the Japanese state to respond to both the pressures on women arising from changing forms and practices of work and the current crisis around social reproduction. Hayashi's assessment of the family-friendly stance of current Japanese labour law is critical, emphasizing how it continues to consign women to the margins of paid work.

Conclusion: a cautionary tale

In the final chapter of *Labour Law, Work, and Family*, Richard Michael Fischl evokes a fantasy world in which gender roles are reconfigured with very different distributional consequences. In this 'women's world' the work involved in caring for children and other family members is supported and absorbed by the state while security needs—fighting fires, policing homes and neighbourhoods—is carried out on an unpaid 'voluntary' basis by men. The result is an equally unequal gendered distribution in which women, not men, come out on top. Fischl's point is not of course to advocate such a transformation but to highlight, in an imaginative and hugely entertaining evocation, the contingency of current demarcations between paid and unpaid work and between public and private spheres, and their gender-disadvantaging consequences.

As virtually all of these contributions indicate, the emergence of work/family issues within the discipline of labour law and on the radar of policymakers has not yet led to reforms that challenge the structural causes of gender inequality arising from the conflicting demands of the market and household. Rather, a distinct cleavage seems to be emerging between reforms that merely manage the tension between work and family so as to relieve some of the pressure on women workers on the one hand and proposals that seek more profound distributive change and have as their aim substantive equality for women both at home and at work on the other. Whether more promising outcomes from the standpoint of gender equality lie in the future will depend on the acceptance of a much wider definition of the concept of work and a willingness to mount fundamental challenges to work norms and practices, both established and emerging, at home and in the labour market.

Finally, it seems fitting to finish the Introduction with a reflection on the role of work/family conflicts in the production of this book. For it has become unavoidably clear to us that it is not only *about* the relationship between work and family; the book is itself marked by that relationship. Myriad work and family conflicts were themselves played out in very concrete ways. The number of points at which family concerns, and issues of care in particular, interfered with the completion of the manuscript has been nothing short of astonishing: both the editors and a very high percentage of the contributors had serious family issues which could not be put to one side or consigned to someone else and simply had to be negotiated (and sometimes renegotiated) in the course of completing the book. The extent to which they played havoc with efforts to comply with the most basic of work-related demands—adhering to a schedule, for example—was, to say the least, in itself deeply instructive of the salience and importance of work/family issues. They also served as a persistent reminder that such conflicts cannot be regarded as exceptional, but rather have now to be regarded as 'normal', part of the structure of everyday working life.

Part I

Situating Debate about Work and Family

2

Work, Family, and the Discipline of Labour Law

JOANNE CONAGHAN*

An alternative labour law cannot be constructed out of nostalgia ... it has to be grounded in a close analysis of the present and an understanding of the past.[1]

I INTRODUCTION

Of what does the subject of labour law comprise? How do we identify its boundaries? What constitutes its rationale? Who is properly subject to its governance? These are questions that are fundamental to labour law, questions which seek to delineate its scope, content, and purpose(s). They are also questions which, in current times, seem increasingly difficult to address in light of the declining explanatory power of those dominant conceptual and ideological frameworks within which such enquiries have traditionally been located.[2]

The object of this chapter is to suggest that a focus on the operation of the work/family dichotomy in labour law offers us a window through which to (re)view and (re)consider these labour law fundamentals. My purpose is not to offer a comprehensive picture or analysis of the field but rather to trouble and disrupt the pictures and analyses which currently abound. Nor is this an act of wanton destruction. On the contrary, it is offered as a positive move, a way of making space for new visions and directions to emerge. Labour law is arguably in need of new visions and directions. There is a growing sense, evident in the academic literature, that it has lost its way; in particular, that it has been harnessed

* I wish to thank Emily Grabham and Paddy Ireland for their comments on an earlier draft of this chapter, Peter Cane for engaging with me on questions of theory and theorizing, and Karl Klare, always, for his friendship and inspiration.

[1] Hepple, B., 'The Future of Labour Law', *ILJ*, 24 (1995), 303, 305.

[2] For analyses of the erosion of dominant labour law discourses across a range of jurisdictions in the context of radical changes in the organization of work, see e.g. Collins, H., 'The Productive Disintegration of Labour Law', *ILJ*, 26 (1997), 295; Klare, K., 'The Horizons of Transformative Labour and Employment Law', in J. Conaghan, R. M. Fischl, and K. Klare (eds.), *Labour Law in an Era of Globalization* (Oxford: OUP, 2002), 3; D'Antona, M., 'Labour Law at the Century's End', ibid., 31; Mitchell, R., 'Introduction: A New Scope and Task for Labour Law', in R. Mitchell (ed.), *Redefining Labour Law: New Perspectives on the Future of Teaching and Research* (Melbourne: Centre for Employment and Labour Relations, 1995), vii.

to the service of competing economic and political agendas which have undermined its integrity and 'vocational' character.[3] In this context, a focus on work and family serves a dual purpose. First, it locates a consideration of labour law fundamentals within a highly contemporary labour law theme. Secondly and simultaneously, it offers the possibility of new insights by adopting a standpoint, an angle of vision, which departs from more conventional approaches to the subject. The idea is to flush out features currently in shadow by focusing on areas which have traditionally occupied the margins.

I want to begin, however, by considering labour law theory in general, for the tradition of labour law theorizing may be part of the problem to be confronted in our efforts to make sense of current events and developments. It may also account, to a significant degree, for the neglect of gendered aspects of the discourse which a focus on work and family, inter alia, reveals. In this context, it may be suggested that labour law theorists have allowed the pursuit of disciplinary coherence and unity to get in the way of more complex and nuanced theoretical approaches to the subject. Another way of putting it, drawing upon the work of Hugh Collins,[4] is to acknowledge that a particular understanding of 'theory' in labour law has rendered us 'deaf ' not only to alternative *theories* but also to alternative understandings of *what* theoretical work entails.

II THEORIZING LABOUR LAW: IN PURSUIT OF UNITY AND COHERENCE

An attraction to notions of unity and coherence, that is, to the idea that different concepts relate to one another in a particular way and by reference to a set of norms, criteria, or purposes which account for that ordering, is clearly detectable in labour law. Indeed, it is a characteristic feature of legal reasoning in general to seek to link the disparate 'data' comprising legal rules and decisions within an overarching conceptual framework which confers both meaning and legitimacy. However, a pronounced concern with notions of unity and coherence in labour law may be attributable to the need, in the early days of this very modern discipline, to establish an 'identity' for labour law, to reconfigure it as a unified subject of study distinct from the mere remnants of public and

---

[3] For an articulation of labour law's vocational qualities, see Collins, H., 'Labour Law as a Vocation', *LQR*, 105 (1989), 468. This theme is taken up in Gahan, P. and Mitchell, R., 'The Limits of Labour Law and the Necessity of Interdisciplinary Analysis', in Mitchell, above, n. 2, 62, and also in Conaghan, J., 'Labour Law and New Economy Discourse', *AJLL*, 16 (2003), 9, 18–27.   [4] Collins, above, n. 2.

private law of which it then comprised.[5] An important additional element, in a British and European context, was the scholarly work of Otto Kahn-Freund. His attribution of a 'primary purpose' to labour law, formulated in terms of the legal regulation of social power,[6] and his compelling articulation of collective *laissez-faire* as a descriptive and prescriptive account of British labour law in the mid-twentieth century[7] set a precedent in terms of theoretical breadth and influence which still exercises a grip on modern labour law scholarship, leaving many labour lawyers with a nostalgic yearning for the certainty in scope, content, and purpose which Kahn-Freund's account appeared to offer.

The dissolution of collective *laissez-faire* as an organizational and interpretative framework in a British context, and the corresponding decline of similar[8] theoretical approaches elsewhere may be said to have left labour law in a theoretical vacuum, in the sense that the discipline lacks a comprehensive theoretical framework to rival the explanatory and normative power of Kahn-Freund's. There have of course been many analyses of salient themes in modern labour law, highlighting, for example, the increasingly pronounced emphasis on macro-economic considerations[9] and renewed engagement with rights discourses.[10] Most prominently, commentators have noted the reorientation of much of contemporary labour law debate around the broad theme of globalization,[11] effecting in

[5] See e.g. Lord Wedderburn, writing in 1965, asserting the 'coherence of labour law' in spite of the fact that 'writers on the subject face the paradox that their subject has, until recently, been thought by most lawyers not to exist at all', Wedderburn, K. W., *The Worker and the Law* (Harmondsworth: Penguin, 1965), 7, 9.

[6] 'The principal purpose of labour law . . . is to regulate, to support and to restrain the power of management and the power of organised labour', Kahn-Freund, O., *Labour and the Law*, 2nd edn. (London: Stevens & Sons, 1977), 4.

[7] Kahn-Freund, O., 'Legal Framework', in A. Flanders, and H. A. Clegg (eds.), *The System of Industrial Relations in Great Britain: Its History, Law, and Institutions* (Oxford: Basil Blackwell, 1954).

[8] In which the key point of similarity may be said to lie in the industrial pluralist orientation of most twentieth-century labour law traditions. See above, n. 2.

[9] The implication of labour law in macro-economic strategies is comprehensively tracked in a British post-war context by Davies, P. and Freedland, M., *Labour Legislation and Public Policy* (Oxford: Clarendon Press, 1993). For a more contemporary analysis, emphasizing competitiveness, see Collins, H., 'Regulating the Employment Relation for Competitiveness', *ILJ*, 30 (2001), 17. For parallel shifts in Australian labour law discourse highlighting labour law's job creation/labour market regulation functions, see Arup, C., 'Labour Market Regulation as a Focus for Labour Law Discipline', in Mitchell, above, n. 2, 29, and Howe, J., 'The Job Creation Function of the State: A New Subject for Labour Law', *AJLL*, 14 (2001), 242.

[10] See e.g. in a British context, Ewing, K. D. and Hendy, J. (eds.), *A Charter of Workers' Rights* (London: Institute of Employment Rights, 2002); at European Union level, Hervey, T. and Kenner, J. (eds.), *Economic and Social Rights under the European Union Charter of Fundamental Rights* (Oxford: Hart Publishing, 2003); and, internationally/globally, Hepple, B. (ed.), *Social and Labour Rights in a Global Context* (Cambridge: Cambridge University Press, 2002). [11] Conaghan et al., above, n. 2; Hepple, above, n. 10.

the process an eclipse of national labour law discourses in favour of supra-national narratives, and the displacement of traditional labour law aspirations by the increasingly hegemonic imperatives of neo-liberalism.[12] This has yielded gloomy reflections about the 'death'[13] or 'end'[14] of labour law, generating calls for its resuscitation in the face of an apparently imminent demise. Labour law scholars are urged to 'reinvent',[15] 'redefine'[16] and even 'transform'[17] the subject in the wake of its 'productive disintegration'.[18] However, none of the efforts to date has served to bestow upon labour law a new sense of its distinct character, its uniqueness as a 'vocational' subject. Nor do they compel a unified understanding of labour law so that each of the separate 'pieces' of the labour law puzzle may be said to fit together in a particular way. On the contrary, what characterizes much of labour law scholarship today is its fragmentation, the dissolution of unity in favour of discrete subject specialities within a general field whose core content is the subject of contestation and whose outer boundaries remain largely undetermined.[19]

Given these features of labour law as a disciplinary tradition, it is easy for labour law theorists today to become caught within an all-or-nothing dilemma: either to come up with a coherent, comprehensive account of the field in the tradition of Kahn-Freund and his contemporaries, or abandon theoretical endeavours altogether as futile and self-defeating. In addition, the seeming impossibility of unity and coherence in the context of radical and relentless changes in the terrain has arguably encouraged a turn away from theory and towards more identifiably politicized engagements with current law and policymaking,[20] a trend compounded

---

[12] See esp. the work of Canadian scholar, Harry Arthurs, e.g. 'Labour Law without the State', *University of Toronto L. J.*, 46 (1996), 1 and 'Reinventing Labor Law for the Global Economy', *Berkeley J. Emp. & Lab. L.*, 22 (2001), 271.

[13] Ewing, K. D., 'The Death of Labour Law?', *OJLS*, 8 (1988), 293; Davis, D. M., 'Death of a Labour Lawyer?' in Conaghan et al., above, n. 2, 159.

[14] e.g. Hepple, above, n. 1, 305, asking: 'Have we reached the end of labour law?'.

[15] Arthurs, above, n. 12.   [16] Mitchell, above, n. 2.

[17] Klare, above, n. 2. See also, Fredman, S., 'The Ideology of New Labour Law', in C. Barnard, S. Deakin, and G. Morris (eds.), *The Future of Labour Law* (Oxford: Hart Publishing, 2004), 9.   [18] Collins, above, n. 2.

[19] Until recently, the 'essential' content of British labour law privileged collective over individual labour issues. However, over the last two decades the marked shift towards individual employment rights in the context of the widespread weakening of collective bargaining arrangements has called into serious question the continued centrality of collective concerns, evidenced by the decreasing coverage of collective issues in textbooks and course outlines. This said, the perception that collective issues constitute the terrain of 'real' labour lawyers arguably retains considerable hold on the normative structuring of the discipline.

[20] See esp. here the work and publications of the UK-based Institute of Employment Rights (IER); see further www.ier.org.uk. See also Ewing, K., 'Democratic Socialism and Labour Law', *ILJ*, 25 (1995), 103, for an account of the political tradition within which the IER project was conceived.

by the collapse, post-1979, of a political consensus with regard to the regulatory role of collective labour strategies,[21] requiring labour lawyers to adopt a defensive stance in relation to the discipline which sits uncomfortably alongside theoretical efforts to disarrange and reconstruct the field. In many instances too, labour lawyers have been deflected from theory by the practical need to do a lot more law. As the scale and intensity of legal regulation of workplace relations has increased, the primary theoretical language of collective autonomy and industrial pluralism has given way to a more complex grammar of legal terms and technicalities, producing a generation of new labour lawyers with a quite different focus and disciplinary orientation.[22]

Within this broad climate of theoretical depletion, the landscape of labour law is being reconfigured with hitherto 'undiscovered' aspects coming sharply into view. Among these is a concern with the reconciliation of work and family responsibilities or, more broadly, with ensuring a proper balance between 'work' and 'life' activities. This was clearly not an issue which engaged the theoretical interest of Kahn-Freund. Yet, since the publication in Britain of *Fairness at Work* in 1997, signalling an intention on the part of the newly elected Labour Government to relocate work/family considerations at the centre of employment policy,[23] the 'work/life balance' has become a 'hot topic' in British law and policy-making, compelling significantly greater scholarly engagement on the part of labour lawyers.[24] A similar preoccupation is detectable in European law and policy,[25] and indeed across a range of jurisdictions.[26] However, the reasons for prior neglect of work and family issues by labour lawyers

[21] See Hepple, above, n. 1, esp. at 305. For a broad account of the decline of 'countervailing workers' power' (CVWP) as a regulatory strategy in post-war western industrialized economies, see Klare, K., 'Countervailing Workers' Power as a Regulatory Strategy', in H. Collins, P. Davies, and R. Rideout (eds.), *Legal Regulation of the Employment Relation* (The Hague: Kluwer Law International, 2000), 63.

[22] It is notable that most of the leading theoretical interventions in British labour law continue to come from the generation of scholars trained in the intellectual tradition of Kahn-Freund. This is despite the fact that labour law discourse as a whole has become increasingly disassociated from the social theoretical premises upon which it was constructed.

[23] Department of Trade and Industry, *Fairness at Work*, Cm 3968 (London: TSO, 1998); see esp. ch. 5.

[24] See e.g. the substantial chapter on work/life issues in Collins, H., Ewing, K. D., and McColgan, A., *Labour Law: Text and Materials* (Oxford: Hart Publishing, 2001), 371–477. The degree of engagement should not be overstated. The tendency of most textbooks is still to assign such issues relatively little consideration.

[25] For an account of the development of work/life strategies in an EU context, see Caracciolo di Torella, E., 'The "Family-Friendly" Workplace: The EC Position', *International Journal of Comparative Labour Law and Industrial Relations*, 17 (2001), 325, and also McGlynn, in this volume.

[26] See essays in this volume, and also Berns, S., *Women Going Backwards: Law and Change in a Family-friendly Society* (Aldershot: Ashgate Publishing, 2003); Williams, J., *Unbending Gender: Why Family and Work Conflict and What to Do about It* (New York: OUP, 2000).

are worthy of some attention as they are closely linked, I believe, to the dominant theoretical tradition of labour law, both substantively and methodologically.

The *substantive* content of the dominant theoretical narrative was predicated upon the bifurcation of industrial relations and, thereby, labour law, into two distinct groups—capitalists and workers—with conflicting interests. This effected the absorption and eclipse of work/family issues within a general model of class conflict played out exclusively in the workplace and in which differences between workers—including gender differences—were largely ignored.[27] At the same time, *methodologically*, a perception that work/family issues raise particular, that is, women-related, rather than general, that is, worker-related, concerns, allowed labour law theorists largely to ignore the presence and operation of work/family considerations in labour law on the grounds that they had little to contribute to the overall project of unity and coherence in the field. In other words, the historical neglect of what might be described as 'feminist' issues in labour law is, in part, attributable to an allegiance among labour law scholars to a particular idea of theory. According to this idea, the purpose of theoretical work is to render the subject of study *coherent*—by identifying norms or criteria by reference to which its contours may be delineated and its contents normatively endowed—and *unified*—by providing a conceptual map which enables each of its components to be located in relation to one another. The result is a theoretical tradition strongly focused on producing the most authoritative, all-encompassing account of the field, one which aims to present labour law within a framework which explains it comprehensively or nearly so, and which is able to pronounce with confidence upon its primary purposes and essential structures.[28] As it was widely assumed that consideration of what we now understand as 'work/family' issues—for example, issues relating to the regulation of women's hours in factories or the legal status and treatment of part-time workers—could never possibly produce such an authoritative and all-encompassing account, they were, at best, relegated

[27] See Conaghan, J., 'The Invisibility of Labour Law: Gender-Neutrality in Model-Building', *International J. of Sociology of Law*, 14 (1986), 377.

[28] As in Kahn-Freund's assertion that 'The main object of labour law is and I venture to say always will be, to be a countervailing force to counteract the inequality of bargaining power which is inherent and must be inherent in the employment relation', Kahn-Freund, above, n. 6, 6. There was unquestionably a time in labour law's infancy when such an uncompromisingly assertive approach to identity and function facilitated the development of a novel legal discourse in the face of strong pressure, from within and outside the discipline of law, to suppress it. Labour law's struggle to be born in less than auspicious legal and political circumstances is captured in Kahn-Freund's fascinating account of the Weimar years and, in particular, in his analysis of the theory and jurisprudence of his mentor, Hugo Sinzheimer. See further Kahn-Freund, O., 'Hugo Sinzheimer 1875–1945 (1976)' in R. Lewis, and J. Clark (eds.), *Labour Law and Politics in the Weimar Republic* (Oxford: Blackwell Publishers, 1981).

to the margins of labour law or, at worst, positioned as aberrant or deviant.

While it is questionable whether, even with this conception of theory, work and family issues were properly assigned such incidental status, I want to suggest a different understanding of theory, one which does not aspire to unity and coherence but which nevertheless purports to offer a better understanding of the world of work. This is a conception of theory which seeks out multiple standpoints, offering richer insights into the operation and effects of a range of regulatory mechanisms currently implicated in the governance of labour. The idea of standpoint signals recognition of the impossibility of non-situated knowledge. Accepting that knowledge derives from, and is constituted by, social practices, institutions, and engagements, and that knowledge acquisition is inevitably a process of interaction between the knower and the context in which she knows, the concept of standpoint essentially seeks to get at the specificity or particularity of the contexts in which knowledge is formed and produced.[29]

It follows that even theoretical knowledge is marked by the standpoint of its author(s) and origins, while, as the product of particular social and institutional conventions about what constitutes theory, it is located in and constituted by those conventions. Furthermore, as the conditions which generate a particular theory (or a particular approach to theory) change, there is a risk that the theoretical project will ossify—become stuck—so that norms and assumptions which are necessarily contingent become represented as universal truths, establishing an unquestioned, taken-for-granted discursive and conceptual underpinning.

One way to avoid or minimize this risk of getting stuck is to seek out perspectives eclipsed by the dominant narrative, to continually survey the field from a marginalized point of view. Such acts of displacement help to bring into focus the parameters which bound the field, present-ing new possibilities for reorienting and remapping the terrain. While this may yield multiple, complex, and even contradictory pictures, it may also serve to sharpen our critical focus by highlighting the contingency and incompleteness of the dominant point of view. In other words, it is the *habit* of theory which is important, the continued effort to reflect upon

---

[29] It does not follow from this that all perspectives are indistinguishable in terms of their authority or usefulness or that we cannot agree upon measures by which different kinds of knowledge may be evaluated. While recognition of the social nature of knowledge does entail reassessing approaches to knowledge formation and validation, it does not require the wholesale rejection of epistemological projects. Feminist standpoint epistemol-ogy is one route towards a 'post-foundationalist' understanding of knowledge, focusing upon its relationship to context, subject-identity, and power. See generally Harding, S., *The Feminist Standpoint Theory Reader: Intellectual and Political Controversies* (New York: Routledge, 2003).

the forms of our engagement, not to produce the best, most comprehensive, most authoritative and far-reaching account of the field, but rather to instil good practices of critical interrogation and reflection, including a willingness constantly to reassess the categories and concepts which ground our analyses as well as the allegiances which underpin them. This is an idea of theory as process, not product,[30] as action, not outcome.[31] It is a view of theory which is endlessly 'interactionist', and in which knowledge—in particular, the categories through which we organize and present 'what we know'—are historically located and diachronically conceived.[32] It is a way of ensuring that our ideas do not go stale, that our frameworks do not entrap us, that we are not rendered 'deaf' to the noise that is all around.

Within this alternative theoretical context, I want to revisit the operation of the work/family dichotomy in labour law and its shift in status from an implicit to explicit feature of the field. My intention is, in part, to illustrate how a focus on work and family can contribute to a better understanding of labour law by reassessing it from the standpoint of those who engage in large amounts of unpaid, caregiving work. At the same time, by invoking a standpoint which is conventionally positioned at the margins of mainstream discourse, I hope to foster a more 'flexible' theoretical environment within which a host of questions which currently bedevil labour law scholarship may be considered.

III WORK AND FAMILY IN LABOUR LAW DISCOURSE

Official and unofficial narratives

Traditionally, in labour law, work and family have been seen as antithetical, as two separate spheres which occasionally collide particularly where women's employment is at issue. Within this frame of reference, the competing concerns of work and family are posited as difficult if not impossible to reconcile, requiring women to 'choose' between their family responsibilities and their desire to engage in paid work.[33] Increasingly,

---

[30] Bottomley, A., 'Theory is a Process not an End: A Feminist Approach to the Practice of Theory', in J. Richardson and R. Sandland (eds.), *Feminist Perspectives on Law and Theory* (London: Cavendish, 2000), 25.

[31] As in the Aristotelian-derived notion of *praxis*, understood in terms of 'doing' not 'making'.

[32] See here the writings of E. P. Thompson on the nature of theory, esp. 'Caudwell', *Socialist Register* (1977), 228 and *The Poverty of Theory* (London: Merlin, 1978), discussed in Ireland, P., 'History, Critical Legal Studies and the Mysterious Disappearance of Capitalism', *MLR*, 65 (2002), 120, 128.

[33] See e.g. the comment made by Wood J. in *Clymo* v. *Wandsworth London BC* [1989] IRLR 241 when he rejected a claim of indirect sex discrimination based on the denial of a woman's request to work part-time after having a baby: '... in every employment ladder from

however, this view is being challenged both by the practical demographics of women's ever-increasing workforce participation, and by the related recognition at a policy level that some degree of reconciliation between work and family responsibilities is desirable. In Britain, this has translated into two basic concerns which have driven New Labour policy: first, a desire to smooth the path to paid work for parents and others with caring responsibilities; and secondly, a concern to facilitate a better balance between 'work' and 'life' more generally, particularly in light of the deleterious social effects of a 'long hours' working culture. The development of this agenda is, in part, a response to wider economic, industrial, and demographic changes but it is also an attempt to harness those changes to progressive social aims, specifically the inclusion of disadvantaged people into the economic benefits of society and the promotion and reinvigoration of ideas of citizenship and public space.[34] In the UK this has resulted in a range of policy initiatives and legal reforms both within, and beyond, labour law aimed at 'chang[ing] the culture of relations in and at work . . . to reflect a new relationship between work and family life'.[35]

According to this 'official' narrative, work and family are spheres which have only lately converged as a consequence of problems generated by the increased participation of workers with caring responsibilities in paid work. Prior to these developments, the two spheres are commonly understood to have operated autonomously: they served different social functions, met different human needs, and involved the pursuit of different kinds of activities. They were, for all practical and conceptual purposes, separate realms, overlapping occasionally and only minimally.

Such a view of the relationship (or lack thereof) between work and family has long informed labour law policy and discourse. Hence the absence of any sustained consideration of the conflicting needs of work and family in early labour law theory. The operating assumption was that, financial provision aside, *concrete* family needs were and should be met outside the 'world of work'. Thus, no conflict was deemed to arise. This was reflected in working arrangements and in the laws developed to regulate those arrangements. Both proceeded on the basis that workers were, and should be, *exclusively* available to their employers for the

the lowliest to the highest there will come a stage at which a woman who has family responsibilities must make a choice' (at 248). On the rhetoric of choice in this context, see further below.

[34] See further, Conaghan, J., 'Women, Work and Family: A British Revolution?', in Conaghan et al., above, n. 2, 53; Driver, S. and Martell, L., 'New Labour, Work, and Family', *Social Policy & Administration* (2002), 46; and on New Labour law generally, Fredman, above, n. 17. For an assessment of parallel developments in Australia, see Chapman and Owens, in this volume.   [35] Tony Blair, 'Foreword', *Fairness at Work*, above, n. 23.

duration of their working time, generally conceived in terms of a full-time, long-term commitment to paid work.[36] 'Work' was thus premised on the assumption that 'workers' were free of child-care and other caring responsibilities. Indeed, it is this assumption which current policy interventions seek to dislodge.

However, behind this official narrative of late convergence is another, 'unofficial' story of long-term interdependence and mutual reinforcement. According to this subversive tale, what the current preoccupation with work/family issues reveals is the extent to which the form work has taken *to date* is reliant upon a specific conception of the family and of the social allocation of activities within and across the two spheres. In particular, for workers to be free to engage in paid work on an exclusive, timed work basis, arrangements must be in place to ensure that other essential social tasks, particularly those associated with the short-term and long-term reproduction of labour, continue to be carried out. In this sense, productive and reproductive concerns necessarily intersect and demand mutual accommodation and, in this context, the work/family divide emerges as a specific expression of this accommodation rather than as a natural or universal feature of social order. Moreover, once this functional and inter-constitutive relationship is recognized, work and family can no longer be posited as distinct and unrelated[37] and their appearance as such is revealed to be the product of the particular way in which work is organized and the mechanisms and institutions—including law—which support and nurture that organizational form.[38]

Thus, the unofficial narrative repositions work and family as fundamentally connected in terms of how they are conceived, how they function, and where their boundaries lie. Moreover, at the core of this

---

[36] The idea that paid work should be carried out exclusively and not in tandem with other 'life' activities is reflective of a shift in notations of time from 'task orientation' to 'timed work' in early industrial capitalism. In this way, a worker's time became a commodity which the employer purchased and did not wish to waste. See further Thompson, E. P., 'Time, Work-Discipline and Industrial Capitalism', in *Customs in Common* (Harmondsworth: Penguin, 1991), 352.

[37] See e.g. Rittich, K., 'Feminization and Contingency: Regulating the Stakes for Work for Women', in Conaghan et al., above, n. 2, 117, stating that 'unpaid work is integral to the performance and structure of productive activity in the market' (at 122). See also Conaghan, J., 'Feminism and Labour Law: Contesting the Terrain', in A. Morris and T. O'Donnell (eds.), *Feminist Perspectives on Employment Law* (London: Cavendish, 1999), 13.

[38] Nancy Fraser has described this organizational form as the 'male breadwinner-female homemaker' model, and identifies the family wage as evidence of the formal recognition of the interdependence of work and family concerns in the context of twentieth-century industrial capitalism; see Fraser, N., *Justice Interruptus: Critical Reflections on the 'Postsocialist' Tradition* (New York: Routledge, 1997), ch. 2. The recognition of the normative power of this model in structuring understandings of work and family is not the same as asserting that, as a matter of fact, all men and women until recently conformed to it. As Fraser observes: 'countless lives never fit this pattern' (ibid., 42).

relationship are considerations of care, which necessarily accompany the social organization of economic activity.

It is only in the context of the need for changes in organizational form generated by the demands of major industrial restructuring on a global scale,[39] in turn producing concerns about how care needs can be met in the wake of the collapse of the 'male breadwinner-female homemaker' model along with the decline of the welfare state,[40] that the conceptual and functional intimacy between 'work' and 'family' has begun to surface. But make no mistake, it has always been there. What has happened is that the *implicit* relationship has become *explicit* at the point at which it is required to undergo a process of substantial renegotiation.

There is another dimension to this unofficial narrative which the official account of separation and division has served to suppress. The work/family divide upon which traditional labour law rests is resolutely gendered. More specifically, a gendered allocation of labour, particularly in the family domain, has served as a key mechanism enabling some workers, that is, men, to engage in paid work on an unencumbered, time-exclusive basis. This gender dimension is rarely if ever made explicit. In the official narrative, the fact that the realm of paid work has been predominantly populated by men while the sphere of family has been the (unpaid) labouring domain of women is regarded as incidental, carrying no significant analytical consequences. One would not deduce from labour law discourse that, as Kerry Rittich observes, work is 'a deeply gendered activity'.[41] It is considered perfectly possible, for example, to analyse the regulatory position of part-time workers with minimal (if any) reference to the gendered nature of part-time work. While gender may be relevant to distributional considerations, in the sense that the poor treatment of part-time workers is acknowledged to have a differential gender-based impact, there is nothing specifically gendered about the legal conceptualization of part-time work *per se*—or so the official narrative would have us believe.

---

[39] A key feature of economic restructuring has been a demand for greater labour market flexibility. This has impacted significantly on the gender division of labour (Walby, S., *Gender Transformations* (London: Routledge, 1997), chs. 2 and 3). The gendered implications of the rise of precarious work are explored by Rittich, above, n. 37, as well as being the subject of a collection of forthcoming essays in J. Fudge and R. Owens (eds.), *Precarious Work, Women and the New Economy: The Challenge to Legal Norms* (Oxford: Hart Publishing, 2005).
[40] Current concerns about care provision are neatly captured by the notion of a 'care deficit'. The idea is that, as women shift their labour from the unpaid care work to the waged economy, a care deficit emerges. See e.g. Bunting, M., 'The Hidden Toll We Pay', *The Guardian*, 21 June 2004. The concept of care here should be construed broadly to embrace not just obvious 'care' considerations such as the provision of child-care, eldercare, and care for the disabled, but also issues such as declining fertility rates (with corresponding implications for immigration policy).   [41] Rittich, above, n. 37, 122.

But, of course, once we acknowledge the centrality of care-based considerations in the structure and performance of productive activities and in particular, once we recognize the relationship between working time norms and care needs in this context, it is difficult to conceive of part-time work without reference to gender. To work part-time is to strike a different balance in the allocation of time to work and life activities than is reflected in the full-time, 'typical' norm. Although we often think of part-time work as an attempt to bridge the work/life separation, it is, in fact, an *endorsement* of that separation, while offering a specific, 'atypical' accommodation which, historically, only women, by virtue of their caring responsibilities, have been required to make. This coercive dimension is often concealed by a rhetoric of choice which positions women's engagement in part-time work as a 'lifestyle' issue which flows from their decision to have children. The deployment of the language of choice thus operates to disguise the gendered structural constraints within which 'choice' is exercised, facilitating the evacuation of gender from the analytical frame. However, part-time work is gendered in a more fundamental sense. The subjection of work to measurement in units of time is a product of particular needs which emerged in early industrial capitalism and which eventually found expression in a gendered social order which facilitated the separation of work and life and thereby enabled capital to purchase and consume labour on a time-exclusive basis.[42] We would not need a concept of part-time work without a social and conceptual separation of work and life, and we would not have such a social and conceptual separation without a gendered allocation of labour.[43] In this sense, and analytically speaking, a full understanding of part-time work as an operative category in labour law discourse requires attention to gender because without it one cannot properly account for the conditions in which a notion of part-time work becomes meaningful. At the very least, this demands consideration of the gendered allocation of labour and its historical and contemporary role in structuring norms of working time.[44]

[42] Thompson, above, n. 36.

[43] Again, this is not to say that a gendered allocation of labour is necessary to the social and conceptual separation of work and life in any absolute sense—one could just imagine an allocation of labour which met the interdependent needs of production and reproduction but which was not gender-based. Rather, it is to emphasize that the form which the organization of labour in fact took, particularly with regard to working time norms, was and remains deeply gendered.

[44] I explore the close relationship between gender and working time further in 'Time to Dream: Flexibility, Families, and Working Time', in Fudge and Owens, above, n. 39. See also Fudge, in this volume.

Work, family, and sex (in)equality

The centrality of gender to work/family considerations tends to bring to the fore sex inequality concerns. For example, it is common to view 'family-friendly' policies as sex equality initiatives, that is, as measures to improve women's social and economic status vis-à-vis men.[45] It is less common to see the family-friendly agenda as a product of economic developments which are driving significant change in social and legal forms and in relation to which family-friendly policy may be better understood as a governance technique for managing the difficulties which economic restructuring has generated. This is not to say that consideration of work/family issues does not have important sex equality implications. Indeed, few labour lawyers today would dispute the relevance of the work/family dichotomy to a better understanding of sex-based inequality, both in a labour market context and more generally. For example, a focus on the interdependence of work and family is a feature of many analyses of the failure of sex discrimination legislation adequately to address issues of sex inequality in the workplace. Challenging the official narrative of separation and independence, feminist commentators have highlighted how the 'public' (that is, paid work) focus of anti-discrimination legislation has allowed gender inequities in the 'private' sphere of the family to flourish unchecked.[46] This has resulted in the infliction of a 'double burden' of domestic and work-based responsibilities on women, as well as placing practical and legal obstacles in the way of their economic advancement which are not easily recognized, let alone addressed by, the official work/family narrative.[47]

Increasingly, too, attention is being paid to the ideological and discursive effects of the official narrative in relation to women workers. The denial of any functional or conceptual relationship between the realms of work and family inevitably structures and shapes the form, content, and relative weight of arguments arising from consideration of work/family issues in an employment context. In relation to business decision-making, for example, such a denial renders family considerations formally irrelevant to the needs and concerns of the business enterprise. This resonates with an economic conception of family-based activity

[45] For a strong critique of this view in an EU law and policy context, see McGlynn, in this volume.

[46] See e.g. Conaghan, above, n. 27; see also Fredman, S., *Women and the Law* (Oxford: Clarendon Press, 1997), esp. 413–16.

[47] The limits often placed on atypical workers' access to employment protection is a commonly cited example in this context: the legal privileging of an 'ideal worker' who can move seamlessly and without encumbrance between the 'separate spheres' of work and family has inevitable gender equity implications; see Williams, above, n. 26, chs. 3 and 4.

as *external* to the processes of production, and, therefore, not a *cost*
which employers should rightfully bear.[48] A related element here is the
characterization of caring work carried out in a family context as 'unpro-
ductive', that is, as yielding no economic value. This is an assumption
which feminist economists have increasingly challenged, highlighting
the economic importance, indeed, centrality of labour-reproducing work,
and fundamentally undermining the traditional discursive privileging
of 'productive' over 'reproductive' labour.[49] Within the context of labour
law and policymaking, the reformulation of unpaid caring work as
'productive' of economic value and the corresponding repositioning of
such productive work as a legitimate 'cost' of doing business, greatly
enhances the rhetorical and political power of arguments for better workplace accommodation of child-care and other caring needs, to the obvious
benefit of women, who remain our primary carers. In short, attention to
the unofficial narrative of work and family as conceptually, functionally,
and discursively interdependent is of enormous value in terms of
accounting for sex inequality and in devising arguments and strategies
to combat and alleviate it.

The key issue however, for present purposes, is whether the unofficial narrative can yield broader insights for the discipline of labour law,
insights which go beyond a consideration of law's implication in
women's disadvantage. In the final part of this chapter, I hope to show
how work/family considerations bear strongly on debate about the
autonomy and scope of labour law as well as raise uncomfortable questions about its normative purposes and basic legitimacy. At the very
least, the articulation of the unofficial narrative of work and family is a
salutary reminder that all is not necessarily what it seems and that how
things appear is contingent upon the way we look at them in the first
place. To put it more concretely, a deconstruction of the work/family
dichotomy in labour law reveals the dependency of our understanding
on the particular conceptual framework(s) we invoke, with corresponding limitations on that understanding effected by the importation of

[48] Fisk, C., 'Employer-Provided Child Care under Title VII: Towards an Employer's Duty
to Accommodate Child Care Responsibilities', *Berkeley Women's Law Journal*, 2 (1986), 89, is
an early example of the now commonly posited feminist argument that the exclusion of
reproductive considerations from the sphere of production enables employers to 'externalize'
the economic costs of care.
[49] There is now a wealth of literature in feminist economics addressing issues arising
from the relationship between productive and reproductive activity, including the pioneer-
ing work of Marilyn Waring, *If Women Counted* (San Francisco: Harper & Row, 1988). For a
useful collection of essays see 'Special Section: Towards a Gendered Political Economy', *New
Political Economy*, 3 (1998), 181–278, including essays by Diane Elson, Georgina Waylen, Jean
Gardiner, and Jane Humphries. See also, Rittich, K., *Recharacterizing Restructuring: Law,
Distribution, and Gender in Market Reform* (The Hague: Kluwer Law International, 2002),
ch. 6, esp. 182–96.

taken-for-granted assumptions we neither acknowledge nor seek to challenge.

The dissolution of labour law's subject

In his opening address at the INTELL7 conference in Kyoto in the spring of 2004,[50] Makoto Ishida posed the question: 'To whom does labour law belong?' On the face of it, this is an odd question to pose. Why should law belong to anybody? At the same time, for those steeped in the labour law tradition, there seems to be a ready answer. Labour law belongs to labour, or more specifically to 'dependent labour', that is, to those workers who are in 'an economic relationship which in some way involves the exchange of *personal service or services* for remuneration'.[51]

This focus on dependent labour provides the discipline of labour law with both its core content and its normative justification. The outer boundaries of labour law may be becoming increasingly blurred, but the centrality of the employment relationship, what Kahn-Freund famously characterized as the 'cornerstone of the edifice',[52] is rarely questioned.[53] The economic relationship between worker and employer, howsoever conceived, is the glue which holds the structure in place. For this reason, labour law is almost exclusively concerned with paid work. From the individual contract of employment to the right to strike, the paid worker is the core unit upon which the regulatory framework is built and in relation to which it purports to act.

The primacy of the employment relationship also provides labour law with its normative base, captured in the notion that labour is not—or at least should not be treated as—a commodity. This concern with the commodification of labour is at the heart of Kahn-Freund's attribution of a 'primary purpose' to labour law, framed in terms of protecting

---

[50] *Labour Law without Boundaries*, 7th Meeting of the International Network on Transformative Employment and Labour Law (INTELL), Ritsumeikan University, Kyoto, Japan, 26–9 Mar. 2004.

[51] Deakin, S. and Morris, G., *Labour Law*, 2nd edn. (London: Butterworths, 1998), 1.

[52] Kahn-Freund, O., 'Blackstone's Neglected Child: The Contract of Employment', *LQR*, 93 (1978), 508.

[53] Hugh Collins, in an introductory text on employment law, has recently observed: 'Employment Law has evolved as a distinct subject of legal scholarship. It is also investigated under several other labels: labour law, industrial law, and social law. Different names for the subject betray contrasts in emphasis and scope. The primary focus of the subject, however, always concerns the contractual relation of employment, which is the legal expression of the economic and social relationship through which work is performed', Collins, H., *Employment Law* (Oxford: Clarendon Press, 2003), 5.

workers from the risks of exploitation acknowledged to be inherent in the employment relationship.[54] It also accounts for labour law's 'vocational' character,[55] and for the dominance of a scholarly tradition which is politically progressive and broadly redistributive.[56] Even as the normative contours of labour law have expanded expressly to encompass the economic purposes which labour law can and, it is increasingly contended, should serve, a concern with the commodification of labour ensures the continued presence of ethical and justice considerations in labour law scholarship and a close association between labour law discourse and wider engagements with 'fundamental' or 'social' rights.[57]

It thus becomes clear that the scope of labour law and its normative foundations are closely bound together in a focus on, and concern with, the paid labour relationship. This has had a number of consequences in terms of labour law as a discipline. First, labour law is not primarily or even predominantly about the world of work. It is about *paid* work and, indeed, about particular forms of paid work. As Davies and Freedland observe, there are many kinds of 'work contracts' which fall outside the sphere of labour law and are more properly assigned to commercial or consumer law.[58] There are also work contracts which look like they should belong in labour law but struggle to do so. This fosters the creation of hierarchies within labour law with those relationships conforming most closely to the classic notion of employment, understood in terms of domination and subordination, attracting the highest level of protection, while arrangements deviating from the traditional form are often required to settle for much less. The difficulties here have been exacerbated by the proliferation of 'non-standard' forms of work, widening the range and proportion of workers likely to fall outside the mantle of legal protection.

The inequities resulting from the imperfect operation of labour law's traditional mechanisms for identifying and protecting vulnerable workers has generated a number of efforts to redefine the legal criteria by which the work relationship may best be characterized. So, for example, one strategy is to look for similarities between the employment relationship and other work relationships, making a case for the extension of

---

[54] Above, n. 28.   [55] Collins, above, n. 3.

[56] Klare, above, n. 21 and id., above, n. 2.

[57] As Collins, above n. 53, summarizes: 'Employment law addresses the paradox encapsulated in the slogan "labour is not a commodity". It regulates employment relations for two principal purposes: to ensure that they function successfully as market transactions, and, at the same time, to protect workers against the economic logic of the commodification of labour'.

[58] Davies, P. and Freedland, M., 'Employees, Workers and the Autonomy of Labour Law', in H. Collins, P. Davies, and R. Rideout (eds.), *Legal Regulation of the Employment Relation* (London: Kluwer Law International, 2000), 267.

legal protection on grounds of fairness, rationality, and coherence.[59] However, in the context of the widespread growth of non-standard forms of work, such an approach cannot fail to privilege and reinforce 'standard' employment by making it the measure, the norm, of work in general. As is often pointed out, this is an inherent flaw in equal treatment models of protection. Another approach is to distinguish between different features of the work relationship which might ground an argument for protection, producing a normative ordering of reasons corresponding to the actual or desired level of protection extended to different kinds of workers.[60] Alternatively, or additionally, efforts to classify workers (with corresponding legal consequences) may be based on the relative needs of different kinds of workers in the broader context of economic concerns such as competitiveness and profitability.[61] It might be argued that in devising a regulatory regime the vulnerability of 'flexible' workers must be balanced against the economic benefits which flow from flexibility and which depend on lowering not raising the overall level of protection. It is in this kind of discursive context that the cleavage between the ideology of competitiveness and the economic reality of increasingly precarious working arrangements begins to surface.[62]

In any event, what is often envisaged is a kind of gradated system in which some kinds of workers have considerably more rights than others and in which a key ideological determinant of how rights are allocated is the degree of correspondence to the traditional norm of employment.

[59] See e.g. Freedland, M., *The Personal Employment Contract* (Oxford: OUP, 2003).

[60] See e.g. Davidov, G., 'Who is a Worker', *ILJ*, 34 (2005), 57, attempting to make sense of the thorny distinction between the legal categories of 'employee' and 'worker' in British labour law. Davidov identifies two characteristics of vulnerability—subordination and economic dependency—and argues that while employees are characterized by both features, workers are, or properly should be, characterized by the economically dependent nature of their work relationship. This provides both a justification for different levels of legal protection and a means of identifying membership of the relevant categories. See also Davies and Freedland, above, n. 58, distinguishing between legal and economic subordination, in which the latter category corresponds, more or less, with Davidov's notion of economic dependency.

[61] See e.g. Caruso, B., 'Immigration Policies in Southern Europe: More State, Less Market?', in Conaghan, et al., above, n. 2, 299. Caruso's focus here is on striking the right balance between formal immigration policy and the practical reliance of some southern European states on informal markets. However, his approach is illustrative of one which looks at the question of levels of legal protection not solely from the perspective of worker vulnerability but also with regard to broader macro-economic objectives.

[62] The notion of 'flexicurity' is sometimes used as a rhetorical device here by which to negotiate and legitimate the precarious world of work which flexibility has arguably spawned. For a trenchant critique of 'flexicurity' rhetoric, see Fredman, S., 'Women at Work: The Broken Promise of Flexicurity', *ILJ*, 33 (2004), 299. See also the essays collected in Fudge and Owens, above, n. 39, all of which focus on the gender implications of the spread of precariousness.

This norm was captured in Kahn-Freund's articulation of the employment relationship in terms of subordination and inequality of bargaining power but has been adapted in the development of legal doctrine to place often strong obstacles in the way of some workers seeking protection, regardless of the real degree of vulnerability.[63]

The idea of distinguishing between different kinds of workers in terms of their legal status and entitlements is not one with which labour lawyers are entirely comfortable.[64] It sits uneasily with a set of disciplinary assumptions strongly premised upon the commonality of workers' interests. Moreover, the lack of an identifiable subject may be thought to threaten the autonomy of labour law as a discipline.[65] Davies and Freedland do not think these concerns present an insurmountable obstacle to the adoption of a more 'flexible and dynamic approach', in which the scope and subject of legal protection vary, depending on the purpose and the substantive content of a particular regulation (so that, for example, a worker might be the subject of labour law for some purposes and the subject of commercial law or other branches of law for others). Labour law, they maintain, is now sufficiently strong to permit the blurring of disciplinary boundaries which such a tailored approach necessarily entails.[66]

But is their confidence well placed? The reconceptualization of labour law in terms of fluid and fragmented legal subjects does *not* fit easily within the traditional normative and conceptual framework of the discipline which relies heavily on the notion of an ideal homogenized worker. It raises questions, for example, about the constituency, role, and legitimacy of trade unions, in particular about how they can represent workers in the context of legally and socially constructed differences of interests between them. For the same reason, it problematizes the pursuit of collective strategies or at least suggests the need for much more complex, identity- and group-based approaches to labour organization which acknowledge differences between workers and the inegalitarian

[63] An archetypal example here in a British labour law context is the 'casual' worker who is often deemed to lack sufficient mutuality of obligation to qualify as an employee even though in reality she may be both economically dependent and highly vulnerable to exploitation (see e.g. *O'Kelly* v. *Trusthouse Forte* [1984] QB 90). The strictness of the legal tests provides an incentive for employers to 'disguise' employment and thereby escape obligations of protection. For an exploration of these issues in a South African context, see Benjamin, P., 'Who Needs Labour Law? Defining the Scope of Labour Law Protection', in Conaghan et al., above, n. 2, 75.

[64] Although, it must be acknowledged, there has always been a gap between rhetoric and reality here. As Davies and Freedland point out, British law has long distinguished between different types of workers (above, n. 58, 285), including, until relatively recently, formally privileging full-time over part-time employees with respect to access to employment rights. See *R.* v. *Secretary of State for Employment, ex parte Equal Opportunities Commission* [1995] 1 AC 1.   [65] Davies and Freedland, above, n. 58, 286.
[66] Ibid.

consequences which flow from those differences, while simultaneously seeking to identify points of commonality which may form the basis for a politics of solidarity and collective action.[67] Paul O'Higgins has recently acknowledged that the 'welcome entry' of particular groups of workers into the labour force such as 'women, immigrants etc' has contributed to the weakening of trade union power, attributing this effect to the lack of an organizing tradition among these groups.[68] But the problem is not simply one of lack of organization. It is rather that the presence of diversely constituted groups of workers, situated legally, socially, and economically in a hierarchical relation to one another, presents new organizational challenges which the idealized subject of labour law cannot meet. One possible solution, advocated in the context of differences between workers across jurisdictions, is to build a collective agenda around a strategy of core labour rights. The discourse of core labour rights, as well as other ethical engagements with fundamental and social rights, might be understood as one response to the dilemma a more divided and unequal (global) workforce has generated for the labour movement. However, a real risk of 'paring down' labour standards to their core components, particularly against a background consensus in favour of the pursuit of labour market flexibility, is that core labour rights will serve to legitimate rather than diminish inequalities between workers.[69] Moreover, in so far as the legal privileging of some workers over others is grounded in economic norms, for example, in the economic benefits of a flexible workforce or the demands of competitiveness, this can effect the subordination, if not full evacuation of, ethical/egalitarian considerations from labour law discourse not least because it becomes very difficult to justify the stark inequalities which result.

In sum, the collapse of the unitary subject seriously undermines the rhetorical stance of progressive labour law, certainly as it has played out to date, and calls for the articulation of new normative visions which can direct and inform a transformative labour law agenda in an increasingly unequal world. In this context it is imperative that labour lawyers confront directly the inegalitarian effects of current constructions of work and family. Otherwise, any normative reconstructive project is doomed

[67] See e.g. Ontiveros, M., 'A New Course for Labour Unions: Identity-based Organizing as a Response to Globalization', and Selmi, M. and McUsic, M., 'Difference and Solidarity: Unions in a Postmodern Age', in Conaghan et al., above, n. 2, at 417 and 429 respectively.

[68] O'Higgins, P., 'The End of Labour Law as We have Known It', in Barnard et al., above, n. 17, 289, 291.

[69] See further Rittich, K., 'Core Labor Rights and Labor Market Flexibility: Two Paths Entwined?', in International Bureau of the Permanent Court of Arbitration (ed.), *Labour Law Beyond Borders: ADR and the Internationalization of Labour Dispute Settlement*, papers emanating from the 5th PCA International Law Seminar, 7 May 2002 (The Hague: Kluwer Law International, 2003), 157.

to reproduce the inequities of the old. Thus, while the idea of distinguishing between workers may seem alien to labour law 'as we know
it',[70] a focus on the work/family dichotomy tells us that this has long
been one of its most entrenched features. More importantly, the work/
family dichotomy situates labour law within a very different normative
framework from that which is normally invoked. From the perspective
of unpaid caregivers, labour law becomes repositioned as a mode of
regulation with concrete distributive effects, not only in relation to
employers and workers, but also between and among workers (paid
and unpaid). To put it another way, the allegedly benign or vocational
purposes of traditional labour law are called into serious question when
its gendered distributional consequences are highlighted. What becomes
clear is that labour law has long operated within the context of a highly
oppressive gendered division of labour which it has actively supported
and reinforced.

The dilemma which labour lawyers face today in terms of an apparent
need to distinguish between different kinds of workers with distributive
consequences privileging some at the expense of others, is merely the
outward expression of an aspect of labour law which has always been
there. To date the conceptual separation of the work/family dichotomy
has facilitated the denial of this somewhat unpalatable truth. Although
labour law is not and never has been neutral as to outcomes between
workers we have been able to proceed, more or less, as if it is. The
challenge now is how to apply this new understanding of the past to the
problems of the present.

Labour law without boundaries?

Labour law is beset by boundaries. The traditional delineation of its
contours is strongly reliant upon the dichotomized pairing of concepts
hierarchically positioned in relation to one another: public/private;
work/family; paid/unpaid; employed/unemployed; formal economy/
informal economy; typical/atypical workers; standard/non-standard
work; regulation/deregulation; citizens/aliens, to name but a few. The
invocation of these pairings maps neatly on to the inside and outside of
labour law, with the first concept in each of the pairings belonging
'inside' and the second falling 'outside' the labour law frame.

An inescapable consequence of boundaries is the construction of
hierarchies and exclusions. A bounded labour law cannot fail to privilege
some workers over others. Indeed, as we have seen, a bounded labour

---

[70] O'Higgins, above, n. 68.

law is directly implicated in the construction of differences between workers, for example, in the construction of workers as paid or unpaid, as employed or unemployed, as typical or atypical, and as citizens or aliens.[71] Moreover, these differences, while the product of legal, political, cultural, and economic choices, are nevertheless a means by which particular costs and benefits are spread among workers: they are strongly distributive in their concrete effects.

This suggests that an egalitarian labour law should seek to move beyond boundaries; a transformative agenda is to be boundary-less. And, as virtually all of labour law's boundaries are currently in flux in the context of radical changes in the world of work, the time for a labour law without boundaries, along with the progressive opportunities this presents, may be close at hand.

Consider once again the distinction between paid and unpaid work. It has been argued throughout this chapter that labour law is implicated in the construction and perpetuation of a conceptual and discursive separation of work and family which has served completely to exclude unpaid work from the scope of labour law's progressive aspirations, while placing a large class of people, namely women, in a position of economic dependence and vulnerability. At the same time, it has been suggested that those progressive aspirations have been rendered problematic, not just because they have been historically pursued to benefit paid workers at the expense of unpaid workers, but also because, even among paid workers, labour law is more and more implicated in effecting and legitimating inegalitarian outcomes.

This has led some scholars to advocate a widening ambit for labour law which reaches beyond the employment relationship to embrace issues pertaining to the labour market more generally.[72] Such an approach has the (potential) virtue of combining distributive considerations, for example, in relation to labour market access and strategies for job creation, with economic concerns about the operation of the labour market in the context of a wider agenda of growth and competitiveness. While clearly there is real risk here that the latter will eclipse the former, it is also the case that this broader focus brings into the frame of labour law

[71] There is a whole other agenda here, paralleling and intersecting with the critique of the work/family dichotomy which explores the boundary between citizen and alien in relation to work issues and the role of labour law, both past and present, in constructing some workers as deserving and undeserving of the 'economic' benefits of citizenship. See generally Bosniak, L., 'Critical Reflections on "Citizenship" as a Progressive Aspiration', in Conaghan et al., above n. 2, 339.

[72] See e.g. the essays in Mitchell, above, n. 2, esp. Arup (above, n. 9) and Gahan, P. and Mitchell, R., 'The Limits of Labour Law and the Necessity of Interdisciplinary Analysis', 62. See also Collins, above, n. 3, and Deakin and Morris, above, n. 51, 1.

a host of excluded constituencies, including the unemployed (or those in and out of employment),[73] immigrant workers, those working in informal, unregulated markets, *and* women engaged in unpaid caregiving work. Once labour law is formally extended to issues of access to paid work, the gendered allocation and distributive effects of unpaid work cannot fail to come clearly into view.

This poses both an opportunity and yet a further risk. The opportunity is the possibility of reconceiving work in ways which truly advance the goals of a progressive labour law agenda, in which work is no longer deeply implicated in inequality and oppression but plays a key role in the promotion of individual and collective human flourishing. This requires a radical shift away from a 'factory vision' of work, with its sharp spatial and temporal delineation of labour activities. As Karl Klare observes: 'The object of study must be not just the workplace but *work's place* in personal, social, and economic life, in social reproduction, and in offering possibilities for and imposing constraints upon human self-realization'.[74] Or, to invoke the rhetoric of the ILO, the concern must be with securing 'decent work',[75] not just work that pays well (or pays at all) but work which promotes human dignity and fosters solidarity in the context of a broader recognition of the interconnectedness of all labour activities, productive and reproductive.[76]

The risk, of course, is that the current openness of labour law to the concerns of unpaid workers, manifest in the form of an institutional and political preoccupation with family-friendly policies, will become merely a technique of governance, a way in which states manage the tensions arising from the collapse of a particular historical accommodation of productive and reproductive needs stemming from an earlier period of industrialization.[77] It is therefore important to view the debate about work and family in the wider context of rapidly rising inequalities in wealth and income worldwide and a seemingly irreversible decline of union power. A world of precarious women workers, moving seamlessly and silently between their productive and reproductive tasks, is not a world that will deliver decent work (although it may well prove to be the 'family-friendly' future). Nor is it a world in which collective labour strategies will flourish. In short, unless, and until, labour lawyers confront the full consequences of the gender division of labour in terms

---

[73] See generally Williams, L., 'Beyond Labour Law's Parochialism: A Re-Envisioning of the Discourse of Redistribution', in Conaghan et al., above, n. 2, 94.

[74] Klare, above, n. 2, 20.

[75] See further International Labour Office, Report of the Director-General, *Decent Work* (Geneva: International Labour Conference, 87th Session, 1999); International Labour Office, Report of the Director-General, *Reducing the Decent Work Deficit: A Global Challenge*, Report 1(A) (Geneva: International Labour Conference, 89th Session, 2001). [76] Ibid.

[77] See Conaghan, above, n. 44, and also Fudge, in this volume.

of effecting and entrenching inegalitarian work relations, any project of progressive transformation through labour law is likely to founder.

V CONCLUSION: REIMAGINING THE WORKER

It takes an act of the imagination to bring the unpaid worker into the sphere of consideration of labour law. But, if labour law as a discipline is to have a normative dimension, if it is to move beyond the mere facilitation of techniques of governance, that is precisely what is required.

There is, however, a particular danger associated with this strategy and, indeed, with any strategy which focuses on differences between workers. The danger is that we will lose sight of capital or, more precisely, that we will omit consideration of the role of capitalist social relations in positioning workers as unequal in relation to one another. Rather than seeing work relations in terms of capital and labour, quintessentially captured in the employer–employee relationship, we will instead invoke the state as both the derivation of and solution to problems of inequality and disadvantage in a work-based context. In this way, for example, 'social' rights conferred by the state emerge as a way of addressing issues relating to the work/life balance. Citizenship becomes the route to our individual and collective advancement.

This cannot be viewed as anything other than a worrying development particularly in the context of strategies to promote worker solidarity in the face of global economic exploitation. It is hardly surprising, therefore, that many labour lawyers seek to hang on to the paid labour relationship as a way of anchoring labour law discourse in an analytical frame in which capital (understood as employers) formally features. Within such a frame, the 'worker' is always understood relationally, and it is that relational context which gives rise to the risk of commodification of labour and, consequently, to exploitation. Thus, as Davies and Freedland observe:

> The whole business of identifying the worker is . . . a matter of recognising a person as being in a particular relationship which qualifies him or her as having the capacity of a worker; the term 'worker' depicts a relational capacity, as surely as does that of 'spouse' or 'cousin'.[78]

According to this understanding, it might be more difficult to characterize unpaid caregivers as 'workers', as their work is not carried out in a relational context or at least not in the context of a formal relationship of economic subordination and dependence.

---

[78] Davies, P. and Freedland, M., 'Changing Perspectives upon the Employment Relationship in British Labour Law', in Barnard et al., above, n. 17, 129, 131.

However, leaving aside the question of whether or not domestic labour is expressive of gender-based relations of subordination and dependence (which feminists have long argued is the case), the assumption that unpaid workers are not economically related to processes of production and, therefore, at risk of, if not subject to, economic exploitation, is plainly unsustainable. If the current crisis of work and family tells us anything, it tells us that the dichotomy between 'paid' and 'unpaid' work is a product of legal and social forms which belie their interdependence in the context of productive activities. In the context of progressive labour strategies, to focus only on those relationships which law acknowledges as economic and labour-related is to allow the legal form to shape the normative agenda rather than the normative agenda to (re)shape the legal form. In the same way, to assume that a shift away from employment (and therefore employer) facilitates the evacuation of capital from the scene of labour relations is to mistake the employment relationship for the range of institutions, structures, practices, and discourses which situate capital and labour in relation to one another, creating the conditions which render workers vulnerable.[79]

It is time then for workers to regroup. It is time for collective labour to reconceive its understanding of itself. And it is time for labour lawyers fundamentally to revise the parameters of the discipline.

[79] This recognition extends to the problematization of employer as well as worker, a project which is already underway in labour law. See ibid.

3

Equity or Efficiency: International Institutions and the Work/Family Nexus

KERRY RITTICH

A variety of international institutions have discovered that women are a focal point in the transformation of the economy, and one of the keys to enhanced growth. The result is a burgeoning series of investigations into the question of women's economic activity and labour market participation, and a range of different analyses of the factors—institutional, cultural, economic, legal—that enhance or impede it. In most, if not all of these analyses, managing the relationship between work and the family, and coming to grips in a comprehensive way with the problem of care, turn out to be central concerns.

For example, the World Bank has issued an analysis of the integration of gender equality into development efforts, *Engendering Development: Through Gender Equality in Rights, Resources and Voice*,[1] which makes the integration of women into markets the engine of both enhanced development and greater gender equality. A deep consciousness of the conflicting demands of work and the family pervades the comprehensive report of the European Commission on the challenge of regulating labour markets in the new economy.[2] The OECD has devoted significant attention to the question in its annual *Employment Outlook*,[3] and has work programmes devoted to the examination of 'Family-Friendly Social Policies', and 'Early Childhood Education and Care'.[4] The UNDP, too, has identified the 'care' deficit as a critical issue in its *Human Development Reports*.[5] And these are only some of the most prominent examples.

The amount of interest in women's labour market participation is unprecedented at the international level, as is the range of institutions now displaying an interest in the issue. While the ILO and the international human rights treaty bodies have long addressed such issues, they

[1] World Bank, *Engendering Development: Through Gender Equality in Rights, Resources and Voice* (Washington, DC: World Bank, 2001).

[2] Supiot, A., *Beyond Employment: Changes in Work and the Future of Labour Law in Europe* (Oxford: OUP, 2001).

[3] OECD, *Employment Outlook 2001* (Paris: OECD, 2001), esp. ch. 4, 'Balancing Work and Family Life: Helping Parents into Paid Employment'. [4] Ibid.

[5] UNDP, *Human Development Report 1999* (New York: OUP, 1999). See the chapter, 'The invisible heart—care and the global economy'.

have typically done so as a subset of concerns over working conditions or gender equality. In both areas, the work/family nexus was understood to be almost exclusively a women's issue and, until recently, was of interest only to those institutions with mandates to further equality and human rights, or with recognized competence and jurisdiction in relation to work and employment.

Work/family issues have now overflowed their designated international channels. What is noteworthy is that they are not just of interest to the institutions concerned with gender equality, or even to those concerned with work; nor are they necessarily figured as equality or 'social' concerns. The new and important development is that the work/family nexus has entered the consciousness of the international financial and economic organizations. Moreover, the point of entry to these debates is the economy itself: for better and for worse, the rules and institutions governing the work/family nexus are increasingly recognized as integral to a host of 'hard' policy concerns, such as the promotion of economic growth, the enhancement of national competitiveness and productivity, and reductions in levels of 'dependency', and, by extension, the fiscal burdens upon the state. It is for this reason that work/family issues have gone mainstream.

It is not difficult to imagine the reasons for this turn of events, as accounts of the new economy constitute litanies of gender-associated concerns. The feminization of the labour market, the decline of the family wage, the emergence of the single family household (usually headed by a mother who is, and is expected to be, engaged in labour market work), and the decline and displacement of the redistributive state are central themes in contemporary policy and regulatory debates. They have all converged to focus an unprecedented level of interest on the extent and quality of women's labour market participation.

However, it would be a mistake to imagine that the new salience of work/family concerns, especially outside the institutions and domains that have traditionally been preoccupied with them, necessarily reflects a moment of enlightenment about gender equality or a new interest in the social dimension of a market-centred world. And, to the extent that it suggests a convergence of thinking among market reformers and social justice activists about 'the way forward' in current reform efforts, the very salience of work/family issues can be deceptive. There are very different motivations, starting points, and institutional agendas in play in respect of the work/family conflict which reflect concerns that are at once distinct, overlapping, diverging, and conflicting. For feminists and others concerned with gender equality, addressing work/family conflict remains principally an essential aspect of eliminating gender bias in labour markets and social and economic life more broadly. Elsewhere, it is connected to the goal of transforming women into more productive workers in order to generate greater growth. In some quarters, it is an ineluctable aspect of (re)solving the crisis of the welfare state and ensuring income security in post-industrial economies. In others, it is anxiety over birth rates and declining numbers of children, the reflection of a systemic incapacity to both work and reproduce. Elsewhere, it is an essential element of establishing a new normative and institutional structure of production and exchange in the new economy. And there are as many ideas about how, and how not, to address the issue as there are about why it is important to do so. Even the very language and terms in which the work/family nexus is discussed vary radically from arena to arena. So while it is clear that there seems to be greater convergence upon the work/family nexus among the international institutions, and more, rather than less, agreement as to its importance, little else, whether in the way of normative assumptions, conceptual framework, structural analysis, or programme and prescription, is necessarily shared.

This chapter investigates this phenomenon, with a view to uncovering why the interest in the work/family interface has emerged within the international financial institutions (IFIs) at this point in time. It considers the different terms and frameworks in which work/family issues are analysed, the new policy and regulatory prescriptions that are now being generated that bear on the intersection of market with non-market obligations, and the stakes for those, typically women with obligations of care, who are likely most directly to experience their effects. What emerges is that work/family issues have not simply registered in new ways on the international plane; rather, the IFIs have become newly important to the way that work/family concerns are represented and resolved. Because their analysis diverges from that of other scholars and institutions, the work/family nexus itself needs to be understood as a dense transfer point at which a number of projects and concerns intersect, sharp conflicts are visible, and out of which a range of possible outcomes seem both possible and likely.

There are key positions and templates on issues from gender equality to the goals of market societies which inform the perception of the work/ family nexus, animate the policy and regulatory debates, and shape the reform trajectories now under debate across the international institutions. These frameworks—the objectives and concerns that are raised, the language in which they are addressed, and the policy/regulatory instruments that seem alternatively available or unavailable to address them—matter acutely in terms of the approach adopted to the work/ family interface. These frameworks, in turn, rest upon myriad intermingled assumptions, both normative and empirical, about the effects of labour market and other forms of regulation; about the proper function of the state, in respect of objectives ranging from the generation of economic growth to the provision of social security; about the nature of markets and productive activity; about the appropriate forms of equality; and even about the organization of social and economic life.

Discussions around the work/family nexus are typically conducted either in the language of equality and social justice or in terms of efficiency and productivity. However, terms like 'equality' and 'efficiency' soon reveal themselves to be unstable and problematic points of reference. This is not simply because their relative importance as values is contested. Rather, the concepts themselves and their policy and regulatory implications are contested in ways that turn out to be intensely relevant to the questions that arise at the work/family nexus. Gender equality in market societies, for example, might be determined by the access of women to educational and work opportunities at the formal level, or it might be measured in terms of the substantive economic equality between men and women, or by something in between these two positions. In regulatory or institutional terms, gender equality might be pursued through the increased participation of women on the terms of work now on offer to men, the incorporation of a range of measures to accommodate women's ongoing family obligations, or it might entail the transformation of the norms and institutions governing work and welfare in a more radically egalitarian direction. The endorsement of gender equality only marks the beginning of a series of further conceptual debates and institutional decisions that are critical to the actual outcome for women. Any discussion of efficient labour markets involves similar complexities. The rules, institutions, and policies which enhance efficiency and productivity at work are a subject of intense debate at both the normative and empirical levels.[6] However, what efficiency itself 'is' is also contested, in ways that make all the difference to the experience of women in labour markets.[7]

All of these complexities are visible in the current discussions on gender equality in the international institutions, and all of these questions converge, as does the relationship between equality and efficiency itself, at the work/family nexus. A central problem is this: if the efficiency calculus is arbitrarily limited so that non-market costs and externalities are excluded, 'efficiency-enhancing' policies may not only produce perverse

---

[6] For a review, see Deakin, S. and Wilkinson, F., 'Labour Law and Economic Theory: A Reappraisal', in H. Collins, P. Davies, and R. Rideout (eds.), *Legal Regulation of the Employment Relation* (London: Kluwer Law International, 2000), 29.

[7] Elson, D., 'Labour Markets as Gendered Institutions: Equality, Efficiency and Empowerment Issues', *World Development*, 27:3 (1999), 611.

results on their own terms, that is to say they may fail to generate the positive economic outcomes their proponents predict. Rather, those who work outside as well as inside the market, regularly traversing the border between the 'productive' and 'reproductive' spheres, will be compelled to absorb disproportionate costs and risks, a situation that both reflects and creates ongoing disadvantage for women both at work and at home.

For these reasons, neither the commitments to equality nor efficiency in the end generate any single set of policy prescriptions, nor are the two objectives easily separated from each other. As much as equality and efficiency have been, and remain, associated with particular policy and regulatory positions which are clearly visible within different international institutions, completely opposing policies can be, and are being, generated in the name of each. This has become more evident as market reformers have begun to address equality concerns, while those interested in distributive justice have started to frame their claims in terms of costs and benefits. Once again, these developments are both unusually visible and highly important around the work/family nexus. Thus, the World Bank now advocates the removal of a range of labour market rules including protective regulations and paid maternity leave for women, not merely on the grounds of efficiency but because of their supposed contribution to gender inequality.[8] Others make the opposite argument, attempting to document the potential contributions of redistributive measures such as paid family leave, a classic target of market reformers, to a goal reformers themselves profess to endorse and promote, the enhanced participation of women in labour markets.[9] To complicate things further, new terms and objectives are now circulating in debates around labour market reform that cannot be safely or solely associated with either. The goals of social inclusion and the focus on the enhancement of human capital, for example, may sound both in the register of greater equality and greater efficiency, and women's labour market participation is a focal point in each.

Yet while at this stage, the arguments have become complex, neither the players, the positions they articulate, nor the arguments behind them are equally influential in the debates. The only constant is the significance of work/family issues, especially for those most directly affected: enormous consequences flow from the management of change at the ideological, policy, and regulatory levels.

[8] World Bank, *Integrating Gender into the World Bank's Work: A Strategy for Action* (Washington, DC: World Bank, 2002).
[9] Lester, G., 'A Defense of Paid Family Leave', *Harvard Women's Law Journal*, 28 (2005), 1.

48 *Kerry Rittich*

I INTERNATIONAL INSTITUTIONS: THE LABOUR MARKET DEBATES

The ILO has long been identified as the international institution with normative, technical, and legal authority in respect of work, including the development of labour standards. Despite the efforts to confirm this authority in the context of debates over labour standards in the global economy,[10] in recent years the international economic and financial institutions have also become significant sites of research, debate, and prescription on matters of labour market regulation, social protection policy, and other questions related to the status of workers, as they have with other issues associated with global economic integration. Although they were virtually irrelevant to these debates but a few years ago, the IFIs in particular have become important players in debates over labour market regulation and social protection policy, weighing in on domestic policy, and regulatory questions in both material and rhetorical ways.[11]

The reasons for their engagement and influence are complex. Some of it arises simply from the new interest in international institutions and supra- or transnational solutions generated by the perceived regulatory weaknesses of the nation state in an economically integrated world. As has been widely noted, the new possibilities of exit afforded to capital have placed enhanced pressure on states to create 'business-friendly' regulatory environments. Yet the growing gap between the world of production and the existing regulatory and protective schemes is also producing pressure to reform and restructure, rather than simply dismantle, such schemes in order better to ensure the welfare and economic security of the growing numbers of un- or inadequately protected workers and citizens. The ongoing potential for social dumping and competitive 'deregulation' among states suggest that labour market and social protection, if not necessarily regulated in conventional ways, can at least be usefully analysed and coordinated at the supranational level.[12]

However these factors alone would not account for the preoccupation of the IFIs with labour issues. Here, what is significant is the role that the

[10] WTO, Singapore Ministerial Declaration, Doc. WT/MIN(96)/DEC/, reprinted in 36 *Int'l Legal Materials* 218, 221 (Jan. 1997).

[11] World Bank, *World Development Report 1995: Workers in an Integrating World* (New York: OUP, 1995).

[12] Because of the move toward fully integrated markets, the possibilities of supranational coordination and soft regulation of labour and social protection policy have been most fully explored and developed in the European Union. For discussions of the European Employment Strategy and the Open Method of Coordination, see Trubek, D. M. and Mosher, J. S., 'New Governance, Employment Policy and the European Social Model', in D. M. Trubek and J. Zeitlin (eds.), *Governing Work and Welfare in a New Economy: European and American Experiments* (Oxford: OUP, 2003).

IFIs play in the general matter of global economic governance. The IFIs have assumed a major role in articulating the norms and institutional parameters which should govern state regulatory practice in the new economy. Because of their institutional implications, and because they are centrally implicated in the normative shifts described next, labour market regulation and social policy reform now routinely figure at the centre of these governance debates.

The debates around governance have taken on heightened significance because the practical concerns and incentives to coordinate or harmonize regulatory practice in a globally integrated economy have coincided with marked normative shifts and ideological conflict around the role of the state and the very purposes of regulation and governance. There are many explanations for these shifts, and debate and conflict over these issues are visible well beyond the IFIs in multiple arenas both domestic and international. However, at the international level, the IFIs have been important drivers of new regulatory projects and authors of the ideology and logic behind them. These institutional and ideological projects are important to both the framing of work/family issues and their management at the policy and regulatory levels, as the approaches of the IFIs to the work/family conundrum are deeply dependent on their orientation toward a more general issue of labour market institutions and social protection and insurance schemes in the new economy. Their views on these issues, in turn, are connected to quite fundamental commitments around governance and the role of the state in economic life. Thus, understanding the diverse approaches to work/family issues on the international plane, and the different trajectories for solving the current dilemmas on work/family issues that are currently proposed, requires at least a basic appreciation of the other concerns and commitments that animate the international institutions. Moreover, these norms and claims emerging from the IFIs now coexist uneasily with a set of other international norms around labour and social protection promulgated by older, if currently less influential, international organizations such as the ILO. Hence, what is emerging at the international level is a split between competing normative and regulatory frameworks in respect of workplace regulation and social policy.

On one hand, the IFIs are attempting to promote a new economic and social welfare order based upon an altered, and much confined, role for the state in the attainment of citizens' income security and greater effort, responsibility, and assumption of risk on the part of the individual worker or household. Although the IFIs were born out of a consensus that a strong regulatory and redistributive role for domestic states was necessary to international economic and political stability,[13] the institutions themselves now subscribe to the view that transactional ease and the facilitation of investment must be the overarching concerns for states in the domain of economic policy and regulation and institutional design.[14] They have become forceful proponents of a reconfigured 'market-friendly' and 'enabling' state, regulatory frameworks which are focused on the correction of market failures, and the pursuit of individual welfare and economic security largely through participation in labour markets. As described below, their gaze has now extended to social issues. But where social concerns figure in their agenda, it is largely to the extent that they either impede or promote the project of economic growth.

On the other hand is a range of international institutions—the ILO, UNDP, the UN human rights bodies—that have long promoted social objectives in different ways. Although they have distinct institutional concerns and mandates which might bring them into contact with work/family issues from different angles, what tends to unite these institutions in contemporary regulatory and policy debates is a concern about the 'social deficit' within the emerging market-centred structure of the international order. In general, they are seeking to alter the normative orientation of global regulatory efforts to make them less exclusively focused on efficiency enhancement and more attuned to human welfare and development and other, now excluded or demoted values and objectives, including solidarity, cohesion, and social inclusion; long-term political and social stability and sustainability; equality, whether along regional, gender, or any number of other axes; and human rights.

Out of these conflicting general orientations have emerged two dominant approaches to labour market policy, regulation, and institutions. The first is the promotion of labour market flexibility through reforms to, or the elimination of, labour market institutions. In the view of the IFIs and the OECD, many labour market institutions introduce rigidities into labour markets that impair the competitive performance of economies and create protected classes of workers to the detriment of others in the process. The second is the call for respect for workers' human rights and the introduction of human rights norms into the operation of global labour markets. The ILO now seeks to gain acceptance of the view that certain labour rights identified as basic or 'core' in the

[13] Kapstein, E., 'Distributive Justice as an International Public Good: A Historical Perspective', in I. Kaul (ed.), *Global Public Goods: International Cooperation in the Twenty-First Century* (Oxford: OUP, 1999), 88.

[14] See e.g. World Bank, *Doing Business in 2004: Understanding Regulation* (Washington, DC: World Bank, 2004); IMF, *World Economic Outlook: Advancing Structural Reforms* (Washington, DC: IMF, 2004), ch. III, 'Fostering Structural Reforms in Industrial Countries', online at www.imf.org.

Declaration on Fundamental Principles and Rights at Work[15] must be recognized as human rights and form part of the constitutive framework of the global economy.[16] Human rights scholars, and UN treaty bodies, for their part, make the case for recognition of a still broader list of worker entitlements, including many which have historically been supported by the ILO.[17] Although they are not entailed by each other, these two basic orientations toward labour market regulation have historically been associated with particular positions on the provision of welfare and social protection as well. In general, those who favour labour market flexibilization or 'deregulation' also favour restrictions on state provision of social benefits and transfer payments, while those who favour human and labour rights typically defend a broader protective and redistributive role for the state. The ILO, for example, is now organizing its response to the social deficit in terms of the promotion of decent work, an agenda which involves, in addition to core labour rights, the promotion of employment, social protection, and an enhanced voice for workers.[18]

However, for a variety of reasons, the distinctions between these two agendas are becoming somewhat muddied. In the wake of a range of criticisms of the dominant approach to market reform in the 1990s, the IFIs have now formally endorsed a 'kinder, gentler' approach to economic development, one that incorporates human rights and a range of social concerns into market reform and integration agendas.[19] As a result, they now purport to pursue a merged economic/social agenda which involves recognizing social development and respect for human rights both as independently valuable ends and because of their contribution to economic growth.[20] The ILO, for its part, now pays much greater attention to the exigencies of economic growth and often speaks the language of efficiency and competitiveness too.[21]

For example, the Bank claims to recognize human rights obligations including core labour rights, at least to the extent that they are linked to,

[15] ILO, Declaration on Fundamental Principles and Rights at Work, 86th Session, Geneva, June 1998, online at www.ilo.org.
[16] UN, Report of the World Summit for Social Development: Copenhagen Declaration and Programme of Action, 6–12 March 1995, UN Doc. A/Conf.166/9.
[17] Alston, P., ' "Core Labour Standards" and the Transformation of the International Labour Rights Regime', *EJIL*, 15 (2004), 457.
[18] ILO, Report of the Director General: *Decent Work*, 87th Session, Geneva, June 1999, online at www.ilo.org; ILO Director General, *Reducing the Decent Work Deficit: A Global Challenge*, 89th Session, Geneva, June 2001, online at www.ilo.org.
[19] World Bank, 'Ten Things You Should Know about the CDF', online at www.worldbank.org.
[20] For a theoretical discussion of this development, see Amartya Sen, *Development as Freedom* (Oxford: OUP, 1999).
[21] ILO, *A Fair Globalization: Creating Opportunities for All*, Final Report, World Commission on the Social Dimensions of Globalization, 24 Feb. 2004, online at www.ilo.org.

and compatible with, its institutional mandate to promote economic growth. Similarly, the OECD professes allegiance to *both* ideals, flexibility *and* basic human rights, arguing that there is no inherent conflict between respect for core labour standards and concerns around competitiveness and comparative advantage in the global economy.[22] Moreover, the Bank has also endorsed gender equality as an aid to growth, while at the same time arguing that market-centred growth, accompanied by a limited set of legal reforms, enhanced 'voice' for women, and some re-allocation of resources is the most promising vehicle by which to promote gender equality.[23] As a result, while greater labour market flexibility on the one hand and enhanced rights, security, and empowerment for workers on the other remain relatively distinct institutional orientations, at this point, the proponents of flexibility often speak the language of the social too, endorsing not only labour market 'deregulation' but a limited number of worker rights and gender equality too.

While this seems to suggest the emergence of overlapping agendas and a convergence of objectives at one level, below the surface agreement often dissipates. This is because the real debate is not only over the place and weight of abstract values such as workers' rights and gender equality or the need to recognize the social dimension of economic growth, but rather the way that these objectives are conceptualized and the means available to pursue them. This becomes clear once we try to imagine the place of work/family issues in this merged social and economic agenda.

II THE WORK/FAMILY NEXUS IN CONTEMPORARY LABOUR MARKET AND WELFARE DEBATES

It has become unavoidably clear that household issues, particularly obligations of care to dependent household members and the division of unpaid labour between men and women, figure in increasingly central ways in debates over the transformation of work, reforms to labour and employment regulations, and the future of the welfare state, all issues that the IFIs regard as key 'structural' concerns in the new economy.[24]

The emerging social welfare deficit which the changes in production, household structure, and labour market demographics have provoked is

---

[22] OECD, *Trade, Employment and Labour Standards: A Study of Core Workers' Rights and International Trade* (Paris: OECD, 1996); OECD, *International Trade and Core Labour Standards* (Paris: OECD, 2000).

[23] World Bank, above n. 1. For an analysis of this project, see Rittich K., 'Engendering Development/Marketing Equality', *Albany Law Review*, 67 (2003), 575.

[24] See IMF, *World Economic Outlook: Advancing Structural Reforms* (Washington, DC: IMF, 2004), ch. III, 'Fostering Structural Reforms in Industrial Countries', 103–46. Available online at www.imf.org.

often referred to as the 'crisis of the welfare state'. As Esping-Anderson has pointed out,[25] the 'crisis' said to be afflicting the welfare state is better understood as a crisis of the post-war welfare regimes as a whole. The replacement of 'state' with 'regime' as the object of attention is important: it reflects the fact that welfare and income security are the joint products of (at least) three institutions, the state, the market, and the family, each of which performs an important role, either explicitly or implicitly, in securing these objectives. Because of normative changes in the realm of governance and the role of the state, transformations in the organization of production, and revolutions in family structure and stability, each institution is now undergoing significant change. These tectonic shifts are beginning to make clear what was formerly much more obscure: this is how deeply interdependent the functioning of these institutions is, and how much each relies upon a set of assumptions about the nature, concerns, and operation of the others. One result of these myriad intersecting changes is the disruption of the assumption that family concerns could be a) safely cabined from those of the market, or b) dealt with, 'business as usual', in the conventional way. As a result, the settled assumption that there are *a priori* distinct realms of state, household, or market responsibilities is now in question.

The post-war welfare state in industrialized economies typically comprised an interlocking set of labour market institutions, social insurance, and social protection schemes, as well as public goods and services such as health care and education either provided or funded by the state. Although they took a surprisingly wide variety of forms in market societies, these different arrangements could plausibly be described as variations on a basic theme. All involved some division of labour and allocation of responsibilities among the three institutions.

As feminist critics first pointed out, and as Esping-Anderson himself now acknowledges, what was most missing from standard accounts of welfare states in industrial societies, including his own path-defining work,[26] was an appreciation of the role of the family as an ongoing provider and residual source of welfare. The post-war compact and the regimes that developed out of it were replete with assumptions, both empirical and ideological, about the nature of the labour force, the parties for whom income protection and social insurance were appropriate, and the extent to which it was necessary for the state to ensure the provision of particular goods and services. At every level gender structured the

---

[25] Esping-Anderson, G., *Social Foundations of Post-industrial Economies* (Oxford: OUP, 1999).
[26] See *The Three Worlds of Welfare Capitalism* (Princeton: Princeton University Press, 1990), in which Esping-Anderson develops a typology of the main forms of the welfare state in industrial capitalism.

design of institutions: women (and children) stood in a mediated position within this structure; limited categories apart, the expectation was that their welfare could be secured through the male breadwinner, as dependants and members of his household.

Yet however unacknowledged, the efforts to secure welfare through labour market institutions, and various state entitlements, policies, and programmes, were in fact dependent upon the presence and indeed continuity of a certain family or household structure that enabled, and indeed encouraged, the presence of unpaid workers at home doing a variety of tasks. Such workers were indispensable to the capacity of the labour market worker to perform his role; they were also vitally important to the economy as a whole. But presumptions about the existence and activities of unpaid workers also helped demarcate the responsibilities assumed by the state from those which devolved to the household. In many states, it was never seriously contemplated, for example, that care, or resources for care, be comprehensively provided to those no longer able to care for themselves, those never able to do so without assistance, or small children before the age of school. Home care for those who were ill was also limited. Even in its more elaborated forms, the welfare state was never intended to 'do it all'; with respect to many services, it was never expected to provide more than residual support. While the market provided an alternative to those in a position to purchase such services, there was no presumption that this would be the norm. Rather, the residual source of welfare was the family or household, with many services to be provided on an unpaid basis by women.

The degree of 'familialization'—the extent to which welfare regimes rely upon the family and unpaid family workers as sources of welfare—varies greatly, something that is unsurprising given that the division of labour between the family, the state, and the market is an artefact of history, politics, and ideology rather than a fact of nature.[27] However, regimes which repose significant responsibilities in the family necessarily presume the presence and availability of someone who is in a position to assume these responsibilities; because of the gender order in respect of unpaid work, in practice they turn out to be highly disadvantageous for women. Thus, the demands of gender equality alone compel a revisiting of the post-war social compact. But because of changes ranging from the demographic shifts in the labour market to the reorganization of production, virtually all of the assumptions that made familialization a workable, if inequitable, strategy have now been destabilized in any event. The workforce has been feminized in primary, rather than merely

---

[27] Rittich, K., *Recharacterizing Restructuring: Law, Distribution and Gender in Market Reform* (The Hague: Kluwer Law International, 2002), ch. 5.

secondary, ways; families and households now take a variety of forms; households are increasingly unstable; the 'family wage' has largely disappeared; and 'normal' long-term jobs and their benefits are increasingly scarce in emerging sectors such as service work.

Whatever the degree of urgency generated by this state of affairs, it is enhanced by a cross-cutting set of concerns about the demographic profile of the labour market. Industrial states are increasingly concerned about ageing populations, low levels of labour force participation, and the growing financial demands on state programmes and entitlements as baby boomers retire. Such trends are creating fears about the sustainability of even 'basic' social programmes, usually identified as the pensions of current workers. They are also placing in doubt the continued availability of services such as health care. The concern over these issues can be acute, as almost all states are also experiencing fairly dramatic declines in fertility rates too. For non-settler states in Europe and Japan, this is producing a social and cultural, as well as a potential economic, crisis.

It is widely recognized that responding to these structural changes and redressing the systematic inequities for those with caregiving obligations requires a reallocation of costs and risks among the three institutions, the state, the market, and the individual or household.[28] Costs of care now borne largely by women need to be more widely assumed, and the economic risks associated with maternity and parenting need to be protected against. Indeed, it seems necessary to reassess in a thoroughgoing way the assumptions about the risks and needs of the 'normal' worker that are now reflected in labour market institutions, social protection and insurance schemes.

The most popular responses to the work/family crisis involve the commodification of unpaid work—paying the worker to perform the work herself or devising a scheme which effectively means that someone else is paid to do the work—and/or the reallocation of unpaid work between men and women. But unless the ambitions and scope of gender equality are themselves to be curtailed, what is required is not simply the transformation of unpaid into paid work or even a better distribution of unpaid work between men and women. Rather, what is involved is a deep challenge to workplace norms, the organization of work and labour markets, and the structures and forces that position different groups in relation to those norms and in labour markets in different ways.

It is not merely feminists who now recognize that all this requires dispensing with the ideal of the unencumbered worker and normalizing the performance of unpaid work and the presence of a variety of other

---

[28] Supiot, above, n. 2; Esping-Anderson, above, n. 25.

events, risks, and obligations in the life of the market worker.[29] However, this is the point at which work/family issues become indissolubly linked to wider regulatory developments. For solving the crisis also involves troubling the increasingly popular idea that only a minor or residual role for the state is required in the provision of goods and services, whether on the theory that someone else will continue to provide them or the belief that the market itself will generate the required services and/or induce a reallocation of unpaid work between men and women.[30]

Addressing work/family concerns requires tackling a number of interlinked conceptual and institutional issues at the public/private divide: how to link now excluded activities, namely unpaid work, to economic activity in the market and how to reconstruct the division of labour between the state, market, and individual for the achievement of economic security, inclusion, and solidarity. These concerns too lie at the centre of current debates on the normative structure of the market economy.

III EQUALITY AND EFFICIENCY: CONVERGENCE OR CONFLICT?

The entry of vast numbers of women into the paid labour force has placed immense pressure on the capacity of women (and households) to perform their designated roles as unpaid providers of care. But at the same time it has also highlighted the significance of women as economic actors. Women, it appears, have become enormously important to the economy in both positive and negative ways, as workers and as potential welfare claimants.

To the extent that they devolve, or even increase, the responsibility for care to individuals, welfare and labour market regimes impair both women's capacity to participate in labour market activity and their ability to maintain and increase their human capital.[31] Yet enhancing the degree and quality of labour market participation is emerging as a central policy objective across the industrialized and developing world. And as discussed below, human capital is increasingly recognized among policymakers as a key input to economic growth everywhere. Hence, to the extent that high-skill, high-wage labour market participation figures not only as the principal source of welfare but also as the engine of

---

[29] For an extended consideration of this theme, see Supiot, above, n. 2.

[30] See World Bank, above, n. 1.

[31] They may also have a variety of other effects, including depressing the birth rate. See Esping-Anderson, G., 'Towards a Post-industrial Gender Contract', in P. Auer and B. Gazier (eds.), *The Future of Work, Employment and Social Protection: The Dynamics of Change and the Protection of Workers* (Geneva: ILO, 2002), 109.

economic growth, failing to revisit the structure of familialization begins to appear to be economically counterproductive as well as inequitable.

And this is only part of the story. To the extent that they can neither support themselves and their children through wage labour (an increasingly typical scenario) nor through a male breadwinner (also a typical situation, for reasons described), women stand to make ongoing claims against the state for support. One option is simply to refuse such claims and tolerate relatively high levels of poverty among women and children; this appears to be the position implicit in the current policy of the USA.[32] However, another is to enhance the terms and conditions on which women participate in markets, not only to advance equality and inclusion, but because the failure to do so will inevitably just increase the claims against the state in any event, often in ways that are more costly in the end.

Although there are other connections too, shifting gender norms and practices thread their way ineluctably through all these issues. Thus, it is unsurprising that active intervention in gender norms and practices in labour markets and social protection also turns out to be part of the response: solutions such as increasing employability and reducing levels of dependency converge around the strategy of increasing the labour market participation of women. It turns out that this objective is tightly interconnected with issues of gender equality in the labour force and a host of issues around the provision of child-care and control over working time, in short, the work/family conundrum.[33]

The lack of attention to work/family and gender equity issues within the IFIs until recently suggests that, standing alone, such issues do not rank very high in the policy calculus. However, to the extent that they are directly related to economic objectives, gender equity and work/family issues stand to rise on the agenda. This makes it tempting to conclude that there may be some degree of convergence between equality concerns on the one hand and competitiveness and growth agendas on the other. Here is where the problems arise. Even where there is agreement about the objective (facilitating women's labour market participation)—whether in light of the myriad intersecting economic, social and cultural transformations afoot, because of the welfare crisis described above, or because of the enhanced focus on anti-discrimination that is arguably also part of the current normative landscape—its realization is anything but straightforward. The reason is that, at least within the IFIs, responses to the work/family conflict are embedded within a wider regulatory project. This larger regulatory project, too, is essentially concerned with the allocation of costs and risk. It, too, represents an

---

[32] For further discussion, see Williams, in this volume.

[33] OECD, *Employment Outlook 2001* (Paris: OECD, 2001), ch. 4, 'Balancing Work and Family Life: Helping Parents into Paid Employment'.

active effort to alter institutional norms and reconfigure the current public/private divide, in part by changing the roles of the market, the state, and the individual in the provision of welfare. However, it is animated by assumptions and objectives, many of which are not obviously compatible with the objectives described above. In particular, it seeks to individualize the assumption of risk, rather than share or socialize risk more broadly. It aims to reduce the role that labour market institutions and other market rules play, confining them to the correction of market failures. And it aims to alter (re)distributive objectives themselves, whether they be greater gender equality or greater income equality in general, by shifting the focus from substantive equality to equality of opportunity and by reducing both the ambitions and the role of the state in ensuring individual and household welfare and economic security.

IV GOOD GOVERNANCE AT WORK

For at least a decade, the IFIs have promoted reforms in at least two areas fundamental to the work/family nexus: labour market rules and institutions and policy concerning social insurance and social protection. This is part of a larger project to reconfigure the role of the state in the economy by shifting the logic of intervention and altering and confining the purposes for and circumstances under which the state 'acts'.[34] The dominant view within these institutions is that part of the necessary reconfiguration of institutions and rules in a globally integrated market involves 'deregulating' labour markets so as to enhance the flexibility of employers in deploying their labour as well as their other assets. Thus, the IFIs advocate a series of reforms that would lower protective regulations for employees, limit job security provisions, and decentralize collective bargaining. In their view it is also important to limit access to income replacement schemes in order to keep downward pressure on wages and increase the incentives to engage in productive work; this is the so-called drive to 'make work pay'.[35]

---

[34] For a recent summary of the logic behind 'structural' reforms, see IMF, *World Economic Outlook: Advancing Structural Reforms* (Washington, DC: IMF, 2004), ch. III, 'Fostering Structural Reforms in Industrial Countries', online at www.imf.org. For an extended discussion, see Rittich, above, n. 23, ch. 2.

[35] IMF, *World Economic Outlook: International Financial Contagion*, May 1999, esp. ch. 4, 'Chronic Unemployment in the Euro Area: Causes and Cures', online at www.imf.org. For an attempt to model the effects of such reforms, see IMF, *World Economic Outlook*, Apr. 2003, ch. IV, 'Unemployment and Labour Market Institutions: Why Reforms Pay Off', online at www.imf.org.

Arguments for similar reforms can be found in OECD, *The OECD Jobs Study—Evidence and Explanations*, Part I: *Labour Market Trends and Underlying Forces of Change*; Part II: *The*

The recent recognition of formal anti-discrimination norms aside, the main effect has been to exclude considerations other than efficiency maximization from the design of labour and other market institutions, and to demote and displace the distributive dimension both of labour law and the private law rules of property and contract that become the default legal regimes governing work as a result. It is worth stressing that primacy of efficiency over other values—distributive justice, equality, social solidarity—is already built into the regulatory structure at this stage. What is important, however, is that this occurs in the mode of technical reforms that are simply designed to render markets more effective and functional, and that the revaluation of regulatory purposes that occurs in the process and the distributive effects that might be generated are thereby obscured. However, the significance of the change can be at least partly captured by contrasting the account of labour market institutions generated by the IFIs with the traditional justification for labour law rules. Labour standards and labour market regulations are imagined not as they are from within the discipline of labour law, as modes of reallocating bargaining power and entitlements to workers so as to ensure a better distribution of the gains of productive activity, but as interventions that distort the operation of markets and constitute impediments to efficiency. Income replacement schemes are seen not as an essential part of the provision of economic security and the preservation of the social and economic fabric, but as the source of unsustainable fiscal burdens. The upshot is that, although employers and capital holders can expect to see tangible gains in both power and income as a result of these reforms, rules and institutions that serve the distributive interests of workers have little if any place in the new regime because of their supposed adverse impact on the maximization of investment and growth.

These assumptions have obvious implications for both workers and labour market regulation. Rather than aspire to greater economic security through improvements in their collective bargaining position, enhanced employment standards, 'redistribution' or even demand-side management of the economy through fiscal and monetary policy by the state, workers are compelled to rely upon their individual rights and assume new responsibility for successfully marketing their skills in a dynamic and unstable economic environment.

The good governance agenda in respect of labour markets represents a particular set of institutional ideals and normative commitments. All states have political constraints and path dependencies at the institutional level which would necessarily complicate its implementation and

Adjustment Potential of the Labour Market (Paris: OECD, 1994) and OECD, *Making Work Pay: Taxation Benefits, Employment and Unemployment* (Paris, 1997).

diversify its effects. Moreover, some form of regulatory change is almost certainly required in light of the massive transformations to the economy and the new issues they have generated in the world of work. However, it is unresponsive to some of the central problems of the new economy. In addition to those issues that arise around the work/family divide, are the balance of power between workers and employers, as well as other distributive justice issues among workers, both within industrialized economies and between the north and south. While the IFIs advocate the reduction of workplace standards and the elimination of labour market institutions to deal with distributive concerns among workers, there simply is no obvious way to respond to the disadvantage of workers vis-à-vis their employers from within this analytic framework and on the basis of these normative commitments; indeed, the governance agenda itself makes this problem worse. The same is arguably true with the disadvantage of those who perform unpaid work.

From the standpoint of distributive justice, this agenda represents a problematic vision of economic and social organization and institutional responsibility. At base, it is a criticism not simply of labour market institutions that need alteration in light of changed circumstances, but of the very purposes of labour market institutions *tout court*. It substitutes the goal that risks should be shared and that inequality among workers and citizens be mitigated with the idea that risks and costs should be individually assumed and inequality tolerated. As many have now noted, the effect, and indeed the idea, of such reforms is to 'recommodify' labour, that is, to increase the exposure of workers to market forces and to make them more rather than less dependent upon their own efforts to ensure their well-being, all in the name of greater growth and, in theory, a larger pie for workers as a whole. In this world, market work effectively becomes the new social right (and duty) and the household and civil society, rather than the state, increasingly becomes the real social sector. To the extent that such changes place downward pressure on wages and benefits, they are likely both to intensify the pressure to participate in markets and increase the degree of reliance upon unpaid household services as well as 'voluntary' service provision in the third sector, civil society. This is ultimately one of its most powerful connections to the work/family conflict, a phenomenon that continues to play out in a distinctly gendered way.

V RECENT COMPLICATIONS: THE ROLE OF HUMAN CAPITAL

It is not difficult to imagine how the norms and assumptions now organizing market reforms might row away from, rather than towards, a solution to work/family conflicts, at least if equality is understood to be the dominant concern. The governance project as a whole is designed to substantially reorder the entitlements, benefits, and burdens of individual citizens. In general, the commitment to labour market 'deregulation' and minimal safety nets exacerbates, rather than ameliorates, income insecurity for workers. It also constrains the use of policy and regulatory tools that might otherwise be available to respond to the changed circumstances of the post-industrial economic order, including the feminization of labour and the resulting care deficit/crunch.

However, it may also pose formidable barriers to reconfiguring roles, expectations, and entitlements in ways that are not simply more equitable but more workable. Despite the current direction and content of the governance agenda, the actual regulatory and policy implications of the new market-centred order are turning out to be complicated and deeply contested rather than straightforward. The fostering of market participation and the reliance upon 'market solutions' to problems of economic security and social justice makes the governance agenda more problematic, even in terms of its own objectives, than it first appears. One reason is that reliance upon markets to generate welfare and security merely throws up a new set of issues around the following questions. What actually would constitute 'equality of opportunity' in contemporary labour markets? What are the conditions under which individuals thrive in post-industrial economies and globally integrated markets? What are the connections between the security of individuals and the competitiveness of states and firms in such a world? Moreover, what happens if equality itself is not an impediment to but is instead positively correlated with efficiency and productivity?

Addressing, let alone answering, these questions involves tackling a set of complex normative and political issues. What, for example, is the metric or measure of 'success' once both social and economic objectives such as gender equality are acknowledged ends of economic reform? Even putting these aside, the centre of gravity in thinking is no longer located in (neo)classical strategies of 'deregulation', privatization, and liberalization alone.[36] Within the IFIs, there is recognition that institutions matter and that the state has an important role to play in securing the conditions of growth.[37] And however inconsistent with the regulatory ideal, myriad policy and programmatic 'interventions' seem to be

[36] E.g. a recent report revisits one of governance's foundational planks, privatization, concluding that its merits may have been oversold, particularly in the absence of adequate and timely regulation. See World Bank, Policy Research Report, *Reforming Infrastructure: Privatization, Regulation and Competition* (Washington, DC: World Bank, 2004), available online at www.econ.worldbank.org.

[37] World Bank, *World Development Report 1997: The State in a Changing World* (Washington, DC: World Bank, 1997); World Bank, *World Development Report 2002: Building Institutions for Markets* (New York: OUP, 2001).

Kerry Rittich

indicated to respond to market failures and externalities of various kinds. The door has already been opened on these issues, and there is no stopping the analysis in a way that seems non-arbitrary. The result is a growing tension in the programmatic commitments of the labour market agenda and the emerging demands of the new economy.

VI HUMAN CAPITAL

Part of the tension and instability relates to the discovery of the importance of 'human capital' to economic growth. In the current narrative, competing in the new economy requires superior skills and knowledge. While in the old industrial order, those with limited skills could still expect to do reasonably well, in part through the regulatory and protective mechanisms embedded in labour market institutions and the social state, the new economy is destined to widen the cleavages between those with and without skills. The result is a bifurcation of the labour market into winners and losers and the creation of social divisions that the nation state is no longer able to mediate. Yet while the state can, and should, no longer aim to guarantee particular social outcomes, still less equalize the position of its citizens, current thinking suggests that the chances of those citizens in the market can be substantially enhanced by greater investments in education and training and by the creation of institutions that encourage greater labour market mobility.[38] The arguments for investment in human capital intensify to the extent that their value is not limited to the individual worker but extend to firms and to the health and competitiveness of economies as a whole. Thus, the enhancement of human capital becomes a pressing public policy issue as it approaches conventional wisdom that it is necessary to support such *other* pieces of conventional wisdom circulating about the new economy, including the need for 'life-long learning', an indispensable element to building a 'knowledge-based' economy,[39] itself now identified as the road to success in a global economy. The only serious debates, in the view of many, are how best to achieve these goals.[40]

The discovery of human capital has already brought some significant shifts to the governance debates within the IFIs. One is that issues once confined to the arena of social, distributive, and egalitarian concerns have entered into the calculus of economic growth. Suddenly child poverty

[38] This is the 'third way' debate.
[39] World Bank, *World Development Report 1999–2000: Knowledge for Development* (New York: OUP, 1999).
[40] Courchene, T. J., 'Human Capital in an Information Era', *Canadian Public Policy*, 28 (2002), 78.

might be a matter of economic, as well as social, policy, as the capacity of the future worker, and by extension prospects for future growth, stand to be impaired by a lack of adequate food, health, and educational resources at an early stage. Similarly, the exclusion of large parts of the population, such as women, from full participation in the economy and the polity is not simply a matter of gender justice or even social cohesion and solidarity, but a matter of limiting dependency and enhancing growth. Moreover, the debates over human capital have a distinctly gendered dimension. The Bank, for example, has concluded that women are disproportionately more inclined to 'invest' in their children than men, and observed that investments in women seem to generate greater economic returns as well.[41] Indeed, gender equality has become a banner issue in this regard: no longer merely a social justice or human rights issue, the empowerment of women through market participation is simply a component of rational economic strategy.[42]

VII ANALYSING THE TRENDS AND PROSPECTS

If the result is at least an instrumental interest in work/family issues and gender equality within the IFIs, in part due to the current narrative about the route to growth in a competitive global economy, because of the larger governance agenda, it is easier to say what it does not than what it does involve. It is not, for example, simply a case of incorporating international human rights norms and labour standards into the agenda, following the analysis and implementing solutions already mapped out by feminist and gender scholars, or even accepting the recommendations of those who have engaged in detailed studies of the general problem of the transformation of work and welfare regimes and concluded that successfully managing the work/family conflict is central to dealing with the challenges of the new economy.[43] While the reasons are surely varied, one possibility is that to some degree they all trench on regulatory and institutional territory that has already been demarcated as undesirable, if not as off limits, for reasons of efficiency even where the result might be improved gender equality. In particular, they typically posit a role for the state that is at odds with current regulatory and governance norms within the IFIs. While the benefits of women's labour market participation and the problems engendered by work/family

---

[41] World Bank, above, n. 1; id., above, n. 8.

[42] World Bank, above, n. 1; OECD, *Employment Outlook 2001* (Paris: OECD, 2001), ch. 4, 'Balancing Work and Family Life: Helping Parents into Paid Employment'.

[43] Supiot, above, n. 2; Esping-Anderson, above, n. 26; OECD, *Employment Outlook 2001*, above, n. 42.

conflict bring to the surface policy conflicts within those norms, so far the narrative about labour market reform does not reflect this.

If it retains its status as a focal point in the analysis of labour markets regulation, the demands of human capital may ultimately unsettle the current reform agenda. For example, there are powerful arguments that labour market regulation may be needed, not only to correct market failures[44] and take account of labour market norms[45] as labour economists have long argued, but to induce firms to pursue a high-skill, high-productivity route to success rather than the alternative.[46] However, so far any significant reconsideration of current institutional ideals has been avoided. The result instead is a distinct set of responses, arguments, norms, and strategies within the IFIs to manage the work/family divide, many of which depart in significant ways from those reflected in other analyses and advocated by other international institutions.

VIII INCORPORATING THE SOCIAL

How might work/family concerns play out in the current narratives around good governance and the prescriptions of the IFIs in particular? Here, it seems useful to begin to distinguish them from the approach typically taken by the other international institutions and the wider social justice constituencies, many feminists included.

Within the ILO and among the human rights treaty bodies, labour market protection schemes, paid maternity and family leave, and provision for child-care all surface as elements of ensuring adequate human rights and social protection to vulnerable groups. Either they are human rights, social rights, women's rights, workers' rights, or simply an aspect of the general right to equality guaranteed under all human rights law.[47] On this basis, it may be argued that particular legislative or regulatory schemes that lie at the work/family nexus are rights in themselves or that they are part of an integrated approach to human rights, a position compelled by the recognition that all rights are now 'universal, indivisible and interdependent and interrelated'.[48]

[44] Deakin and Wilkinson, above, n. 6.

[45] Solow, R., *The Labour Market as a Social Institution* (Cambridge, MA: Basil Blackwell, 1990).

[46] Bernard, C. and Deakin, S., 'Corporate Governance, European Governance, and Social Rights', in B. Hepple (ed.), *Social and Labour Rights in a Global Context* (Cambridge: Cambridge University Press, 2002), 122.

[47] See UN Charter, 26 June 1945, 1 U.N.T.S. xvi, Arts. 13 and 55; UN Universal Declaration of Human Rights, in particular Arts. 2 and 23.

[48] Vienna Declaration and Programme of Action, para. 5, *Report of the World Conference on Human Rights: Report of the Secretary-General*, UN Doc. A/CONF.157/24 (part I), 13 Oct. 1993.

The 'rights' paradigm diverges in profound ways from the approach to legal and regulatory issues under the governance paradigm. While those differences cannot be explored in any depth here, it seems important to highlight two fundamental points of divergence.

One of the ways that rights-based approaches depart most clearly from the governance agenda is in respect of the role of the state in securing social outcomes. All rights-based strategies at international law are predicated on state responsibility at some level. Indeed, state action or 'intervention' may also be required; thus, the presence of a state with some degree of regulatory, protective, and redistributive capacity may be the (unarticulated) condition of possibility for the fulfilment of particular rights. For example, Article 11 of the Convention on the Elimination of All Forms of Discrimination Against Women (CEDAW), states that parties are obligated to ensure a range of employment-related rights to women. This includes taking measures 'to encourage the provision of the necessary supporting social services to enable parents to combine family obligations with work responsibilities and public life, including in particular through promoting the establishment and development of a network of child-care facilities'. The CEDAW Committee also issued general recommendations on topics related to women's role in the economy, including remuneration for unpaid work.[49] The ILO, for its part, has a number of conventions detailing the obligations of states in relation to their workers which bear in central ways on the work/family divide.[50] Moreover, many provisions involve substantive rather than merely formal obligations. To put it another way, rather than mere 'enablement', the state assumes obligations to ensure particular outcomes.

The other way in which the agendas diverge is in respect of the general status of such rights within market reform and development undertakings themselves. It is important to note that under the rights paradigm, issues are framed as entitlements. All debates about what it means to respect, protect, and ensure workers' rights and women's rights aside— questions which currently preoccupy those grappling with the social deficit and the implications of social rights in the context of globalization and development—framing claims as rights is intended to ensure that they have foundational rather than merely instrumental status in regulatory decisions.

[49] General recommendation, No. 16, Tenth Session, 1991, 'Unpaid Family Workers in rural and urban family enterprises'; General recommendation, No. 17, Tenth Session, 1991, 'Measurement and quantification of the unremunerated domestic activities of women and their recognition in the GNP', available online at www.un.org.

[50] See e.g. ILO Convention 156, Workers with Family Responsibilities Convention, 1987; Convention 183, Maternity Protection Convention, 2000, available online at www.ilo.org.

The logic that governs work/family issues, their status within the universe of regulatory concerns, and their ultimate disposition look very different from within the IFIs. Social concerns may now merit attention both as individually valued ends and because of their strategic connection to goals such as enhanced labour market participation.[51] However, much of the interest remains derivative: they are of interest to the extent that they are connected to economic growth or because, like the social deficit in general, they require attention if the general project of market reform and economic integration is not to be subverted. In any event, they are carefully designed so as not to interfere with what are perceived to be the demands of growth.

The recent incorporation of the 'social, structural and human' dimensions of development and the explicit recognition of human rights as a means and end of development might appear to have boosted the status of rights arguments and, with it, the prospects for resolving conflicts at the work/family divide in a way congenial to gender equality concerns. There are analytic, historical, and political reasons for scepticism about the possibility of relying upon rights claims alone to further distributive agendas for workers in the global economy.[52] However, the problems begin at an earlier point, as it would be an error to assume that within the IFIs all, most, or even many social concerns are conceptualized as matters of right: except for a limited category of entitlements comprising formal equality for women and core labour rights for workers, they are a matter of economic policy not fundamental rights.[53] While gender equality may have been normalized as an element of good governance, a broad range of specific entitlements and institutions, including those bearing in central ways on the work/family nexus, have no such status; indeed, many are targets for elimination on efficiency grounds. Thus, although both rights arguments and the social dimension of development have a place within reform schemes, neither necessarily means that the institutions and policies by which economic development goals are furthered have themselves been seriously altered, or altered in 'progressive' ways.

It is important to recall that it is an established part of the governing economic narrative, one with a longer pedigree and more secure

[51] The formal incorporation of social concerns, including human rights, into the current development paradigm is relatively recent; it can be dated from 1999. See World Bank, *Comprehensive Development Framework* (Washington, DC: World Bank, 1999).

[52] For a discussion of some of these problems, see Rittich, K., 'Core Labour Rights and Labour Market Flexibility: Two Paths Entwined?', in International Bureau of the Permanent Court of Arbitration (ed.), *Labour Law Beyond Borders: ADR and the Internationalization of Labour Dispute Settlement*, papers emanating from the 5th PCA International Law Seminar, 7 May 2002 (The Hague: Kluwer Law International, 2003), 157.

[53] On this, see the distinction between economic policy and 'rights' that are key to gender equality in World Bank, above, n. 8.

methodological moorings within the IFIs, that labour market institutions and robust social entitlements function as disincentives to work, impair the efficient allocation of labour resources, and thus constitute an impediment to growth.[54] These presumptions do not appear to have been disturbed, despite the new attention to social concerns and women's labour market participation.

The result is quite contrasting social regime ideals. For example, reform proposals from within the gender equality and wider social justice constituency would commonly include the following elements: public law entitlements based on human rights or constitutional norms to non-discrimination for women; legislation and administrative apparatuses to enhance the capacity of women and other workers to bargain collectively; provisions protecting both job and income entitlements for child and maternity-related leave; access to social insurance schemes such as pensions and unemployment insurance on non-disadvantageous terms to workers engaged in part-time, intermittent or other forms of non-standard employment; welfare entitlements adequate to support those engaged in non-market care work; and the provision of public goods and services ranging from funded day care to housing that reduce the economic pressure on women who, whether they work in the labour market or not, continue to fare more poorly than men.

The IFIs have no such elaborate social scheme, partly because a central part of their project is to dismantle such regimes and replace them with more market-friendly and market-centred alternatives. There is a focus on a limited set of individual worker rights which guarantee non-discrimination in education and job opportunities. To the extent that a need for social protection remains, the preference is for arrangements that, rather than being generally available to workers, are more finely calibrated to individual levels of workplace participation and remuneration.

For example, the Bank has endorsed a concept of social protection that is focused on improving the economic security of the individual worker over her lifetime through 'social risk' management.[55] However, the explicit trade-off is a reduced focus on mitigating the risks that actually materialize or improving the fortunes of particular groups of workers or the workforce as a whole. While some redistribution from the better off to the truly disadvantaged is envisioned under this model, social risk management is promoted partly on the basis that it can lead

[54] See IMF, *World Economic Outlook: International Financial Contagion*, May 1999, ch. IV, 'Chronic Unemployment in the Euro Area: Causes and Cures'.
[55] Holzmann, R., Sherburne-Benz, L., and Tesliuc, E., *Social Risk Management: The World Bank's Approach to Social Protection in a Globalizing World* (Washington, DC: World Bank, 2003).

to better welfare outcomes *without* the necessity of actually redistributing income.

The result is a fairly stark contrast between the classic Keynesian
approaches to labour market regulation and social protection reflected
in the norms and preoccupations of the ILO and the UN human rights
bodies on one hand and the IFIs and good governance norms on the
other.

IX MARKETING GENDER EQUALITY

All of these trends described above are visible in the World Bank's strategies to promote gender equality and women's labour market participation. The Bank now endorses gender equality, having recognized that it
is both 'good for growth' and an end of development on its own.[56] The
Bank is particularly interested in encouraging women's labour market
participation, the more efficient and productive uses of women's time
and work, and the assumption of greater risk on the part of women in
order to generate greater market rewards. Indeed, through changes to
legal entitlements, enhanced voice, and investments in human capital, the
Bank places women's capacity to compete better in markets at the centre
of its efforts to 'engender' development. However, its principal interest
apparently lies in making the 'business case' for gender equality, that is,
establishing that gender inequality introduces a range of inefficiencies
into the organization of productive life, and that gender equality can
enhance growth without increasing costs.[57] Moreover, the model of
gender equality that it has endorsed and now advances brackets the
question of substantive economic equality between men and women.[58]
And although some changes to legal rules are envisioned to promote
gender equality, formal anti-discrimination norms aside, they do not, in
general, include alterations to those governing market transactions.

The result is assiduous efforts to get women into markets—by eliminating direct discrimination and formal barriers to access to education and
jobs; enhancing investments in women's human capital; and by ensuring
that women have access to resources and credit, especially through
microcredit lending schemes—so that women too can be ideal labour
market entrepreneurs. However, these are accompanied by a series of
barriers and resistances to alternative proposals. Not only do these
commitments limit or block the project of furthering gender equality in
labour markets by other means, they virtually compel the abandonment

---

[56] World Bank, above, n. 1; id., above, n. 8.   [57] Ibid.
[58] World Bank, above, n. 1.

of substantive economic equality between men and women. They also create blind spots to the reasons why, under such a system, many women might never realistically be expected to perform as 'ideal' workers.

With respect to unpaid work, the Bank places its greatest hope in market forces, holding that the increased participation of women in the labour force can be expected to alter the gendered division of household labour. For example, in *Engendering Development*, the Bank argues, *inter alia*, that enhancing women's participation in the market can be expected to lead to a substitution of unpaid with paid work, as well as a better allocation of unpaid work between men and women.[59] Note the direction of causation that is implied: it is women's participation in markets that changes the allocation of unpaid work between men and women, not a reallocation of burdens through institutional or structural reforms that enables higher levels of market participation on the part of women.

What perhaps best characterizes the approach to work/family issues is an attitude of marked diffidence about how to approach them or whether, beyond reliance upon market forces, to do anything at all. Reducing the cost to women of their household roles *is* identified as a key issue in the Bank's policy research report on gender and development. However, the mechanisms for doing so remain problematic, particularly those that concern care, resulting in a qualified endorsement of strategies to spread the cost of care, accompanied by a caution that the costs of labour market solutions are likely to outweigh their benefits.[60] For example, *Engendering Development* observes that the availability of low-cost care appears to be beneficial, but reserves its position on how it is to be provided. Tellingly, when it comes to the official Bank statement on mainstreaming gender equality,[61] the issue is simply absent.

Here, the earlier discussion on governance and labour market regulation seems to hover in the background. In its broader concerns to promote efficient markets, the Bank already has an institutional position that has broad implications for the routes by which social objectives, including gender equality and the resolution of work/family conflicts, can be pursued. The Bank has decisively concluded that, a defined set of exceptions aside, regulation is generally bad for growth. Thus, it is simultaneously 'for' the strengthening of private law rules and 'against' labour market institutions, on the basis that these rules enhance competitive markets and competition among workers.

The observations that might be made at this point mirror the earlier observations about the prospects for achieving distributive justice for workers under the labour market governance agenda. Whatever other concerns may be involved, if the question is not merely how to ensure

---

[59] Ibid.   [60] Ibid., 23–4.   [61] World Bank, above, n. 8.

women's participation in labour markets but how to do so in ways that do not systematically disadvantage women, all evidence is that the risks and costs associated with childbearing and care have to be pooled and shared. The Bank claims to endorse a different, more equal division of labour between men and women in the market and a redistribution of labour and power at home. However, it has no structural analysis that links this issue in a comprehensive way to the organization of work or to economic life more broadly, and no institutional response to the current (mis)allocation of the costs and risks of child-care as between women and men. Moreover, the IFIs have no response to the equality concerns engendered by the increasing pressure to work longer and longer hours *other* than the idea that women, too, should now be in the market on terms similar to men.

There are a number of empirical objections that could be made to the idea that market forces will undo the current gender division of unpaid labour. First is simply the fact that there is not much evidence that it is happening, even though the entry of women into paid work has been dramatic in the last generation.[62] And as the OECD observes, the increase in single family households headed by women probably means that, even where there are some shifts in the traditional allocation of household work between men and women, women in the aggregate are likely now doing more, not less, unpaid work. Moreover, an institutional response involving some combination of leave entitlements with publicly provided child-care appears now to be positively correlated with higher labour force participation by women.[63] Indeed, the issue has been identified as the single most important determinant of women's labour market participation.[64]

The effort to promote market solutions to the gender division of unpaid work exemplifies a more pervasive problem with reliance upon market forces in the abstract to promote greater gender equality or any other social objective. The Bank envisions markets as engines of gender equality; it also makes a robust case for the possibilities of win-win solutions in the drive for equality and efficiency. This is important for positive and negative reasons, both because such possibilities may really exist, and because where market forces are deemed sufficient to generate desirable outcomes, additional policy, regulatory, and institutional changes appear unnecessary; indeed, they may become part of the problem.

But whatever these transformative possibilities, the analysis of market incentives is clearly incomplete without an analysis of the power of different types of market institutions and incentives to also subvert

---

[62] ILO, *Yearbook of Labour Statistics* (Geneva: ILO, various years).

[63] OECD, *Employment Outlook 2001* (Paris: OECD, 2001).

[64] Esping-Anderson, above, n. 26.

equality objectives. It must be observed that the relatively deracinated institutional approach to equality is also puzzling. For reliance on market forces divorced from their institutional underpinnings has now been discredited as a mode of generating positive economic change. Elsewhere in reform literature, and even elsewhere in the Bank's gender analysis, institutions and the incentives they generate are at the centre of the analysis,[65] raising the question, why not here?

A basic issue for work/family issues, and the gender equality concerns to which they give rise, lies with the incentive structure generated by the more intense commodification of labour and the productivist approach to work. Absent countervailing forces, the commitment to competitive, efficient labour markets should be expected to generate greater inequality both in general and along gender lines. Intensified reliance upon 'deregulated' markets ensures both that labour is recommodified *and* that workers will see widely varying returns for their efforts. For example, the pressure to work long hours which, unless restrained by other means, is inherent in the commitment to competitive labour markets generates greater rewards for those who can and will do more paid work, a division of job opportunities, and various forms of workplace segregation and hierarchy. Moreover, because these developments take place against the background of a pre-existing gender order around work, both paid and unpaid, they might also be expected to generate a more intensified division of labour at home, larger income differentials between men and women, and perhaps disincentives to have children as well. Under such schemes, workers are induced to either prioritize market work, and enjoy the market gains, or not to prioritize market work, and suffer the consequences.[66] This is not only the effect; it is the idea. If this is the very ground upon which ideal labour market institutions are configured, then the question becomes not only what specific work/family policies and regulations are available in the circumstances, but what are the possibilities that, even if specific institutional changes were implemented, they might actually overcome these structural tendencies embedded in the regime as a whole?

The issues of gender disadvantage arising around the work/family nexus are relational, which is to say that they cannot be solved without considering the norms around work and labour markets, the disparate ways that workers may be positioned in relation to them, and the relative capacities of workers to fulfil them.[67] And they are structural, in the sense

[65] World Bank, above, n. 36.

[66] It is of course true that, according to other values and scales, there are losses associated with prioritizing market work as well.

[67] Day, S. and Brodsky, G., 'The Duty to Accommodate: Who Will Benefit?', *Canadian Bar Review*, 75 (1996), 433; Minow, M., *Making All the Difference* (Cambridge, MA: Harvard University Press, 1990).

72 *Kerry Rittich*

that all of these issues, in turn, are linked to the incentives for action, the allocation of risks and entitlements, and the distribution of costs and benefits in the institutions that govern markets and non-market life.

This is not news. The Bank itself has articulated the importance of norms and institutions to the general question of gender equality;[68] moreover, its project for mainstreaming gender equality reflects an appreciation of the broad range of areas, including macro-economic concerns, that might be relevant to improving gender equality. Yet for the most part, the plan to 'engender' development holds stable the market norms and institutions in which women are to perform as economic actors. This suggests either that there is an incomplete understanding of the extent to which gender equality might be connected to the laws and institutions that structure market transactions and/or that there is a set of other concerns that overrides the objective of gender equality at a particular point, notwithstanding the story that the Bank itself now tells about its importance to economic development.

X CONCLUSION

The conceptions of both equality and efficiency and the particular routes and institutions by which they should be pursued that now inform the analysis of labour markets within the IFIs have potentially profound effects on the disposition of work/family issues. The heightened emphasis on contractual relations among workers and employers governed by commercial norms, the distrust of labour market regulation, and the efforts to reduce the redistributive functions of the state all converge to discredit most strategies to reconstitute the work/family divide in a transformative way no matter how much they might otherwise be indicated for maximizing the labour market participation of women or otherwise advancing gender equality. Similarly, the emphasis on individual worker rights, along with the displacement of questions of bargaining power, and the focus on economic security through individual effort and financial contribution all make it difficult to imagine how any reallocation of risks and costs, whether between workers and employers or among workers who are very differently situated in relation to market opportunities, might ever be effected. Whatever their relation to aggregate growth, such strategies seem unresponsive to both the efficiency and the equality concerns raised by the work/family conundrum.

However, if general governance trends seem critical to the disposition of work/family conflicts, then it is also true that by exposing the deep

[68] World Bank, above, n. 8.

interconnections between social and economic issues, work/family issues also seem to call into question core commitments of the governance agenda. The idea that it is possible to remain neutral concerning, or actually promote, the interests of workers and women while simultaneously advancing a particular institutional order designed to empower investors and privilege efficiency over distributive objectives *and* the claim that the resulting regulatory order is actually neutral and efficient, are problematic for reasons that have only been suggested here. Moreover, the categorical claims about the expected effects of reforms should give pause to anyone who is familiar with the vagaries of adjudication or the complexity of determining what the law actually is in any particular jurisdiction. Effects can be not only difficult to ascertain; they will almost certainly vary widely across different contexts.[69]

However, two things might be emphasized. The first is that, although it is defended in the name of enhanced labour market efficiency and higher levels of employment, the governance agenda represents something much more than that; it is also a social and political vision. Distributive decisions are embedded within the matrix of economic rights and rules that now have pride of place; they are also implicit in those that have been rejected. Critical decisions about the powers and entitlements of the contracting parties, the allocation of economic risk among workers, and the distribution of the rewards of production are made when labour market institutions are dismantled and employer contractual entitlements strengthened. They are not merely 'economic' or technical in either their design or effect.

The second broad observation is that even the commitment to growth through competitive markets might lead to quite different policies than those with which it is now associated. Even if the general position on legal and institutional reform were to remain intact and unexamined, the countervailing arguments for reallocating the costs and risks associated with care might still be compelling where they are conclusively linked to productivity. Similarly, nothing seems more central to a market-centred vision of economic welfare than a thick rather than minimalist understanding of the elements of equal market opportunity. At the end of the day, the work/family nexus remains a site at which a highly significant and interrelated set of issues that bear on workplace vulnerability, equality, the enhancement of human capital, and productivity intersect. If women really are the 'axial principle' of the new economy,[70] as we are increasingly informed, then we should expect work/family concerns to

---

[69] See e.g. World Bank, *Doing Business in 2004: Understanding Regulation* (Washington, DC: World Bank, 2004), which describes labour market institutions as 'recent', attributes their emergence to the desire to correct market failures, and exhibits basic confusion about the connection between regulatory form and substantive outcomes.

[70] Esping-Anderson, above, n. 26.

be at the forefront of policy and regulatory shifts. Indeed, the experiments around extensions of leave, including paid leave, and the efforts to ensure that flexibility norms operate at least minimally to the advantage of workers that are now underway in so many jurisdictions, despite the economic and ideological pressure to create more business- and investment-friendly regulatory regimes, suggest nothing so much as countervailing pressure on the dominant institutional model precisely at this point.

In addition, the role and determinants of human capital remain inadequately theorized, notwithstanding the enormous emphasis now placed upon human capital in contemporary labour market debates and economic growth. One source of ambiguity concerns whether, and what, costs associated with the development and support of human capital really should be counted as economic investments. This is acutely important to work/family issues. It is already recognized that much human capital development occurs promoting the families and households.[71] Women's distinctively important role in that health and education of family members has already been recognized too. What remains is to extend the insights: the human capital lens provides a potentially unlimited basis for establishing linkages between unpaid domestic work and market outcomes, as many activities in the home can be plausibly linked, in both positive and negative ways, to the capacity of present and future workers. Moreover, there are precedents for such moves. With respect to public expenditures, for example, the Bank has no trouble apprehending that it might be important to direct infrastructure investments to reducing the time that women spend collecting water; the fact that it detracts from more productive uses of women's time seems obvious.[72] There is no reason, but for current norms and conventions, that the same logic might not inform the question of care.

Externalities and market failures are also arbitrarily recognized and ignored. For example, the 'efficiency' of labour market institutions such as paid leave for a variety of care-related activities might be calculated with reference to the full spectrum of effects that are generated both inside and outside the market, and arguments for reallocating costs and risks associated with the family obligations could be framed in terms of the internalization of the costs of production. These moves seem especially compelling, once it is recognized that we have *already* made the decision that all citizens are now presumptively market workers. Even the wisdom of replacing broad-based social protection with 'social risk' management might be problematic, if it turns out that the failure to broadly insure against risk restrains people from making investments

[71] Courchene, above, n. 40.   [72] World Bank, above, n. 8.

and choices that would otherwise be productive in the long term. In short, there is no shortage of arguments internal to the governance logic itself that might be marshalled in favour of a different, or simply a more diverse, set of approaches to issues at the work/family nexus.

Yet, this seems utopian. If progress in terms of equality is now increasingly tied to efficiency concerns, we are unlikely to see change without a recognition that there are economic *costs*, costs that extend beyond women, associated with the failure to recognize the value of unpaid work. Notwithstanding the presence of old and new arguments and evidence linking 'soft' social and egalitarian objectives to 'hard' economic outcomes such as improved domestic growth rates, there remain entrenched perceptions that regulating for equality undermines efficiency.[73] For this reason, proponents of alternatives should expect to meet a set of well-rehearsed arguments that such solutions are undesirable and/or untenable in the new economy; that they seek to bring back the bureaucratically cumbersome Leviathan state; that they would cost too much and kill growth; and that they harm the very groups they purport to assist. Moreover, advocates of heterodox approaches may be required not merely to make the case that such efforts can be reasonably expected to aid productivity and growth, but to establish empirically that they do so. One of the great victories of good governance rhetoric has been to establish as *doxa* that labour market 'deregulation' generates positive economic outcomes, something that may place a sizeable, perhaps insuperable, bar to those seeking reforms that run counter to them. It is often difficult to establish the precise link between particular legal or institutional reforms and specific social or economic outcomes, as the myriad contingencies involved mean that there is inevitably an element of speculation and calculated risk. Establishing proof has just become more difficult in any event in light of new studies funded by the Bank that purport to establish in empirical terms the broad proposition that regulation is bad for growth and has other undesirable side effects:[74] this means that countervailing evidence will always be at hand.

Equality and efficiency may be win-win strategies as market reformers are now fond of claiming. However, whatever the overlap between them, it is doubtful that we are in a world in which 'social policy . . . becomes progressively indistinguishable from economic policy',[75] unless that means that social justice concerns are simply to be merged into efficiency concerns. Real conflicts, distributive conflicts, continue to exist. Moreover, they are being created in the course of reform.

[73] ILO, *Time for Equality at Work* (Geneva: ILO, 2003).
[74] World Bank, *Doing Business in 2004*, above, n. 14, ch. 3, 'Hiring and Firing Workers'.
[75] Courchene, above, n. 40.

At the end of the day, the most striking thing about debates around the work/family nexus remains the starkly different languages and templates in which they are now framed. Not only do international institutions often support different institutional projects, they perceive the work/family nexus—and labour market regulation and gender equality too—through fundamentally different lenses. Any movement seems likely to require each side to engage more deeply with the terms of reference and the argumentative strategies of the other, and to confront more directly the relationship and potential conflict between their normative commitments to equality and efficiency. There are critical implications for both sides in this debate. One is that insistence upon 'rights' means a capacity to ignore the economic consequences of normative and institutional decisions, as if those effects were in some sense apart from the realization of the rights themselves. The other is that engaging in cost/benefit analysis necessarily means demoting or rejecting distributive concerns.

Once it becomes evident that there is more at stake in the regulation of labour markets and the provision of social protection and insurance than merely promoting efficient transactions, a number of questions seem salient. One is why, if questions of equality and distributive justice are necessarily engaged in market reform, efficiency should dominate the debate to the exclusion of other concerns. A second is why economic and financial institutions, as between other actors and institutions both domestic and international, should have a privileged position in relation to the determination of the reform trajectory. Yet a third is whether work/family issues, like other critical regulatory questions in the new economy, belong in the realm of technical expertise rather than either fundamental rights or democratic politics.

Part II

Reimagining the Worker

4

Work/Family, Australian Labour Law, and the Normative Worker

ANNA CHAPMAN*

I ANALYSING THE AUSTRALIAN WORK/FAMILY PROBLEM

Work/family issues have become a major topic of interest and discussion in Australia. Rarely does a week go by without a news service carrying a story exploring the reasons why professional women are deferring decisions to have a baby, or considering the implications of long working hours and absent fathers and the lack of affordable child-care places. The Sex Discrimination Commissioner, the trade union movement, and all major political parties have now developed policies and programmes of reform to address the problems that are seen to arise at the intersection of paid market work and caring and domestic responsibilities.

Academics, too, have been keen to explore the work/family phenomenon. The Australian literature is grounded in a range of disciplines, adopting different approaches and levels of explanation. Broader developments in the Australian labour market are important in most accounts, particularly the substantial increase over the past thirty years in the number of women, especially mothers, in paid work.[1] Also seen as important are shifts in labour market regulatory thinking and structure, away from centralized standard-setting through industrial awards in favour of decentralized enterprise bargaining against a safety net of minimum standards. Many scholars interpret these developments as accountable for worsening work and family outcomes, as hours of work, shift allocations, leave arrangements, wages, and type of engagement become, increasingly, matters for negotiation rather than prescriptive standard-setting.[2]

* This chapter draws on my doctoral studies in the Centre for Socio-Legal Research at Griffith University. I thank Rosemary Owens, Joanne Conaghan, and Kerry Rittich for their encouragement and thoughtful comments on a draft of this chapter, and the participants of INTELL7 for welcoming my original paper. Any errors remain mine.

[1] In June 2000, 61% of married women with dependent children were participating in the paid labour force: Australian Bureau of Statistics (ABS), *Labour Force Status and Other Characteristic of Families*, Cat 6224.0 (Canberra: ABS, June 2000).

[2] See e.g. Strachan, G. and Burgess, J., 'The Incompatibility of Decentralised Bargaining and Equal Employment Opportunity in Australia', *BJIR*, 38 (2000), 361.

What typifies much of the Australian literature, and especially scholarship that situates its analyses primarily in the paid labour market, is an understanding both that the work and family problem is a relatively new phenomenon, and that it is properly understood as an inevitable conflict between the competing demands of two separate spheres of life. Labour law, with its ambit lying in the public world of the market, has also tended to constitute work and family problems as being the product of relatively recent social change, bringing family responsibilities into conflict with the demands of the market. In this framework, and with Australia's relatively recent emphasis on enterprise bargaining, industrial law becomes about responding to these developments by facilitating employers, employees, and trade unions in reaching their own agreements regarding these matters above a set of minimum standards.

This chapter attempts to take a different approach to analysing the current Australian work/family phenomenon. Rather than starting from an understanding that this is a relatively new problem of conflict between two separate spheres, the analysis seeks to reveal how labour law is itself constitutive of current problems. To do this the existing situation must be placed in a context of (at least) the twentieth-century breadwinner and family wage tradition of Australian industrial relations. Do the gendered assumptions of the breadwinner/homemaker model and family wage of the twentieth century continue to shape labour law today? What does labour law assume about its subject worker, and his/her relationship to family and domestic work?[3] How have these understandings developed over time, and across different areas of Australian labour law, such as award-making, enterprise bargaining and anti-discrimination law?

This chapter begins the work of addressing these questions by drawing on various moments in Australian labour law that reveal something of the law's subject. In particular, the analysis exposes some main ways in which the assumptions of the breadwinner model of work and family, formally adopted in the Australian system of industrial relations in 1907, continue to exert a profound influence over the shape of legal regulation today. For example, a breadwinner/homemaker framework appears to underlie the fragmentation of the labour market, and labour standards, into a (standard) full-time/(non-standard) part-time dualism that marginalizes female part-time and casual employees, whose form of

---

[3] This approach comes from an understanding that all doctrinal categories or areas of law, including labour law, construct their own understanding of the legal person—the subject—'who is deemed to act in certain ways, to wield certain rights and to assume certain responsibilities': Naffine, N. and Owens, R. J., 'Sexing Law', in N. Naffine and R. J. Owens (eds.), *Sexing the Subject of Law* (North Ryde, NSW: LBC Information Services, 1997), 3, 7. See also Naffine, N., 'Sexing the Subject (of Law)', in M. Thornton (ed.), *Public and Private: Feminist Legal Debates* (Melbourne: OUP, 1990), 18.

engagement in paid labour marks them as mothers first, and workers second. Whilst it is true that in Australia, as elsewhere, the limitations of the breadwinner model and its legacy have become more visible as greater numbers of women have entered the paid labour market, and as other pressures such as labour market restructuring and neo-liberal thinking challenge the rationale of the labour law tradition, it is a mistake to see work and family as a new phenomenon, or problem.

Many scholars, in Australia and elsewhere, have explored a paradigmatic worker of labour law, workplace cultures, and industrial relations practice that is inimical to the interests of women workers. The ideal worker of labour law is invariably identified as a full-time employee working under a contract of employment on a continuous and permanent basis, from young adult years until retirement. What characterizes these accounts is a strong sense that the legal regulation of (paid) labour markets is built on an understanding of work and the worker that is gendered male. More recent scholarship has focused attention on a particular aspect of this gendering process—the normative assumptions about the interconnections between the market worker and the worker's family. For example, in *Women Going Backwards*, published in 2002, Sandra Berns writes about how Australian labour markets and law assume a worker who is 'unencumbered' by family or domestic responsibilities.[4] Similar normative concepts have been identified in many other industrialized countries.[5] This chapter seeks to build on this body of scholarship through focusing on ways in which Australian labour law constitutes the relationships of the ideal worker and his/her family and domestic work.

This chapter commences its legal story of the paradigmatic worker of Australian labour law in the origins of the system of compulsory arbitration established in the early twentieth century. Following this, the analysis turns to examine Berns' account of the unencumbered worker of contemporary Australian labour markets and legal regulation. This work provides the conceptual underpinning for the chapter. From here the chapter focuses on some contemporary aspects of the Australian labour

---

[4] Berns, S., *Women Going Backwards: Law and Change in a Family Unfriendly Society* (Aldershot: Ashgate Publishing, 2002). Berns uses this term throughout her text. It first appears in the preface (at vi) in relation to her concept of the unencumbered citizen.

[5] See e.g. Conaghan, J., 'Women, Work and Family: A British Revolution?', in J. Conaghan, R. M. Fischl, and K. Klare (eds.), *Labour Law in an Era of Globalization: Transformative Practices and Possibilities* (New York: OUP, 2002), 53; Rittich, K., 'Feminization and Contingency: Regulating the Stakes of Work for Women', in ibid., 117; Williams, J., *Unbending Gender: Why Family and Work Conflict and What To Do About It* (New York: OUP, 2000); Appelbaum, E., Bailey, T., Berg, P., and Kalleberg, A. L., 'Shared Work/Valued Care: New Norms for Organising Market Work and Unpaid Care Work', in H. Mosley, J. O'Reilly, and K. Schomann (eds.), *Labour Markets, Gender and Institutional Change* (Cheltenham: Edward Elgar, 2000).

market and legal regulation, as revelatory of a subject worker who is not
encumbered in the labour market by family and caring work.

II THE AUSTRALIAN BREADWINNER OF THE TWENTIETH CENTURY

Commentators identify the Australian system of compulsory arbitration
of industrial disputes, established at the federal level through a 1904
statute, as a key aspect of the social settlement brokered in the first
decade of the twentieth century. Along with restrictions on (non-
European) immigration, arbitration ensured relatively high minimum
wage rates and security of employment for workers in Australia. In
return, a third aspect of the settlement—high tariffs—protected domestic
markets, and profit levels, for the Australian manufacturing industry. In
this framework, arbitration was a central arm of social protection, with
social security providing residual relief for those who, for reasons seen
as socially acceptable at that time, did not themselves engage in the
labour market, or were not able to be dependent on a labour market
wage.[6]

The normative model of the family at the time—a marriage relationship between a full-time male breadwinner and a female homemaker and
mother—provided a central ideological theme underpinning this social
settlement. A breadwinner/homemaker structure of work and family was
institutionalized in the federal arbitration system through a 1907 case
known as the *Harvester* judgment.[7] The specific issue before the court
related to the interplay between tariffs and wages. Commonwealth excise
legislation provided tariff protection to manufacturers on condition that
the wage rates they paid to unskilled labourers were 'fair and reasonable'. Higgins J., the President of the Arbitration Court, determined that
in order to satisfy this test, a wage must be sufficient to support the
'labourer's home of about five persons' in conditions of 'frugal comfort'.[8]
The court assumed that the worker was the sole wage earner for himself,
his wife, and two or three children. This needs-based family wage
approach to setting minimum male wages came to form the basis for
Australia's wage fixation system for most of the twentieth century.[9]

Harvester legally institutionalized gender inequality in basic wages.
What had been market practice at the time became legal practice in the

---

[6] See generally Hancock, L., Howe, B., and O'Donnell, A. (eds.), *Reshaping Australian
Social Policy: Changes in Work, Welfare and Families*, Growth 48 (Melbourne: Committee for
Economic Development of Australia, Nov. 2000); Castles, F., 'The Institutional Design of the
Australian Welfare State', *International Social Security Review*, 50 (1997), 25.

[7] *Ex parte H. V. McKay* (1907) 2 CAR 1 ('*Harvester*').   [8] Ibid., 6.

[9] Hunter, R., 'Women Workers and Federal Industrial Law: From *Harvester* to Comparable
Worth', *AJLL*, 1 (1988), 147.

arbitration system.[10] A direct consequence of the *Harvester* family wage was that minimum wages for women were set on the assumption that when women did engage in market work, they were supporting themselves alone. In the *Federated Clothing Trades* Case of 1919 Higgins J. determined that the minimum rate for adult women ought to be 'the sum per week necessary to satisfy the normal needs of an average female employee, who has to support herself from her own exertions'.[11] After an investigation of what that might be, the court set a female basic wage at just over half the male rate. Some thirty years later the female minimum was increased to seventy-five per cent of the male rate.[12] Gender differentials between wage rates were sustained over the decades through a highly gender segregated labour market. From the early days where women worked alongside men they were granted the same pay, lest their lower rate lead to a loss of breadwinner jobs to them.[13] The legacy of the family wage, and the undervaluation of the type of market work that women have predominantly engaged in, continues to be felt today, both in the ongoing struggle for equal pay and in Australia's high rates of gendered occupational segregation.

The breadwinner/homemaker model of work and family shaped the legal regulation of the labour market in the early twentieth century beyond wages policy. *Harvester* reinforced the association of men with the public world of market work and women with financial dependence and the responsibilities of family and home. This gender division in household work remains resistant to change today with women continuing to shoulder a substantially larger share of family and caring work.[14] A good example of the normative force of the homemaker ideal in the first half of the twentieth century lies in the rules that existed until 1966 in the Commonwealth public service that imposed bars on the employment of married women. Indeed, the rules provided that women employees were deemed to have 'retired' upon marriage.[15] The breadwinner/homemaker

[10] Ryan, E. and Conlon, A., *Gentle Invaders: Australian Women at Work*, 2nd edn. (Melbourne: Penguin Books Australia, 1989), 84; Bennett, L., 'Legal Intervention and the Female Workforce: The Australian Conciliation and Arbitration Court 1907–1921', *International Journal of the Sociology of Law*, 12 (1984), 23.

[11] *Federated Clothing Trades* v. *J. A. Archer* (1919) 13 CAR 647, at 691.

[12] *Basic Wage Inquiry 1949–50* (1950) 68 CAR 698.

[13] *Rural Workers' Union* v. *Mildura Branch of the Australian Dried Fruits Association* (1912) 6 CAR 62.

[14] Regardless of whether women engage in paid market work, they continue to do considerably more domestic and family work than men. See generally Craig, L., *The Time Cost of Parenthood: An Analysis of Daily Workload*, Discussion Paper 117 (Sydney: Social Policy Research Centre, University of NSW, 2002); Bittman, M., *Juggling Time: How Australian Families Use Time*, 2nd edn. (Canberra: Australian Government Publishing Service, 1992).

[15] Section 49 of the Commonwealth Public Service Act 1922 (Cth), repealed by s. 4 of the Public Service Act 1966 (No. 2) (Cth).

model is also illustrated in two award test cases brought in the 1920s seeking reductions in working time. The underlying assumption of the parties, and the court, in these cases was that when workers were not at work, they were engaged in leisure. Paid work and leisure were assumed to constitute the worker's day, and household and caring work were assumed out of existence. Higgins J. postulated: 'The feeling [of workers] is that all the energies of a man's waking hours should not be given to the making of a living; that he should have some energy left for other and higher things—art, education, science, literature, even hobbies and amusements, as he selects'.[16]

The *Harvester* family wage concept was always deeply flawed as a model for ensuring social protection. It institutionalized sex discrimination and a hetero-normative model of the family in the industrial relations system. It severely undercompensated female-headed households, as it overcompensated the apparently forty-five per cent of male workers at the time who were not married.[17] From the early 1970s, the indefensibility of the *Harvester* approach became more visible, especially as greater numbers of women entered the paid labour market and second-wave feminism became an effective voice in the political sphere. Changes in the social security system and family law presented further challenges to the breadwinner/homemaker form. In 1973, income support was extended to all female sole parents, including mothers who had never been married. Previously, income support was limited through a widows' pension to selective categories of women who were seen as socially deserving, such as widows and 'deserted' wives.[18] Two years later, no-fault divorce became available.[19] These developments went towards recognizing women-headed households as sustainable family units.[20]

The family wage concept was finally formally abandoned by the Industrial Relations Commission in a series of equal pay cases culminating in the 1974 *National Wage Case*.[21] In this decision the Commission

[16] *Australian Timber Workers' Union v. John Sharp and Sons Limited* (1920) 14 CAR 811, at 847. See also *Amalgamated Engineering Union v. J. Alderdice and Company Pty Ltd* (1927) 24 CAR 755; *Standard Hours Inquiry* (1947) 59 CAR 581.
[17] Whelan, D., 'Women and the Arbitration System', *Journal of Australian Political Economy*, 4 (1979), 59, 65.
[18] Social Services Act (No. 3) 1973 (Cth). Widows' pensions were provided through the Widows' Pensions Act 1942 (Cth).
[19] Family Law Act 1975 (Cth). This Act provided for divorce based on one year's separation.
[20] The developments did not however unambiguously break with the breadwinner/homemaker tradition. For example, and as Berns points out, the 1973 supporting mothers benefit contained no requirement that the recipient seek work in the labour market, thereby reinforcing the idea of mothers as homemakers, and not as labour market participants. See Berns, above, n. 4, ch. 6.
[21] *National Wage Case 1974* (1974) 157 CAR 293. This case followed equal pay test cases in 1969 and 1972: (1969) 127 CAR 1142; (1972) 147 CAR 172. See generally Hunter, above, n. 9.

made clear its break from the social protection role of arbitration established by *Harvester* in stating that '[t]he Commission has pointed out in the past that it is an industrial arbitration tribunal, not a social welfare agency. We believe that the care of family needs is principally a task for governments and not the Commission'.[22] From this point, minimum wage rates were not differentiated by sex. Formal equality had been achieved, and workers were to be paid as individuals on the basis of work value, rather than on the basis of the supposed needs of male breadwinners and single women.[23]

III THE UNENCUMBERED WORKER OF CONTEMPORARY AUSTRALIAN LABOUR MARKETS

As Sandra Berns points out in *Women Going Backwards*, two central assumptions underlay the Australian twentieth-century breadwinner/ homemaker model. The first, reinforced through the family wage concept of the *Harvester* case, was that the breadwinner was financially responsible as the sole wage earner for his family. By paying the market worker a family wage *Harvester* explicitly supported the financial dependence of the private sphere of the family on the public waged labour market. The second assumption was implicit in *Harvester*, and was not clearly articulated or critiqued in labour law until feminist scholars began to look at these issues relatively recently. This assumption was that the breadwinner had no responsibility to actually do the caring and domestic work of the family because this was taken care of by the full-time homemaker wife. Through the breadwinner/homemaker bargain then, market work and the family existed in a complex interdependent relationship, marked by the financial dependence of the homemaker on the worker and the dependency of the market worker on the domestic and family work of the homemaker.[24]

The late 1960s and early 1970s equal pay cases are seen by Berns as central in displacing the first assumption of the breadwinner model that the worker of the labour market was financially responsible as the sole wage earner for a family.[25] Market workers were no longer to be assumed to be supporting a family. The second assumption underlying the breadwinner/ homemaker model was however untouched by these equal pay cases.[26] For Berns, this second assumption continues to hold sway to this day.

---

[22] *National Wage Case 1974* (1974) 157 CAR 293 at 299.
[23] The relationship between formal equality and the abandonment of the family wage concept in 1974 is discussed further below.   [24] Berns, above, n. 4, 4–5, ch. 6.
[25] Ibid., 27.
[26] e.g. working hours were not revised downwards in recognition of the abandonment of the model that assumed that market workers had the support of a full-time homemaker.

It is this second assumption, and labour law's separation of production from reproduction, that is the subject of contemporary feminist interest and analysis. Berns' thesis regarding the labour market is that the bread-winner of the twentieth century has largely 'metamorphosed' into the unencumbered worker of today—a normative worker who has neither financial responsibility to provide for a family nor actual responsibility for family and domestic work.[27] For Berns, today's ideal worker continues to behave in the market as if he (or she) has a homemaker wife.[28]

Berns situates the downfall of the family wage and the emergence of the unencumbered worker within the broader political tradition of liberalism and classical and neo-classical economic theory, and specifically in the simplified model of the abstract liberal citizen and rational economic actor—the formally equal individual of the public sphere. In particular, she positions the fall of the family wage in a context of the growing acceptance during the 1960s of the value of formal equality in the public sphere.[29] Berns explores how the liberal tradition constitutes its formally equal citizen (and worker) of the public world as devoid of gender, racial, class, or family context. The main identity of the liberal citizen (and worker) lies in absence rather than presence—an apparent lack of markers signifying particularity. For liberalism, differences in gender, race, class, and family context belong in the world of the social, family, and the home, and not the market.[30] 'All the ties and obligations constitutive of the social, the indicia of difference, must be left behind if people are to meet as equals in the public sphere'.[31] Berns draws on the work of John Rawls in *Political Liberalism* to illustrate liberalism's public citizen. She writes that Rawls' understanding of the liberal citizen 'as a free and equal moral person capable of being self supporting over a complete life' represents both that engagement in the paid labour market is normative, and, secondly, that the citizen faces no impediments to such participation, such as the particularities of caring or domestic work.[32]

In her text, Berns discusses a linguistic and social process that she identifies as differential gendering.[33] This practice identifies difference in a way that naturalizes and universalizes the point from which difference is measured. For example, when we identify and study particular groups of workers, such as women workers, their gender (and often family circumstances) assumes primacy both linguistically and socially, leaving the normative figure of the worker ungendered. In this way men

---

[27] Berns uses the word 'metamorphosed' on p. 167 of her text: Berns, above, n. 4.
[28] Berns makes this point in relation to the unencumbered citizen: ibid., 43.
[29] Ibid., 166.   [30] On Berns' unencumbered citizen, see generally ibid., 16–20, ch. 2.
[31] Ibid., 36.
[32] Rawls, J., *Political Liberalism* (New York: Columbia University Press, 1993), discussed in Berns, above, n. 4, 18.   [33] Berns, above, n. 4, 4–6.

and male workers disappear from view and analysis, to be replaced by the universal figure of the worker. Thus, differential gendering explains the dichotomies of workers/women workers, and more recently in Australia, workers/workers with family responsibilities. The category of 'worker' assumes primacy as the universal figure of the labour market, and the categories of 'women workers' and 'workers with family responsibilities' are constituted in their difference as outsiders to the labour market (and labour law). Berns writes that through differential gendering, 'masculinity is simultaneously affirmed (as universal) and rendered invisible (and thus located beyond analysis)'.[34]

Berns examines the fields of industrial relations law and policy, anti-discrimination law, family law, and the tax/transfer system to reveal how they interconnect in complex, and sometimes contradictory, ways to produce the unencumbered citizen of the liberal nation state. The text positions itself as an exploration at the theoretical and conceptual level, rather than as an empirical examination of legal rules. For example, the text finds strong evidence of an unencumbered subject of industrial relations policy in the construction of (federal) government-funded child-care as being part of family policy under the family services portfolio, rather than as being included in the industrial (or workplace) relations portfolio.[35]

Berns finds further support for her theory of the unencumbered worker in various other observations. One matter is the fragmentation of the labour market into a core of unencumbered workers and a periphery of secondary workers, such as part-time employees and casuals, who are often visibly encumbered by the particularity of family work.[36] In addition, the text highlights that enterprise bargaining has continued to marginalize the sex equality agenda in the labour market, and that the flexibility that has been delivered is largely employer-driven. The relative lack of provisions such as paid maternity and parental leave in enterprise bargaining agreements further bolsters Berns' thesis of the unencumbered worker.[37] Berns makes the argument that with the spread of working hours into evenings and weekends, employers often seem to assume in enterprise bargaining that workers are available to work at any time, and on short notice, reflecting a view of the worker as an individual with few commitments outside market work.[38] Finally, an unencumbered

---

[34] Ibid., 6.   [35] Ibid., 165.   [36] Ibid., 155–6.

[37] Ibid., 4–5, 162–3. For example, one study has found that only 13.5% of registered collective agreements contained at least one measure that the researcher identified as genuinely useful for parents and other carers, whilst only 11.6% of registered individual agreements included one or more such clauses: Whitehouse, G., 'Industrial Agreements and Work/Family Provisions: Trends and Prospects under "Enterprise Bargaining"', *Labour & Industry*, 12 (2001), 109, 113–15.   [38] Berns, above, n. 4, 14–16.

norm of workplace cultures appears evidenced in men's reluctance to take up measures, where they exist, such as parental leave and family leave.[39]

The remainder of this chapter builds on Berns' work by expanding on some of these observations. The gendered fragmentation of the labour market into a core of full-time employees and a periphery of part-time and casual workers is explored first. This is followed by an examination of how anti-discrimination values have been marginalized in the enterprise bargaining framework of Australian industrial relations, and what this reveals about the normative worker of enterprise bargaining. Finally, the Sex Discrimination Act 1984 (Cth) is examined to uncover a paradigmatic figure of work relations that is constituted as being without family responsibilities.

IV THE BIFURCATION OF THE AUSTRALIAN LABOUR MARKET AND LABOUR LAW

The traditional breadwinner/homemaker household, with a male partner as the sole wage earner and a female partner as a full-time homemaker, is still a strong model of labour force participation for families in Australia. In 2000, it accounted for just over thirty-four per cent of working families with dependent children. A second main path followed by families has been called a 'one plus' model, where one partner (invariably the male) works in the market full-time (defined as thirty-five hours or more per week), whilst the female partner engages in paid work on a part-time basis (defined as less than thirty-five hours per week). This model accounts for almost thirty-one per cent of working families. A third model, where both adults are in full-time waged work, comprised approximately twenty-three per cent of all working families. One-parent families, with the parent in paid work, accounted for just over twelve per cent of such working families.[40]

Both the continuing strength of the traditional breadwinner family, and the emergence of the 'one plus' model, reinforce women's primary attachment as being to the home and family, and men's to the public world of the labour market. Women are family carers first, and waged workers second, if at all.

---

[39] Berns, above, n. 4, 5–6.

[40] Buchanan, J. and Thornthwaite, L., *Paid Work and Parenting: Charting a New Course for Australian Families*, A Report Prepared for the Chifley Research Foundation (Sydney: University of Sydney, Aug. 2001), 19–20, esp. Table 4 (p. 20). It is unclear how the data used in this study categorized same-sex families.

The growth of the 'one plus' model is symbiotically related to employer demands for greater labour supply flexibility from the mid-1980s. Indeed, some Australian commentators discuss how employers were able to mobilize successfully the rhetoric of the family-friendly workplace to bolster their claims for flexibility and choice.[41] The demands of business for labour flexibility have aligned easily with government policy promoting part-time employment for mothers as a suitable and desirable way of addressing work/family conflict.[42] This policy underlies the approach to part-time and casual employment taken in the 1996 Workplace Relations Act. The Act removed existing provisions in industrial awards that limited the number of part-time and casual employees that an employer could engage. In addition, the Act ensures that awards contain provisions providing for regular part-time employment, where deemed appropriate by the Industrial Commission.[43]

Berns understands the development of part-time work for women as a fragmentation of the labour force into a core of normative (male) unencumbered full-time workers, and a periphery of (female) secondary or contingent workers, who are often visibly marked by family and domestic responsibilities.[44] There is much support for the view that the labour market continues today to require that full-time workers behave as if they have a homemaker wife taking care of family and domestic work. Indeed, in many ways this supposition has become stronger in relation to full-time workers, with working hours increasing substantially in Australia over the past twenty years,[45] and work intensification and pressure characterizing workplaces.[46] In this environment, part-time work for mothers becomes the obvious policy response of a conservative government seeking to disrupt existing power relations in the market, and the family, as little as possible. Even though the working lives of

---

[41] Berns, above, n. 4, 2; Hunter, R., 'The Mirage of Justice: Women and the Shrinking State', *Australian Feminist Law Journal*, 16 (2002), 53, 57; Junor, A., 'Permanent Part-time Work: Rewriting the Family Wage Settlement?', *Journal of Interdisciplinary Gender Studies*, 5 (2000), 94, 105.

[42] Reith, P., 'Delivering on Work and Family: The Workplace Relations Act 1996', *Australian Bulletin of Labour*, 25 (1999), 221. The author of this article was, at the time, the federal Minister for Employment, Workplace Relations and Small Business.

[43] WR Act, ss. 89A(4)(a), 143(1C)(b). Prior to the 1990s the trade union movement and the Industrial Commission were both antipathetic to part-time employment, seeing it as undermining the male breadwinner full-time norm: Owens, R., 'Women, "Atypical" Work Relationships and the Law', *Melbourne University Law Review*, 19 (1993), 399, 407–8.

[44] Berns above, n. 4, 155.

[45] Working hours have become a major industrial issue in Australia, with full-time employees working an extra 3.1 hours per week more than they were in 1982. Most of this is unpaid. Campbell, I., 'Extended Working Hours in Australia', *Labour & Industry*, 13 (2000), 91, 93–4.

[46] Watson, I., Buchanan, J., Campbell, I., and Briggs, C., *Fragmented Futures: New Challenges in Working Life* (Annandale, NSW: Federation Press, 2003), 95.

full-timers may be difficult, and indeed becoming more consuming, full-time standard employment remains at the centre of labour law's gaze, especially its protective vision. Workers engaged on a full-time basis under contracts of employment of indefinite duration attract the strongest and broadest range of legal entitlements and protections, which often increase with length of continuous service. These include, for example, award rights to paid annual, sick, bereavement, family, and long-service leave, rights on redundancy, and protection from unfair and discriminatory dismissal. These workers are the ones around whom labour law has been built.

Contingent and precarious workers are frequently referred to in Australia as atypical or non-standard workers, words that emphasize (and may further entrench) the typicality of the full-time worker.[47] Such workers remain at the periphery of labour law's protective function. Contingent work, such as part-time and casual employment, is often characterized by insecurity over continuing engagement and hours and shifts worked. This work is often poorly remunerated with little possibility of career progression. Relatively low unionization levels also characterize these groups, undermining their effectiveness in collective bargaining.[48] Although part-time employees generally have access to award leave entitlements on a pro rata basis, casuals usually do not.[49] Part-time employees are often able to seek redress in relation to unfair and discriminatory dismissal, whilst casuals employed for less than twelve months cannot bring an application in relation to unfair dismissal.[50]

Even where initiatives have been introduced into labour law to assist employees to manage their family commitments around their working lives, these schemes are sometimes marked by the normative strength of the full-time ideal in ways that undermine their effectiveness. An example of this lies in the entitlement to unpaid parental leave following the birth of a child. This legislative right, enacted at the federal level through a 1993 statute, provides a right to unpaid maternity and paternity leave of fifty-two weeks (in total) for full-time and part-time employees who have completed twelve months' continuous service with their employer.[51]

[47] Owens, R., 'Decent Work for the Contingent Workforce in the New Economy', *AJLL*, 15 (2002), 209, 212–14.

[48] See generally Junor, A., 'Permanent Part Time Work: New Family/Friendly Standard or High Intensity Cheap Skills?', *Labour & Industry*, 8 (1998), 77; Owens, above, n. 43, 407–11.

[49] As against this, awards usually require a wage loading to be paid to casuals.

[50] WR Act, ss. 170CB, 170CBA, 170CE(5), (5A), (5B). See also s. 492 for the position in Victoria.

[51] The current provisions are WR Act, Part VIA, Division 5, Sch. 14. These provisions further reflect the *Harvester* model by limiting entitlements explicitly to the child's mother and her spouse. Notably, the concept of spouse is not defined in the WR Act. Although it is likely to include a heterosexual de facto spouse, it is unlikely to cover a same-sex spouse, as same-sex marriages are not recognized in the Commonwealth legal system. Some states do, however, recognize, for a range of purposes, same-sex de facto relationships.

Prior to 2001, casuals were excluded from this right.[52] Given gendered labour force participation characteristics, it is likely that more fathers than mothers will be eligible for this right to unpaid parental leave, especially prior to 2001, as women are more likely to be casuals than men, and also less likely to accumulate twelve months' service than men, due to time out of the workforce for family-related reasons.[53] The irony of this is twofold. Not only are men least likely to feel able to take unpaid leave, as in most couples they remain the highest income earner, in Australia, as elsewhere in the world, the bulk of the work of caring for young babies invariably falls to mothers. A second example relates to family leave. Following an award test case initiated by the trade union movement in 1994, the federal Industrial Commission drafted standard award clauses that permit employees to use their aggregated entitlements to paid sick leave and bereavement leave (to a maximum of the equivalent of five days per year) to care for a sick family member.[54] Permanent part-time employees have a pro rata entitlement to family leave, whilst casuals have no entitlement. As most casuals are women, men are again more likely to be entitled to this work and family measure than are women. Not only do these examples reveal the pervasiveness of the standard/ contingent framework of labour law, they highlight the limitations of reforms built on this gendered structure.

Several Australian scholars, in addition to Berns, have explored the relationship between part-time work (including casual work) and a normative subject of Australian labour law and labour markets who works on a full-time basis without constraint due to family or domestic work. Rosemary Owens, in important early Australian investigations of women, atypical work, and labour law, examined the ways in which the labour market and labour law continued to privilege typical full-time employees over atypical workers.[55] In one article Owens argued that the promotion of atypical work as a step forward for women is deeply problematic because it continues to structure women's lives through understandings about women's proper (natural) roles in the family and

---

[52] In 2001, the right to unpaid parental leave was extended through the federal award system to casuals with more than 12 months' continuous service: *Re Vehicle Industry Repair, Services and Retail—Award 1983* (2001) 107 IR 71.

[53] Owens makes a similar argument regarding the preconditions that attached to the 1979 award entitlement to unpaid maternity leave: Owens, above, n. 43, 415–16.

[54] *Family Leave Test Case—November 1994* (1994) 57 IR 121; *Family Leave Test Case, Supplementary Decision* (1995) AILR 3-060; *Personal/Carer's Leave Test Case—Stage 2—November 1995* (1995) 62 IR 48. Notably, family leave extends to cover caring for a member of the employee's 'household'. This concept was adopted by the Industrial Commission for the purpose of covering non-normative caring relationships, such as those arising in same-sex families.

[55] Owens, R., 'The Peripheral Worker: Women and the Legal Regulation of Outwork', in Thornton, above, n. 3, 40; Owens, above, n. 43.

the home.[56] Beth Gaze reveals the normative strength of the full-time paradigm of Australian labour markets in the lack of a labour market model, understanding, and legitimacy for part-time work. She illustrates her argument by drawing on the university as a workplace, where part-time faculty must negotiate anew their responsibilities in relation to research, teaching, and administration, as there is no default labour market framework for part-time work to fall back on.[57] Anne Junor explores the potential offered by permanent part-time employment to alleviate work and family conflict in Australia, whilst moving towards the longer-term goal of gender equity. She notes the highly gendered character of part-time employment and investigates whether permanent part-time employment for mothers is a residue of a male breadwinner/female homemaker model, and whether it might provide the basis for a new and more equitable gender settlement. Junor concludes that the dualism of (male) full-time/(female) part-time does not itself transcend the breadwinner/homemaker model, and as such can only be one part of a broader strategy for a new gender settlement in Australia.[58]

V THE ANTI-DISCRIMINATION AGENDA IN THE ENTERPRISE BARGAINING FRAMEWORK

An unencumbered worker norm can be seen in the way in which anti-discrimination principles have been marginalized in the industrial relations framework. From the enactment of the first anti-discrimination statutes in Australia in the mid-1970s, industrial law and anti-discrimination values were widely viewed as operating in separate spheres, and indeed institutionally involved different state agencies and enforcement regimes. This division began to break down in the early 1990s with anti-discrimination values being imported into the industrial system.[59] Some tentative steps were taken in 1992, and a year later, a broader set of rules was enacted by the federal Labor government.[60] The current industrial relations legislation—the Conservative government's Workplace Relations Act 1996 (Cth)—does little to build on the 1993 amendments. Indeed, in

[56] Owens uses the concept of the sexual contract, drawing on the work of Carol Pateman in *The Sexual Contract* (Cambridge: Polity Press, 1988), ch. 5: Owens, above, n. 43, 422.

[57] Gaze, B., 'Working Part Time: Reflections on "Practicing" the Work-Family Juggling Act', *Queensland University of Technology Law & Justice Journal*, 1 (2001), 199.

[58] Junor, above, n. 41.

[59] Nevertheless, the separation of industrial law and anti-discrimination law remains. For example, the Sex Discrimination Act 1984 (Cth) (SDA) still retains an exemption in s. 40 in relation to sexually discriminatory practices of an employer done in direct compliance with an award or registered collective agreement.

[60] Industrial Relations Reform Act 1993 (Cth).

some important respects, the existing provisions are weaker than the framework introduced in 1993. Notably, even though it is now generally believed that work and family outcomes are deteriorating in Australia, there have been no amendments over the past seven years to the Workplace Relations Act designed to address a situation that is seen by some as approaching a crisis.

The current rules in the Workplace Relations Act charge the Industrial Commission with the task of ensuring that the content of registered collective agreements does not discriminate on a prohibited ground.[61] Grounds include sex, sexual preference, family responsibilities, and pregnancy. The way that the Commission approaches this task in relation to collective agreements gives rise to some concerns. It generally accepts the agreement, and the parties' submissions in relation to it, at face value with little further investigation into potential issues of discrimination. Importantly, there is generally no examination of how the agreement might operate in the particular workplace in question.[62] The statutory rules pertaining to a new type of agreement introduced with the 1996 scheme—a registered individual agreement called an Australian Workplace Agreement or AWA—contain even weaker anti-discrimination provisions. There is no legislative requirement that AWAs be scrutinized prior to approval to ensure that they are non-discriminatory towards women or workers with family responsibilities. Rather, AWAs must merely contain a prescribed anti-discrimination clause.[63] Not only is this standard clause worded very generally, but the existence of this clause does not necessarily mean or guarantee that the rest of the agreement is non-discriminatory.[64]

There are some provisions in the Workplace Relations Act relating to consultation in enterprise bargaining processes that warrant examination. The current provisions have their origins in the 1993 amendments of the Labor government. They require employers to take reasonable steps to ensure that a proposed collective agreement is explained to employees before they agree to it.[65] The legislation requires that the explanation must

---

[61] WR Act, s. 170LU(5). An exemption exists in relation to the 'inherent requirements' of that employment, or on the basis of religious teachings or beliefs in relation to the employment of a member of staff in a religious institution: WR Act, s. 170LU(6)(b), (c).

[62] This is my conclusion from a brief survey of 20 recent case decisions. It is consistent with the conclusions of earlier research: Charlesworth, S., 'Enterprise Bargaining and Women Workers: The Seven Perils of Flexibility', *Labour & Industry*, 8 (1997), 108; Charlesworth, S., *Stretching Flexibility: Enterprise Bargaining, Women Workers and Changes to Working Hours* (Sydney: Human Rights and Equal Opportunity Commission, 1996), 10.

[63] Where the agreement does not explicitly include this clause, it is implied into it. WR Act, s. 170VG(1), Workplace Relations Regulations, reg. 30ZI(1), Sch. 8.

[64] Importantly, AWAs attract certain requirements of confidentiality and secrecy regarding their content, making it difficult to assess their impact and effect: WR Act, ss. 83BS, 170WHB. But see also s. 170VG(2).   [65] WR Act, ss. 170LJ(3), 170LK(7).

be appropriate for the employees, having regard to their particular circumstances and needs, especially those employees who are women, young people, and people from non-English speaking backgrounds.[66] The point has been made that this type of legislative provision means little in the absence of broader mechanisms to ensure genuine participation and representation in bargaining processes by all employees.[67] Notably, the Workplace Relations Act does not ensure such broader processes. Another limitation with these statutory provisions lies in the way the Commission monitors compliance with them. The Commission's approach is almost perfunctory, invariably accepting, without further inquiry, the employer's usually very brief explanation of how the particular needs of employees in these three groups were taken into account in the consultation process.[68] In some cases, employers have indicated that these employees received the same explanation and information as the workforce as a whole, suggesting that the particular needs of women workers, young people, and people who have English as a second language may not in fact have been taken into account at all.

This consultation requirement provides an excellent example of the process of differential gendering explained by Berns.[69] Each of the three groups—women employees, young workers, and employees from non-English speaking backgrounds—are defined by their difference from an assumed universal figure of the worker who is genderless, and without the particularities of age or language. Indeed, the specificity of workers in these three categories is made explicit in the legislation, which refers to their 'particular circumstances and needs'.[70] The identification of the three groups in the legislation, through a process of differential gendering, simultaneously affirms the universal worker as genderless and without age and language, and at the same time sends a clear message that the workers in the three groups are non-normative.

The statutory rules in the Workplace Relations Act that impose anti-discrimination principles onto the content of collective agreements and AWAs, in addition to the requirements about consultation, fall far short of an attempt to recognize, or facilitate recognition, that work and family are not separate spheres, but are interconnected in complex and dynamic ways. The legal rules themselves are weak, and the enforcement

[66] WR Act, s. 170LT(7)(a). There are no equivalent consultation requirements in relation to AWAs. But see s. 83BB(2).
[67] Owens, R., 'Law and Feminism in the New Industrial Relations', in I. Hunt and C. Provis (eds.), *The New Industrial Relations in Australia* (Annandale, NSW: Federation Press, 1995), 36 (writing about the 1993 Industrial Relations Reform Act provisions).
[68] This is my conclusion from a brief survey of 20 recent case decisions. It is consistent with the conclusions of the earlier research conducted by Charlesworth, above, n. 62.
[69] Berns' understanding of differential gendering is explained above. See Berns, above, n. 4, 4–6.   [70] WR Act, s. 170LT(7).

procedures adopted by the Commission in relation to them exacerbate their limitations. They are not capable of generating a displacement of the breadwinner tradition of market work. They make no real attempt to do so. Indeed, the consultation requirements explicitly work to further entrench a male (adult and Anglo) norm as the universal subject of enterprise bargaining.

VI THE SEX DISCRIMINATION ACT 1984 (CTH)

In 1990, Margaret Thornton wrote about a 'benchmark' figure of Australian anti-discrimination law, who she described as 'likely to be a white, Anglo-Celtic, heterosexual male who falls within acceptable parameters of physical and intellectual normalcy'.[71] Evidence of Thornton's benchmark person emerges most clearly in the concept of direct discrimination articulated in the various anti-discrimination statutes. Direct discrimination generally arises when the discriminator treats the complainant less favourably than, in circumstances that are the same or are not materially different, the discriminator treats, or would treat, a comparator person.[72] In a complaint of sex discrimination brought by a woman, the comparator employee will be a similarly situated male employee. In a complaint of discrimination on the ground of race brought by an Indigenous employee, the comparator will be a non-Indigenous employee. Through this process of comparison, across the different grounds, Thornton's benchmark class is constituted as normative in the labour market. Their workplace experiences provide the benchmark against which differential treatment is measured, and discrimination is defined.[73]

The Sex Discrimination Act 1984 (Cth) prohibits direct discrimination on a range of grounds, including family responsibilities. These provisions were introduced in 1992. In a complaint of discrimination on the ground of family responsibilities the comparator is a similarly situated employee without family responsibilities. This comparator is Berns' unencumbered worker, established as normative in the labour market through the Sex Discrimination Act. Had Thornton been writing today about the benchmark figure of anti-discrimination law, no doubt she would have also identified the characteristic of being without family responsibilities. The provisions in the Sex Discrimination Act relating to family responsibilities

---

[71] Thornton, M., *The Liberal Promise: Anti-Discrimination Legislation in Australia* (Melbourne: OUP, 1990), 1.   [72] See e.g. the SDA, ss. 5(1), 6(1), 7(1), 7A.
[73] This point originates from MacKinnon, C., *Towards a Feminist Theory of the State* (Cambridge, MA: Harvard University Press, 1989); MacKinnon, C., *Feminism Unmodified: Discourses on Life and Law* (Cambridge, MA: Harvard University Press, 1987).

reveal an unencumbered norm of Australian labour markets in another way. The legislation provides a very narrow legal entitlement regarding family responsibilities. The ground covers only direct discrimination, and only in relation to dismissal from employment.[74] In this way, the Sex Discrimination Act protects only a very limited space for family context in the workplace. It aims merely to ensure that encumbered workers are not dismissed when a worker without family responsibilities would not be. In constituting a contained and relatively small area of legitimacy for the family encumbrances of workers, the legislative scheme confirms that the appearance of family context elsewhere in the employment relation is inappropriate.

A final way in which the Sex Discrimination Act is built upon, and rein-scribes a separation of market and home, lies in the exclusion from the Act of unpaid work within the family.[75] In this way, the fiction of the home and the family as being beyond regulation by law is maintained. In addition to excluding unpaid work within families, the Sex Discrimination Act continues to exclude some work performed in a commercial context in the home.[76] These exclusions reflect both the malleability of liberalism's public/private divide, and the strength of the ideology surrounding the home and domestic sphere, as being untouched by law.

VII CONCLUSIONS

This chapter poses some (ambitious) questions about the normative person of Australian labour law and, in particular, that subject's relationship to family and domestic work. The analysis commences in the breadwinner/homemaker tradition of Australian industrial law and, in particular, the family wage of the 1907 *Harvester* case. It attempts to shed some light on the contemporary subject of labour market legal regulation by focusing on three present day phenomena, namely, the fragmentation of the labour force and labour standards into a dualism of standard/ non-standard work, the marginalization of anti-discrimination values in

[74] Other aspects of paid work, such as recruitment, hiring, promotion, and training are not covered (unless the employer's actions can be shown to constitute constructive dismissal): SDA, s. 14(3A). The concept of family responsibilities is defined in s. 4A (and see the definition of de facto spouse in s. 4(1)). These provisions are explicitly limited to heterosexed family forms.
[75] The Act covers employment, commission agents, contract workers, and partnerships. All these presuppose a legally enforceable common law contract: SDA, s. 4(1).
[76] Section 14(3) of the SDA excludes sex discrimination in employment that relates to performing domestic duties in the residence of the respondent. Section 35 provides an exemption in relation to sex discrimination in paid work, where the duties of the position involve the care of a child or children in the place where the child or children resides or reside.

enterprise bargaining, and the test of direct discrimination in the Sex Discrimination Act 1984 (Cth). Each of these matters reveals a normative worker who largely acts in the labour market as if he (or she) has a home-maker wife at home.

Much work remains to be done to fully bring into vision the subject of Australian labour law. This chapter is a small step along that path. In particular, several research questions follow from the ones investigated here: have the paradigmatic assumptions regarding the worker and the worker's family responsibilities developed evenly across different areas of labour law, such as industrial law and anti-discrimination law? What factors and processes account for uneven developments? A sub-set of questions arises in relation to labour law's vision of the normative family and caring relationships of its worker. The subject worker and his family of *Harvester* were constituted culturally as heterosexual, and Anglo-Celtic. Does labour law continue to assume a heterosexed normative family, in an Anglo-Celtic form? Arguably, current analyses are only beginning to skim the surface of these difficult and perplexing questions.

5

The Right to Flexibility

HUGH COLLINS*

European governments regard greater flexibility in labour markets as a key ingredient to the achievement of greater business competitiveness, full employment, and growing prosperity. Policies favouring flexibility have been central to the European Union's employment strategy introduced by the Amsterdam Treaty,[1] with detailed policy prescriptions initiated at Luxembourg in 1997,[2] then developed at Lisbon in 2000 with the Open Method of Co-ordination,[3] and most recently relaunched with reformulated guidelines in 2003.[4] Through the Open Method of Co-ordination for the employment strategy, the European Union sets an agenda and exerts peer pressure on Member States to adopt these policies in national legislation, active manpower expenditures, and social practice.[5] There is clearly a large measure of consensus across the political spectrum that these policies or guidelines are desirable and form part of what can be

---

* Thanks are due to the editors, Emily Jackson, and Claire Kilpatrick for comments, and to Anna Edwards for research assistance.

[1] Treaty of Rome (as amended), Title VIII, Art. 125: 'Member States and the Community shall, in accordance with this Title, work towards developing a co-ordinated strategy for employment and particularly for promoting a skilled, trained and adaptable workforce and labour markets responsive to economic change . . .'.

[2] Council Resolution of 15 Dec. 1997 on the 1998 employment guidelines, OJ C 30, 28.1.1998, p. 1.

[3] Treaty of Rome (as amended), Art. 128; Hodson, D. and Maher, I., 'The Open Method as a New Mode of Governance', *Journal of Common Market Studies*, 39 (2001), 719; Regent, S., 'The Open Method of Coordination: A New Supranational Form of Governance?', *European Law Journal*, 9 (2003), 190; Trubeck, D. M. and Mosher, J., 'New Governance, EU Employment Policy, and the European Social Model', in C. Joerges, Y. Mény, and J. H. H. Weiler (eds.), *Mountain or Molehill? A Critical Appraisal of the Commission White Paper on Governance*, John Monnet Working Paper No. 6/01 (European University Institute, Florence, 2001); the details of the OMC process have been streamlined following a review: European Commission, 'On Streamlining the Annual Economic and Employment Policy Coordination Cycles', COM (2002) 487 final; Watt, A., 'Reform of the European Employment Strategy after Five Years: A Change of Course or Merely of Presentation?', *European Journal of Industrial Relations*, 10 (2004), 117, 128–30.

[4] Council Decision of 22 July 2003 on guidelines for the employment policies of the Member States (2003/578/EC), OJ L 197/13, 5.8.2003; Watt, above, n. 3. The new guidelines are expected to remain constant for a period of three years.

[5] Szyszczak, E., 'The Evolving European Employment Strategy', in J. Shaw (ed.), *Social Law and Policy in an Evolving European Union* (Oxford: Hart Publishing, 2000), 197; Biagi, M., 'The Impact of European Employment Strategy on the Role of Labour Law and Industrial Relations', *International Journal of Comparative Labour Law and Industrial Relations*, 16 (2000), 155; Ashiagbor, D., 'EMU and the Shift in the European Labour Law Agenda: From "Social Policy" to "Employment Policy" ', *European Law Journal*, 7 (2001), 311.

described as a European model of the social market. National governments are encouraged to orient their interventions in labour markets towards these policy goals, and they usually try to present their actions as consistent with the guidelines, even if local political considerations and labour market institutions lead to divergences in interpretation and implementation.[6] Although the employment strategy is mostly expressed at a high level of generality, as in the 2003 'three overarching and inter-related objectives of full employment, quality and productivity at work, and social cohesion and inclusion', the policy goals certainly point to the need for particular changes in the law at national and sometimes transnational levels.[7] This chapter explores the potential legal implica-tions of the 2003 guideline on 'adaptability' in the labour market, and in particular its agenda with respect to flexibility, because one of those implications seems to reveal implicitly a radical proposal to transform the legal structure of the contract of employment.

The contract of employment has provided the predominant legal conceptualization of employment relations in Europe.[8] Labour laws typically adopt this legal institution as a starting point, and then seek to replace or modify certain aspects of the contract by regulation. The argument of this chapter suggests that to fulfil the most recent ambitions of the European employment strategy with respect to the guideline on flexibility, it will be necessary not merely to modify the institution of the contract of employment, but rather to introduce a seismic shift in some of its key elements. This radical reconstruction of the legal institution can be expressed briefly by the novel legal idea of an employee's right to flexibility. In order to appreciate the significance of the challenge posed by the most recent evolution in the policies regarding flexibility to the traditional legal framework, it is useful at the outset to examine some foundational elements of the legal institution of the contract of employment.

I TIME IN THE CONTRACT OF EMPLOYMENT

Control over the time of the worker lies at the heart of the contract of employment. The contract sets a framework for the timing of work, the

[6] For an assessment of the impact on legal regulation in Member States: Mosher, J. S. and Trubek, D. M., 'Alternative Approaches to Governance in the EU: EU Social Policy and the European Employment Strategy', *Journal of Common Market Studies*, 41 (2003), 63, 73–6.
[7] The Employment Strategy expressly rules out the possibility of harmonization of laws based upon this Title in the Treaty (Art. 129), but transnational measures fulfilling those policy goals can usually be presented by the Commission under Art. 137.
[8] Veneziani, B., 'The Evolution of the Contract of Employment', in B. Hepple (ed.), *The Making of Labour Law in Europe* (London: Mansell, 1986), 31.

total hours of work required in a given period, and the duration of the employment relation. In the historical evolution of the contract of employment, it was this element of the employer's control over time conferred by the terms of the contract that provided a crucial distinguishing feature of this legal institution from other contracts for the performance of services.

The advent of the factory and the office accelerated a division in space and time between workplace and home. The workplace became a separate space, geographically distanced from home, and separated from other life activities by a gateway that permitted both entry and exclusion from work. The creation of a workplace also enabled employers to construct new methods for measuring performance of work. Instead of payment systems connected exclusively to the number of units produced or tasks completed, contract performance could be measured by reference to time spent within the workplace combined with the employer's ability to observe and monitor effort in the performance of work.

The creation of the workplace established the conditions necessary for the widespread use of a particular type of contract for the performance of work. The ancient common law structure for the regulation of domestic service, the master and servant relation, was exported to the new geographical space of the workplace.[9] The contract of employment could assume the form of payment of wages for hours of work, that is the worker's presence in the workplace. This domestic service model replaced the previous dominant legal form for craftsmen, skilled workers, and other independent contractors engaged in industrial production, which rendered payment conditional on measurement of output or the completion of a particular task. The ability to direct, supervise, and monitor work performed in the workplace enabled employers to ensure that they received productive work in return for the wage. Their powerful sanction against poor work and absenteeism was exclusion from the workplace, with the consequent removal of the worker's main source of income.

This new contractual relation produced in response to industrialization was eventually named the contract of employment.[10] At its core was a bargain about time. The employer purchased a worker's time rather than products of his or her labour. Managers had to estimate in advance how

[9] Fox, A., *Beyond Contract: Work, Power and Trust Relations* (London: Faber, 1974), ch. 4.
[10] Deakin, S., 'The Evolution of the Contract of Employment 1900–1950: The Influence of the Welfare State', in N. Whiteside and R. Salais (eds.), *Governance, Industry and Labour Markets in Britain and France: The Modernising State in the Mid-Twentieth Century* (London: Routledge, 1998), 212; Deakin, S., 'The Many Futures of the Contract of Employment', in J. Conaghan, M. R. Fischl, and K. Klare (eds.), *Labour Law in an Era of Globalization: Transformative Practices and Possibilities* (Oxford: OUP, 2002), 177.

much time would be required to achieve the desired level of production and when the work would be required, and then employ workers with appropriate skills for the requisite period. To perform this function efficiently, managers had to be able to insist on the implementation of their precise calculations. They had to be able to fix the total hours of work, the timing of work, and the number of workers through contracts of employment. This specification of the timing and duration of work provided the sharpest distinction between contracts of service and contracts for services. Whereas independent contractors could determine their hours, methods of working, and the rhythm of work, employees had to conform to the precise requirements of the employer, as expressed in the contract. This contrast in control over time was a crucial ingredient of the 'control' test used by the law for distinguishing between employees and independent contractors.

In pursuit of productive efficiency, managers bargained for contracts that both fixed hours of work to suit the demands of the business and also permitted termination of contracts on short notice to avoid the costs of surplus labour power. Casual work, offered for short periods of time as required, with payment by the hour, tended to fit the employer's need for efficient production. But to recruit and retain the best workers, especially when they were organized by trade unions for the purpose of collective bargaining, employers needed to offer more substantial promises of job security and standard hours. Legislation also qualified the power of employers to determine the time and duration of employment through contracts by the imposition of compulsory obligations in order to give a degree of protection to employment security. As a result, the bare form of casual work was not in practice the standard pattern of the contract of employment, but rather the default outcome when workers lacked any significant bargaining power at all. Even so, the typical standard contract of employment still provided the employer both with the initiative to fix the hours and timing of work according to the needs of production, and also with the ability to terminate the employment relation on short notice when labour power became surplus to requirements.

The continuing presence of the employer's power effectively to determine working time and the duration of employment through its bargaining power over the specification of the terms of the contract goes a considerable way towards explaining the difficulty experienced by lawyers in trying to articulate a modern conception of the employment relation. Modern legal analyses of the contract of employment try to capture the social expectations of job security by emphasizing its long-term relational dimension,[11] and its legal expression in the idea of 'mutuality

---

[11] Freedland, M. R., *The Personal Employment Contract* (Oxford: OUP, 2003), 90.

of obligation'.[12] Yet the basic elements of the institution of the contract of employment always permitted the employer to try to bargain for exclusive control over the duration and timing of work, even though the social expectations emphasized the permanence of work and its limit to normal hours. Thus, even today, a permanent job is rarely more than a contract of indefinite duration terminable in most instances by a fairly short notice period or even 'at will'. The terms of the contract do not reflect the social expectations of permanence, regularity, and stability. The institution of the contract of employment permits an employer to construct a job package to suit its production needs, and subject to statutory controls at the margins and collective bargaining, the employee has to take or leave the package on offer. The legal institution of the contract of employment therefore provides a structure through which employers can achieve productive efficiency by controlling the lever of working time. It is not without irony that when employers use their bargaining power to determine working time in the contract so that they merely offer casual work, as required, that this type of work is sometimes excluded from the coverage of employment protection laws on the ground that it lacks the necessary 'mutuality of obligation' for an employment relationship.[13] The absence of mutuality in the sense of a long-term commitment by the employer to provide work is clearly just an extreme manifestation of the underlying structure of the contract of employment that provides the employer with the facility to determine in the first instance working time and the duration of employment.

With that background concerning the legal institution of the contract of employment in mind, we can consider the evolution of the employment strategy of the European Union, particularly with respect to ideas concerning labour market flexibility. The following account draws a distinction between two phases in the evolution of these policy ideas.

II MANAGERIAL FLEXIBILITY AND FAIRNESS

In the original language of the European Union's employment strategy, the policy of flexibility was primarily directed at the aim of modernizing work organization and forms of work. The early formulations of the strategy in 1998 and 1999 emphasized 'four pillars': improving employability, developing entrepreneurship, encouraging adaptability of businesses and their employees, and strengthening equal opportunities policies for women and men.[14] The third pillar concerning adaptability

---

[12] *O'Kelly* v. *Trusthouse Forte plc* [1983] ICR 728, CA.
[13] *Carmichael* v. *National Power plc* [1999] ICR 1226, HL.
[14] Council Resolution, above, n. 2.

was largely concerned with labour market flexibility. This policy included the promotion of 'flexible working arrangements, with the aim of making undertakings productive and competitive and achieving the required balance between flexibility and security'. The emphasis, through repetition, was on flexibility in the terms on which work was offered. In other words, employers should be permitted to offer jobs in non-standard forms, such as part-time and temporary work, or variable hours of work, and with indeterminate job descriptions, with a view to obtaining managerial flexibility with respect to the amount and use of labour power. This policy prescription was clearly influenced by perceptions of 'Eurosclerosis' in the form of rigidities in the labour market, which when combined with weaknesses in the supply side, appeared to lead to high levels of unemployment.[15]

Viewed in this context, the European Union's employment strategy on labour market flexibility was correctly regarded with suspicion by workers and their representatives. It could be interpreted as a policy designed to remove or reduce restrictions built up over more than a century through legislation and collective bargaining on the employer's power to press for casual and temporary employment in various forms. Even if what was intended did not go so far as the promotion of casual work, the emphasis on flexibility certainly embraced the use of non-standard forms of work such as part-time work, temporary jobs, and flexible working patterns.

Resistance on the part of workers to this kind of flexibility is understandable. These different forms of numerical and functional flexibility may lead to a stressful combination of an enlargement of job responsibilities with weaker employment security. Flexibility can also require variable hours of work, unsocial hours, alterations in the place of work, and more generally the absence of clear contractual entitlements for employees. By strengthening the employer's discretionary powers and the ability only to pay for labour as required, the legal regime heightens the employee's sense of insecurity and subordination. At its most extreme, flexibility leads to contracting out of employment protection laws altogether by the adoption of forms of contracts for services which elude the legislative categories governing the scope of protection of employment laws. Greater flexibility in these senses may be conducive to better competitiveness for business, at least in the short term, but this

---

[15] Although perhaps an apt analysis of some of the causes of high unemployment in some Member States, it is far from clear that the policy prescriptions made sense in some European economies with their lower wages and extensive informal and temporary work relations: Seferiades, S., 'The European Employment Strategy Against a Greek Benchmark: A Critique', *European Journal of Industrial Relations*, 9 (2003), 189; Mosher and Trubek, above, n. 6, 74 (Italy).

efficiency may perhaps only be gained at the price of a weakening of the commitment of the workforce to co-operative industrial relations.

In response to this problem of securing co-operation and in order to secure long-term competitiveness in business, most governments and employers recognize that greater managerial flexibility must be combined with a greater commitment on the part of employers to fair treatment of the workforce and to respect for workers' need for economic security.[16] Even with weak bargaining power, employees can still damage productivity and competitiveness by their failure to co-operate fully in efficient production. To obtain this co-operation, if firm contractual commitments are not made, the employer must at least commit itself to fairness in the conduct of the undertaking and the exercise of managerial power in order to obtain full co-operation from the workforce. The difficulty lies in giving content to this notion of fairness towards employees.

Granting flexibility to employers seems to rule out the traditional safeguards for fairness in the workplace: a precise job content, fixed contractual entitlements and duties, and legal guarantees of job security.[17] Answers to the need to find new dimensions of fairness have been sought in such legal initiatives as requiring greater sharing of information with the workforce,[18] clearer procedures for the implementation of organizational changes,[19] more comprehensive anti-discrimination laws,[20] better legal protection against arbitrary treatment through dismissal laws,[21] and the extension of employment rights to non-standard workers.[22] These techniques for expressing and implementing the value of fairness all present a counterbalance to the employer's power to insist through the terms of employment upon flexibility on the part of the workforce. By controlling the employer's discretionary power to direct the workforce and determine requirements for labour power, if only at the margins, these measures, either directly or indirectly, serve to reassure employees that the employer will not engage in opportunism or undermine reasonable

[16] Collins, H., 'Regulating the Employment Relation for Competitiveness', *ILJ*, 30 (2001), 17.

[17] Marsden, D., *A Theory of Employment Systems: Micro-Foundations of Societal Diversity* (Oxford: OUP, 1999).

[18] Directive 98/59 (collective redundancies), Art. 2; Directive 2001/23 (transfers of undertakings), Art. 7; Directive 2001/86 (employee involvement in the European company); Directive 2002/14 (information and consultation).

[19] Directive 98/59 (collective redundancies), Art. 4; Directive 2001/23 (transfers of undertakings).

[20] Directive 2000/43 (equal treatment irrespective of racial or ethnic origin); Directive 2000/78 (general framework for equal treatment in employment).

[21] Although the general law of dismissal is not covered by EU legislation, dismissals for particular reasons can be forbidden, e.g. Directive 2000/78 (equal treatment), Art. 11 (victimization); Directive 2002/14, Art. 7 (protection of employees' representatives).

[22] Directive 99/70 (fixed-term work); Directive 2003/88 (working time).

expectations of stability in employment. These ideas about how to secure fairness as a counterbalance to increased flexibility seem to have been what was intended by the formulation in the European Union's employment policy quoted above that flexibility should be balanced by 'security'.[23]

III FLEXIBILITY AND THE BALANCE BETWEEN
WORK AND PRIVATE LIFE

The employment strategy of the European Union and its Member States seems now to have taken a different course. Faced with the criticism that the original employment policy failed to evidence sufficient concern that good or decent jobs should be created,[24] the guidelines were altered in 2003 to reduce the stress on flexibility, and to emphasize instead, as well as the retained commitments to full employment and the strengthening of social cohesion and inclusion, the revised goal of improving quality and productivity at work. The change almost certainly reflects as well a new emphasis upon linking the employment strategy to a concern for social inclusion and social cohesion.[25] Nevertheless, the need to encourage flexibility remains a key ingredient in this reformulated employment strategy. The new guidelines call for Member States to promote the 'diversity of contractual and working arrangements, including arrangements on working time, favouring career progression, a better balance between work and private life and between flexibility and security'.[26] But what exactly are the policies that this new guideline requires governments to promote?

The new guideline envisages that employers should offer a diversity of job packages. These packages might include variations in hours of work, the timing of work, or different working arrangements, such as working from home for part of the time. According to the guideline, this diversity in job packages is expected to help to achieve three goals: career progression, a better work/life balance, and a better balance between flexibility and security. In other words, the diversity of job packages is

[23] The meaning of 'security' in the context of European employment policy may perhaps be elucidated by the discussion in the Supiot Report of 'active security': Supiot, A., *Beyond Employment: The Transformation of Work and the Future of Labour Law in Europe* (Oxford: OUP, 2001), 196–200.

[24] Ball, S., 'The European Employment Strategy: The Will but not the Way?', *ILJ*, 30 (2001), 353.

[25] Atkinson, T., 'Social Inclusion and the European Union', *Journal of Common Market Studies*, 40 (2002), 625; for an examination of the meaning of these terms in the context of employment law: Collins, H., 'Discrimination, Equality and Social Inclusion', *MLR*, 66 (2003), 16, 21–6.

[26] Council Decision of 22 July 2003 on guidelines for the employment policies of the Member States (2003/578/EC) OJ L 197/13, 5.8.2003.

encouraged because it seems to have the potential both to promote competitiveness and productivity, and, at the same time, to create jobs which workers will regard as good quality jobs. Workers will regard these diverse job packages as good jobs because the packages contain the potential for career progression, offer better possibilities for balancing the demands of work with other responsibilities and individual interests, and yet preserve also an unspecified though adequate degree of employment security. This formulation retains the continuity with the previous policy of seeking a balance between flexibility and fairness. What is different in the new description of the European employment strategy is the presentation of diversity in job packages as in itself having the potential to improve the quality of jobs.

At first sight, this linkage between diversity in job packages and improvements in the quality of jobs seems improbable. Experience suggests that much of this diversity might in practice consist of the creation of temporary, part-time, low-skilled jobs on low pay. Such developments in the labour market would be a reversion to the elementary model of casual employment that social legislation and bargaining has sought to reduce or eliminate. These kinds of jobs, though often better than nothing, hardly qualify as the good jobs envisaged by the European Union's employment strategy. They do not seem to offer any prospects of career progression. Nor do they obviously improve the balance between work and private life except perhaps for those workers, such as students, who genuinely seek a part-time, temporary job. It is true, of course, that diversity in job packages might produce other kinds of variations that might be attractive to some workers, such as job shares or independent contracting in the form of consultancies. Even so, judged in comparison with the standard job package, offering full-time work, for an indefinite duration, with prospects for progression up the grades of an internal labour market, the non-standard job packages will usually seem relatively unattractive to most workers. So how can the governments of the European Union now believe that diversity in job packages will in fact improve the quality of jobs?

The key assumption of the policy seems to be that diversity in job packages will enable workers to achieve a better balance between work and private life, as a result of which it is supposed that they will be more productive, more satisfied with their jobs, and experience less stress. Good jobs, on this view, are not merely those positions which pay well, but must also comprise jobs that contribute optimally to an individual's well-being. This welfare calculation involves not only an assessment of the job's intrinsic qualities and its financial and psychological rewards, but also of how work contributes to, and is compatible with, every other aspect of an individual's life. A good job usually contributes significantly to an individual's well-being, but if the total hours, the timing, and the pressure of work effectively prevent a person from pursuing other interests and responsibilities, the job may in fact have severely damaging effects on well-being. These effects may be revealed in feelings of stress or depression, which can harm both work performance and personal relationships. The proposed solution is to reconfigure the notion of a good job as one that provides an adequate level of income, offers the possibility of career progression, and at the same time permits the individual to achieve a sense of well-being through the realization of a satisfying balance between work and private life.

In this context, the phrase 'private life' needs to be understood broadly to refer to most aspects of a person's activities outside working hours. These personal activities are not confined to family responsibilities or care for dependants, though certainly those are an important and demanding aspect of private life. Private life can include other kinds of relationships, having the time to see your friends or to be with someone you love. Furthermore, the term 'private' seems misleading to the extent that it implies that the contrast is between work and home life. The private activities that contribute to a person's well-being might include an employee's desire to spend more time on other kinds of work, such as voluntary charitable work, public or community service, local politics, pursuing educational interests, or even running a small business on the side. Moreover, it should be recognized that a person's well-being may require several shifts in the balance between work and private life during a lifetime. New parents may want to change their hours of work radically during the early years of childrearing. Older workers may shift their preference for having greater leisure time by reducing the hours of work without leaving the workforce entirely. Indeed, there seems no strong argument to confine the range of reasons for which employees might wish to alter their hours of work in order to achieve a better balance between work and private life. The aim is to find the balance between work and private life that establishes the optimal level of well-being for each individual. It seems to follow that any reason for varying hours of work, which an employee believes is likely to contribute to his or her well-being, is likely to be a valid reason.

It is also important to recognize the concept of diversity in job packages extends beyond many of the well-established categories of flexibility such as part-time work, temporary work, and casual work. Diversity in job packages can experiment with all the variables in the measurement of work. One variable is fractional work: an employee agrees to work for a particular fraction or percentage of the standard full-time job, such as one-third or four-fifths. The fraction could be varied at periodical intervals, such as reductions during school holidays.

Another variable concerns the period of measurement of hours. For example, in the case of annualized hours, over the course of a year the employee performs the same number of hours as those performed by a standard full-time worker, but in any given week the hours rise and fall according to the needs of the worker and the business. Flexibility can also be obtained by variations in the time of day when work is performed. Under flexitime arrangements, the employee has no set start or finish time but is required to work the agreed hours during the week or month. Similarly, the contract may provide for a compressed working week, under which the employee works the same number of hours as a standard full-time worker, but perhaps in the space of four days in a week, or nine days in a fortnight. Breaks in the continuity of work, such as career breaks, sabbaticals, or routinely only working during school terms, can also provide a technique to promote flexibility. The place of work is also another important variable for this expanded concept of flexibility. The employee may be able to work more conveniently and efficiently for at least part of the week from home. No doubt this list does not exhaust the possible variables in the creation of a diversity of job packages.

Bearing in mind both this wide definition of how the balance between work and private life should be conceived, and the breadth of the notion of diversity in job packages, it should be appreciated that these issues concern all participants in the labour market. No doubt the issue of the work/life balance especially concerns particular sections of the workforce, such as lone parents, who may encounter substantial obstacles in holding down a standard job whilst providing adequate childcare. Nevertheless, the concern to establish quality jobs, which achieve a satisfactory balance between work and private life, should apply to everyone. We can identify the relevance of this concern, for instance, in that sector of the labour market, which, from many points of view, is the most privileged. Many managers, professionals, and highly skilled workers earn well above average wages and enjoy considerable job security and good career prospects. Nevertheless, their well-being may be damaged by their work's interference with their private life, even to the extent that their dissatisfaction with their work/life balance may reduce their productivity at work. For example, in Britain the average working week is close to forty hours, and for highly skilled workers and professionals the average is closer to forty-five hours. About a quarter of professionals and managers work in excess of forty-eight hours a week. Many members of these groups would prefer to work shorter hours, or to phase their work during the week in ways that would enable them to participate better in family life or other pursuits, or, over a longer period of time, to increase and decrease their working time according to their changing personal circumstances. But these variations may not be possible either because of the employer's rigid terms of employment, or because these employees believe, probably correctly, that requests for reduced hours would damage their long-term career prospects.[27] The concern about the balance between work and private life therefore applies to these relatively privileged groups. Indeed, all participants in the labour market may have, from time to time, particular concerns about an unsatisfactory balance between work and private life.

It follows that the link drawn in the European Union's employment strategy between the quality of jobs and the diversity of jobs available makes sense in the context of the growing concern about establishing an optimal balance between work and private life. But the creation of diversity in job packages also retains its importance as a method for increasing productivity and competitiveness. Instead of these improvements in efficiency being achieved simply by the employer being able to reduce labour costs through techniques of numerical and functional flexibility, the diversity of job packages is expected to help the employer's business in a more subtle way. By facilitating a better balance between work and private life through an offer of diversity in job packages, employers will be able to improve productivity, it is believed, by attracting and retaining good workers, and by keeping them better motivated and more willing to co-operate whilst working. With these assumptions, flexibility can be presented as a win–win policy: employers improve productivity, innovation, and competitiveness; employees have good quality jobs that suit their personal needs to earn an income but also to engage fully in other aspects of private life without excessive stress.

No doubt the credibility of the assumptions of this new version of the economic strategy on flexibility can be challenged. My concern here is not with making any such assessment of the theory of the connection between competitiveness and the work/life balance, but rather to consider the implications of the policy for the regulation of the employment relationship. Even so, it is perhaps worth noting that the policy hypotheses do have some empirical support, and as a result, in a UK context, are likely to be maintained by government for some time, enough time at least to have a noticeable impact on the law. Support can certainly be found for the claim that firms that operate 'family-friendly' measures can benefit in various ways from the retention of skilled and experienced workers.[28]

[27] Kodz, J., Harper, H., and Dench, S., *Work-Life Balance: Beyond the Rhetoric*, Institute for Employment Studies, Report 384 (Brighton: Institute for Employment Studies, 2002) (summary available at www.employment-studies.co.uk).
[28] Lewis, S. and Lewis, J. (eds.), *The Work-Family Challenge: Rethinking Employment* (London: Sage, 1996); Dex, S. and Scheibl, F., 'Flexible and Family-Friendly Working Arrangements in UK-Based SMEs: Business Cases', *BJIR*, 39 (2001), 411; Department of Trade and Industry, *Best Practice in Your Business: Flexible Working* (London: DTI, 2004), also

Similarly, businesses that offer some flexibility in hours may be able to improve recruitment by exploring a wider pool of talent, and also may be able to reduce absenteeism.[29] Surveys in this field tend to provide support for the assumptions behind the new approach to flexibility. In one survey, two-fifths of full-time workers agreed that if they were given more control over their time at work they would be more productive.[30] Better control over hours of work also seems likely to increase contentment in a job and to reduce levels of stress.[31] Two surveys of employees commissioned by the UK government both support by large majorities the views that everyone should be able to balance their work and home lives in the way they want to, and that people work best when their work/life balance is satisfactory.[32] No doubt these surveys should be treated cautiously: most people will see positive benefits arising from less time at the office or in the factory (assuming that pay remains constant or does not diminish sufficiently to affect lifestyle significantly). The degree of benefit to both employers and employees from any scheme of increased flexibility will no doubt turn on how carefully the diverse job packages have been tailored to the particular needs of both parties. Although such benefits will be discovered, research will no doubt also reveal instances where the risks of flexibility for workers are also fully realized by the loss of job security and reduction of income. This is not the place, however, to embark upon a thorough evaluation of what is necessarily a patchy, probably inconclusive, pool of evidence about the advantages of diversity in job packages. The question here is rather what are the legal implications of the pursuit of this new conception of the policy of labour market flexibility?

available at http://www.dti.gov.uk/bestpractice/assets/flexible.pdf; Woodland, S., Simmonds, N., Thornby, M., Fitzgerald, R., and McGee, A., *The Second Work-Life Balance Study: Results from the Employer Survey: Main Report* (London: DTI, 2003), ch. 10 (http://www.dti.gov.uk/er/emar/errs22MainReport.pdf) provides more balanced survey evidence from employers. For US examples of reduced staff turnover, see Berg, P., Applebaum, E., Bailey, T., and Kalleberg, A. L., 'Contesting Time: International Comparison of Employee Control of Working Time', *Industrial and Labor Relations Review*, 57 (2004), 331, 346.

[29] Suff, R., 'Managing Attendance the Flexible Working Way', *IRS Employment Review*, 798 (2004), 19.

[30] Jones, A., *About Time for a Change* (London: The Work Foundation, 2003), 10 (available at http://www.theworkfoundation.com).

[31] Jones, above, n. 30, 11; Thomas, L. T. and Ganster, D. C., 'Impact of Family Supportive Work Variables on Work-Family Conflict and Strain: A Control Perspective', *Journal of Applied Psychology*, 80 (1995), 6.

[32] Hogarth, T., Hasluck, C., Pierre, G., Winterbotham, M., and Vivian, D., *Work-Life Balance 2000: Results from the Baseline Study*, DfEE Research Series, No. 249 (London: DfEE, 2001); Stevens, J., Brown, J., and Lee, C., *The Second Work-Life Balance Study: Results from the Employees' Survey*, DTI, Employment Relations Research Series No. 27 (London: DTI, 2004).

IV BEYOND FAMILY-FRIENDLY REGULATION

When examining the legal implications of this policy evolution in the European Union regarding labour market flexibility, it is easy to miss the potential transformative effect on employment law. For a generation now, legislation in Europe has interfered with the power of the employer effectively to determine the content of job packages in order to respond to the needs of women and families. Mandatory rights in connection with pregnancy leave and maternity leave provided women with flexibility to take time off around the time of the birth of a child. These measures were generally conceived in Europe as part of the principle of ensuring the equal treatment of women in the labour market, or more precisely equal opportunity.[33]

By the time of the early formulations of the European Union's employment strategy, however, the gender equality policy had expanded to a more ambitious agenda of reconciling work and family life.[34] This policy included a raft of 'family-friendly' measures in employment law, such as parental leave, maternity pay, as well as the need for governments to make available affordable, accessible, and high-quality care services for children and other dependants.[35] Most of these 'family-friendly' policies still, however, address primarily the position of women in the labour market. In particular, the improvements to earlier legislation regarding maternity leave,[36] rights to maternity pay,[37] and the introduction of a right to parental leave,[38] aim to reduce the number of women who leave the labour market for a long period of time on the birth of a child.[39] The logic and policy behind family-friendly measures also requires some limited

---

[33] Although for the practical reason of using the qualified-majority voting system, many Directives in the 1990s were presented as concerned with encouraging improvements, especially in the working environment, to protect the health and safety of workers under Art. 118a (now Art. 137). See e.g. Directive 92/85/EEC on improvements in the safety and health of pregnant workers.

[34] European Commission, *Incorporating Equal Opportunities for Women and Men into all Community Policies and Activities* Com (96) 67 Final CB-CO-96-083-EN-C (Luxembourg: European Commission, 1996); Perrons, D., 'Flexible Working Patterns and Equal Opportunities in the European Union', *The European Journal of Women's Studies*, 6 (1999), 391.

[35] Conaghan, J., 'Women, Work, and Family: A British Revolution?', in J. Conaghan, R. M. Fischl, and K. Klare (eds.), *Labour Law in an Era of Globalization: Transformative Practices and Possibilities* (Oxford: OUP, 2002), 53.

[36] The Maternity and Parental Leave Regulations 1999 (SI 1999/3312), Part II, as amended by SI 2002/2789.

[37] Social Security Contributions and Benefits Act 1992, Part XII; Statutory Maternity Pay (General) Regulations 1986 (SI 1986/1960) (as amended, particularly by SI 1994/1367, SI 2000/2883).

[38] The Maternity and Parental Leave Regulations 1999 (SI 1999/3312), Part III, as amended by SI 2001/4010; based upon EC Directive 96/34.

[39] Employment Act 2002, ss. 17–21.

rights to be accorded to men, in order to enable them to help their female partners to stay in work. In particular, new provisions include the right to unpaid parental leave for up to thirteen weeks to care for a child under five years old,[40] the right to paternity leave for two weeks on the birth of a child,[41] together with an entitlement to a minimum level of payment by the employer during that paternity leave,[42] and the right to take time off in the event of family emergencies applies equally to men and women.[43]

The underlying objective of these measures goes beyond a concern for formal gender equality towards a more explicit labour market policy of increasing the participation of women. In addition, the broader ambition of enabling parents of young children to achieve a better balance between work and childrearing begins to figure in the policy objectives. The emphasis of the policy behind these recent family-friendly measures is to enable parents of pre-school age children to keep their position in the labour market whilst making adequate provision for childcare. By granting limited rights to fathers, the legislation pokes a finger at the ideology of the sexual division of labour, though ultimately in preserving much of the inequality of parental rights, particularly with respect to paid leave, the current British legislation still tends to endorse the male breadwinner model. The absence of paid parental leave for fathers, except for two weeks of a subsistence-level payment on the birth of a child, seems destined to ensure that few fathers will decide to forgo their normal income at a time when family expenditure has increased and the mother's income has been reduced. Comparative studies reveal that it is only in countries where parental leave is paid at a level related to normal earnings that there is a high take-up of the right to parental leave, but even in those countries it is rare (apart from in Sweden) for fathers to take leave.[44]

Although innovative in many respects, these family-friendly measures in employment law still use the technique of providing some basic statutory rights, which are mandatory in the sense that the employer is

[40] The Maternity and Parental Leave Regulations 1999 (SI 1999/3312), Part III, as amended by SI 2001/4010, based upon EC Directive 96/34. The precise entitlements to leave can be adjusted either by collective agreement or workforce agreement, but the default position limits the amount of parental leave in any one year to 4 weeks.
[41] Employment Rights Act 1996, ss. 80A–C, inserted by Employment Act 2002, ss. 1–2; the Paternity and Adoption Leave Regulations 2002 (SI 2002/2788).
[42] Social Security Contributions and Benefits Act 1992, Part 12ZA, inserted by Employment Act 2002, s. 2.   [43] Employment Rights Act 1996, s. 57A.
[44] *Equal Opportunities Review*, 66 (1996), 22, cited in McColgan, A., 'Family Friendly Frolics: The Maternity and Parental Leave, etc. Regulations 1999', *ILJ*, 29 (2000), 125, 140. European Commission, *Reconciliation between Work and Family Life* (Brussels: European Commission, 1998); Social Security Select Committee, Ninth Report, 1998–9 Session, *Social Security Implication of Parental Leave*, 1 HC 543.

required to comply with them. The underlying legal framework that the employer has the power effectively to determine the contractual job package remains, subject only to the mandatory family-friendly rights that must be observed. Running in tandem with these employment law measures has been a push across Europe to improve the provision of childcare, again with a view of ensuring the continuing participation of the parents of young children in the labour market. There is a strong statistical association between the availability of affordable or subsidized childcare and women's labour market participation; and there is another strong association between women's labour market participation and lifetime earnings. The loss of earnings for women from the lack of available or affordable childcare has three main components: earnings during lost years out of the labour force; lost hours by taking part-time work; and lower pay, perhaps in part-time work, but also because of exclusion from career improvements of wages. In comparison to most other European countries, the losses to women in the UK are particularly severe. 'Comparing the child-free scenario with that of bearing two children at ages 25 and 28, the simulations put a mother's loss of employment at eight years in Britain, ten in Germany, two in Sweden and none in France.'[45] In order to justify the provision of nursery education, therefore, governments can point not only to the advantages to women of greater lifetime earnings, but it can also be argued that the cost of public provision of nursery care can be offset by benefits of economic growth and higher taxation revenues accruing from a larger, better paid, labour force through the greater participation of women.

These policies of public provision of childcare also share the legal assumption that the employer can determine unilaterally the contractual job package that is offered. They tend to reinforce the priority of the employer's demands for presence in the workplace at times that fit the demands of production. The problem of reconciling the competing demands of private life and work is addressed in childcare policies by increasing the social division of labour. Childcare becomes paid work for a segment of the workforce, releasing parents to take other forms of paid work. Whilst this reconciliation of the demands of work and home is feasible, though expensive, to my mind it accepts too readily the notion that employers have no responsibility to create family-friendly working arrangements through the job packages offered. At the same time, it accepts too readily the idea that a satisfactory reconciliation of the competing demands of family and work will be found in transferring care

[45] Joshi, H. and Davies, H. 'Day Care in Europe and Mothers' Forgone Earnings', *International Labour Review*, 132 (1992), 561.

to paid workers during the working day. The policy ignores the possibility that parents might wish to spend more time with their young children.

The most recent formulations of the European Union's employment strategy, however, seem to embrace a more ambitious goal and require a rather different approach to legal regulation. In these formulations, as we have seen, the concern for the balance between work and private life has become partly detached from issues of gender equality and women's participation in the labour market. Although those concerns still exist, the policy to secure a better balance between work and private life is now presented as an essential ingredient in the search for competitiveness through labour market flexibility. There are two crucial changes. First, the policy applies to all workers and to any kind of reason that they may have to alter their work/life balance, not merely to adjustments for the benefit of those workers with family responsibilities. Secondly, and more radically, the policy requires employers to offer diversity in contractual job packages, in order to satisfy the needs of all workers for a satisfactory balance between work and private life.

V TRANSFORMATION

The radical nature of this policy needs to be emphasized. It marks a transformative break with the legal tradition of the contract of employment. As we have observed, in the past the employer largely determined the terms of the job package offered to workers, and pressed for the productively efficient structure of casual work as far as possible. As parties to a contract, employees have always enjoyed the formal legal right to negotiate for their own particular package of terms. In practice, of course, the legal right is not matched in most instances by sufficient bargaining power to resist the employer's offer of terms on a 'take it or leave it' basis. The new employment policy concerning the balance between work and private life envisions a reversal of this pattern, because it expects employers to offer job packages to suit the work/life needs of workers, not merely those that serve productive efficiency. It contests the assumption on which the contract of employment has evolved, which is that it is for the employer to offer a package of terms that serves its productive needs, and for the employee to bargain for marginal adjustments in favour of fairness and security. The policy rather envisages that employers should offer job packages that somehow combine the vectors of productive efficiency and the work/life needs of workers, and should not be permitted to restrict the offer to standard packages that fit the needs of the business alone.

Another way in which to highlight the radical implications of this new approach to flexibility in the employment strategy is to contrast it with the family-friendly provisions that grant parents time off from work. The notion of a legal right to time off work, either paid or unpaid, assumes that the employer is entitled to insist upon the continuation of its standard job package. The legal right to time off merely grants a special privilege to the worker to cease to perform work for a temporary period without terminating the employment relation. In contrast, the new conception of flexibility insists that the employee should be able to challenge the standard job package itself, to influence what are the normal hours of paid work, so that 'time off' is transformed into time that was never required under the contract of employment at all. Although this new approach does not go so far as to impose upon employers the costs of helping with childrearing of employees, it does compel employers to consider the need to organize job packages for paid work around the family responsibilities and other private life needs of the workforce.

As a practical matter, the policy therefore necessarily envisions the creation of a mechanism to increase the bargaining power of workers so that they may secure changes in the standard job package offered by their employer. Since the type of package required by each worker to improve his or her personal work/life balance may differ, it is not possible to impose by general rules what kinds of packages should be offered by an employer. Instead, each package has to be tailored to the needs of the individual, whilst at the same time, of course, permitting the employer to protect its interests in productive efficiency. Therefore, what the new employment strategy on flexibility appears to envisage is a bargaining process, but one in which the employee enjoys a strengthened hand, which empowers him or her to insist on a package of hours of work that improves the balance of work and private life for that individual. To obtain that bargaining power, the position of the employee must be strengthened either through harnessing collective workforce pressure or by the introduction of individual legal rights (or some combination of the two). The critical change to be highlighted is that the law must channel freedom of contract in the design of job packages, so that employees obtain a strengthened bargaining position to demand his or her preferred diversity in the job package offered by the employer. Instead of the employer being permitted (subject to the observance of mandatory statutory rights) to offer terms of employment suited to its production needs, the flexibility policy now envisages that the employee should be in a position to make a compelling counter-offer of the terms on which he or she will be prepared to work in order to achieve a satisfactory balance between work and life.

Such a radical transformation of the employment relationship poses difficult questions about how it might be successfully implemented. Employment law is surely not going to ignore the employer's continuing need to ensure efficient production. It is unlikely to force employers to concede working arrangements that lead to significant reductions in productive inefficiency. After all, one important motive for the new policy of flexibility is to improve competitiveness and productivity, not to damage it. So the practical question becomes: how can the law devise a framework for the employment relation that, on the one hand, gives sufficient weight to the employer's need to organize production efficiently, and on the other hand, grants employees the effective bargaining power to adjust their job packages to achieve a better balance between work and private life? A number of legal models are worth evaluating as potential means for implementing this transformation of the employment relation.

VI PRACTICAL IMPLEMENTATION

What these models for legal intervention in pursuit of the new employment strategy of flexibility have in common is an attempt to increase the bargaining power of the employee to press for some particular kind of flexibility in working arrangements. These models would all need to include one common element, which can be mentioned conveniently first. Assuming that an employee makes a request for a variation of a job package, it would be necessary to offer protection for the employee against possible retaliatory action by the employer. Employees would not want to ask for flexibility if their requests could be met by the employer imposing some kind of detriment or dismissal. Even where employers have voluntarily introduced such schemes, workers may be reluctant to take them up for fear of signalling an unwillingness to work hard and be co-operative. 'If workers are ambivalent about their right to be sick, it is not surprising that they often fear repercussions for using family-oriented provisions which are constructed as a concession for those who cannot conform to "normal" working patterns.'[46] In short, as is the case for the enjoyment of other employment rights, there needs to be protection against victimization or retaliatory action in the event that an employee seeks to vary the standard package of terms of employment.

Three kinds of models can be considered as practical ways of implementing the new policy on flexibility and diversity in job packages. The

---

[46] Lewis, S., ' "Family Friendly" Employment Policies: A Route to Changing Organizational Culture or Playing about at the Margins', *Gender, Work and Organization*, 4 (1997), 13, 15.

principal difference between the possible models turns on the type of legal duty imposed on the employer. These models are framed primarily in terms of individual legal rights. It is likely, however, that superior outcomes for employees could be achieved through collective bargaining or some other kind of partnership arrangement that agrees to the creation of a variety of job packages. This collective approach may also prove more satisfactory and less complex and costly for employers than having to respond constantly to individual requests for diverse variations in job packages. Through a collective agreement, for instance, the employer could agree rules governing fractional work or annualized hours, which could then be applied to all requests for variation.[47] In addition, collective bargaining can provide a fair procedure for securing trade-offs between different kinds of flexibility, such as the ability of workers to trade excess hours in one period for additional leave in another.[48] But any such collective bargaining would certainly be strengthened and better focused by its grounding on a framework of legal rights for individual employees. We need to question, however, whether the traditional patterns of collective bargaining would prove adequate for the agreement of rules about work/life balance issues. Unions are associated, perhaps unfairly these days, with the idea of a pressure group seeking to protect the standard employment package. Evidence from the 1998 British Workplace Employee Relations Survey suggests in fact that, 'Although unions were negatively associated with the availability of work-at-home arrangements and flexible working hours options, they appear to have increased the availability of three other policies designed to help workers balance the demands of work and family: parental leave, special paid leave, and job-sharing options'.[49] A collective or participatory approach towards establishing diversity of job packages may require the broadening of access to the bargaining table, in order to permit other groups, such as lone parents, the elderly, and the part-time workers, to have an effective voice in the design of work.[50]

Model 1: bargaining in good faith

One possibility is to require the employer to negotiate about the proposed variation or flexible arrangement in good faith or by reference to some analogous standard. In the Framework Agreement on Part-time Work, for

---

[47] This emphasis on collective consultation and agreement is strongly supported by the UK government's advisory body: ACAS, *Changing Patterns of Work* (Feb. 2004) (www.acas.org.uk/publications).

[48] E.g. the German system of 'working time accounts': Berg et al. above n. 28, 344–5.

[49] Budd, J. W. and Mumford, K., 'Trade Unions and Family-Friendly Policies in Britain', *Industrial and Labor Relations Review*, 57 (2004), 204.   [50] Supiot, above, n. 23, 92.

instance, there is a legal duty on employers to 'give consideration to requests by workers to transfer from full-time to part-time work that becomes available in the establishment (and vice-versa).'[51] This is a very weak requirement, so weak in fact that the UK government seems not to have implemented it in legal form at all. But the idea of a duty to consider in good faith a request for flexible working would set the stage for a negotiation process that was something more than a casual rejection of the request. At the least, this requirement of negotiation in good faith or some similar requirement could impose a duty on the employer to listen to the request, examine its implications, and to put forward counter-proposals, including, of course, outright rejection of the request. Whether or not this duty would provide the employee with a significant improvement in bargaining power must, however, still be doubtful. An employer could pass through the motions of negotiation without ever giving an inch.

The legal duty to bargain in good faith might be more effective, however, if it was placed in the context of collective bargaining over the introduction of new flexible working arrangements. For example, if the union proposed new arrangements such as flexitime or annualized hours, a legal duty to bargain in good faith in response to the union's request might overcome any resistance of the employer to examine the full implications of the proposal carefully. After all, if the limited empirical evidence is correct, once the employer has incurred the expense of introducing the new flexible scheme, the employer should benefit in the long-term from improvements in efficiency and productivity. What may be required, therefore, is a legal incentive to overcome the initial reluctance to incur the expense of trying a new scheme for organizing working time.

Model 2: rejection only on objective grounds

A second model tries to control the bargaining process more closely by specifying that the employer can only reject a request for flexible working on certain specified grounds. This model has been employed in the UK in connection with variations in terms of work requested by parents of young children. A parent of a child aged up to six (or of a disabled child up to sixteen) has the right to ask an employer to vary hours of work (and times and place of work).[52] A 'parent' for these purposes is defined quite broadly to include guardian, foster parent, and a partner of a 'parent', who has or expects to have responsibility for the upbringing

---

[51] Directive 97/81, Appendix, Clause 5.3. (OJ L 14, 20.1.98, p. 9).
[52] Employment Rights Act 1996, Part VIIIA, inserted by Employment Act 2002, s. 47.

of the child. The parent must also be asking for the variation in hours for a particular purpose: 'to enable him to care for' a child.[53] There is no limit on the kinds of changes in hours that may be requested, provided that they fit within this purpose. A detailed procedure applies to this 'right to ask'.[54] The employer can only refuse the application on certain specified grounds. These grounds, however, are drawn broadly to include 'additional costs', 'inability to re-organise work among existing staff', and detrimental impact on quality or performance.[55] Breach of the right entitles the employee to seek up to eight weeks' pay in an employment tribunal.[56]

The first study of the impact of this law finds that there has been a significant increase in the willingness on the part of employers to accept flexible working requests.[57] Before the legislation was introduced, about 20 per cent of such requests for flexible working were rejected by employers, whereas the rejection rate declined to about 11 per cent afterwards. This variation may of course be explained in part by changing attitudes of employers towards requests for flexibility or a misunderstanding of the law. It is noticeable, for instance, that the rejection rate was much the same regardless as to whether the employee who made the request actually qualified for the right or not. So the alleged causal link between the legislation and the growth in flexible working patterns is not clearly established.

The extent to which this model for the legal right will improve the bargaining position of individual employees depends critically on how the permitted grounds for rejecting requests for flexibility are framed and interpreted. Almost any change in working practices may impose, at least initially, additional costs on the employer. Flexible working is likely to have consequential effects for other workers such as the need to reorganize their schedules or reallocate tasks. If employers are permitted to use such grounds for rejecting requests for variations in job packages, the legislation is unlikely to strengthen significantly the bargaining position of employees. It would be possible under this model, however, to narrow the grounds on which employers may reject requests for flexibility, so that the employer would have to point to significant, long-term extra costs, or the impossibility of reorganizing the performance of work. In Germany, for instance, the revised Federal Childcare Payment and Parental Leave Act (Bundeserzihungsgeldgesetz), gives a right to take parental leave for a period of up to three years after the child's birth.

[53] Employment Rights Act 1996, s. 80F(1)(b).
[54] Flexible Working (Procedural Requirements) Regulations 2002, SI 2002/3207.
[55] Employment Rights Act 1996, s. 80G(1)(b).   [56] Ibid., ss. 80H and 80I.
[57] Palmer, T., 'Results of the First Flexible Working Employee Survey', DTI, Employment Relations Occasional Papers (London: DTI, 2004), available at www.dti.gov.uk.

During the period of leave the job is suspended but there is a right to return and a prohibition on dismissal. Both parents can take leave at the same time. Regarding flexibility, parental leave can be taken in the form of part-time work of fifteen to thirty hours per week, and the employer can only reject a request for part-time work if this creates considerable problems for the company.[58] This sort of stringent test clearly makes it almost inevitable that the employer will have to agree to proposals for fractional working.

Model 3: duty of reasonable accommodation

A third model for a legal implementation of the policy of diversity in job packages would be to place employers under a duty of reasonable accommodation of the needs of employees. This model differs both because it might be more selective about the types of reasons for which an employee might be permitted to make a request for flexible working owing to its reference to the needs of employees, and because it would create a strong presumption that the employer should respond positively to such requests. An analogous duty of reasonable accommodation can be found in the provisions governing disability discrimination, under which the employer is under a duty to make reasonable accommodations to the needs of disabled employees.[59] A similar duty on employers also arises in connection with the test for whether indirectly discriminatory rules can be justified on business grounds.[60] The issue of costs for the employer in making adjustments is handled through a standard such as reasonableness, or as part of a test of proportionality. As in the disability legislation, the employer would be expected to accept reasonable costs in order to make adequate provision for the needs of the worker to make adjustments to his or her balance between work and private life.

This third model, with its duty of reasonable accommodation, seems likely to impose the most stringent requirement on the employer, and consequently is more likely to strengthen the bargaining position of the employee in pressing for a request for variation. It also introduces a potential scope for collective negotiation about the extent of reasonable

[58] European Foundation for the Improvement of Living and Working Conditions, 'New Provision on Parental Leave and Childcare Payment' (www.eiro.eurofound.ie).

[59] Directive 2000/78 establishing a general framework for equal treatment in employment and occupation, Art. 5, OJ 200 L 303/16; Disability Discrimination Act 1995, s. 6.

[60] Conaghan, J., 'The Family-Friendly Workplace in Labour Law Discourse: Some Reflection on *London Underground Ltd v Edwards*', in H. Collins, P. Davies, and R. Rideout (eds.), *Legal Regulation of the Employment Relation* (London: Kluwer, 2000), 161, 165; Collins, H., 'Discrimination, Equality and Social Inclusion', *MLR*, 66 (2003), 16, 37–8; Jolls, C., 'Anti-discrimination and Accommodation', *Harvard L. R.*, 115 (2001), 642.

adjustments to of the needs of private life and efficient ways in which to accommodate them. By limiting the reasons for variations to the needs of the employee, however, this model might take a narrower view of the issues posed by the policy of flexibility than the other two. For instance, an employee may wish to alter hours of work to fit in with convenient transport patterns, as in the case where the bus to work only runs once an hour, so the employee always arrives forty-five minutes early or fifteen minutes late. If the employee requests a later or earlier start, can this be described as a need of private life, or is it merely a matter of convenience? The general ambition of the employment strategy to improve the work/life balance for everyone should encourage a broad view of the needs of employees to alter hours of work, and not permit the dismissal of some requests as merely matters of convenience. In the example of the bus journey for instance, such a request should be regarded as a need of the employee, because in practice it probably determines the hours at which the employee has for leisure in the evenings—having to rise an hour earlier prevents the employee from going to bed late.

The purpose of elaborating these different models is to explore the practical implications for employment law of finding ways in which to implement the new policy of flexibility. This basic structure of initiating a bargaining process between employer and employee about diversity in job packages can be constructed in different ways that will affect both the degree of bargaining power of the employee and the extent to which the interests of employees in enjoying aspects of their private life will be protected from the demands of work.

Beyond the construction of this negotiation process, employment law may need to address difficulties that will arise from particular kinds of diversity in job packages. For instance, where the flexibility involves working from home for part of the week, usually involving what is labelled 'telework', it will be important to ensure that the worker continues to enjoy the same benefits and employment rights as those of comparable workers at the employer's premises. The European Framework Agreement on Telework[61] provides a voluntary code agreed between employers and unions on the relevant principles, which the social partners intend, if possible, to implement themselves without introducing legal rules. If this framework becomes effective, it should meet the principal difficulties experienced by teleworkers with regard to such matters as health and safety, career progression, monitoring of performance, and the allocation of costs.

---

[61] Brussels, 16 July 2002.

Another type of specific problem concerns job packages that involve a break in the continuous performance of work.[62] This problem arises in connection with maternity leave, career breaks of various kinds, or prolonged absences on account of the sickness of the worker or a dependant. By breaking the continuity of employment in the sense that no work has been performed, the legal inference may be that the job has been terminated or at least suspended. The apparent consequence may be that the worker loses seniority rights or fails to qualify for various statutory protections. In the UK, although the legislation usually preserves continuity of employment through short breaks, it may not at present protect the position of workers who take career breaks other than those connected with maternity. It may not be appropriate for the legislation to insist that all career breaks taken for whatever reasons should not affect seniority rights and qualifying periods for statutory rights. But legislation should certainly require the potential implications of career breaks on such matters to be disclosed and made clear to the employee before the decision to take a break is made.

A further general problem that diversity in job packages may provoke is a decline in the use by employers of time as the principal measurement of productive work. In response to calls for flexibility in hours of work and the ability to work from home, employers may seek increasingly to measure outputs rather than time. Pay for completed tasks tends to transfer the risk of difficulties encountered in achieving satisfactory performance of work to the workers. Such difficulties might include the illness of the worker or dependants, breakdowns of machinery such as IT equipment, problems in obtaining adequate co-operation from other employees or linked businesses. Although the new style of flexibility envisaged in the employment strategy may not risk a reversion to precarious forms of employment, it may provoke a reversion to the pattern of transferring unexpected costs of production onto the workforce entailed by the use of task-performance contracts.[63] Thus the search for mechanisms to induce the creation of quality jobs in the European labour market may prove long and hard.

VII CONCLUSION

Standing back from these technical questions of how the law can best help to implement the new European conception of flexibility, what

---

[62] Kilpatrick, C., 'Gender and the Legal Regulation of Employment Breaks', in J. Fudge and R. Owens (eds.), *Precarious Work, Women and the New Economy: The Challenge to Legal Norms* (Oxford: Hart Publishing, 2005, forthcoming).

[63] Collins, H., 'Independent Contractors and the Challenge of Vertical Disintegration to Employment Protection Laws', *OJLS*, 10 (1990), 353, 362–5.

seems to be becoming clearer is that we are beginning to witness a transformation in the legal construction of the employment relation. The need for reasons of efficiency to permit the employer to determine the content of job packages has been challenged, not merely on the grounds of its indirect discriminatory effects on women and the difficulties it presents to working parents, but also on the more fundamental ground that it prevents all workers from achieving the optimal balance between work and private life. It is argued that improvements to this work/life balance will, in fact, improve efficiency and competitiveness by increasing participation in the labour market and by enabling workers to be more productive when they are working, because they will suffer reduced stress and be willing to be more co-operative. These claims for improvements in efficiency arising from granting employees a right to determine their own job packages have not been adequately tested and may not apply across the board to all economic sectors. Nor is it clear that the change in business culture that has led employers to be more willing to engage in negotiations about flexibility at the request of employees has, at the same time, overcome the widespread assumption by employers that employees who do not want a standard full-time job and who are unwilling to put in extra hours are not well motivated and deserving of career progression.[64]

Despite these necessary reservations about the practical effects of the new ideas about flexibility in the European employment strategy, what is clear is their potential transformative effect on the legal construction of the contract of employment. The model under which the employer, by virtue of superior bargaining power and the need to respond to production requirements, can determine unilaterally the content of job packages has always been contested by organized labour. Legislation has created various mandatory rights that also impinge on the employer's freedom to set the terms of employment. What the new measures regarding the balance between work and private life seem to envisage is that individual employees should be given the negotiating strength to insist upon the creation of job packages which suit their personal needs rather than the employer's view of the imperatives of productive efficiency. In effect, the employee may be granted a legal right to flexibility according to his or her personal needs, and the employer either has to accommodate this right in the terms of the contract of employment or find pressing objective business reasons for rejecting its acceptance in the particular case.

[64] Lewis, S., ' "Family Friendly" Employment Policies: A Route to Changing Organizational Culture or Playing about at the Margins?', *Gender, Work and Organization*, 4 (1997), 13, 16.

6

Recommodifying Time: Working Hours of 'Live-in' Domestic Workers

GUY MUNDLAK

I INTRODUCTION: LIVE-INS' OVERTIME EXCEPTION

Overtime regulation typically does two things. First, it sets limits to the length of the working day and working week. This is usually done by establishing what a standard working day/week is, as well as the maximum number of hours the employer can employ the worker over and above the standard. Secondly, it requires the payment of higher wages for these overtime hours. The core of this regulatory arrangement exists in most countries, with variations from one country to another. One type of variation concerns the extent to which these regulations apply to all workers. While coverage is often universal, in all countries there are various exceptions. They may be for certain types of occupations, for various sectors, in situations of derogation by collective agreement, and more. Most of these exemptions indicate that a uniform arrangement of time is difficult to prescribe.

The exception of live-ins from working-time regulation is one of the more common exceptions found in comparative studies.[1] Live-ins are workers who reside in the household where they work. In most cases they are employed in domestic household chores (for example, cleaning, cooking and serving) and in care work (for children, disabled family members, and the elderly). They differ from other workers in the same occupations who come and go from the workplace to their places of residence.[2] Live-ins are therefore characterized by a combination of two features: their occupation and their residence in someone else's home, which is also their workplace.[3]

---

[1] See EIRO, *Overtime in Europe* (July 2003). Online at www.eiro.eurofound.ie.

[2] They differ from, but also share some features in common with, people who reside in the workplace and even conduct similar duties, but for whom the workplace is not a residential home (e.g. a dormitory). Similarly, they differ greatly from people who work out of their own homes, although home-workers also share some of the problems identified in this chapter. To avoid overly fine distinctions, I will adhere only to the fundamental distinction between domestic and care workers who are 'live-ins' and those who are 'work-outs', i.e. who work outside their homes.

[3] The term 'live-ins' is chosen here as a relatively neutral reference to this type of employment. Alternative terms often conceal either positive or negative implications, or are

A closer look at the application of overtime regulation to live-ins suggests that the exception of live-ins takes different forms. In some cases, albeit rarely, the law applies overtime law equally to live-ins and other employees. In these cases the major problem of overtime arrangements is that they are difficult to enforce and are therefore, like other legal arrangements that are formally applied to 'peripheral workers', merely the 'law in the books' but hardly the 'law in action'.[4] However, it is more common to find some kind of exceptional treatment of live-ins in overtime legislation. Sometimes, live-ins and their employers are exempted from time regulation altogether. At other times, their standard working day or working week is longer than the general rule. In these cases, overtime payment is slashed because the longer hours performed by the live-in are part of the standard working day/week. A third variety of statutory exception consists of applying time regulation in general, but exempting the employer from overtime payments. In these cases, the constraint on employing the live-in for many hours is based on a general prohibition but not on any economic incentive in the form of increased overtime payment. Obviously, the problem of enforcement in such situations is even more difficult. Finally, in all of these situations there are also differences stemming from whether a minimum wage and overtime are calculated on the basis of hours worked, or whether a monthly salary is permitted. When wages are paid as a monthly salary, overtime exceptions provide a particularly strong incentive for around-the-clock employment. Employers simply seek to get the most for a lump-sum payment.

Overtime regulation and its exceptions are reflective of embedded values regarding working time. More generally, working-time regulation has stood at the centre of law's attempt to decommodify two alleged commodities. First, working-time regulation was intended to decommodify time in response to the centrality of time-oriented valuation that was so central to the Industrial Revolution.[5] Secondly, working-time regulation is part of the decommodification typical of the welfare state. Decommodification in this sense suggests that one's life chances are not wholly contingent on market forces, but are associated to the same extent with a set of rights and entitlements granted by the state.[6] Responding

sometimes formally used in law to distinguish a particular status. These differences between the terms may change from one country to another. Such terms include au pairs, nannies, domestics, and even servants.

[4] ILO, *Towards a Fair Deal for Migrant Workers in a Global Economy* (Report submitted to the International Labour Conference, 92nd session, 2004), 41–71.

[5] Thompson, E. P., 'Time, Work-Discipline and Industrial Capitalism', *Past & Present*, 38 (1967), 56, 63.

[6] Esping-Andersen, G., *Social Foundations of Post-industrial Economies* (Oxford: OUP, 1999).

to these two complementary objectives, working-time regulation reflected industrial practices and demarcated different types of time, assuming clear boundaries between what have become the commonplace categories—'work' time and 'leisure' time. Thus, the division of every working person's time into these particular niches becomes not solely the outcome of contractual negotiations, but also a social construct reflecting the desirable balance between work and other activities.

The carving out of exceptions to working-time regulation consists of the regression of the two interrelated projects of decommodification. Although it has been claimed in the past that both projects are gendered and lean towards the model of a male breadwinner, the withdrawal of regulation is certainly no triumph for the working women (and some men) who are employed as live-ins. Similarly, the traditional distinction between 'leisure' and 'work' underlying working-time regulation was hardly reflective of women's experiences, but the exceptions to working-time regulation do not attempt to provide a more sensible construct that fits the different perceptions of time held by men and women. Moreover, working-time regulation or deregulation does little to affect the entrenched structures in society, whether gender-, class-, or race-based, which make the qualitative meaning of time so different to the various groups. Thus, commodified or not, time seems to be a manipulatable subject of regulation that is used to advance the interests of the regulator. For those at the periphery of the labour market, the question is not whether 'to regulate or not to regulate', but how regulation merely serves to advance social objectives within the social construct of time.

Labour and welfare law govern the relationship between employers, employees, and the state. It will be argued here that recommodifying is part of the legal arrangements that construct the labour market's periphery, where workers with the fewest rights are concentrated. At the periphery, live-ins cater to the interests of both employers and employees at the core of the labour market. Despite legislative and judicial rhetoric to the contrary, the application of the overtime exception to live-ins is rooted in the fact that they are largely women, foreign, and poor. The exception pits the interests of the poor against those of the rich, and of 'foreigners' against those of citizens. Yet more peculiarly, it undermines potential solidarity between women as it nests within, and even entrenches, skewed gender relations. It presents the overtime exception as a solution to an inevitable conflict between career women and women employed in domestic help, but does not recognize the fundamental flaw in the time/leisure distinction.

II LIVE-IN WORKERS: WHO THEY ARE AND WHAT THEY DO

Live-ins are engaged in domestic and care work, and their tasks usually include either cleaning and serving, or care for children, disabled, and elderly family members, or both. The phenomenon of live-in workers is not new. The contemporary practice of employing live-ins is a variation of the common law servant, but live-in arrangements can also be traced back to earlier feudal practices. Whereas there was a move away from live-in arrangements during most of the twentieth century, towards the end of the century the live-in arrangement began gaining in popularity[7] as the result of two complementary processes. On the 'demand' side, as the number of dual-career families increases, there is a growing demand for live-ins who can take full responsibility for all household and care tasks. On the 'supply' side, globalization processes that reduce the transaction costs of transborder migration increase the numbers of live-ins who seek work in more prosperous economies. As the employment of live-ins in the developed countries has increased, it is no longer restricted to wealthy manor owners, but extends to the homes of young dual-career professionals.[8]

The growing reliance of families on live-ins entails their engagement as the only household employee. This distinguishes them from the servants of the manor, who were part of a team in which there was a highly structured hierarchy and division of labour. The modern live-in is the epitome of multitasking. She is secluded from fellow workers, and her employment as a live-in is expressly designed to eliminate any artificial divisions of labour. If she can physically complete a task, it is part of her job definition. Being the multitasker she is, the live-in worker is also secluded from other employees who are similarly situated. Moreover, as many live-ins are migrant workers, they are also removed from their natural community and surroundings to begin with. They are in touch with their community only on their days off, or only with those who are employed in the same neighbourhood, through daily encounters in the park, shopping centres, and the like.[9]

---

[7] See a historical description in Graunke, K. L., ' "Just Like One of the Family": Domestic Violence Paradigms and Combating On-The-Job Violence Against Household Workers in the United States', *Michigan Journal of Gender & Law*, 9 (2002), 131, 136–50.

[8] Sassen, S., *The Mobility of Labor and Capital: A Study in International Investment and Labour* (New York: Cambridge University Press, 1988); Hochschild, A. R., 'Love and Gold', in B. Ehrenreich and A. R. Hochschild (eds.), *Global Woman: Nannies, Maids and Sex Workers in the New Economy* (New York: Metropolitan Books, 2002), 15.

[9] For more extensive studies of live-ins, see the ethnographic accounts in Romero, M., *Maid in the USA* (New York: Routledge, 2002); Parreñas, R. S., *Servants of Globalization* (Stanford: Stanford University Press, 2000); Sotelo, P. H., *Domestica: Immigrant Workers Cleaning and Caring in the Shadow of Affluence* (Berkeley: University of California Press, 2001).

From the live-in's point of view, her company, her employer, her home, and her work are all one and the same. The nature of the work performed by the live-in, complemented by the multiple dimensions of seclusion, suggests that being a live-in worker is more than a job. It is a way of life, temporary perhaps, but not necessarily short-term. It assumes that the place, task, and time are all detached from labour market and other social norms. Unlike the traditional worker, the live-in does not provide the employer with a definite period of time in which the worker's services are for the employer to use, but is viewed as someone whose time is at the disposal of the employer almost wholesale.[10]

Peggie Smith nicely demonstrates the strong roots of timelessness, multitasking, and solitude that characterize live-ins, in reference to a study by Emily Blackwell, conducted in 1883:

She abandons family life, having no daily intercourse with her relatives as do out-door workers living in their own homes. She loses her personal freedom, for she is always under the authority of the employer. She can never leave the house without permission; there is no hour of the day in which she is not at the bidding of her mistress; there is no time in her life, except [a] few … seasons of absence, for which she may not be called to account.[11]

Yet the basic structure (or 'structurelessness') of this particular employment relationship remains even today. In one interview with a woman who employs a live-in in Israel, the worker's schedule and tasks were described in the following mundane manner:

At 7:15 she leaves her room and comes downstairs. She gets two hours of rest in the middle of the day when the baby is asleep. When he wakes up I am already back from work. She goes up to her room around 20:30, sometimes a bit earlier. If she didn't have the time—she does the ironing in her room or folds the laundry, while watching TV. She really is part of the family.[12]

Live-ins also describe their work in terms of a continuous time commitment:

I begin at seven in the morning. I change her, feed her. Give her all the injections and medication. Then I clean the apartment. When you take care of an elder, the

---

[10] This chapter is concerned with time management, but much of it is also applicable to the study of space regulation. For example, the absence of boundaries raises issues of privacy. Does a live-in have a place of her own, which is not under the employer's control although it may be on the employer's legally owned premises? In general, employees' spatial privacy rights are limited, but when work and off-work sites merge, the general rules of privacy at work have to be reconsidered. Employers usually consider them to have been abolished altogether, just like time regulation. What live-ins may require, then, is strict, even if artificial, prescriptions of spatial privacy, just like strict, artificially determined time limitations that forestall the absorption of the live-in into the family's day.

[11] Blackwell, E., 'The Industrial Position of Women', *Popular Science Monthly*, 23 (1883), 380, cited in Smith, P., 'Regulating Paid Household Work: Class, Gender, Race, and Agendas of Reform', *American University Law Review*, 48 (1999), 851, 871.

[12] Interviews conducted May 2002.

first thing that you need is patience. For example, when you feed her it can take up to an hour...I wake up at four in the morning just to check that the woman is alive.[13]

Daily schedules are also related to the duration of placement:

Then there's the problem of hours which seem to get more flexible (that is, longer) the longer you work for the family. There's also the problem of being asked to do work—dog walking, ironing, serving at dinner parties—that was not part of the job description and was not included in the original salary. And if the job can be flexible, the salary is often inflexible...Then there is the problem of summers. Many families offer nannies a Hobson's choice: either go away with them and be trapped in some all-white resort, or take token wages while they're gone... Basically I am on call around the clock. I feel like my life isn't mine even when I am home.[14]

Time is also an issue in formal contracts and rules, as described in a handbook issued by a Hong Kong employment agency:

Learn to *clock watch*. Schedule your time and work...During your *free time, rest if you must, but be ready to answer the door or telephone*. Sew clothes or other special chores like re-potting some plants and cleaning kitchen cupboards.[15]

While the double bind that has been highlighted over the years has been that which requires a difficult juggling act between work outside and inside the home,[16] the live-in experiences a double bind of her own. If she works too fast, she will be asked to do more. If she works too slowly, she will be reprimanded for not working well enough. It is precisely because she has nowhere else to go, that she is not expected to schedule her time. Any scheduling and planning is considered as undermining the nature of her work.

Similar descriptions appear in numerous ethnographic studies of domestic care and live-in arrangements. Common to all of them are the descriptions of a boundaryless relationship. The live-in is conveniently (to the employer) internalized into the household and no longer viewed as an external agent. There are no clear boundaries between working time and 'leisure' time. There is no clear demarcation of the tasks to be performed. A central tenet that surfaces time and time again in interviews worldwide is the 'you are part of the family' claim.[17] The employee is

[13] Parreñas, above, n. 9, 159.

[14] Chever, S., 'The Nanny Dilemma', in Ehrenreich and Hochschild, above, n. 8, 35.

[15] Constable, N., 'Filipina Workers in Hong Kong Homes: Household Rules and Relations', in Ehrenreich and Hochschild, above, n. 8, 121.

[16] Hochschild, A. R., *The Time Bind: When Work Becomes Home and Home Becomes Work* (New York: Metropolitan Books, 1997).

[17] On the 'you-are-part-of-the-family' claim, see Bakan, A. and Stasiulis, D. (eds.), *Not One of the Family: Foreign Domestic Workers in Canada* (Toronto: Toronto University Press, 1997); Gregson, N. and Lowe, M., *Servicing the Middle Classes: Class, Gender and Waged Domestic Labour in Contemporary Britain* (New York: Routledge, 1994).

claimed to be part of the family rather than an arm's length contractual agent, and her work is therefore considered as part of the ongoing family routine. However, the 'you are part of the family' shibboleth does not capture the reality in which the responsibilities and rights of the live-ins are hardly typical to family members. Live-ins' position within the family seems to be a combination of adults' responsibilities (many) and children's rights (few). Moreover, the mutual emotional attachment and moral responsibilities that bind the family together are wholly absent from the relationship between the live-in and the family.

III THE EXEMPTION OF LIVE-INS FROM TIME REGULATION

The boundaryless relationship between the live-in and her employer undoubtedly results in friction, and the relatively common abuse of rights. A similar abuse of rights is typically encountered by migrant workers in various occupations, as well as by women employed in hierarchical situations and peripheral workers in general. The boundaryless relationship merely amplifies the problems. The employee cannot easily retreat from her work. As a migrant worker she fears deportation. As a woman she fears abuse. As a peripheral worker she cannot easily access the courts or other venues to claim her rights, nor are her alternatives in the labour market good enough to merit taking action and helping herself. In addition to these three characteristic weaknesses, the live-in does not have an alternative home. There is no place to which she can escape. While the public/private divide is often portrayed as a patriarchal legal construct, in this context it is the absence of a public/private distinction, which is detrimental to the live-in's rights.[18]

However, the typical barriers to claiming their rights do not undermine the general principle that live-ins are employees, entitled to full employment rights. Admittedly this claim may seem merely theoretical at times, but it generally represents the prevalent national statement of 'the law'.[19] However, the law on overtime poses an exception because it explicitly creates a double standard that does not conform with the generally universal (that is, broadly applicable to all employees) nature

[18] In a sense, the boundaryless relationship with her employers puts the live-in in a position similar to that of abused children, whose major source of support potentially is the abuser.
[19] It should be emphasized that, to the extent that the employee is a migrant worker, the premise of equality is true only with regard to employment rights. It is scarcely the rule with regard to social security or welfare rights, health care, and education. The claim here, then, is that the live-in *qua* employee deserves all the rights accorded to employees in the system.

of employment standards. In some countries, this is but one of many exceptions to the universal nature of employment law. In the USA, for example, live-ins are also denied the freedom to organize under the NLRA.[20] In other countries, such as Israel, this constitutes practically the only formal exception to the universal applicability of labour law.[21] The law is explicit in holding live-ins to be different from other employees. As regards other issues, live-ins *qua* women and *qua* migrant workers are formally entitled to all rights. This exception therefore begs close scrutiny of the justifications asserted on its behalf.

An anecdotal survey of the current legal situation in several countries demonstrates the variations of the exception and its alleged justifications.[22] Such a comparison must obviously be read with caution for two reasons. First, it is not intended to demonstrate similarity in the law across regimes, but that different legal arrangements have a similar functional and expressive outcome. Secondly, the phenomenon of live-ins is very different in the countries surveyed, and it is reported to be less common in Australia and the United Kingdom (although on the rise), while more visible and prevalent in the United States, Canada, and Israel. The comparison does not claim that labour law in general, and working-time regulation in particular, create the use of live-in arrangements. They may provide some incentives, but are not sufficient in themselves. In the present context they merely reflect societal values regarding the nature of live-ins' work, and—more generally—the nature of time and work.

A comparative overview

The United States of America

At the federal level, the exemption of live-ins from the Fair Labor Standards Act (FLSA) is not across the board. It is limited to time arrangements in general and overtime payments in particular. Until 1974, all domestic workers were exempted from the application of the FLSA. In 1974, most domestic workers were included, and since then they have been entitled to the minimum wage according to the law.[23] Where there is a difference between live-ins and live-outs is with regard to overtime arrangements, where only the latter are covered.[24] The separation

---

[20] National Labor Relations Act, 29 USC 152(3) (1994).

[21] Mundlak, G., 'Neither Insiders nor Outsiders: The Contractual Construction of Migrant Workers' Rights and the Democratic Deficit', *Tel Aviv University Law Review*, 27(2) (2003), 423.

[22] The countries chosen for this comparison are all common law countries. For a discussion of labour law exceptions regarding domestic workers in general, see also Blackett, A., *Making Domestic Workers Visible: The Case for Specific Regulation* (Geneva: ILO, 1998).

[23] Workers performing care work for the elderly or the infirm and those performing casual babysitter services are still exempt. See 29 USC s. 213(a)(15) (1994).

[24] 29 USC s. 213(b)(21) (1994).

between the minimum wage and overtime suggests that employers by law must pay their live-ins the minimum wage per hour worked, but not overtime pay. Thus, the many hours worked by live-ins are compensated according to the minimum wage, but no more. Beyond the FLSA, various states exclude live-in domestic workers from overtime arrangements in various ways, ranging from the simple application of the federal arrangement, to a specifically carved-out exception of live-ins from overtime, or the more generalized exemption of domestic workers from state regulation.[25] Exceptional treatment that applies to live-ins may also be the result of exceptions that segment broader groups of which live-ins are part—for example, workers employed in a workplace with only a handful of employees or less, or domestic workers.[26] The diversity of means for excluding live-ins from overtime pay indicates that even a rather technical piece of labour law is based on a surprisingly elaborate set of provisions—the definition of 'employee', the scope of the minimum wage, the application of time regulation, and the particular arrangement for overtime pay. The complex nature of overtime therefore makes it rather easy to conceal the statutory legitimacy of the differentiation of benefits granted to live-ins.

Canada

Most live-in arrangements in Canada fall under the auspices of the Live In Care Program, which allows migrant domestic workers entry into the country. The employment standards applied to these workers are those detailed in the general labour standards legislation in the various provinces. While the live-ins generally are entitled to equal rights under labour law, there are differences among the provinces and also changes over time. Some provinces explicitly exclude live-ins from overtime arrangements.[27] Others apply overtime arrangements. These are sometimes

[25] In New York the arrangement matches the federal arrangement (NY CLS Labor Sec. 220); Delaware excludes live-ins from the category of 'employees' (19 Del. C. Sec. 901); some states allow a greater degree of 'flexibility' in contractual arrangements negotiated with domestic workers, as is the case in California (Cal. Lab. Code Sec. 511); Pennsylvania excludes domestic workers from time regulation altogether (43 Pa. Cons. Stat. Ann 103(b)). Similar arrangements are found in other states and the legal exclusion is of particular interest for its expressive value. For example, in Florida, ' "Employment" *does not include...domestic servants in private homes'* (emphasis added) (Fla. Stat. S. 440.02(17)(c)(1)). This explicitly states, in a nutshell, the social view of the servants' role in the household.

[26] For a survey of the various states' regulations, see Young, D., 'Working Across Borders: Global Restructuring and Women's Work', *Utah L. Rev.*, 1 (2001), 29–30.

[27] e.g. the Newfoundland Labour Standards Act (OC 96-291), s. 25, and the Consolidated Newfoundland and Labrador Regulation 781/96, s. 9(2); Alberta Regulation 14/97; under the Employment Standards Act, s. 6; there are also particular regulations for caregivers who work full day shifts—Alberta Regulation 14/97, s. 43.4. These are not directly related to the issue of live-ins but the differentiation among the two groups is indicative of the rationale. While 24-hour shifts do entitle caregivers to some level of overtime, a live-in arrangement does not. This suggests that the rationale is predominantly related to the intimacy-and-trust argument, specified in the following section.

equivalent to those of other workers, and sometimes they are based on a longer definition of the 'standard work-week' or 'work-day', or otherwise provide only partial rights to overtime pay.[28] Quebec, for example, generally subscribes to the view that labour standards apply equally to immigrant domestic workers, but exceptionally entitles live-ins to a lower minimum wage and prescribes a longer working week for them compared to other caregivers.[29] The arrangement which singles out the live-in also grants her particular benefits, such as a guarantee of free room and board. Thus, live-ins are entitled to overtime pay, but the economic value of their benefits is distinct from that of other workers. This package of advantages and disadvantages has been criticized, it being maintained that '[T]he advantage of free room-and-board begins to fade in view of the hours actually worked. The experience of these workers shows that overtime, resulting from the obligation to live in the home of the employer, is rarely paid'.[30] The consequences of the long hours of work have also been recognized in various judicial decisions, which have noted that long hours exploit the live-in, deny her the possibility of contact with the community outside the employer's home and, consequently, also the practical possibility of applying for immigrant status.[31]

The United Kingdom

A generalized approach to the regulation of time is also a relatively recent addition to British labour law and somewhat foreign to its working culture.[32] Under pressure from the European Union, and in order to comply with the EU Working Time Directive, the Working Time Regulations were passed in 1998.[33] However, overtime pay remains largely a matter of individual or collective bargaining, and a relatively significant proportion of workers work unpaid overtime.[34] It is therefore difficult to argue that live-ins are treated exceptionally. Obviously, they are not covered by collective agreements, but other than that, their statutory rights are very weak, if not non-existent, like those of other employees in the UK. However, their exceptional treatment and the legal perception of the

---

[28] e.g. legislation in British Columbia defines 'domestic workers' at the initial stage of the statute, but does not refer to domestic workers in its current version, hence applying equal rights to domestics. R.S.B.C. 1996, c. 113, s. 1; also, see the Ministry of Skills Development and Labour Guidelines, as published online at http://www.labour.gov.bc.ca/esb/domestics/obligations.htm#hours.   [29] The Act Respecting Labour Standards, R.S.Q. c. N-1.1.

[30] Langevin, L. and Belleau, M., 'Trafficking in Women in Canada: A Critical Analysis of the Legal Framework Governing Immigrant Live-In Caregivers and Mail-Order Brides' (Status of Women Canada, 2000) (www.swc-cfc.gc.ca).

[31] *Mustaji* v. *Khi Yoeng Tijn*, British Columbia Supreme Court, 1995 ACWSJ 630473.

[32] Barnard, C., Deakin, S., and Hobbs, R., 'Opting Out of the 48 hour Week: Employer Necessity or Individual Choice?', *ILJ*, 32 (2003), 223.

[33] The Working Time Regulations, SI 1998/1833 (later amended).

[34] Arrowsmith, J., *EIRO Comparative Study on Overtime: The Case of the UK* (EIRO, 2003), 7.

live-in's time can be identified indirectly in the minimum wage context. For example, a case decided by the EAT was concerned with a (partial) live-in worker who was paid on a daily basis.[35] Although her daily wage divided by the number of hours worked seemed to fall below the minimum wage threshold, the court ruled that her work was not 'time work' that could be calculated by the hour. Instead, her work was considered to be 'unmeasured work'. The Working Time Regulations also exempt unmeasured work. The court explained that she was not employed on the basis of hours worked and that her working hours could not be clearly distinguished from her idle hours, in which she was not required to do any work.

Australia

The dominant form of overtime regulation in Australia is through awards.[36] Live-in housekeepers are governed by particular awards usually designed for domestic workers in general, in which there are particular clauses that prescribe the rights of live-ins.[37] While the awards grant live-ins certain benefits in recognition of the special responsibilities and hardships that are inherent in the occupation of housekeeper, they do not grant overtime payment. Some awards distinguish between general home-care workers, for whom there is a schedule of wages and overtime benefits, and those who are employed for twenty-four hour shifts, who are entitled only to the basic wages.[38]

Israel

Time is regulated in Israel by a law that dates back to 1951.[39] The law applies to all workers, but there are several exceptions of a general nature, of which the two most important have been used to exclude live-ins from overtime regulation. The Tel-Aviv District Labour Court has ruled that the exception pertaining to workers whose working time cannot be monitored also applies to live-ins. Similarly, the exclusion of workers whose work is of a high-trust nature also applies to live-ins, because they are being relied upon to perform the most intimate tasks.[40] This decision

[35] *Walton* v. *Independent Living Organisation* [2003] EWCA Civ. 199. The live-in in this case is not typical of those discussed in this chapter. She was not a migrant worker, and she was also employed for only three days a week, and therefore had her own home during the rest of the week.

[36] Buchanan, J. and Bearfield, S., *Reforming Working Time: Alternatives to Unemployment, Casualization and Excessive Hours* (Melbourne: Brotherhood of St Laurence, 1997).

[37] AW772275 Community Service (Home Care) (Act) Award 1988 (consolidated by AW816351CRA).

[38] Australian Industrial Relations Commission, Home and Community Care Award 2001, s. 19.

[39] Hours of Work and Rest Law (1951). The overtime arrangements are detailed in ch. 4, and the exceptions are listed in s. 30(a).

[40] Tel-Aviv Labour Court, Case 911652/99 *Todroangan—Moshe Maayan* (unpublished, 3.3.2001).

was given at a time when the labour court has just begun to engage in judicial law-making with regard to the vast number of migrant workers in Israel. On appeal, the majority of the National Labour Court held that the working time of live-ins cannot be measured but must be valued, and drawing on a rough estimate the court gave the live-in a supplement of thirty per cent of her wages.[41] The dissenting opinion suggested that overtime regulation should be applied to live-ins just as it applies to other workers. Despite the general claim that migrant workers deserve the same employment rights as other workers, this is almost the single exception to the formal statement of the equal applicability of the law. At the same time, the National Labour Court's remedy, and—more so—the dissenting judge's opinion, are the sole examples, in this brief comparison, of a formal statement in favour of granting live-ins overtime pay.

In summary, this limited comparison demonstrates that live-ins' overtime is frequently not compensated. Even when the formal statement of the law (albeit not necessarily its practical implementation) guarantees migrant workers, live-ins, and domestic workers equal rights in the sphere of labour standards, overtime tends to be an exception. Sometimes the exception is extended to broader groups of workers, while at other times it segregates the very particular group of live-in domestic workers.

Yet even this limited comparison does not reveal the full extent of the exceptional treatment of live-ins. While the description here focuses on the direct provisions regarding overtime benefits, there are other components in time regulation that have the effect of making overtime payment a rarity. For example, there is the simple question of 'hours worked', which is a matter for controversy. When the live-in is 'just there' or merely 'watching the children', when she is 'around the house' or is asked to run an errand or take something up on the way to her own room—are these work hours, or merely the acts of someone who 'blends into the family'?[42] The common formulas developed in various countries are generally similar—'the actual time spent on duty performing job activities' (USA), or hours of work versus 'hours the worker is present and responsible for chores of a family nature' (France), or 'hours of work are those in which the employee cannot do as he pleases' (Israel).[43] These definitions are all vague and easily manipulable. Generally, sleeping time, mealtimes and breaks are either unpaid or can be negotiated by contract; considering the bargaining position of live-ins, most cannot be

---

[41] National Labour Court, Case 1113/02 *Todroangan—Moshe* Maayan (unpublished, 27.1.2004). While the comparative analysis is not concerned with the court's formulation of its position, it should be noted that the 30% supplement to the wages is a creative judicial solution that has no basis or mention in the statute.   [42] See Blackett, above, n. 22.

[43] On France, see ibid.; United States—29 CFR § 78; Israel NLC 1973/2–4 Avraham Ron—The Municipality of Mitzpe Ramon 4 PDA 386.

reasonably expected to bargain overtime provisions, thereby making them potentially available to their employers for work and chores of a family nature at all hours. Thus, even a statutory guarantee of overtime pay is not sufficient, if the live-in's working time is discounted and held to be 'leisure' or something other than work—such as 'unmeasured work' or 'responsibilities of a family nature'.

A critique of the overtime exception and its justifications

Traditionally, the overtime exception was part of a broader approach that withheld employment regulation from live-in arrangements. The relationship between the live-in and the family for which she works—so the argument went—cannot be captured in conventional terms of 'employer' and 'employee'. The high level of intimacy and the sanctity of privacy distinguish it from other employment situations. This argument has been refined somewhat since other employment standards have begun to be applied to the live in.

Currently, one justification holds that while the live-in is an employee, a special state of trust obtains between the parties. It would therefore not be appropriate to count the hours of work, which is more typical of managerial practices in manufacturing or in professions that bill their hours.[44] A second justification holds that it is impossible to measure the amount of time worked by the live-in. The boundaryless relationship in which working time and leisure time are not neatly demarcated denies the existence of measurable time that lies at the basis of overtime arrangements. The difference between these two justifications is that the former holds that it is *inappropriate* to require overtime payment, while the latter holds that it is *not feasible* to measure working time in such a relationship. Both justifications can account for the general applicability of employment standards on the one hand, nevertheless exempting live-in workers from overtime payment on the other. This exception is not because live-ins are not employees. Nor is it because they are not as deserving as other employees. They are. It is merely a 'technical adjustment' to the law of

[44] Christine Jolls presents a slightly different variation of this argument. She holds that *minimum wage regulation* is not necessary when the occupation requires a high level of trust. In such cases, the employer has an incentive to pay high wages as a way of fostering a more trustful relationship and a higher degree of commitment on the part of the worker. See Jolls, C., 'Fairness, Minimum Wage Law and Employee Benefits', *New York University Law Journal*, 771(1) (2002), 47. Such a rationale may be applied to the regulation of overtime as well. However, as mentioned above, overtime regulation is intended to do more than merely increase the employee's wages, and in fact increased compensation is only an incidental outcome. Moreover, this argument may seem feeble when the employer has alternative means of obtaining the worker's commitment—e.g. by threatening to contact the immigration authorities.

minimum employment standards which stems from the particular problem of regulating time in this work relationship.

The two justifications for the overtime exemption are not particularly convincing. First, the high-trust relationship draws on exemptions that are generally applied to high-ranking, salaried officials. These are workers who, despite their formal status as 'employees', have interests that are closer to those of the shareholders than to those of other employees. The exemption may also be applied to white-collar professionals whose workday cannot be expected to be based on the concept of shift-work, as it extends throughout the whole of the day. These 'employees' resemble independent contractors who manage their own balance between work and leisure time, and whose profit depends on their investment of time. Unlike employees whose earnings are adjusted to the number of hours worked, these workers' earnings are generally in recompense for an overall commitment to the tasks performed, and the time worked is in fact whatever is necessary to advance and complete their tasks. The juxtaposition of high-ranking managers, engineers engaged in research and development, and domestic live-ins is an odd one. Sociologically, these are different types of workers. The assumption that the exempted employee is akin to the shareholder hardly seems appropriate in the case of the live-ins. The argument that the work of exempted employees cannot be broken up into units of time is irrelevant as well. If the live-in were to be replaced by two or three live-out domestic workers working several hours a day, there would be no problem measuring the work performed in hourly units. While complicated managerial tasks arguably cannot be broken up into units of time, cleaning and care work can be easily scheduled. The problem is that such scheduling would undermine the live-in's economic advantage to the employer. The second justification for the exemption, which holds that the working time of a live-in cannot be measured, is equally problematic. This type of exemption may be suitable for travelling sales agents whose whereabouts throughout the day are unknown. But the working time of the live-in is easily gauged. The work is performed within the 'establishment' and is highly visible. It is true that some employers do not want to deal with measuring and recording working time. However, this is also true of employers in industry, who prefer to forgo the use of the classic time clock because it clashes with the organizational culture the employer wants to promote. Just because the employer forgoes the measurement of time, this would not appear to justify a blanket exemption of live-in workers from overtime arrangements.

The weakness common to both justifications is indicative of the basic fallacy that underlies them. Both justifications assume a boundaryless workplace. The first assumes there are no clear boundaries between the employer and the employee, who are in fact viewed as inseparable and symbiotically linked. The second assumes there are no boundaries between working time and leisure time. However, these assumptions do not reflect any intrinsic truth regarding the relationship between the live-in and her employer. The high-trust argument is based on the 'we are all a family' fallacy, which has been used to deny the live-in her privacy and her autonomy. It is hardly a truism; it is actually a legal myth or fable. It is a clear example of demarcating the household as private sphere to deny the public protection that is typical to labour law.[45] Similarly, the absence-of-supervision justification adopts a view benefiting the employer, who is always in favour of greater flexibility and less precision in defining the employment contract.[46] The reason there are no boundaries between work and leisure time is because the law does not require them. If the law were to mandate pay for overtime, very clear boundaries might be expected to emerge.

The overtime exemption therefore is not an obvious legal response to an objective problem. The proposed justifications emphasize administrative problems and conceal a more fundamental prejudice.[47] Arguably, the real reasons must be sought in the live-in's gender, foreignness, and class.[48] A sociological explanation of the law also points of the absence of solidarity, and the 'divide and conquer' effects of these legislative arrangements which guarantees their perpetuation over time.

From legal justifications to explanations

Live-ins are women

What seems to be a better explanation for the overtime exception is that most live-ins are women. While some men work as live-ins, mostly performing care work for adult disabled males and elderly males, the

---

[45] Olsen, F., 'The Family and the Market: A Study of Ideology and Legal Reform', *Harvard Law Review*, 96 (1983), 1497; for a similar claim—'nobody talks about the politics of housework anymore'—see Ehrenreich, B., 'Maid to Order', in Ehrenreich and Hochschild, above, n. 8, 85.

[46] Offe, C., *Disorganized Capitalism* (Cambridge: MIT University Press, 1985), 14.

[47] A similar use of administrative justifications is analysed with regard to other exceptions that are applied to live-ins, such as the American NLRA's exception regarding the domestic workers' freedom of association. See Smith, P., 'Organizing the Unorganizable: Private Paid Household Workers and Approaches to Employment Representation', *North Carolina Law Review*, 79 (2000), 45, 63.

[48] The need to emphasize these interrelated features of live-ins has been highlighted by several authors. See e.g. Macklin, A., 'Foreign Domestic Workers: Surrogate Housewife or Mail Order Servant', *McGill Law Journal*, 27 (1992), 681; Banks, T. L., 'Toward a Global Critical Feminist Vision: Domestic Work and the Nanny Tax Debate', *J. Race and Justice*, 3 (1999), 1; Fitzpatrick, J. and Kelly, K., 'Gendered Aspects of Migration: Law and the Female Migrant', *Hastings International & Comparative Law Review*, 22 (1998), 47.

employment practices of the occupation are largely determined in accordance with the dominant gender employed.[49] Male live-ins are therefore employed according to standards that were socially designed for women.

The gendered composition of live-ins affects their employment standards in various ways. Live-ins perform the tasks that are stereotypically considered either part of women's innate nature or the result of social indoctrination. Consequently, the work they do is not perceived as a 'job'. This in large part explains the high-trust justification. Live-ins are not doing a 'job' because they have a high-trust, intimate relationship with their employers. This intimacy belongs to the sphere of relationships between a woman and her family (spouse, children, and parents). The care and the intimacy are deemed part of the general way in which women interact with those who are dependent on them (or on whom they are dependent). The vague boundaries are a result of what society thinks is the identical nature of what live-ins do for others and what they do for themselves.[50] To be clear, there is nothing about work at home, care work, or any other occupation for that matter, which is innately a woman's job. Nor is there anything intrinsic in the work itself that explains why women do it much more than men. Any reference to this division of labour is merely a reflection of a well-documented reality, and not of ideals. Social constructs could be much different,[51] but the point is that they are not, and as will be argued here, the overtime exception for live-ins is merely one more example of a legal rule that is being used to preserve the status quo rather than question it.

Clearly, over the years, women have succeeded in breaking down occupational barriers and stepping into jobs that were predominantly occupied by males. Yet the live-in's occupation is the clearest example of 'women's work' done for money. The job consists of cooking and laundering, and the live-in still does the same things (cooking and laundry) for herself when she is off the job. Women who perform 'women's work' as labour—as a paying job, rather than as unpaid work within the home—receive relatively low market wages. Yet when they are live-ins they are not even considered to be fully marketing their work, because they have moved their home along with their work. As long as women's household work remains in the social perception as some form of

---

[49] This point is evident in comparable-worth studies where gendered occupations are determined by the dominant gender, and a minority employment of the other gender has but little influence. See Rhoads, S., *Incomparable Worth* (Cambridge: Cambridge University Press 1993), 7–40.

[50] For a critique of the separation between the intimate (designated as 'spiritual') and economic dimensions of household labour, see Roberts, D., 'Spiritual and Menial Housework', *Yale J. of Law and Feminism*, 9 (1997), 51.

[51] See e.g. Fischl, in this volume.

volunteer care work, altruism, or just pure fun, then the live-in's house-hold work is viewed as some kind of hybrid, halfway between the marketing and non-marketing of women's work.

The gender argument in itself is not sufficient. There are live-ins, most of them women as well, who are highly paid and can bargain for their rights assertively. These are the high-wage 'nannies'.[52] They are employed to do care work, and they too perform 'women's work'. This is a separate niche within the live-in labour market, and the problems of other live-ins are not necessarily alien to them either. They, too, have to cope with solitude, the awkward balancing of intimacy and the work relationship, and employers' intrinsic desire to make the work schedule and work definition more flexible. But the mental and tangible resources they have to cope with these pressures are relatively high, because these nannies are neither foreign nor poor.

Live-ins are foreigners

Domestic workers who work on an hourly basis do not live-in. They come and go at fixed times as contractually negotiated. It is the employ-ment relationship that brings them and their employers together, and the rest of the time they are apart. When off the job the domestic employees resort to their own world. Many employers are not even aware of that world. They do not always know where their domestic workers live, what their neighbourhoods look like, or what the domestic worker's family concerns are. When on the job, the parties' relationship is 'professional'. The parties agree to a general time frame. Within that time frame, the use of the employee's time is determined on the parties' implicit and explicit agreements regarding the positive and negative incentives to elicit work (for example, bonuses and monitoring devices).

By contrast, live-ins generally do not hail from the neighbouring town. They prefer a live-in arrangement because they do not have an alternative home in the vicinity. Sometimes they want a live-in arrange-ment to save on the costs of housing. At other times they must accept a live-in arrangement because that is what employers demand. In some countries, the live-in arrangement is even required by the state as part of the immigration requirements. In the case of undocumented migrants, a live-in arrangement is also an asylum of sorts, albeit a fragile one, from the immigration authorities. Given their distance from their own community, the employer is their only home.

---

[52] See McLaughlin, E. and Kraus, N., *The Nanny Diaries: A Novel* (New York: St Martin Griffin, 2002), and the distinction drawn between the high-waged nannies and migrant live-ins in Romero, M., 'Nanny Diaries and Other Stories: Imagining Immigrant Women's Labor in the Social Reproduction of American Families', *De Paul Law Review*, 52 (2003), 809.

Ironically, employers who are concerned with their privacy display a preference for foreign live-ins, because they do not intrude as much as local workers. They are always there, but the common metaphor used for such workers is that they are invisible. This may be because they do not speak the language.[53] Or it is because their personal problems and lives are supposedly 'left behind' and their presence is dedicated only for the purpose of live-in work. Their invisibility is also ascribed to be a cultural matter that the live-ins bring with them from a far and exotic culture. Common then among these reasons is that their foreignness is a fundamental reason for the employers' preferences as well as for the employees' assent to the boundaryless live-in arrangement.

Live-ins as an issue of class

The live-in's gender and foreignness also interact to construct yet a third important explanation for the overtime exemption. Live-ins are generally poor, if not in dire need, and they are willing to compromise over wages that are at the legal minimum (and often even below that). The problem of live-ins therefore must be captured also as a matter of class. Some live-ins work around the clock. Others work on and off around the clock. The cumulative number of hours worked is typically far beyond the 'standard' working day or working week as prescribed in statutes regulating time. Requiring employers to pay overtime would considerably raise the cost of live-ins.

The implication of the overtime exception is that it pushes down the minimum wage. Minimum wage arrangements commonly apply to migrant workers (and obviously apply to women). However, a minimum wage is usually determined either by the number of hours worked or on the basis of a monthly salary. If workers are not entitled to overtime, this means that hourly compensation is directly tied to the *number* of hours worked, but with no extra *per-hour* compensation for the hours worked over and above the regular working day or working week. If the workers receive a monthly salary, this salary will have been calculated for a 'normal' working week worker. But for live-ins the same salary is actually provided for a greater number of hours, thus reducing the wage per hour. Consequently, some countries maintain a contradictory position. On the one hand they apply the minimum wage laws to live-ins, but at the same time they exempt their employers from overtime payment and reduce the minimum wage. A standard argument in support of the payment of the minimum wage to foreign workers is that sub-minimum wages would lead to the preference of migrant workers over local workers,

---

[53] Cf. Rivas, L. M., 'Invisible Labors: Caring for the Independent Person', in Ehrenreich and Hochschild, above, n. 8, 70.

but this is generally not a problem with regard to live-ins. Domestic workers usually prefer a work-out to a live-in arrangement anyway. Instead, it seems that the overtime exception makes it possible to maintain a façade of equal treatment with regard to minimum wages, while allowing a real distinction on the basis of the method the wage is calculated.

One final problem that may be raised with regard to the class argument is that the objective of overtime pay, at least at the formal level, is usually not to increase workers' wages *per se*, but to serve as an incentive against excessive overtime.[54] Consequently, to argue that live-ins cannot capitalize on the benefits of overtime is an argument misdirected. However, this argument is not very convincing. First and foremost, the fact that live-ins do not receive overtime payments does not help them shorten the working day or working week. There is no alternative incentive to ensure that they do not work around the clock. As mentioned above, the *raison d'être* for this arrangement is precisely the live-in's excessively long working hours with no extra pay. Secondly, overtime has become an increasingly significant source of compensation for many workers. Even if overtime payments need to be rethought altogether, denying overtime payment to live-ins is to deprive them of an important source of income which is lawfully available to other workers in the labour market.

On solidarity: who can voice the live-ins' interests?

The intertwining features of gender, class, and alienage makes live-ins exceptionally vulnerable in the labour market. Politically, this arrangement seems to be very convenient for many, and thus relatively secure from change. If live-ins have one characteristic which can potentially be used to promote their rights, it is the fact that they are women. Clearly, the other two axes that prescribe their position in the labour market do not have the same potential, because other poor and migrant workers are not a major source of political power. Women, on the other hand, have gained more influence in the political sphere and can be assumed to promote the live-ins' interests in solidarity. Solidarity, however, is rare. Live-ins secure the traditional division of labour within the household

---

[54] The general rule in democratic regimes, with minor exceptions, is that the state does not determine wages over and above the minimum wage. Given that overtime payments are not limited to low-waged workers, if the objective of statutory overtime payments was to increase wages, then the general rule would have been violated. It is therefore generally agreed that increased overtime payments should be regarded as a deterrent and not as a right in itself. This, of course, does not undermine the obvious conclusion that employees who are employed overtime are better compensated. On the use of overtime as a deterrent, see Schor, J., 'Worktime in a Contemporary Context: Amending the Fair Labor Standards Act', *Chicago-Kent Law Review*, 70 (1994), 157.

but eliminate its disadvantage to women. Given the minor role of men in household chores and family care work to begin with, the live-ins are viewed by the household and by society as predominantly an aid to the women who employ them. Most commonly, it is women who recruit, instruct, and 'manage' the live-ins.

Dual-career families are those in which both partners have a career outside the home. Compared to the traditional division of labour in the household, the exceptional feature of dual-career families is that the woman engages in a dual career of her own—both within and outside the household.[55] Consequently, society perceives live-ins as a means to relieve the *woman* of her dual role. The major advantage of live-ins to the families that employ them is around-the-clock availability; counting their hours would eliminate this advantage. Of course, there are other ways to perceive, encourage, and aid dual-career families. Somewhat too obvious even to mention, the male partner could assume a greater role within the household. Yet very little is done fundamentally to move the dual-career family away from the traditional gender division of labour.[56] Some think the matter is not appropriate for social intervention, and others suggest that there are no practical ways to compel a different division of labour.

Limiting the social response to the traditional division of labour to cost-saving methods, such as the overtime exception, frames the problem in a manner that sets poor and rich women against each other. It allows women, as employers, to develop a greater capacity to overcome the 'double bind' that disadvantages them as employees.[57] The live-ins therefore serve multiple, class-related objectives. To the household, they designate the social status of their employers like other prized commodities such as luxury cars and gadgets. But more particularly, they also have been commonly described as the servants that relieve the 'lady of the house' from the menial tasks.[58] Consequently, they relieve the household from reconsidering the division of labour within it, and maintain the social status quo. Any effort for solidarity among women on these two sides of the live-in relationship risks the token arrangement society and law have crafted to relieve the gender tension, and may result in bringing back the traditional status quo. Career women may not be able

---

[55] Hertz, R., *More Equal than Others: Women and Men in Dual-career Marriages* (Berkeley: University of California Press, 1986). Dual-career households are distinguished from dual-earner households, in which a job held by one or both earners is not perceived subjectively or assessed objectively as a 'career'.

[56] For a review of the vast literature on this issue, cf. Shelton, B. A. and John, D., 'The Division of Household Labour', *Annual Review of Sociology* (1996), 299.

[57] Williams, J., *Unbending Gender: Why Family and Work Conflict and What to do About it?* (Oxford: OUP, 2000).

[58] Macklin, above, n. 48, op. note 307 onwards; Smith, above, n. 11, op. note 51.

to afford it, and because men are not involved they may not sufficiently care. Traditional or modern, the division of labour is structured as the internal affair of women, ignoring the benefits men and employers alike derive from it. Otherwise stated, the overtime exception distances men from the problem and puts in place a divide-and-conquer strategy that undermines the potential for solidarity.

IV THE OVERTIME EXEMPTION: DECOMMODIFICATION AND RECOMMODIFICATION OF TIME

It is the particular nature of the overtime exception to serve to (re)commodify time. The benefit to the employing families, which is ensured by the state, is based on the withdrawal of one of the central pillars of regulation in labour law. Interestingly enough, time regulation has in the past been criticized for being based on men's time schedules and for disadvantaging women. The consequences of the overtime exception to live-ins demonstrate that withholding the regulation of time places some men at a disadvantage as well, though again it is mainly women who suffer the negative consequences. Clearly, whether time is regulated or not, some women will pay the price. The regulation and deregulation of time do not address the underlying problems associated with the time constraints encountered by women, but simply shift them to other women. They maintain the existence of a qualitatively distinct third type of non-valued time. It is the time that oils the ongoing friction between work and leisure.

Time

Oddly, to both Marxists and neoclassical economists, time displays certain features that are attributed to commodities. Its nature as a commodity is that it can be bought and sold, and that every unit of time (for example, an hour) is equally priced.[59] The market trade in time is therefore no different than the market trade in widgets. The difference between Marxist and neoclassical economics lies in their understanding of this market trade.

---

[59] There are classical definitions of commodity that cannot include time, especially from a Marxist point of view; e.g. Polanyi defines commodity as something that is manufactured for the purpose of being sold in the market (Polanyi, K., *The Great Transformation* (Boston: Beacon Press, 1944)). Given that time is not manufactured and is not really sold, only virtually, it is not a commodity. However, if we define a commodity as anything that can be bought and sold, then time can be fitted into this definition.

Marx argues that there is a market for labour power but not for labour services. Once the employer has purchased the workers' power, he seeks to pay employees subsistence wages for their time and to extract from them as many working hours as possible.[60] The more hours the worker can be employed, the greater the rate of exploitation and the profit to the employer. If the employer pays employees by the hour, he has an incentive to avoid the hours of employment in which their productivity declines. The employment of two part-time workers is more productive and profitable for the employer than the employment of one full-time worker, even if the wages for the two part-time employees are less than the subsistence wages. Thus, the employer will seek to increase his profits at the expense of the employees' state of under- or over-employment. The competition over working time is therefore a function of the parties' relative power.

In contrast to Marx's demand-side exploitation theory, the neoclassical economists emphasize a supply-side 'meeting-of-minds' model, in which individual employees' preferences for working time are the driving force behind time distribution. Working time is nullified leisure time, but it is also the time required to earn the amount of money that is needed for consumption. Working time is therefore determined by the needs of consumption.[61] Employers in a competitive market are likely to be responsive to employees' needs because they have to attract the best employees to recruit and accommodate their requirements. Employers, therefore, are not seeking to exploit their workers, but to accommodate them. For the same reason, flexible work schedules are assumed by this school of thought to be reflective of what workers want. Admittedly this is not what some workers want in an ideal world, but contracts rarely display an ideal price either. What is important is that contracts reflect the best price out of a set of feasible options available in the market. There is no exploitation—just a meeting of minds.

Whether one believes in the demand-side or supply-side theories, the exploitation or accommodation theories, the depiction of time in both, one finds, is rather similar. It is possible to replace the employment relationship and the units of time with a supplier–consumer relationship and tangible commodities. If time had been left only to market forces, it would have been assumed that patterns of working time reflect either one process or the other (exploitation or accommodation). For both sides of an otherwise heated descriptive and normative debate, the day is comprised of twenty-four hours and the week of 10,080 minutes, each of which is identical to the others.

[60] Marx, K., *Das Kapital*, ch. 10.
[61] For a review of the neoclassical literature on working time, see Contensou, F. and Vranceanu, R., *Working Time: Theory and Policy Implications* (Cheltenham: Edward Elgar, 2000).

There are various problems with the commodification of time. At the descriptive level one may ask whether time really does conform to the definition of commodity. It is not manufactured, and the consumption of time does not fall neatly into the framework of market-driven supply and demand. If the assumption that time is a commodity is merely a heuristic form of explaining how time is used, a different problem arises, because time may not be commensurable. If a person chooses to work longer hours, does that imply that her value of time can be calculated by comparing her choices to the other alternatives?[62] From a normative point of view—should the trade in time be absolutely permitted (according to the neoclassical view) or absolutely prohibited (as in the Marxist view)? Both views assume it is a commodity, and the different prescriptions are merely indicative of their ideological positions in regard to commodities. Both views, however, do not generate a policy that seeks to decommodify time. This is where the law on working time steers the debate away from the dispute over the appropriate policy on commodities.

The decommodification of time can be seen as an integration of two interrelated statutory projects. The first is that of labour law, which decommodifies various experiences and dimensions of the employment relationship and isolates them from market forces. The regulation of working time described here is closely related to the regulation of time over the life cycle, demarcating childhood time, adult working time and retirement time. Not only time, but such rights as health, safety, privacy, and equality have also been removed from the marketplace. These dimensions of the employment relationship are characterized as being more than just economic rights, but a matter of human dignity. An eighteen-hour working day, just like toiling in a sweatshop without proper ventilation, is not only a matter of inequality in economic bargaining, it is also dehumanizing. Laws regulating working time partially decommodify time-units.[63] This does not mean that they take away time's economic value. Things that are not commodities may have an economic value, but that is not their only value. The law tags some hours as working time, and others as leisure time. The boundary between the two is partially permeable, to the extent that workers may choose to contract some time from the leisure side to the labour side, over and above the standard rate of working time. This is permissible overtime. Hours are

---

[62] Andersen, E., *Value in Ethics and Economics* (Cambridge, Mass.: Harvard University Press, 1993); Sunstein, C., 'Incommensurability and Kinds of Valuation: Some Applications in Law', in R. Chang (ed.), *Incommensurability, Incomparability and Practical Reason* (Cambridge, Mass.: Harvard University Press, 1998), 234.

[63] The distinction between partial and complete commodification is based on Radin, M. J., *Contested Commodities* (Cambridge, Mass.: Harvard University Press, 1996), 102–14.

alienable and can be negotiated, but only according to a mandatory public policy regarding the cost of time. However, there are limits to the extent of overtime a worker may perform, and some hours of the day are slotted in a totally non-commodified manner as inalienable leisure time.

Secondly, the decommodification of time is also an essential component of the welfare state, which partially isolates human experience and opportunities from the functioning of the market. The allegedly meritocratic regime governed by the market gives place to a regime based on principles of democratic participation and social integration. A disabled person who receives aid in kind, or in the form of an allowance or reimbursement from the state, is 'deserving' and entitled because she complies with the social criteria defined by the community, and not because society is engaged in charity or mercy. One's economic and social position is therefore determined not only by markets, but also on the basis of one's attachment to the distributing community.

The welfare state project is therefore closely tied to the labour law project. Like the institutions of the welfare state, labour law seeks to partially isolate individuals from their market power and to guarantee them a minimum level of achievement, rooted merely in their being 'employees'. The two projects are substitutes for each other to an extent. A broader guarantee of minimum rights within the domain of labour law reduces the need for the institutions of the welfare state. Moreover, the decommodification of time provides a qualitative guarantee of individual well-being, civic engagement, political participation, and social interaction, all of which are integral to social citizenship. In this sense, the regulation of working time extends beyond the Marxist/ neoclassical debate, which is framed in terms of the economic value of time.[64]

The achievement of statutory time regulation should therefore be assessed in relation to these two projects of decommodification. The simple assessment, in both spheres, is that time regulation in general, and overtime regulation in particular, have benefited workers. The industrial norms of the past have been outlawed and the workday is more humane and more compatible with human dignity. Together with minimum wage provisions on the one hand and welfare benefits on the other, dignity is also complemented by adequate income. Yet, if time regulation seeks to prohibit or permit overtime, then it is missing some of the adverse implications of this arrangement.

---

[64] Although Marx clearly provides the additional dimensions of alienation that tie the economics of time to a broader view of human experience.

The overtime exception for live-ins: labour market regulation and the exclusion of women

Despite the generally positive assessment, the regulation of time also demonstrates the intrinsic difficulty in advancing the interests of labour. Unlike shareholders, who are presumed to hold the same interests— maximizing their profits—the interests of labour are more diverse.[65] The underlying principle of time regulation is that time should be decommodified to assure the separation and non-marketability of non-working time, such as childhood time, retirement time, and leisure time. Unlike shareholders' profits, which are fully commodified, the 'profits' of labour are rooted in the decommodification of essential non-tangible assets such as time, safety and dignity.

Because of the particular nature of the labour/welfare safety net, regulation does not benefit all. This is well demonstrated by the regulation of time. The traditional gender-based critique of time regulation is that it is based on the male, factory worker model. It assumes two types of time— 'work' and 'leisure'—thus ignoring the fact that there are at least three types of time, one of which applies to women in a predominant manner yet remains invisible in statutory time regulation: 'house and care time'. When a person is not at work he is assumed to be at 'leisure', but for many women, 'leisure' is essentially non-paid work at home.[66] Moreover, the particular arrangements associated with time regulation, such as the right to fringe benefits or the use of working time to determine entitlement to unemployment funds, welfare and the like, have often been geared to exclude women from the primary labour market and squeeze them out to its periphery. The problems are generally slanted in two complementary directions. First, labour law is interested in employment issues, and women who work at home are assumed to be outside the employment sphere. Otherwise stated, if the role of labour law is to decommodify certain dimensions of work, then women's work at home is not commodified to begin with and employment law is therefore irrelevant. Secondly, employment law often takes the convenient, full-time (and indefinite) model of employment, which is disproportionately male, and arranges for its partial decommodification. For example, in most countries overtime is differentiated from extra-time.[67] An employee who has a part-time contract (for example, twenty hours a week) and works extra hours is not entitled to overtime or to any other legal protection.

---

[65] Offe, above, n. 46, 170–219.

[66] Williams, above, n. 57. Williams develops the notion of 'domesticity' according to which the work/family conflict is a driving force of the gender problem.

[67] See EIRO, *Overtime in Europe*, above n. 1, for an explanation of the terms.

Legal protection is extended only to those employed over and above the maximum number of hours prescribed by law. Because more women than men are employed only part-time, time regulation is commonly a means for exclusion.

If the problem is identified as women's economically and legally unrecognized work, some have suggested that women's work at home must be commodified.[68] The argument here is that the only way to achieve recognition of household work is to value it in market terms. The social realization that women have a job at home, as well as outside it, would shape the way the law looks at part-time arrangements and extra work, in which women are over-represented but which fall short of current overtime arrangements. The meaning of commodification of women's work is difficult to pinpoint, but if the decommodification of time by means of regulation is part of the disadvantage law has imposed on women in the labour market, then it is appealing to think that recommodification may be the most appropriate response. However, the overtime exception of live-ins from time regulation demonstrates the weakness of such a response. Basically, the exception makes overtime a matter for contractual negotiation. For most live-ins, this means complete recommodification. In this situation, there are no limits to the contractual definition of the live-in's tasks and time commitment. If the live-in's work and 'leisure' time cannot be delineated, then the parties are allowed to negotiate a full-day commitment. At other times the recommodification is partial. While there are limits to how many hours the live-in may work, the amount of compensation she receives for her work is not subject to any regulation.

The live-in arrangement is an extreme example of the commodification of women's work. If, as a result of recommodification, live-ins are placed at a serious disadvantage, this should also serve as a warning to those who believe that the simple solution to women's unrecognized contribution at home is to translate it into market value. There is no reason to assume that if women's household work (when done in their own household) is commodified then women's bargaining power will immediately improve. The commodification of live-ins suggests that the market valuation of women's work does not capture the true value of their work. Consequently, the devaluation of women's work is one and the same, regardless of whether women's work is relegated to the market,

---

[68] Among those who endorsed policy solutions that resonate with the principle of commodification: Silbaugh, K., 'Commodification and Women's Household Labour', *Yale J. of Law and Feminism*, 9 (1996), 81; Ertman, M., 'Commercializing Marriage: A Proposal for Valuing Women's Work Through Premarital Security Agreements', *Texas L. Rev.*, 77 (1998), 17; Cahn, N., 'The Coin of the Realm: Poverty and the Commodification of Gendered Labor', *J. of Gender, Race and Justice*, 5 (2001), 1.

the public sphere, or the family. Shifting the work from one sphere to another does not resolve the problem of devaluation itself.

Not only does the recommodification of time prove to be a hollow promise for live-ins, the losses extend beyond the live-ins themselves. In the process of shifting time from the family to the market sphere, the fundamental problem is ignored. For example, if the problem is identified as women's (and men's) lack of control over their life's schedules, then live-ins merely augment the problem. They free the wealthier workers to surrender to the market's work schedules, suggesting that around-the-clock work is the labour market norm. The fact that some women can accommodate such demands is also used to argue that there is nothing gendered or discriminatory in such schedules. Consequently, it is legitimate to require all women to accommodate such schedules. The norm, made possible by live-ins' work, is applied to production workers, secretarial staff, and single mothers who are expected to take care of themselves, avoid welfare, and conform with prevailing norms of work. Yet it is these workers who cannot roll the costs of the norms over to others.

The live-in's overtime dilemma is indicative of the basic problem in time regulation, and in labour regulation more generally. Whether time is decommodified or recommodified, there are some women who pay the price. The recommodification of time by means of the overtime exemption plays off women as employers against women as labourers. The conformity of women *qua* household employers to the norms prescribed by the time/leisure dichotomy is based on the availability of care and domestic work performed by others without time constraints. This conflict appears at two levels. First, simple economics demonstrates that the economic value of women's work outside the home, according to the prescription of the market, requires the availability of cheap domestic and care work. Thus, even when overtime is only partially recommodified (that is, readily available but still costly), this objective is achieved. Secondly, women's need to adapt to the increasingly flexible demands of market-compensated labour and 'leisure', and to squeeze in unrecognized care time between the statutory types of time, requires finding a means of escaping the overly simplified construction of time. The overtime exception of live-ins provides exactly this flexibility. In every production system a measure of flexibility must exist. In the family production system, the household has little flexibility because it must adjust to the demands of the market, to domestic household needs, and to the cultural norms of care (parents, especially mothers, must conform to social norms of care and 'good parenthood'). Flexibility is only made possible by the multitasking, full-time, present but invisible live-in, whose time has been recommodified so as to fit into the schedules and meet the needs of all others.

The question is therefore *not* 'commodification or not', but rather who pays the price, and how the social and legal precepts of time allocate resources to the labour market participants (as well as to those excluded from the market). It seems that the failure of the two versions of time regulation illustrated here is that both fail to address the fundamental social, economic, and legal institutions that determined the allocation of all household work to women. Live-ins allow the maintenance of household work as women's work, avoiding the need to bring men into the supply pool of household labourers. The overtime exception further applies a 'divide and conquer' strategy among women, undermining gender-based solidarity. Hence, it utilizes age-old mechanisms of discrimination but does not respond to them.

The overtime exception for live-ins; welfare state institutions and the exclusion of migrants

If women's time, that which does not conform to the traditional division between 'work' and 'leisure' time, cannot be fully valued by either the de- or recommodification of time in law, then it must be treated as a distinct type of time. Yet it is unclear how this should be done. To avoid this trap, the law merely shunts women's time from one category of women to another. When women were disenfranchised and lacked all political power, they were denied rights by the male legislatures that were accountable to the male electorate. Since women won the right to vote and can legitimately raise women's issues and feminist solutions, old solutions must be rethought. Women's time remains an issue that requires public attention, but taking it out of the 'private' sphere of the family, or removing it from the 'private' sphere of the market, are all deemed to be politically controversial. The state does not presume to sponsor child-care, expand the care for the elderly, or intervene in the internal division of labour within the family. By contrast, opening the gates to both documented and undocumented migrant women who work as live-ins is a solution that does not encounter any strong populist objection. This way, the state can provide the overtime exception and continue to ensure that women's time will be cheaper. Live-ins' function in the welfare state is therefore best captured by an insiders/outsiders schema.

The shifting of time serves important functions in the welfare state and therefore accommodates the welfare state's objectives.[69] It has been noted

---

[69] This is best captured by Walzer, M., *Spheres of Justice* (New York: Basic Books, 1984), 56–61. Walzer draws on the analogy of the state and the family—'why are they admitted? To free citizens from hard and unpleasant work. Then the state is like a family with live-in servants'.

that—like labour law—welfare state institutions are gendered and patriarchal in nature.[70] In the past women were encouraged to marry and remain at home. Now the agenda is changing in two complementary ways. The good wife is expected to work as well. Moreover, a growing number of single mothers, who previously relied on welfare, are being required to work. Live-ins are scarcely of any assistance to the second category, but they are an important part of making the first one possible. The overtime exception makes live-ins less expensive. It also has the market effect of reducing the costs of care even in homes that do not employ a live-in. This allows the welfare state to pay less in aid to families that need to care for their children or their ageing parents. It can also promote non-economic aspects of dignity, such as the dignity of people with disabilities, by allowing them to remain at home with a live-in who constantly cares for them, rather than having to be taken to an institution for similar care. Live-ins make possible the values—economic and other—of the modern welfare state.

The problem the overtime exception poses to the decommodification proposed by the welfare state institutions is therefore similar to the one in labour law—it does not *solve* the problem, but merely *shifts* it. Live-ins allow women to take part in waged work, civic life, and politics. These are necessary steps for social inclusion and citizenship. It is the exclusion of live-ins on the basis of alienage that makes all this politically and socially possible.[71] They are not deemed to be deserving as citizens or residents, and the project of social inclusion displays less (or no) concern for their inclusion.

Moreover, while it is sometimes assumed that migrant workers are 'outsiders' who make cohesion among the 'insiders' easier, the growing reliance on live-in arrangements actually segments the insiders and makes social transformation more difficult to achieve. Live-ins provide a convenient solution for dual-career families that are well compensated in the labour market. It is the lesser-waged families and single mothers, then, for whom the need for day-care arrangements becomes a struggle. This can give rise to two-tiered social provision, as is commonly observed in other welfare state institutions such as health care and pensions. Making the live-ins more 'affordable' broadens the segment of the population that seeks privately negotiated solutions, instead of prompting public pressure for universal solutions to one of the most significant barriers to social inclusion. The time exception therefore directly devalues

---

[70] Pateman, C., 'The Patriarchal Welfare State', in A. Gutmann (ed.), *Democracy and the Welfare State* (Princeton: Princeton University Press, 1988), 231, 244.

[71] Carens, J., 'Migration and Morality: A Liberal Egalitarian Perspective', in B. Barry and R. Goodin (eds.), *Free Movement* (Philadelphia: Penn. University Press, 1992), 25–47.

the live-in's work, but also indirectly devalues the welfare state's institutions for social provision.

V CONCLUSION

The overtime exception for live-ins is functional when viewed as a welfare state arrangement as it is in labour law.[72] It has nothing to do with the alleged justifications that the law provides for the exception— such as that their work cannot, or should not, be measured. In both spheres of law, labour and welfare, the distinct nature of the 'third time' is crucial to the smooth functioning of the family, the market, and the state. Dumping the 'third time' on live-ins, who are migrant women workers, frees society from having to make sense of fundamental questions: is the 'third time' necessary or inevitable? How should it be valued? How should it be distributed within the family and between the genders? Should it be embedded in the solidaristic arrangements of the state?

Why should the matter of overtime be of particular interest? Clearly, the problems live-in workers encounter go far beyond this seemingly minor matter. Physical and mental abuse, even employers' power to withhold pay, would seem to merit more attention. These are all serious problems. However, the issue of overtime merits attention beyond its practical significance. The overtime exception very clearly illustrates that matters of inclusion and exclusion are often hidden in the small details of the law. Laws that may seem to favour workers, such as the universal coverage of minimum wage law, are actually detrimental to some. For live-ins, the guarantee of a minimum wage is meaningless without any recognition of their overtime commitment.

The overtime exception further illustrates that, even as law becomes more progressive and aware of women's issues, the fundamental structures of exclusion remain. Law or policy does not easily respond to the challenge raised by the recognition of the 'third time'. The gendered nature of family and work remain. The problem is not merely that of entrenched social values. The fact that the law prescribes the overtime exception indicates that it is the state which is responsible for devising latent mechanisms that are responsible for entrenching the division of labour. Rather than acknowledge the qualitatively distinct time women spend in managing the gap between what is commonly (or cynically) described as work and leisure times, the law merely reshuffles time. It shifts the burden of women's time from some women to others.

---

[72] Cf. to Ganz, H., 'Positive Functions of Poverty', *American J. of Soc.*, 78 (1972), 275.

Regulating time, or deregulating it, has done little to address the broader patterns that have a disparate impact on women: growing pressure in the workplace for employer-managed time flexibility, extensive hours, the stagnating distribution of the 'third time' between men and women, and the availability of quality day-care facilities. The state avoids a right to better compensation for overtime and abstains from guaranteeing a universal right to work part-time. It accepts time arrangements as well as social arrangements as given, and merely seeks to find a cheap way to accommodate the existing arrangements. Absent a response to these problems, women's time remains qualitatively distinct and undervalued.

The live-ins' gender and position in society as migrants are complementary components in the overtime exception 'solution'. Gender, alienage, and class shape an exceptionally vulnerable position in the social hierarchy, and in domestic labour markets.[73] Shuffling women's time from one group of women to another (that is, from women in dual-career families to migrant live-ins) illustrates the fact that whether time is regarded as private or public, whether policy options lean towards regulation or deregulation, and whether time is regarded as a commodity or not, it just doesn't matter enough. Like the equality/difference debate, which has been critiqued as empty, and of little consequence to the underlying problems of women in society,[74] the socio-legal constructs presented here are equally empty.

Consequently, some have argued that commodification of the currently unpaid labour women perform can resolve the work/family problem.[75] The strategic implications of this view impose costs on the poor women who make commodification possible. One response to such a challenge is that reducing the feminist agenda only to strategies that benefit all women alike is not desirable. Not only does it eliminate strategies that can help non-poor women, it also leads to policy options that explicitly target and stigmatize the poor.[76] Others object to commodification of women's currently unpaid work and argue that paid work in the labour market is the only promising strategy.[77] Under this agenda, it is suggested that turning household work into paid work performed by others who are not members of the household is better, because it elevates paid labour market work to be the most valued objective. However, the strategies to ensure its full valuation are remote from the experience of

---

[73] Sotelo, P. H., 'Immigrant Women and Paid Domestic Work: Research, Theory and Activism', in H. Gottfried (ed.), *Feminism and Social Change: Bridging Theory and Practice* (Urbana & Chicago: University of Illinois Press, 1996), 105.

[74] Mackinnon, C., *Feminism Unmodified* (Cambridge, Mass.: Harvard University Press, 1987), 32–45.   [75] Williams, above, n. 57.

[76] Williams, J., 'Care as Work, Gender as Tradition', *Chicago-Kent Law Review*, 76 (2001), 1441, 1455.   [77] Shultz, V., 'Life's Work', *Columbia Law Review*, 100 (2000), 188.

live-ins, such as union organization, lobbying, solidarity, and asserting rights in the courtroom. It seems that without taking the class and the alienage components of the live-in's problem seriously, neither commodification nor decommodification matter. The problem is indeed gendered, but its solution cannot sidestep its class dimensions. A solution that does not address the real difficulties that can be attributed to these other dimensions of the problem is most likely to fail on its own gender-based terms. A solution that avoids the additional dimensions will eventually encounter resistance to the need fundamentally to change the meaning and valuation of women's work and of the 'third time'.

7

The Family Economy versus the Labour Market (or Housework as a Legal Issue)

MARIA ROSARIA MARELLA*

I INTRODUCTION

Freedom of contract is traditionally understood as the major mechanism of self-determination in private law. For this reason, when applied to domestic relations, it should enhance personal autonomy within the family as well and contribute to the modernization of family law and to its proximity to the market model. However, the legal regime governing family relations is traditionally seen as separate from the core of private law, the market, and freedom of contract, because it pursues a different goal—solidarity among individuals as opposed to exchange between them. This is true for the legal regime governing 'informal' domestic arrangements (cohabitation agreements) as well as for the regulation of married couples. In both cases, the position of spouses or partners is constructed as external to the market, and oriented towards the realization of the interests of the family, which, in turn, prevail over the interests of the individual parties.

This analysis challenges such a representation on two bases. The first point is that the solidarity paradigm survives, both in legal rules and social stereotypes, in spite of the progressive reorientation of family law regimes toward the paradigm of private ordering. The solidarity model continues to play a role within the legal regime governing unmarried couples and 'legitimate' families, beginning with the construction of a rigid opposition between (unpaid) housework and (paid) market work. This means that an egalitarian conception of the family is constantly being superseded by an opposing tendency to construe gender roles rigidly, and in a way which posits them as natural to the spouses. The second point is that freedom of contract is *not* the solution, as long as it implies a gender-blind approach. Too often—in legislation, case law, as well as in scholarly analysis—the shift in family law from a patriarchal, communitarian paradigm to a market paradigm represents the husband

* I am indebted to Kerry Rittich and Daniela Caruso for the English editing of an earlier draft. A special thanks to Karl Klare for inviting me to the INTELL6 conference in Catania, Italy, June 2002.

and wife, and men and women, as neutral bargaining parties. It does not take into account how deeply social and legal norms, ranging from gender roles to the opposition between paid and unpaid work as a consequence of the family/market dichotomy, affect the bargaining power of men and women within the family, the market, and society.

This chapter will consider the extent to which freedom of contract *can* be consistent with cultural and social change in family relations. To what extent can private ordering within the family equal self-determination and social enhancement for men and women, both in terms of personal liberty and wealth redistribution? As we shall see, the legal status of housework proves to be crucial here.

II SOLIDARITY V. EXCHANGE IN THE REGULATION OF UNMARRIED COUPLES

With respect to unmarried couples, the separation of the family from the market was first constructed as an opposition between particular domestic arrangements and good mores. In many western legal systems, in Italy as well as in the traditional common law countries, cohabitation agreements were considered void on grounds of public policy; a man's promise financially to support his partner during and after the end of the relationship was conceived of as consideration for the sexual performance of the woman. Such promises were held to be unenforceable because they were rooted in a meretricious relationship. This mode of interpretation has been superseded to an extent as freedom of contract has entered into the analysis. However, in the courts' perception, there is still a fundamental difference between cohabitation agreements and market transactions. The ambivalence of the feminine—housewife on one side, prostitute on the other—still informs judicial discourse and adjudication.

As recently as 1986, the Italian Supreme Court stated that the economic loss suffered by a prostitute as a consequence of physical injury could not be assessed according to her actual income, which was the result of illegitimate transactions established in violation of public policy, but had to be estimated on the basis of the average monthly income of a housewife.[1] Here solidarity plays a role. In the Italian legal system, for instance, cohabitation agreements are, or might be, enforceable as long as they are grounded on a *causa*, a notion roughly comparable with the

---

[1] The amount was assessed on the basis of the social subsidy provided by the state and conferred in some circumstances on non-working people or those performing unpaid work like housewives; Cass., 1 agosto 1986, n. 4927, in Foro it., 1987, I, 493.

common law doctrine of consideration. There is no doubt that valid consideration can be identified in the performance of everyday housework, while detriment can be located in the loss of professional opportunities in the labour market. Nevertheless, concerns about the protection of women are usually addressed outside the market and beyond the boundaries of freedom of contract. Where domestic arrangements are concerned, Italian courts mostly enforce the doctrine of moral obligation (*obbligazione naturale*, Art. 2034 c.c.), where solidarity, *not* bargaining, between the partners is the operative principle. Any transfer of money or conveyance of property between the couple, whether or not for the purpose of maintenance, is interpreted as the spontaneous performance of a moral or social duty inspired by a reciprocal sense of solidarity between the partners. Consequently, there is no enforceable agreement, whatever the original intention of the parties. The only legal effect of this moral obligation is that the payment or the object of the performance can be retained. For example, an Italian court rejected the claim of a woman who had lent a large amount of money to her partner when he was experiencing financial troubles and who subsequently sought to retrieve the money from his heirs upon his death. The court denied that there had ever been a loan, and held that the true ground for the transfer of money was the woman's sense of solidarity with her companion in the framework of their relationship; a moral rather than contractual obligation was in the background.[2] The extreme results of this mode of interpretation in decisions regarding the legal qualification of working activities within the family are discussed further below.

The English 'natural love and affection' model

In most common law jurisdictions, even in the absence of express contracts, equitable remedies like constructive trusts and proprietary estoppel are available to ground compensation for unpaid work and material contributions to the family unit upon the dissolution of the relationship. Here reliance is crucial. Thanks to both remedies, a non-marital partner might be entitled to an equitable share in property accumulated during the relationship, especially in respect of the family home. Apparently, neither concerns for the position of the economically weaker partner, nor an implicit move towards the legal recognition of unmarried couples, are the basis of judicial reasoning in this area. Rather, equitable remedies like proprietary estoppel are available only because of unconscionable conduct on the part of the promissor. In other words, courts are not operating according to a family law *rationale*; rather, legal

---

[2] Cass., 3 febbraio 1975, n. 389, in Foro it., 1975, I, 2301.

protection results exclusively from the application of equitable remedies. Nevertheless, the family/market opposition, as mirrored in the distinction between unpaid and paid work, is still pervasive. The equitable remedy of proprietary estoppel is available, as long as the partner who relied on the promise to share the family property has suffered a detriment as a result of her reliance. The manner in which English courts identify detriment is similar to the Italian notion of the moral obligation between unmarried couples. The solidarity model operates by means of the English doctrine of *natural love and affection*. That is, every kind of work and contribution to the family unit which can be interpreted as a 'natural' expression of love and affection between partners will not be considered a detriment for the purposes of triggering an action of proprietary estoppel. Obviously, typical expressions of natural love and affection are the usual tasks of the housewife—housework and childcare. Accordingly, these activities are not relevant for the purposes of proprietary estoppel: housework equals unpaid work, and women's gender roles continue to be situated outside the market. Conversely, financial contributions towards the purchase of a house as well as typical masculine activities like fixing a fence, building a brick wall around the garden, etc. *are* regarded as a detriment. Consequently, legal protection is here clearly grounded on the distinction between market-like and non-market-like transactions based on love, affection, and solidarity. This reproduces the female/male opposition, both in the family and the labour market. It is not surprising that in an English case involving a gay male couple,[3] the usual categorization was dropped out of a belief that a man's work as a waiter in the restaurant of his partner was part of a labour market transaction.

The stereotype of the home as 'the abiding place of the affections'[4] and the 'currency of familial emotions'[5] also affect the way in which the American legal system conceptualizes housework, both within and outside the marriage. Notably, housework is *not* considered work even if the spouses have negotiated an hourly wage to be paid by the husband for the wife's homemaking. In a recent case, the court refused to treat housework as employment, that is, as paid work, because of the familial context. Specifically, the court decided that the contract between husband and wife lacked consideration because 'the economic exchange between them would be purely illusory'.[6] In the court's reasoning, work performed in the family home is inherently external to the market realm: the woman's labour is conceptualized as the object of her prior obligation

---

[3] *Wayling* v. *Jones* [1995] 2 FLR 1029, CA.

[4] *State* v. *Bachmann*, 521 N. W. 2d 886, 888 (Minn. Ct. App. 1994) citing *State* v. *Cooper*, 285 N. W. 903, 904–5 (Minn. 1939).

[5] Silbaugh, K., 'Turning Labor Into Love: Housework and the Law', *Northwestern U. L. Rev.*, 91 (1996), 1, 4ff.   [6] *State* v. *Bachmann*, above, n. 4, 888.

toward her family. Consequently, the spouses had not shown that their
wage agreement resulted in gain or loss to either person.

(Not only) housework equals solidarity in Italian case law

In this respect Italian case law is even more strict in defining a sharp
boundary between paid and unpaid work. Acts performed in the framework of a *more uxorio* relationship[7] are held to be grounded in *affectionis vel
benevolentiae causa* (that is, made 'in consideration of love and affection')
and should not be remunerated. In fact, unless the performer proves that
a proper labour contract was established between the parties, the court
will presume that because of their intimate relationship, the work was
intended to be gratuitous. For example, a woman who had been working for years as a nurse in the consulting room of a doctor was held to
be no longer entitled to her salary from the moment she became engaged
in a *more uxorio* relationship with the doctor.[8] In the *ratio decidendi* of the
Supreme Court, notions of 'solidarity' and 'gratitude' were crucial in
setting aside the presumption of paid work. In fact, the normal legal presumption was flipped in this context: in order to establish her case, the
plaintiff had to prove she *was* a regular employee. In more recent cases,
women's work in their partners' enterprises is normally characterized as
unpaid. We find the same *ratio* in the case of a woman who had been
working for a long time in her partner's fish-breeding factory[9] and in the
case of a woman who not only had been working on her partner's farm,
but had also lent him money. In both cases, there was no remuneration
and no money back;[10] everything melts into the blob of solidarity.

III AGREEMENTS IN CONTEMPLATION OF DIVORCE AND THE
FAMILY/MARKET DISTINCTION

This section briefly analyses the effect of a market or private ordering
paradigm in contrast to the solidarity paradigm in the framework of
marriage, with specific reference to the enforceability of prenuptial
agreements in contemplation of divorce.

The family law regime is widely believed to be situated at the
periphery of private law and external to the legal structures governing

---

[7] i.e. a 'relationship between cohabiting partners acting like spouses'.
[8] Cass., 7 luglio 1979, n. 4221, in Foro it., 1979, I, 2315.
[9] Cass., 17 febbraio 1988, n. 1701, in Foro it., 1988, I, 2306; see also Cass., sez. Lav., 14
giugno 1990, n. 5803.
[10] Trib. Torino, 24 novembre 1990, in Giur. it., 1992, I, 2, 428, n. OBERTO.

the market—contract, property, and tort law. As far as they impinge on family law rather than market transactions, each of these private law institutions follows different rules. This is the case because, in the family law framework, relations between individuals are supposed to be shaped by the solidarity paradigm. And the solidarity paradigm is, indeed, expected to be fulfilled by the law—whether in a legislative or judicial context—through the mechanism of familial *status* as opposed to freedom of contract.

In the Italian legal system, patrimonial transactions between spouses are not included in the general notion of contract. Moreover, the structure of marital property is defined by mandatory rules. According to the Civil Code, spouses can choose between different regimes: shared property or separate property. However, their choice as to regime does not amount to a contract. On the contrary, it is consistent with the notion of *Rechtsgeschaeft*: an empty box in which all other agreements, whether involving patrimonial issues or not, as well as declarations of will other than contracts can be accommodated. Through this technical strategy, familial agreements on marital property are not governed according to a market paradigm. In other words, the position of the spouses, unlike in the market, is defined by mandatory rules based upon personal and inalienable status whose entitlements and obligations can barely be modified at will. Moreover, although the spouses can establish agreements on personal or patrimonial issues, these agreements are much less stable than regular contracts, in so far as they can only be enforced as long as the circumstances upon which they were entered into do not change. In fact, they are presumed to be grounded in solidarity rather than in the individual allocation of risk.

Within this framework, prenuptial agreements are considered void by Italian courts because they treat marital status as a commodity. The legal regime governing divorce cannot be derogated from, as long as it promotes, and establishes, a bond of 'post-marital' solidarity. It is debatable whether Italian divorce law, as opposed to freedom of contract, truly promotes solidarity between the former spouses. A divorce regime may be more likely to promote solidarity if it considers not only the wife's domestic contribution but also her investments in the human capital of her husband as assets to be shared upon the dissolution of marriage. However, this is not the view taken by Italian courts, where the alimony obligation is usually not assessed on the basis of the husband's earnings and career prospects, even though they can also be regarded as a product of the wife's labour. This is the reason why contracts may be useful instruments to remedy defects in the existing scheme of family entitlements. I will return to this point below.

IV THE CONTRACTUALIZATION OF THE MARITAL RELATIONSHIP: FREEDOM OF CONTRACT V. FAIRNESS?

Let us go now to my second point: the extent to which freedom of contract is a possible answer to issues of self-determination in family law. Towards this end, it is helpful to consider the American model in contrast to the Italian model. In the United States of America, freedom of contract within marriage is largely unquestioned and American courts regularly enforce support-waiver agreements. Particularly since the enactment of the Uniform Premarital Agreements Act (UPAA) in 1983, few doubt that freedom of contract between spouses is almost limitless, at least concerning economic matters. The question that arises is no longer to what extent the family law regime differs from the market and contract law, but rather, whether freedom of contract within the framework of marriage promotes gender justice or, conversely, produces new forms of female exploitation. This is a thorny topic, which has been the subject of intense exploration on the part of feminist legal scholars. Certainly, a family law regime based on status leads to rigid gender roles which are hard to shake off. On the other hand, the mere move towards the market is not sufficient to free women from those gender roles, and the social stereotypes, that heavily affect their bargaining power in relation to men.[11]

One of the original aims of feminist scholars was to bridge the gap between the family law regime and the market by revealing the ideological roots of the family/market dichotomy.[12] This analysis disclosed the family's proximity to the market by demonstrating, for instance, that both institutions have been alternatively ruled by the same policies, *laissez-faire* and state intervention, although in different moments of their recent history. For this reason, solidarity cannot be seen as a value exclusively epitomizing the family realm, as both individualism and altruism underpin the law of contracts on the one hand,[13] while familial relations and dynamics are likely to reveal egoistic motives on the other.[14] Thus, the internal diversity of both family and market values plainly reveals the inadequacy of traditional explanations.

[11] In the European literature, see e.g. Frost, L., 'The Deregulated Sex: On the Privatization of Marriage', in R. de Lange and K. Roes (eds.), *Plural Legalities: Critical Legal Studies in Europe* (den Haag: Recht en Kritiek, 1991), 43.
[12] Olsen, F., 'The Family and the Market: A Study of Ideology and Legal Reform', *Harv. L. Rev.*, 96 (1983), 1497.
[13] Kennedy, D., 'Form and Substance in Private Law Adjudication', *Harv. L. Rev.*, 89 (1976), 1685.
[14] Rhode, D., *Justice and Gender* (Cambridge, MA: Harvard University Press, 1991).

However, the dichotomy continues to influence courts and legislatures and impose severe costs on women. From the marginalization of the family with respect to the marketplace springs the rigidity of gender roles within the family and its hierarchical internal order, as well as the unequal footing of men and women in the marketplace. Although they are construed as segregated, the economies of the household and the market are strongly interdependent in ways that mutually reinforce their inner structures of inequality. As a result, the strict division of labour between men and women within the former context heavily influences employment, career, and earning opportunities of men and women in the latter.[15] Moreover, the strict social roles that are triggered by family legal structure further disempower women by forcing them into rigid identities of 'mothers' and 'wives' that limit their social mobility, their life prospects, and their personal liberty within and outside the family.[16]

The deconstruction of the family/market dichotomy strategically aims at breaking up the vicious circle that incessantly reproduces these patterns of gender inequality within society. However, the outcomes of the 'contractualization' of family relations, as the diffuse enforcement of the UPAA in the USA indicates, show that freedom of contract has not empowered women.[17] If, in theory, freedom of contract has redistributive potential in the framework of family life, in reality it has not had this effect thus far. More precisely, freedom of contract does not appear to promote a fair distribution of family wealth between the sexes. In addition, when enforcing freedom of contract in family matters, courts do not consider wealth redistribution as an issue! In the era of the contractualization of family relations, the formalist, gender-blind approach prevails on the grounds of promoting fairness. In the transition from illegal transactions to ordinary contracts, the enforcement of marital agreements is now supported by the formal equality of the contracting parties and by the rational choice principle. If courts engage a will theory perspective, there is no reason to treat the parties differently; whatever each party has bargained for is presumed to result from his or her own rational choice in accordance with individual wealth maximization.

[15] Willikens, H., 'Law, Gender Relations and the Interdependence of Exchange Economy and Household Economy', in de Lange and Roes, above, n. 11, 158; Rittich, K., 'Feminization and Contingency: Regulating the Stakes of Work for Women', in J. Conaghan, R. M. Fischl, and K. Klare (eds.), *Labour Law in an Era of Globalization* (Oxford: OUP, 2002), 117.

[16] Frug, M. J., 'A Manifesto: A Postmodern Feminist Legal Manifesto (An Unfinished Draft)', *Harv. L. Rev.*, 105 (1992), 1045.

[17] Atwood, B., 'Ten Years Later: Lingering Concerns about the Uniform Premarital Agreement Act', *J. Legisl.*, 19 (1993), 127; Brod, G., 'Premarital Agreements and Gender Justice', *Yale J. Law & Feminism*, 6 (1994), 229; Silbaugh, K., 'Marriage Contracts and the Family Economy', *Northwestern U. L. Rev.*, 93 (1998), 65; Younger, J. T., 'Ante-nuptial Agreements', *William Mitchell L. Rev.*, 28 (2001), 697.

In the last decade, American case law has moved in this direction. When the American courts began to enforce prenuptial agreements, they generally adopted the 'fairness approach' which involved the implementation of protective doctrines such as unconscionability, misrepresentation, and duress. To be sure, courts at the same time claimed to be in favour of both the private ordering of the family *and* the requirements of substantive justice in family relations. The effect of this policy was to submit marital agreements to both a substantive and a procedural test of fairness in order to prevent the weaker party from being worse off as a result of the contractual arrangement. However, over time, freedom of contract in family matters tended to be interpreted in a more formalistic way: women's formal equality in the labour market became the argument according to which it was possible to dismiss any protective doctrines in favour of the rational choice paradigm.[18] The jurisprudence under the UPAA, now adopted by roughly half of the states, has also moved steadily towards a point at which a substantively unfair agreement is much less likely to be invalidated. According to the provisions of section 6 (a)(2) of the UPAA, substantive unconscionability does not affect the enforceability of an agreement unless there is evidence of inadequate knowledge of the other party's financial position or of the parties' legal entitlements. That is, a substantively unfair agreement is enforceable, regardless of the financial or emotional position of the party who agreed to it, if no misrepresentation of any kind can be proven.[19]

The enforcement of cohabitation agreements also reflects this trend. The leading case, *Marvin* v. *Marvin*,[20] affirmed the enforceability of cohabitation agreements by highlighting their similarity to ordinary contracts, commercial transactions included. Since *Marvin*, courts have tried to connect domestic agreements to formal requirements which have the consequence of favouring the stronger bargaining party.

In Germany, courts have been moving in the opposite direction. Prenuptial agreements, support waivers included, are legal and enforceable

---

[18] *Simeone* v. *Simeone*, 581 A.2d 162, Pa. 1990.

[19] The UPAA's disregard of the difference between pre-marital and commercial contracts (especially when 'viewed against the backdrop of persistent gender inequality in the market-place') has been criticized by the Supreme Court of California: *In re Marriage of Susan and Barry Bonds*, 83 Cal. Rptr.2d 783 (1999). In 1998, the American Law Institute (ALI) produced the *Principles of the Law of Family Dissolution*. Chapter 7 of the ALI Principles is a compendium of new guiding policies to govern financial contracting between prospective spouses. It is very different in policy from the UPAA. It aims to realize a new balance between free-dom of contract and fairness, starting from the different treatment of pre-marital contracts with respect to commercial contracts. See Levy, R. J., 'Pre-nuptial Contracts: The American Law Institute's Principles of the Law of Family Dissolution', online at www.civil.udg.es; Bix, B. H., 'Pre-marital Agreements in the ALI Principles of Family Dissolution', *Duke J. of Gender Law & Policy*, 8 (2001), 231.

[20] 18 Cal.3d 660, 134 Cal Rptr. 815, 557 P.2d 106 (1976).

and regulated by the Civil Code. In the past, the German Supreme Court generally adopted a formalistic approach to enforcing these contracts, treating them as expressions of the will of equal parties no matter how unfair their content.[21] However, recently the German Constitutional Court has intervened on the grounds that unfairness in contract law violates the individual right to self-determination and conflicts with Article 2 of the Constitution.[22]

V BARGAINING AND GENDER

There are further structural reasons why freedom of contract in the family context does not fulfil redistributive expectations. As previously noted, both inside as well as outside the family realm, bargaining power is not equally distributed between men and women. This is a result of gendered stereotypes, social roles, and the way that legal regimes create and/or reproduce them, mainly through the family/market dichotomy.[23] Beyond formalistic trends in case law, this inequality in bargaining power helps to explain why freedom of contract *in action* fails to increase women's standard of wealth after divorce.[24]

Bargaining in the shadow of the law

A first, intuitive answer is that the legal regime governing marital property and divorce constructs men's, and women's, freedom of contract and their respective bargaining positions within the market context.[25] In other

---

[21] Dauner-Lieb, S., 'Rechweite und Grenzen der Privatautonomie im Ehevertragsrecht', *Archiv fuer die Civilistische Praxis*, 201 (2001), 295.   [22] BVerfG, 6.2.2001.

[23] Olsen, above, n. 12. For an analysis of the dichotomy between paid and unpaid work as a social construction, see Rittich, above, n. 15, 126 ff.

[24] See Willikens, above, n. 15, 165 ff. for an analysis of possible legal reform strategies that aim to change the gendered division of labour by focusing on the institutions of contract and property.

[25] In all transactions and social relations, individuals' bargaining power is heavily affected by the legal rules operating in the background. Law is a crucial factor in determining the distribution of income between social classes as well as playing a role in the distributive conflict between men and women. In particular, background legal rules structure the alternatives that are open to the parties in given bargaining situations. For example, marriage provisions on maintenance obligations can make unskilled labour less attractive to women and cause them to demand more from their employers to keep them in the labour market. By contrast, making divorce easier may reduce women's bargaining power with employers by reducing their security outside the labour market. Therefore, the family legal regime as well as equal treatment provisions in the labour market are capable of affecting the relations between men and women within and outside the family, between employers and employees, between workers of opposite genders, between husbands and wives, etc. See further Kennedy, D., 'The Stakes of Law, or Hale and Foucault!', *Legal Studies Forum*, 15 (1991), 327.

words, spouses bargain in the shadow of the law.[26] Statutory laws promote solidarity between the spouses to the extent that the spouse without financial resources is entitled to alimony after the divorce. However, they do not reward domestic work or, more generally, house-wives' contributions to the family welfare in the same way the labour market would. In this way, divorce regimes also reinforce the unpaid/paid work distinction, which, in turn, reflects the family/market dichotomy.

In Italy, statutory law entitles the wife to post-divorce financial support if she is not financially self-sufficient. But the actual amount due is assessed according to the couple's standard of living during the marriage. An increase in the husband's standard of living after divorce will only be taken into account by the court if it is the 'natural and foreseeable' outcome of the wife's activity. Accordingly, the real amount turns out to be uncertain, since it is based on discretionary distinctions between relevant and irrelevant activities which, in turn, reproduce the opposition discussed above between market-like and non-market-like arrangements.[27]

Obviously these background rules will influence the content of the prenuptial agreement; it is extremely unlikely that the party with greater bargaining power, usually the husband, will offer the weaker party, usually the wife, better conditions than those required by statutory law.

Bargaining in the shadow of the market

A second possible answer is that spouses also bargain in the shadow of the market, meaning that their bargaining position within the marriage is influenced by the alternatives open to them outside the marriage.

Bargaining theory holds that an individual's bargaining power is a product of the alternatives available to her or him in the market. For prenuptial agreements, this includes both the labour market and the 'marriage market'. Thus, the bargaining power of the wife with regard to the possible dissolution of the marital relationship is deeply influenced by her ability either to be economically independent after divorce or to enter a new and profitable marriage. According to a recent American study,[28] both prospects are much more favourable for men than for women. Thus, it is unlikely that a woman who is outside the labour market or who has reduced her professional commitments because of her domestic duties will be able to find a job whose income allows her to maintain the same standard of living as she experienced during the marriage.

---

[26] Mnookin, R. and Kornhauser, L., 'Bargaining in the Shadow of the Law: The Case of Divorce', *Yale L. J.*, 88 (1979), 950.

[27] Cass., 20 marzo 1998, n. 2955, in I contratti, 1998, 472.

[28] Wax, A. L., 'Bargaining in the Shadow of the Market: Is There a Future for Egalitarian Marriage?', *Virginia L. Rev.*, 84 (1998), 509.

Moreover, cultural factors seem to prevent women from bargaining at the same level as men in contemplation of divorce. They also affect the potential for an egalitarian marriage. It is a commonplace that women 'age' earlier than men and that they become less attractive marriage partners as beauty, sex appeal, and reproductive capabilities fade away. In addition, as women usually retain custody of children after divorce, their chances of a new profitable marriage are further reduced. A shortage of favourable alternatives in the marriage market renders women weaker than men on the bargaining scene.

The 'snowball' effect

I now wish briefly to summarize my points in order to highlight how the family/market and unpaid/paid work oppositions can have a 'snowball' effect on women's position in society.

The original exclusion of women from the market, through the characterization of domesticity as women's 'proper' realm, has affected women's bargaining potential in so far as it has produced deeply rooted social stereotypes.[29] Legal rules and social biases create what Carol Rose calls the presumption of 'women's greater taste for cooperation'.[30] If solidarity is the paradigm of family relations and the family law regime, and if domesticity is women's natural sphere, so women's solidaristic attitude works inside and outside the family, the market, and the workplace to generate a set of cultural assumptions which lead people to *think* that women are more naturally cooperative. This ultimately affects the gendered allocation of assets. Let us consider some examples. First, in a market transaction with a man, a woman is supposed to care more than her contractual partner about the relationship. Whether or not this is true, she will bear the costs of keeping the contractual relationship alive and, as a consequence, the deal will cost her more. She may be better off because of it, but not *as much* better off as her partner. Also, because of her lower share of the outcome of past bargains, the woman already has relatively fewer assets than the man and is a riskier prospect for a lender. In order to secure a loan, she may have to put more money down or pay higher interest rates or face other unfavourable terms. This pattern could have considerable effects on assets and entitlements in a number of areas. Secondly, let us consider now the domestic economy of housework.

---

[29] As I emphasize in this section, the behaviour and attitudes of private actors in their institutional/professional roles, as well as social stereotypes and the legal rules that affect them, also have a disciplinary effect. See Kennedy, above, n. 25.

[30] Rose, C., 'Women and Property: Gaining and Losing Ground', *Virginia L. Rev.*, 78 (1992), 421. (1992); ead., 'Bargaining and Gender', *Harv. J. L. & Pub. Policy*, 18 (1994), 547. The arguments presented immediately below draw from Rose's article.

Because of her cooperative inclinations, the wife (or unmarried partner) will invest more than the husband in their common welfare and, as a result, will contribute more to the domestic economy. So, the reward for her cooperation is negative. Thirdly, consider the labour market. For many reasons, women's taste for cooperation can make them less attractive than men to prospective employers. Men's reputation for toughness or meanness (as opposed to cooperativeness) can make them appear more stable and reliable. Additionally, an employer may take into account a woman's sense of obligations to third parties, especially children.[31] In particular, because men are not usually engaged in unpaid work and are not often required to stay at home to take care of the children, they may appear more attractive to employers. Finally, there is a more profound reason why a man may look better to the employer: he may appear to be a stronger candidate and better educated because he *might actually* be a stronger candidate and better educated. Women's supposed cooperativeness—because it is not rewarded in the marriage or in the market—can induce others, especially family members, to invest less in women's human capital. Men's better chance of success can persuade families to invest more in their sons' rather than their daughters' education. This reduced investment can, in turn, impede women's chances to develop professional skills that would increase their employability. As a result, women will have fewer chances of profitable employment and poorer alternatives to marriage. Without attractive alternatives, a woman is more likely to enter a non-egalitarian marriage where she will be engaged in unpaid housework to a much greater extent than her spouse. Her commitment to the household will further reduce her prospective chances in the labour market. Consequently she will have less bargaining power than her husband within the marriage as well.

VI BEYOND A GENDER-BLIND APPROACH: FREEDOM OF CONTRACT, RECOGNITION, REDISTRIBUTION

Let us go back to the last critical question: can the privatization or contractualization of family relations redistribute power and assets between men and women? Could it promote self-determination in family relations? If rigid solidarity/bargain, family/market dichotomies reinforce the opposition between unpaid and paid work and eventually the construction of male and female identities within society, can the

---

[31] Rose, C., 'Women and Property: Gaining and Losing Ground', *Virginia L. Rev.*, 78 (1992), 421. (1992); ead., 'Bargaining and Gender', *Harv. J. L. & Pub. Policy*, 18 (1994), 547. The arguments presented immediately below draw from Rose's article.

privatization of the family and the move to freedom of contract promote social change, by breaking up the rigidity of gendered social roles and redistributing resources and social power between genders?

Currently, scholarly discussion around domestic agreements, and particularly pre-marital agreements, concerns, on the one hand, the degree of protection for women as weaker parties in the transaction[32] and, on the other hand, the conception of contract that does or should underpin the private ordering of family relations.[33] I believe that the issues are closely related. This is because the problem of women's protection/exploitation in family matters is an instance of the 'difference dilemma'.[34] This dilemma—the impossible alternative between women's formal equality and women's substantive difference—reproduces the solidarity/bargain opposition; it will continue to do so as long as the solution is sought in the tough alternative between legislative paternalism and freedom of contract. As such, I would rather deal with the second crucial question: what kind of balance between freedom of contract and fairness can we establish in contract law?

Freedom of contract as the right to self-determination

The problem of fairness in contract law was openly faced by the German Constitutional Court for the first time in 1993[35] and more recently in 2001,[36] specifically with respect to marital agreements. In the latter case, the suit concerned a prenuptial contract waiving spousal and child support obligations after divorce. The woman was pregnant and already had a child at the time she gave her consent to the arrangement. The Court held that the contract was unfair and void because it violated the woman's freedom of contract as an expression of her fundamental right to self-determination protected by Article 2 of the German Constitution. As the Court affirmed, contractual terms cannot conflict with fundamental rights. Valid and enforceable contracts flow from each party's free will and self-determination; conversely, unfair contractual terms are the outcome of one party's interests imposed upon the other and amount to an unjust infringement of the other party's right to self-determination.

In fact, substantive inequality, in the form of different economic and social conditions, produces unfair transactions. In the most recent

---

[32] Cossman, B., 'A Matter of Difference: Domestic Contracts and Gender Equality', *Osgoode Hall L. J.*, 28 (1990), 305.

[33] Scott, R. E. and Scott, E., 'Marriage as Relational Contract', *Virginia L. Rev.*, 84 (1998), 1225.

[34] Cossman, above, n. 32, and Minow, M., *Making all the Difference* (Cambridge, MA: Harvard University Press, 1992).   [35] BVerfG, 19.10.1993.

[36] BVerfG, 6.2.2001, in NJW, 2001, 957; BVerfG, 29.3.2001.

decision on the matter, the Court explicitly referred to the traditional family, which is characterized by conventional gender roles and a sharp distinction between housework and 'breadwinning', as the typical context for unfair agreements and fundamental rights violations.[37] The same decision concludes by stating the existence of a duty on judges to oversee the content of contracts as part of their broader obligations in relation to safeguarding fundamental rights. I would argue that this approach is a fair starting point toward a non-gender-blind approach to domestic contracts, although one could challenge such a doctrine on the grounds that it undermines certainty in transactions of this nature.

Freedom of contract and recognition

In the framework of fair arrangements, freedom of contract can enhance personal liberty and promote social change. In recent times, it has become increasingly common to assume that courts should enforce contracts with respect to all types of social relations, as long as they do not break conventional moral standards and do not frustrate norms of fairness.[38] In this light, 'contracts should be regarded as a facility for expanding valuable choices and as providing the necessary security for the pursuit of more detailed plans in life'.[39]

For unconventional couples or families—including but not limited to same-sex couples—the adoption of a private ordering paradigm for domestic relations can produce a higher degree of freedom: through contract, the parties are able to shape the meaning of their relationship and determine the terms on which they wish to live together. According to lesbian legal theory,[40] for example, the enforceability of cohabitation contracts forces the legal system to recognize unmarried couples, especially same-sex couples, endowing them with legal significance without defining those relationships or imposing authoritative regulation upon them. Interestingly, freedom of contract here stands for *recognition*[41] and works as a surrogate for status. What about redistribution?

[37] A path-breaker and supporter of a non-gender-blind approach in German scholarship has been Schwenzer, I., 'Vertragsfreiheit im Ehevermoegens- und Scheidungsfolgenrecht', *Archiv fuer die Civilistische Praxis*, 196 (1996).

[38] Collins, H., *The Law of Contracts* (London: Butterworths, 2003), 96.   [39] Ibid., 103.

[40] Testy, K. Y., 'An Unlikely Resurrection', *Northwestern U. L. Rev.*, 90 (1995), 219.

[41] I am referring here, and in the following section, to Nancy Fraser's identification of recognition and redistribution as the two main policies of emancipation, egalitarianism, and political contestation over the last few decades (Fraser, S. N., 'Rethinking Recognition', *New Left Review*, 3 (May–June 2000).

Redistribution and freedom of contract

What happens in terms of redistribution when the legal regime governing
the family embraces a market-like model and the individual positions of
the members of the family are defined through freedom of contract?
I believe that prenuptial agreements, unlike cohabitation contracts, can
promote wealth enhancement and social change mainly through a fairer
redistribution of resources between the spouses.

Redistribution in contract law is a critical question, although one that
is often misrepresented or disregarded as an issue in private law
adjudication. As space precludes consideration of the issue in detail, I will
simply recall what Duncan Kennedy,[42] Hugh Collins,[43] and other scholars
have masterfully demonstrated, which is that even apparently neutral
and merely technical rules in contract law have redistributive effects
between the parties. My only aim here is to stress that the contractualization of domestic relations would not necessarily undermine family
values such as love, affection, and solidarity. Solidarity is not the
prerogative of the domestic realm, nor is altruism. As Duncan Kennedy
has pointed out, contract law embodies a continuous tension between
individualism and altruism.[44] In long-term contractual relations, for
instance, obligations of fair dealing, cooperation, and reciprocity prevail
over the strict observance of contractual terms.[45] Solidarity and altruism,
to the extent that they mean taking into account the reliance of one party
on the other party's promises and behaviour, are values that families
share with contracting parties in the market.

Solidarity in the market does not only mean that freedom of contract
finds its 'natural' limits in the protection of others' fundamental rights,
in accordance with a formalistic interpretation of German constitutional
jurisprudence. Rather, it represents an alternative to the model of autonomy according to which contractual parties are seen as the bearers of
equal rights. In fact, although the image of freedom of contract evokes
the vision of two people negotiating the terms of their agreement as
equals, 'in practice most contracts constitute the opportunity for one
party to create unilaterally a system of rules and governance structures
for the relation'.[46] As such, the election of an autonomy-based contractual theory rather than a 'solidarity' or relational model can be crucial in
terms of entitlements and the distribution of power.

---

[42] Kennedy, D., 'The Political Stakes in "Merely Technical" Issues of Contract Law',
European Review of Private Law, 1 (2001), 7; Italian translation: 'La funzione ideologica del
tecnicismo nel diritto dei contratti' in *Riv. critica del diritto privato* (2002), 317.
[43] Collins, H., *Regulating Contracts* (Oxford: OUP, 1999).   [44] Kennedy, above, n. 13.
[45] Collins, above, n. 38, 104.   [46] Ibid., 105.

Let us consider the example of the unconscionability regime in the American UPAA and compare it with its counterpart in the American Uniform Commercial Code (UCC). I have already illustrated how the UPAA provisions have marginalized the role of unconscionability and other protective doctrines. In this respect it seems that the rhetoric of *laissez-faire* and the sovereignty of the will of the parties is more determinative in family law matters than in the market realm. The provisions of Article 2 of the UCC on good faith and fair dealing in commercial matters allow the courts to refuse to enforce a contract if the contract itself or any clause within it is 'unconscionable at the time it was made'.[47] Unlike the UPAA provision, some courts have held under the UCC that substantive unconscionability renders the provision in question unenforceable *per se*; proof of misrepresentation to the disadvantaged party is not required. In general, case law under the UCC appears to be more flexible regarding procedural defects, avoiding the UPAA's rigid requirement of misrepresentation. Consequently, it seems that in American contract law, the weaker party may be more extensively protected in market transactions than in family agreements. Where should we now locate the solidarity v. exchange model in respect of the traditional family/market dichotomy?

Housework as consideration

I will pass quickly to my final point. Promises of financial support for the period after marriage or cohabitation are often unenforceable for lack of consideration. In Italian case law, one often reads about promises in favour of wives concerning further money or estates as integral parts of the financial support due according to the legal regime of divorce. However, these promises, although not necessarily violating the mandatory regime, are void on the basis that there is no *cause suffisante* in support of them. By disregarding the importance of housework, childcare and other unpaid contributions typically made by women to the family economy and treating them instead simply as instances of love and affection, the family/market conception plays a significant and detrimental role in women's position both within the family and the market. By contrast, these promises should be held as made in consideration of fundamental contributions to the family unit made by the wife across a range of contexts, in accordance with a recent Italian Supreme Court decision.[48] The case involved a complex transaction between spouses. When the marriage was close to the point of breakdown, the husband and wife entered into a marriage covenant

---

[47] § 2-302 UCC. See Bix, B., 'Bargaining in the Shadow of Love: The Enforcement of Premarital Agreements and How we Think about Marriage', *William and Mary L. Rev.*, 40 (1998), 145.   [48] Cass., 12 maggio 1999, n. 4716

excluding community of property; at the same time, under a separate agreement, the husband turned the family house that was under his exclusive ownership into a communal asset. The contract provided that the house had been built by both spouses together. After the divorce, the husband alleged that the agreement concerning the house was void for lack of consideration. The Supreme Court upheld the contract on a technical basis by considering the contribution of the wife to the construction of the house. No inquiry was requested by the court in order to assess the nature and extent of the wife's contribution.

The Canadian Supreme Court, ruling on the marital relation in a different doctrinal context, that of unjust enrichment, found the housekeeping and childcare services performed by the wife to be a benefit to the husband, as he received household services without compensation which, in turn, improved his ability to save money and increase his assets. The court also found that these services represented a detriment to the wife, in that she provided labour without compensation.[49] In English case law, childcare has been taken into account as the central element of consideration in a contract between two unmarried parents concerning child-rearing. In particular, the mother's promise to care for the child has been held to constitute a benefit conferred upon the father.[50] In Dutch case law, the doctrine of *unforeseen circumstances* has been employed in the evaluation of the wife's labour contributions in order to supersede the doctrine of moral obligation.[51]

As these cases indicate, the constitutive elements of consideration, benefit, and detriment are to be found in the reciprocal gains and losses produced in the household and valued within the complex, intricate web of constant exchanges, mutual giving, and support that characterize the family economy and the patrimonial relations between the spouses within it.

VII CONCLUSION

The analysis carried out in this chapter suggests that the contractual regulation of family matters does not necessarily alter the meaning of familial relations nor thwart exchanges of love, counselling, and emotional support among family members. On the contrary, contracts

---

[49] *Peter v. Beblow* [1993] 1 S.C.R. 98, (1993) S.C.J. No. 36, File No. 22258, cited in van der Burght, G., *Shortcomings of the Legislator of a Self Proclaimed Progressive Country*; online at http://civil.udg.es/isfl/EuropeanRegionalConference2003.

[50] *Ward v. Byham* [1956] 1 WLR 496, [1956] 2 All ER 776, CA. But see also Lord Denning's opinion in *Tanner v. Tanner* [1975] 1 WLR 1346, [1975] 3 All ER 776, CA, with reference to the father's obligations towards the mother in consideration of her childcare services.

[51] See van der Burght, above, n. 49, 10.

extend the opportunity to establish meaning in the social sphere of the family as long as they contribute to the pursuit of valuable plans of life. By permitting the construction of family obligations, contracts give greater specificity to people's choices within the family.[52] On the other hand, limits to private ordering in the family are justified as long as freedom of contract is used as an instrument of unfairness and exploitation. In this respect, it has been emphasized how a gender-blind approach to freedom of contract tends to reinforce patterns of inequality within the family and the marketplace.

To the extent that the contractual regulation of family relations is envisaged as a means for expanding free choice, throwing off rigid social roles *and* empowering (or not disempowering) weaker parties, contractual terms should be subjected to attentive scrutiny by courts.

In order to affirm progressive values in the legal system and society, not only should standards like fairness, reasonableness, and good faith be enforced. Although they are powerful tools for promoting social justice in contract law—good faith is generally regarded as the major device to promote contractual fairness—as I have shown above, in American case law, the unconscionability clause has also been profitably deployed for the purposes of securing contractual justice in pre-marital agreements. In a similar vein, the German Constitutional Court has referred to good faith and immorality in contract law as standards that the judge should implement in order to correct unfair distributive schemes and enhance the fundamental rights in agreements between prospective spouses.

However, the enforcement of mere technical rules[53] can also promote a move towards fairness and progressive social change in contract law, and their role in this respect should not be undervalued. The positive requirements of contract enforcement, the finding of consideration, and the intention of the parties to create a legal relation[54] have all been successfully utilized by courts to realize distributive objectives. In practice, all often involve the valuation of women's contributions to the household. The reappraisal of unpaid (house)work emerges as a central factor in realizing contractual fairness in family matters. It also proves to be a crucial issue in distributive conflicts between women and men.

---

[52] Collins, above, n. 38, 103.   [53] Kennedy, above, n. 13.

[54] In fact, this contractual element has been interpreted in opposing ways, in order to support the weaker party in a domestic contract: compare the enforcement of the implied-in-fact contract doctrine in *Marvin* (above, n. 20) with the denial of a party's contractual intention in *Balfour* v. *Balfour* [1919] 2 KB 571, CA.

8

Gender and Diversification of Labour Forms in Japan

MUTSUKO ASAKURA

I LABOUR IN THE POST-FORDISM ERA

The atypical labour problem is a women's problem

The worker image which has been considered the ideal model by labour laws in European countries is the male head of household. These workers have held relatively stable positions, and have worked in forms of labour that make it possible to earn a family wage (a wage high enough to support a family's livelihood).[1] But this worker model, under the Fordist production regime, faced major change in the 1970s. Specifically, forms of labour diversified as never before due to the growth of the tertiary production sector, the new heterogeneity of family structures, women's entry into the workforce, and the externalization of housework and child-raising labour.[2]

In the post-Fordism era, labour forms came to be divided into 'typical' and 'atypical', and the latter grew in all countries. Of course, there were differences in growth trends, depending on the type of atypical labour, because while part-time work started increasing in the 1980s, temporary and agency work began growing in the 1990s. Much of the cause for the growth of atypical labour lies with the labour demand side.[3] This is because international competition has intensified in conjunction with economic globalization, leading to a higher demand for labour that companies can use more flexibly; but the intention to cut personnel costs is an especially big reason. Also at work here are the needs of the labour supply side: it is said that women who choose part-time work of their own accord have a high degree of satisfaction in their work.[4]

---

[1] Supiot, A., *Beyond Employment: Changes in Work and the Future of Labour Law in Europe* (Oxford: OUP, 2001), 24–5. [2] Ibid., 177.
[3] Houseman, S. and Osawa, M. (eds.), *Hataraki-kata no Mirai* (*How People Will Work in the Future: A Comparison of Atypical Labour in Japan, the US and Europe*) (Tokyo: Japan Labour Research Institute, 2003), 6.
[4] A study of individuals in 15 EU countries indicated that about 60% of part-time workers chose this form of employment voluntarily (see ibid., 8).

Meanwhile, the gender division of labour is still deeply rooted and heavily influences the real world and the home, both institutionally and consciously. As such, the growth of atypical labour has an especially big influence on women workers. Relative to women, many men still have typical jobs that are stable and offer comparatively high compensation, while women have increasingly ended up in unstable and poorly compensated atypical jobs. Unless this social construct, known as the gender division of labour, is shaken to its very foundation, events will naturally follow this course. It is overwhelmingly women workers who have suffered the disadvantages that arise from atypical work, and thus it can be said that the problem of atypical labour is a women's problem.

Women's work in Japan

The same phenomenon has occurred in Japan but several characteristics of Japanese labour trends emerge in a comparison with European countries. Let us begin by exploring the changes in the structure of the working population and in the diversification of employment forms over the last thirty years. The percentage of employees in the Japanese working population as a whole (employees, self-employed workers, and family workers) has consistently increased over the last three decades, so that from being around 60 per cent in the 1970s, it has been over 80 per cent since 1995. On the other hand, while close to 20 per cent of these workers were self-employed in the 1970s, the same three-decade period saw that figure drop roughly by half. Similarly, by 2000, the percentage of family workers had dropped to about one-third of that in 1970 (see Figure 8.1).

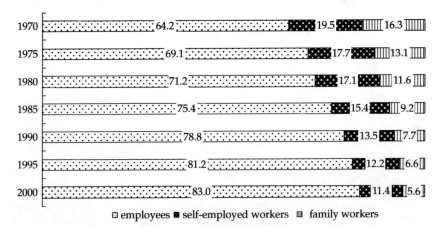

☐ employees ▨ self-employed workers ▥ family workers

FIGURE 8.1: *Japanese working population by status (male and female)*
Source: Statistics Bureau, Japanese Ministry of Internal Affairs and Communications

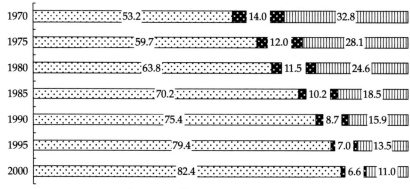

☒ employees ■ self-employed workers ⅏ family workers

FIGURE 8.2: *Japanese working population by status (female)*
Source: Statistics Bureau, Japanese Ministry of Internal Affairs and Communications

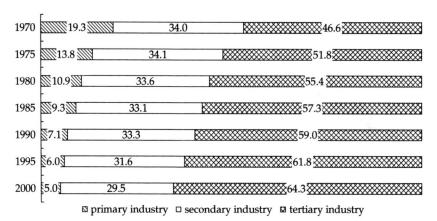

⊠ primary industry ☐ secondary industry ⊠ tertiary industry

FIGURE 8.3: *Japanese working population by industry (major groups)*
Source: Statistics Bureau, Japanese Ministry of Internal Affairs and Communications

As these changes proceeded, the status of women workers changed greatly, exhibiting a shift away from family workers towards employees. In the 1970s, family workers accounted for 30 per cent of all women workers, while under sixty per cent were hired employees. However, in 2000, family workers had fallen to 11 per cent, while employees had climbed to 82 per cent (see Figure 8.2).

In percentages by industry, in the 1970s nearly 20 per cent of workers were in the primary industries, but in 2000 that was somewhat over 5 per cent. Tertiary industries, on the other hand, employed approximately 50 per cent of workers in 1975, but by 1995 had over 60 per cent of workers (see Figure 8.3).

Have there been changes in employment management by companies? Employment management by Japanese companies up to the 1970s consisted of the long-term employment system established after World War Two. This system involved the long-term fostering of male workers as regular workers who were considered central to the organization, and who were vested with the primary working role. Gender-discriminatory employment management by companies (for example, early retirement systems for women) was based on the gender division of labour that pervaded society. Because promotion within the company demanded that employees accept long working hours and transfers anywhere in Japan, career building was, realistically, quite difficult for married women with family responsibilities.

Yet there is no mistaking that major changes are occurring in this long-term employment system. As the prolonged business downturn drags on, Japanese companies have attempted to revamp their management by cutting the number of regular workers through the expansion of diverse forms of labour. A policy statement entitled ' "Japanese Management" for a New Era', which was released in 1995 by the Japan Federation of Employers' Associations (Nikkeiren), recommended that from now on Japanese companies should reduce to very small numbers their regular permanent workers whose contracts did not formally specify terms of employment, while at the same time increasing the numbers of workers with highly specialized capabilities and hiring workers who perform simple tasks as non-regular temporary workers. Since that time, the labour market has actually been proceeding in line with Nikkeiren's policy.

But now, as in the past, women are still not a core presence in Japanese companies. The increase in women workers over the last thirty years is not an increase in regular employees forming the company core, nor in workers with specialized capabilities. These female employees are nothing more than additional non-regular employees with a peripheral presence. Even in present day Japan, men and women have totally different age group profiles for labour force participation rates (see Figure 8.4).

Female participation plots an M shape, peaking in the younger years after high school or college, and troughing during the child-raising years. This is a characteristic of the female labour force seen in Japan, but not in other developed countries. Participation of women in the labour market is very different for unmarried and married women. Although the graph plot for unmarried women is close to that of men, married women have a low participation rate, except for women from about forty to fifty-five years of age, who often work part-time.

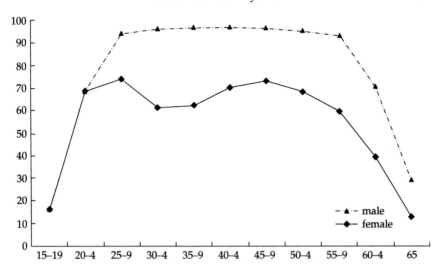

FIGURE 8.4: *Japanese labour force participation by sex and age group* (2004)
Source: Statistics Bureau, Japanese Ministry of Internal Affairs and Communications

Quantitatively, the increase in women workers over recent years is, by and large, an increase in part-time employment by married women.

II THE WIDENING GENDER GULF

In line with the 1995 Nikkeiren policy statement, the labour market trend is clearly moving towards replacing permanent employment with non-regular, temporary employment. Over the last five years regular employment decreased by 1,720,000, being replaced with about two million non-regular temporary workers.[5] Although this trend is observable for both men and women, the trend toward a lower proportion of regular workers among hired workers is far more pronounced among women. Over the same five years, the proportion of women engaged in short-hour work (that is, work comprising fewer than 35 hours weekly) increased by 3.4 per cent, from 35.9 per cent in 1997 to 39.3 per cent

[5] From 1997 to 2001, regular workers decreased from 38,120,000 to 36,400,000, but part-time workers increased by 1,310,000, from 6,380,000 to 7,690,000; part-time student workers increased by 750,000, from 3,070,000 to 3,820,000, and commissioned part-timers and others increased by 10,000, from 2,070,000 to 2,080,000. Statistics Bureau, Ministry of Public Management, Home Affairs, Posts and Telecommunications, *Special Study of Labour Survey* (released every Feb.) (www.stat.go.jp).

in 2001. Among men, the proportion only rose by 0.4 per cent, from 11.5 per cent to 11.9 per cent. Changes of the same magnitude have occurred for temporary employment as well. The proportion of women in temporary employment increased by 2.4 per cent, from 15.7 per cent in 1997 to 18.1 per cent in 2001, but among men the rise was only 1.2 per cent, from 4.3 per cent to 5.5 per cent.[6]

Statistics for dispatch workers show that 65.1 per cent of such workers are women. By type of dispatch worker, women account for 87.4 per cent of registered dispatch workers,[7] and 46.9 per cent of permanent dispatch workers.[8] Women account for a higher proportion of registered dispatch labour which is the more unstable form of employment. There are also clear gender gaps in job type and work content. Men are heavily represented in 'software development', 'machine design', and other specialized work that offers the promise of high incomes. In comparison, women are heavily represented in 'office equipment operation' and 'general clerical work', which are non-specialized and low-paying jobs. This results in a wide difference between the annual income of men and women. Dispatch workers who in surveys answered that they earn between two and three million yen per year make up 43.7 per cent of office equipment operators and 46 per cent of general clerical workers, but a mere 7.8 per cent of software developers and 6.9 per cent of machine designers. On the other hand, dispatch workers responding that they earn at least five million yen annually account for only 1.3 per cent of office equipment operators, and 1.2 per cent of general clerical workers, but 20.6 per cent of software developers, and 28.7 per cent of machine designers. One can discern a clear division between 'women's jobs' and 'men's jobs' in dispatch labour.[9]

With the increase in non-regular labour, the gender gulf further widens in terms of labour forms and compensation. The market for non-regular

[6] From 1997 to 2001, regular workers decreased from 38,120,000 to 36,400,000, but part-time workers increased by 1,310,000, from 6,380,000 to 7,690,000; part-time student workers increased by 750,000, from 3,070,000 to 3,820,000, and commissioned part-timers and others increased by 10,000, from 2,070,000 to 2,080,000. Statistics Bureau, Ministry of Public Management, Home Affairs, Posts and Telecommunications, *Special Study of Labour Survey* (released every Feb.) (www.stat.go.jp).

[7] In this arrangement, workers register with a dispatching agency, and each time there is a request from a company to have workers sent, the agency enters into labour contracts with registered workers and sends them to the requesting company. Since this is an unstable form of employment for workers, the agency engaged in dispatching workers must obtain permits from the Health, Labour, and Welfare Minister.

[8] An arrangement in which agencies send workers they themselves employ to companies when there is a request. Since this is stable employment for workers, agencies engaging in this kind of dispatching need only report it to the Health, Labour, and Welfare Minister.

[9] Ministry of Health, Labour, and Welfare, 'Survey on Dispatch Workers', from *Study on the Private Sector Labour Demand System* (study carried out in July and Aug. 2002 but unpublished).

labour, which is unstable and low paid, has become female-dominated. In fact, although the wage differential between men and women in regular employment tends gradually to close,[10] the differential is widening if non-regular employment is included.[11] The next section examines how Japan's labour law and policy address this widening separation in forms of employment and labour between women and men.

III LABOUR LAW

The creation of a legal system to bring about the principle of equal compensation between regular and non-regular workers is essential in eliminating gender differences at work, but Japanese labour law has inadequate provisions for this. Because of their status, non-regular employees suffer two major disadvantages compared to their regular counterparts: one is fixed-term contracts, and the other is the difference in wages and other compensation. This section discusses how Japan's legal system addresses them.

Legal policy on fixed-term contract workers

Many non-regular workers (including short-hour part-time workers) are employed under fixed-term labour contracts. In recent years some workers who perform key, specialized jobs have fixed-term contracts even though they are called regular contract employees. Under the long-term employment system, fixed-term workers are treated differently from regular workers in terms of wage systems and structures.

In a number of European countries such as Germany and France, entering into fixed-term labour contracts requires employers to clearly show that the work by nature must be temporary (for example, substituting for employees who are taking long-term sick leave, maternity leave, or child-care leave). However, in Japan, as a general rule, hiring fixed-term contract workers is left to freedom of contract as long as the term is not longer than three years (Labour Standards Act, Article 14). Termination during the term of such a contract is limited by the Civil

---

[10] Comparing the ordinary pay of men and women regular employees, women received 63.1% of men's pay in 1997 and 65.3% in 2001. The gender wage differential 'tends to shrink when seen over the long term'; see Ministry of Health, Labour, and Welfare, *Danjo kan no Chingin Kakusa ni kansuru Kenkyukai Houkoku (Research Group Report on Wage Differentials Between Men and Women)* (www.mhlw.go.jp, Nov. 2002), 3.

[11] Comparing the cash pay amounts of men and women workers, including part-timers, women received 50.8% of what men received in 1995, 50.0% in 1999, and 49.8% in 2000. The gulf is, in fact, widening; see Ministry of Health, Labour, and Welfare, *Monthly Labour Statistics Survey* (Jan. 2000) (wwwdbtk.mhlw.go.jp).

Code to 'unavoidable reasons' (Civil Code, Article 628) and although employment during the contract period is guaranteed, it ends upon contract expiration. Because this means that the contractual relationship automatically ends, there is no need for reasonable grounds, which are required for the termination (dismissal) of a regular worker (who has a labour contract without a stipulated term). In reality, fixed-term labour contracts are in many instance repeatedly renewed over long periods of time, but often employment is terminated when employers refuse to renew fixed-term contracts. The bottom line is that fixed-term labour contracts are unstable.

When fixed-term labour contracts are repeatedly renewed, and when workers have significant expectations for employment continuation, case law holds that reasonable grounds are needed to refuse the renewal of fixed-term contracts because the legal principle of abusing the right of dismissal is applied by analogy.[12] Despite the need for reasonable grounds to terminate employment, this does not mean that in situations such as workforce reduction, when someone must be dismissed, terminating the employment of fixed-term workers requires reasonable grounds to the same extent as is required for the dismissal of regular employees. The Supreme Court held that in workforce reductions it is unavoidable that companies will dismiss temporary workers before seeking the voluntary retirement of regular employees.[13] With respect to guaranteed employment, it is clear that the legal status of fixed-term workers is inferior to that of regular employees.

Legal policy on differences in compensation

The Labour Standards Law, the Equal Employment Opportunity Law (EEOL), and other general worker protection laws apply fully to non-regular workers as well, but there are mechanisms that encourage housewives working part-time to limit their work so as not to exceed a certain annual income,[14] which is a pretext for limiting the wages of part-time

---

[12] The Toshiba Yanagicyo Factory case, Supreme Court (22 July 1974) 28 *Saikosai Minji Hanreishyu* 927; the Hitachi Medico case, Supreme Court (4 Dec. 1986) 486 *Rodo Hanrei* 6.

[13] The Hitachi Medico case, above, n. 12.

[14] The tax system allows people whose spouses earn less than a certain yearly amount to receive a tax exemption for their spouses. For this reason, housewives who work part-time tend to keep their annual incomes below a certain amount in order to decrease their husbands' income tax. More than 30% of part-time workers consider adjusting their working hours in this way. Under the social insurance system, people who work less than 75% of the hours of a normal worker, and earn less than 1.3 million yen annually, can be insured under the national pension system without paying premiums themselves. Recently, there have been louder calls to stop giving part-time workers special treatment under the tax and social insurance systems in order to develop part-time labour as a good employment opportunity.

workers. There are also serious problems regarding the employment management of part-time workers. The biggest problem is the huge difference in wages and working conditions between part-time and regular workers. Part-time workers receive hourly wages which are lower than those of regular workers. In nearly all cases, part-time workers receive no pay rises, regardless of the number of years they have worked for a company, and no bonuses or retirement allowances.

The wage differential between part-time workers and regular employees is especially unfair in cases of 'quasi-part-time work', where part-timers work about the same hours as regular employees and perform all but the same work as some regular employees. The only court decision in such a case was that of the Nagano District Court's Ueda Branch in 1996, in which the court handed down a judgment on female 'non-regular workers' who worked in production nearly full-time and performed key tasks, but who received far lower compensation than regular employees. This decision stated that if the wage amount was under 80 per cent of the wage of regular female employees with the same years of service, that would violate the ideal of equal treatment that underlies labour law, and should be deemed to violate public order and good morals (Civil Code, Article 90). Consequently, those employees can demand the payment of damages of up to 80 per cent of the difference.[15]

In some Western countries, part-time workers receive the same hourly wages as full-time workers if they are hired for a job in which the type and level of the required skills are the same. This is because in their labour markets a common wage schedule is created under industryspecific collective agreements, and wages are determined by the job, and/or because the law provides for the principle of equal treatment in proportion to time worked with respect to part-time workers' wages. ILO Convention No. 175, the EU Directive on part-time labour, and other instruments also adopt the basic principle of equal pay for equal work.[16]

However, Japan has no explicit provision prohibiting discrimination against part-time workers. The general theoretical interpretation of 'social status', prohibited as a cause for discrimination by Article 3 of the Labour Standards Act (LSA), which also prescribes the general principle of equal treatment, is that the classification of 'part-time worker' is not

---

[15] The Maruko Keiho-ki case, Nagano District Court, Ueda Branch (15 Mar. 1996) 690 *Rodo Hanrei* 32. This case went to the appellate court, but ended in a settlement that was nearly the same as the District Court decision.

[16] ILO Convention No. 175 (Convention Concerning Part-time Workers); Council Directive 97/81/EC of 15 Dec. 1997 concerning the Framework Agreement on Part-Time Work concluded by UNICE, CEEP and ETUC-Annex: Framework Agreement on Part-Time Work (OJ L 14, 20.1.1998, 9–14).

included.[17] This Article does not restrict differences in treatment based on form of employment. Further, Article 4 of the LSA prohibits wage discrimination between men and women, but because it has not been interpreted as prohibiting indirect gender discrimination, the wage differential between part-time women workers and regular women employees is not illegal. Even the EEOL, which became law in 1985 and was amended in 1997, bans gender discrimination in placement and promotions, but this merely rectifies gender discrimination for those within the same employment management category. While administrative authorities were at first reluctant to interpret differences in treatment between men and women in different forms of employment as illegal,[18] the June 2000 notification 'Matters of Importance Concerning Employment Management Differentiated by Career Tracks' articulated the view that when employment management categories exist in name only and are not rational, and are mere pretexts for rationalizing discrimination against women, different employment management for each track violates the EEOL and should be rectified. This notification suggests that the possibility of dispute over differences in worker treatment which exceed employment management categories including forms of work and employment is not denied even under the EEOL. Nevertheless, with only an interpretative possibility given by the notification, there is no hope that it will be effective in actually eliminating discrimination.

The 1993 Law Concerning the Improvement of Employment Management for Short-Hour Workers (Part-Time Work Law) asks employers to consider the 'balance' between short-hour workers and standard workers, but it is not generally understood that workers can invoke this law to demand equal treatment of employers.[19] For this reason, other than the general principle of 'public order' set forth in the decision on the Maruko Keiho-ki case, it is currently impossible to find provisions based on positive law for bringing about equal treatment for regular and non-regular workers.

---

[17] Unlike the common view of 'social status', I do not think it should be interpreted strictly or in a limited sense. Instead, I believe it is definitely possible to have an interpretation in which the contractual status of workers, which should be regulated in accordance with the demands of society, is included within the scope of 'social status'. Asakura, M., *Rodo to Gender no Houritsugaku* (*A Legal Study of Labour and Gender*) (Tokyo: Yuhikaku, 2000), 440.

[18] According to 'guidelines' based on the EEOL, discrimination against women means giving women different treatment from men in the same employment management category, and that 'employment management categories' are categories such as job type, qualification, form of employment, and form of work. Under this interpretation, part-time women workers and full-time male workers are in different employment management categories, and therefore the EEOL is not violated even if women and men are treated differently.

[19] This law prescribes that proprietors receive administrative guidance pursuant to the law's provision for the obligation to make efforts. However, encouragement by

The voluntariness of choosing non-regular work

Owing to the lack of explicit provisions in law, whether or not Japan should legislate a principle of equal treatment for non-regular and regular workers has become the major focus of controversy in labour law. Here, the matter that must be explored from the perspective of gender is the validity of the explanation that part-time work is the form of employment 'chosen' by women workers who consider family responsibilities important, and that they do not desire the same treatment as regular employees, who are under considerable constraint.[20]

What choices are women actually making about non-regular work? Asking women part-timers why they willingly chose to become non-regular employees yielded these responses: 26.8 per cent said, 'I became a non-regular employee out of necessity because there was no place that conformed to my wishes', while 61.6 per cent said, 'I became a non-regular employee because I wanted to'. However, 42.2 per cent of the latter stated that they would have wanted to be regular employees if they did not have the burdens of child-rearing, housework, and nursing care. This group accounts for 55.6 per cent of the 30 to 34 age group, which is raising children.[21] The gender division of labour is narrowing women's choices. In view of these figures, it is probably no mistake to say that the work choices made by women themselves are not based on true free will, but are none other than forced choices.[22]

There are considerable differences in the reasons that women and men give for choosing agency work. For women, the top two reasons are: 'because

administrative guidance has had hardly any real effect. Nevertheless, in 'Part-Time Labour and "the Ideal of Balance" ', *Minsyoho Zasshi*, 119, (1999), 4–5, Michio Tsuchida argues for an interpretation in which this law's 'ideal of balance' is actively imbued with effectiveness under private law.

[20] Sugeno, K. and Suwa, Y., 'Part-Time roudou to Kintou Taigu Gensoku' (Part-Time Labour and the Principle of Equal Treatment) in I. Kitamura (ed.), *Gendai European Hou no Tenbou* (*Prospect of Modern European Law*) (Tokyo: University of Tokyo Press, 1998) classify part-time work in terms of whether the choice of such work was voluntary. This chapter classifies part-timers into those who voluntarily choose part-time work, and those who involuntarily choose it and argues that the challenge of government policy on the part-time work issue is to give the latter group more discretion in choosing.

[21] See Conference for Gender Equality, Committee of Experts on Basic Issues, 'Measures for Supporting Women's Bid to Work: Interim Summary' (www.gender.go.jp, Oct. 2002), 27, from Japan Institute of Workers' Evolution, 'Study on Diverse Forms of Work' (Tokyo: Japan Institute of Workers' Evolution, 2001).

[22] In relation to Sugeno and Suwa, above, n. 20, I recognize the importance of the policy challenges the authors present but I have argued, nevertheless, that because the choice of 'non-voluntary part-time work' is a 'forced choice', the existence of 'voluntary part-time work' is not a basis for negating the principle of equal treatment; and I have described the same discussion taking place in Britain. Asakura, M., 'Supplementary Opinion on the Maruko Keiho-ki Case', *Rodo Horitsu Jumpo*, no. 1473 (Feb. 2000), 14 ff.

I can choose the kind of work I want to do', at 38.0 per cent, and: 'I wanted to be a regular employee but could not find a job' at 36.6 per cent. For men, the reasons were: 'Because I can use specialized technologies and qualifications', at 38.2 per cent and: 'Because I can use my abilities', at 36.6 per cent.[23] Gender differences in job type and working conditions for agency work are evident in the different reasons for the choices made. As noted previously, the types of agency work often performed by women are office equipment operation and general clerical work, which are conspicuous for their low wages. It is even more evident that these are 'constrained choices'.

Of course, just saying that women's choices are not free will choices but 'forced choices' does not solve the problem, because such an explanation means that women permanently face such forced choices unless we reform the social construct of the gender division of labour. Company responsibility will probably recede into the background. On this point, feminism offers, with respect to legal policy, the following doubts about finding importance in whether women have 'the voluntariness of job choice'.

On the matter of job choice, the conservative view that women are always uninterested in high-paying, high-skill jobs is also asserted in the US as the 'lack of interest' argument, but Vicki Schulz criticizes this view and offers new insight into women's job choice consciousness.[24] As a basis for discussion, Schulz uses a court case which dealt with the question of whether the high-paying commission sales jobs in a company were monopolized by men because of discrimination by employers or simply because of women's work preferences.[25] Schulz claims that women do not have fixed job preferences before entering the labour market, but that such preferences are created by the workplace, which is central to developing workers' autonomy and will to work.[26] As this shows, the question of whether non-regular employment is 'chosen' by

---

[23] Ministry of Health, Labour, and Welfare, above, n. 9.

[24] Schulz, V., 'Telling Stories about Women and Work', *Harv. L. Rev.*, 103 (1990), 1749–843.

[25] *EEOC* v. *Sears, Roebuck & Co.*, 628 F. Supp. 1264 (N.D. Ill. 1986), aff'd 839 F. 2d 302 (7th Cir. 1988).

[26] In this article, Schulz discusses the problem of proving sexual discrimination as follows. Assuming that women's job preferences change depending on their work environment and treatment, even if one admits the fact that job choices are in reality restricted in a society with a gender division of labour, this does not excuse employers. As long as employers do not actively develop employment strategies attractive to women while not being bound to women's pre-existing preferences, no one will think that discrimination has been overcome. If the courts accept the 'lack of interest' theory with respect to women's job choices, then all that employers need do is just satisfy women's non-traditional job preferences. Instead, the courts should render legal decisions that positively affect women's job choices and should institute legal obligations for employers to create a positive employment culture that eliminates gender-based workplace hierarchies.

women cannot be the premise which decisively influences the state of legal policy on non-regular employment; instead, it is the employment management of businesses that deserve our attention.

Reasons for the concentration of women in non-regular jobs

Whether choices are 'forced' or 'voluntary', it is important to examine the underlying reasons why women 'choose' non-regular employment. First, probably no one will object to citing the firmly entrenched gender division of labour mindset that dominates Japanese society. Japan has the largest difference among industrialized countries in how men and women spend their working time. Average time spent on housework in dual-income households is four hours and ten minutes for wives, but a mere twenty-one minutes for husbands.[27] And only 0.44 per cent of men take paternity leave when their spouses give birth.[28] But those male and female attitudes are founded on the social structure. In other words, the gender division of labour mindset is continually being reproduced by Japanese employment practices, which have been built on the assumption of a 'standard family image' based on the gender division of labour, and by the tax and social security systems that are tightly integrated with those practices.[29] The reason that part-time women workers adjust their working hours is not because of simple supply and demand in the labour market, that is, it does not happen as a result of free and autonomous choices by the demand side (businesses) and supply side (workers). Instead, the tax and social insurance systems described above exert a heavy influence.[30]

The second reason is the problematic nature of Japanese companies' employment management itself, especially the strength with which

[27] Ministry of Public Management, Home Affairs, Posts and Telecommunications, *Basic Study of Social Life* (www.stat.go.jp).

[28] Ministry of Health, Labour, and Welfare, *Basic Study of Women's Employment Management* (wwwd.btk.mhlw.go.jp).

[29] As stated previously, Japan's employment practices are undergoing change. Specifically, the seniority element that has influenced the determination of wages and promotions is receding into the background, while the merit system is coming to the fore. However, the rock solid gender structure is actually being maintained and strengthened. Asakura, M., 'Nihonteki Koyo-kanko no Henyo to Gender' ('The Gender Order and Changes in Japanese Employment Practices'), in *21 Seiki ni okeru Syakaihosyo to sono Syuhen ryoiki* (*Social Security and Its Periphery in the 21st Century*) (Kyoto: Horitsu Bunka-sha, 2003), 131 ff.

[30] Osawa, M., 'Hataraku Josei to Zeisei Syakaihosyo' ('Working Women and the Tax and Social Security Systems'), *Modern Esprit* (Apr. 2003), 184. There have been suggestions from various quarters concerning reforms of the tax and social insurance systems, e.g. Conference for Gender Equality, Committee of Experts on Impacts, 'Report on "Lifestyle Choices and the Systems for Taxes, Social Security, and Employment" ' (http://www.gender.go.jp/danjo-kaigi/eikyou/houkoku/index_hei02.html 2002).

regular workers are restricted by their company organizations. Regular employees are assured long-term employment, but on the other hand they are often subject to considerable requirements by their companies beyond the mere provision of labour, such as long overtime hours, elastic pay, and frequent transfers, both within a company and to another company.[31] Such requirements exist not only as virtual employment management, but have also gained legal acknowledgement in the case law. For example, there is a legal doctrine that affirms the broad authority of employers regarding reassignment and transfer (the Toa Paint case, Supreme Court, 14 July 1986, 1198 *Hanrei Jiho* 149). There is also another doctrine stating that employees must work overtime when collective agreements on overtime work stipulate hours of overtime and there is a provision in the works rules stipulating that workers are subject to overtime orders (the Hitachi Ltd case, Supreme Court, 28 Nov. 1991, 45 *Saikosai Minji Hanreisyu* 1270). These doctrines give legal recognition to the aforementioned requirements. Women workers, who because of gender roles must take responsibility for their homes and jobs, are 'forced' to make job choices which avoid the heavy requirements of regular workers. In Japan, there is, therefore, a stronger tendency than in other countries for women to concentrate in non-regular jobs.

The third and biggest reason that women concentrate in non-regular employment is the unfair labour management of Japanese companies, about which the law does nothing. One should recall the fact that nearly 30 per cent of women who choose part-time work responded that they 'unavoidably became non-regular workers'. Japan has no law that completely prohibits discrimination in all labour-related areas,[32] and no fair wage mechanism in the labour market.[33] Further, once women quit their jobs, the path to regular employment is closed so that when they seek re-employment, companies are likely to offer them only non-regular employment. Companies can thereby conveniently secure labour for very low compensation. The fact that the 'freedom' to reduce personnel costs by

[31] Mizumachi, Y., *Part time Roudo no Houseisaku (Law and Policy on Part-Time Work)* (Tokyo: Yuhikaku, 1997), 214.

[32] Japan has not ratified one of the basic ILO conventions, No. 111 (Discrimination in Respect of Employment and Occupation).

[33] Claiming as grounds the fact that Japan has no systems for wages based on job type or job grade, and asserting that Japan has no social foundation that sanctions the principle of equal pay for equal work, some people have adopted a negative take on the principle of equal treatment. However, I take the opposite stance. One can argue that establishing this principle is necessary precisely because the labour market cannot eliminate unfair wages, and the concept of 'equal work', which must be specifically defined when establishing the principle, does not have to be rigidly seen in terms of the 'same job'. Asakura, M., 'Should Wages for Regular and Part-time Workers be Based on the Principle of Equal Pay for Work of Equal Value?', *Japan Labour Bulletin*, 41(8) (Oct. 2002), 8.

paying lower wages for equal work is reserved for companies, and that there is no labour market to eliminate this, is a very Japanese characteristic. Just so long as one makes the form of employment different, it is permissible effectively to discriminate among people who do equal work. It is even possible to argue that what this entails is that the law recognizes a relationship of 'status' which modern labour contract law has been trying to overcome.[34]

The need to institute the principle of equal treatment

A frank examination of the situation as outlined above shows that especially in Japan, legislating the principle of equal treatment for non-regular workers is essential, and there are two ways to do it. One way is to conceive legislation that demands equal treatment of regular and non-regular employees, and the other is to restrict discrimination against non-regular employees through legislation that prohibits indirect gender discrimination because women predominate among non-regular employees. In Japan, efforts are underway in both respects.

Let us examine the first way. When the Part-Time Work Law was enacted, its supplementary provisions called for a review three years after taking effect. Accordingly, a study was launched in 1997 by a Ministry of Health, Labour, and Welfare panel of experts, and after years of discussion the Part-Time Labour Research Group issued its final report in July 2002, stating the need for labour and management to reach a consensus to bring about 'treatment commensurate with work performed' regardless of whether workers are regular or part-time, and the need to create 'Japanese rules for equal treatment' suited to Japan's situation.[35] But because this report stated that speedy legislative enactment of these equal treatment rules would be difficult, amendments were made only in the

---

[34] Yonezu, T., 'Work-Sharing to Rodoho' ('Work-Sharing and Labour Law'), *Kikan Rodoho*, 194 (Oct. 2000), 42.

[35] Final Report of the Part-Time Labour Research Group, *Problems of Part-Time Work and How to Effect Solutions* (www.mhlw.go.jp, July 2002). This report asserts that 'Japanese rules for equal treatment' based on collective agreements would consist in deciding treatment and working conditions for part-time workers and regular employees in the same way, when part-time workers perform the same work as regular employees. Even when that cannot be done, says the report, employers should provide for a balance in treatment and working conditions between part-time workers and regular employees. However, it also states that establishing reasonable differences is permissible 'in situations in which there is no overtime, reporting to work on holidays, reassignment, or transfers'. Thus, when setting up equal treatment rules, one must be cautious from the gender perspective about the idea of using overtime, reassignment, transfers, and other restrictive conditions as criteria. Nakano, M., 'Part time rodo kenkyukai houkoku wo yomu' ('Reading the Final Report of the Part-Time Labour Research Group') *Rodo Houritsu Junpo*, no. 1538 (Oct. 2002), 4.

part-time work guidelines based on the Part-Time Work Law, not in the law itself. It was an unfortunate outcome.

These revised part-time guidelines took effect in October 2003 and the fundamental thinking on short-hour workers who perform the same work as ordinary workers is evident in the requirements imposed upon proprietors: (1) when the breadth and frequency of personnel transfers, changes in roles, and the way personnel are trained, as well as other systems for using human resources, and the operation of those systems are in essence no different from those of ordinary workers, employers shall endeavour to guarantee equal treatment 'after having implemented measures including those to integrate the methods for deciding treatment', and (2) when systems for using human resources and the operation of those systems are different from those of ordinary workers, proprietors shall endeavour to guarantee equal treatment 'based on the degree [of difference]'. A certain measure of progress in discussion leading toward 'treatment commensurate with work performed' has indeed been achieved, but the revised guidelines sanction differentials on the basis of 'systems for using human resources and the operation of those systems' even among workers whose jobs are the same. Furthermore, most part-time workers will likely be excluded as 'workers whose jobs are not the same'. And most of all, administrative guidance based on these guidelines will certainly be inadequate to the task of bringing about equal treatment between part-time workers and regular employees. Low compensation for part-time workers continues.

But there is also some good news. A group of non-partisan Diet members from both Houses, called the 'League of Diet Members for Bringing about Equal Treatment for Part-Time Workers' continued discussions for over two years, leading to the submission of a legislator-introduced Bill to amend the present law to the 159th Diet session in June 2004. The Bill includes a provision that proprietors 'must not treat short-hour workers differently from ordinary workers in terms of wages and other working conditions by reason of being short-time workers'. At the time of writing, it is being heard in the House of Representatives and will be carried over to the next Diet session. Much attention is focused on whether the long-awaited debate on the legislation of the equal treatment principle is about to begin in the Diet.

There has also been some progress toward prohibiting indirect gender discrimination using the other way of legislating the principle of equal treatment. For many years the Japanese government has been disinclined to legislate such a ban on the grounds that 'there is no social consensus.'[36]

[36] The government went no further than a supplementary resolution to the 1997 amendment of the EEOL, stating: 'Further discussion shall be held on indirect discrimination', and the issue was again put off when passing the 1999 Basic Law for a Gender-Equal Society.

Yet international agencies have directed quite severe criticism towards Japan for having done nothing to control indirect gender discrimination. The UN Committee on the Elimination of Discrimination Against Women (CEDAW Committee) stated in its 1995 concluding comments that Japan's government should report on the measures taken to address the indirect discrimination that women face in the private sector.[37] In the 29th meeting of the CEDAW Committee in July 2003, there were a number of critical observations on the lack of legislative progress in Japan, and the concluding comments made to Japan in August 2003 recommended that domestic law incorporate a definition of discrimination against women, including direct and indirect discrimination.[38]

Domestically, a committee of experts called the Equal Employment Opportunity Policy Research Group finally released its report in June 2004. This report discussed the concept of indirect gender discrimination, stating that prohibiting such discrimination is crucial for assuring the equal treatment of men and women in employment, and that 'a forward-looking response is hoped for'. I was one of the members of this group, whose discussion was consistently oriented in the direction of prohibiting indirect gender discrimination. If the tripartite Labour Policy Council starts deliberations and comes to an agreement in response to this report, we can perhaps hope that legislative debate on provisions to ban indirect gender discrimination will be on the agenda in the 2006 Diet session.

[37] UN Doc. A/50/38, para. 636.
[38] UN Doc. CEDAW/C/2003/II/CRP.3/Add.1/Rev.1.

9

Poor Women's Work Experiences: Gaps in the 'Work/Family' Discussion

LUCY WILLIAMS

> Give a man a fish, and he will eat for a day. Teach a man to fish, and he will eat for a lifetime (Chinese proverb).

Mainstream discourse, across the political spectrum, both in developed countries and in so-called 'developing countries',[1] regularly invokes the above Chinese aphorism to privilege waged work within the formal economy ('fishing') as the primary instrument for poverty reduction and to argue that social assistance in the form of monetary grants to support women as caregivers[2] ('giving a fish') is an ineffective, and often destructive and dependency-creating method, of reducing poverty.[3] Recent 'welfare reforms' in the USA and the UK, which predominantly affect poor women and their children (now being touted throughout the globe as successful and therefore being marketed by neo-liberal development policymakers and institutions in developing countries) are based on the assumptions that participation in formal-sector waged work is the path to individual independence, and that welfare receipt is the path to dependence. This framing of the problem assumes an institutional structure within which a breadwinner's labour in the formal sector provides family subsistence. More importantly, it also assumes clear distinctions between formal-sector waged work, informal-sector work, and family work. In this, it fails to recognize the complexity of women's, particularly poor women's, work.

---

[1] I recognize the problematic nature of current terminology used to describe economic levels. I use 'developed' and 'developing' countries quite tentatively, understanding the ways in which that formulation incorporates a Western understanding of development.

[2] Of course, the concept of 'giving a fish' is not limited to the realm of single mothers and their children, but also includes the elderly and the disabled who do not have a legally defined connection to formal-sector waged work sufficient to trigger eligibility for social security benefits.

[3] Although this proverb is open to other interpretations, 'fishing' is widely and commonly understood as going into the paid workforce (or self-employment in the formal sector). See, e.g. in the USA, Senator Robert Dole, invoking this interpretation of the proverb on the floor of Congress, 140 Cong. Rec. S15062-02 (8 Oct. 1994). See also 'Welfare to Work Agencies Work Together to Aid Local Attempts', www.fairmontsentinel.com, 'Columbia Work Initiatives', www.columbiascgateway.com (where so-called 'welfare to work' spokespersons cite the proverb using the same interpretation).

Regrettably, the same premises and failings appear in much feminist and progressive writing in this field, which is preoccupied with the question of how to fashion smoother and more egalitarian links between 'work'—almost always meaning 'paid employment in the formal sector'—and 'family'. To some extent, the mainstream, from liberal to neo-liberal to conservative, has simply co-opted feminist 'work/family discourse', draining it of much of its critical and egalitarian content. That this is possible is due, in part, to the fact that much feminist writing often privileges waged employment as the road to women's independence and self-realization. Although the importance of paid employment reflects a valuable insight under present circumstances, particularly in the developed nations, situating the 'work/family' problem within that context fails to incorporate much of poor women's work.

The simple distinction between 'giving a fish', and 'teaching to fish', as these phrases are commonly understood, does not do justice to the experiences of poor women. My goal in this chapter is to decentre formal-sector waged work in the discussion of work/family tensions, and propose an alternative analysis which expands and complicates our notions of the types of activity that produce value for families.

My approach relies on the following concepts: in this chapter, 'family provision' is the overarching term which includes all effort expended to sustain, nurture, and develop family members. Family provision includes two types of work, which, however, are not mutually exclusive. The first is 'caregiving work', which includes effort expended to sustain and nurture family members, but which does not produce what society recognizes as 'value' or 'potentially commodifiable value'. The second, 'subsistence work', encompasses all forms of effort to produce and provide the means to maintain the subsistence needs of family members, that is, work which produces what society recognizes as value. 'Subsistence work' includes both 'waged work'—employer–employee relationships within the formal sector—and 'non-waged work', which includes both subsistence work in the informal economy, and in-home production for consumption by the family.[4]

I use these terms because the simple categories of 'work' and 'family' do not capture the experiences of poor women for at least three reasons: first, many women and children have historically worked in slave labour, and

---

[4] Some activities cross these categorical lines; e.g. grooming children for school might be seen as both caregiving (nurturing, imparting pride and self-respect) and as subsistence work (socialization as investment in the family's human capital). In addition, the distinction between women's work 'in the home' and women's work 'outside the home', while significant for some analytical purposes, cross-cuts these categories; e.g. in-home craft production for barter or sale would be subsistence work, whereas transporting children to the doctor would be caregiving.

millions still do.[5] Women worked and continue to work as sharecroppers, as field hands or in subsistence farming, in domestic labour, by providing for boarders, taking in laundry, providing informal child-care, bartering goods and services, and working in small family businesses. All these forms of work fall outside the concept of waged work as traditionally understood.[6] While many poor women (at least in the USA) currently do cycle in and out of waged work in manufacturing and, more recently, also in low-wage service jobs, focusing on the waged-work context ignores important problems facing many poor women in the developed world and effectively erases the experiences of most poor women in developing countries.

Secondly, poor women's experiences do not reflect a sharp dichotomy between 'work' and 'family'. Throughout the world, poor women do not have, and never had, a choice but to combine subsistence work with caregiving work. For example, a slave or sharecropper would take her child with her to the field, and nurse him/her while picking cotton or farming. More importantly, a simple work/family distinction for poor women is quite artificial because both subsistence work and caregiving work by poor women are essential for family provision. Poor women have no option other than to do subsistence work of some type, whether low-waged work within the formal sector, taking in sewing, or tilling a vegetable garden for family consumption, in order to provide basic necessities such as food, clothing, and housing for their children.

Thirdly, policy proposals based on a simple work/family distinction must be subjected to serious, critical interrogation. To return to the metaphor contained in the proverb, what if the individual is not capable of, or adept at, fishing? What if she doesn't want, or have time, to fish because she has other pressing obligations which have a higher priority for her, even if the broader community does not economically value those responsibilities? What if there are insufficient fish in the river, fish that have little meat on them, or fish that contain toxins? Indeed, what constitutes fishing, and why has 'fishing' been understood to mean waged work within the formal economy instead of all work?

Exploring these questions in turn raises several additional issues of critical importance to policy debate and research methodology:

1) Within virtually all countries and cultures, poor women have always had to work in ways that do not fit the Western, middle-class ideal

---

[5] 'UN rights commission to appoint expert on human trafficking', 20 Apr. 2004, online at www.un.org; 'UN report spotlights hidden problem of children exploited for domestic labour', 11 June 2004, online at; UN: 'Children working Slave-Like conditions', *Associated Press*, 12 June 2004, online at: www.worldrevolution.org.

[6] See, Klare, K., 'The Horizons of Transformative Labour and Employment Law', in J. Conaghan, R. M. Fischl, and K. Klare (eds.), *Labour Law in an Era of Globalization: Transformative Practices and Possibilities* (Oxford: OUP, 2002), 10.

of full-time caregiving in the home. While both subsistence and caregiving work have been and remain central to poor women's lives, *both* are routinely devalued in the dominant Western view, and particularly by the legal systems of the developed nations.

2) While formal-sector waged work is privileged in legal and political discourse in the developed world and in neo-liberal development policy in the developing world, entrenched legal definitions of work exclude many poor people who are in fact low-waged workers and completely ignore many who perform non-waged subsistence work. Many labour and social welfare laws virtually define poor women out of the labour force—as non-market workers—denying them important legal entitlements and protections. As a result, labour and social welfare laws frequently render poor mothers dependent on state largesse, or 'the dole'.

3) At the same time, labour and social welfare laws efface, and thereby legitimate, the dependent status of waged workers, particularly in low-wage sectors.

4) The quality and components of low-waged and other subsistence work available to poor women failed historically, and fail currently, to provide adequate means of family provision, and create serious and harmful tensions in poor women's lives between their subsistence and caregiving work.

Contemporary discussion of work/family conflicts—as though work and family were mutually exclusive categories—often begins with the assumption that, in recent decades, the waged workforce has 'become feminized'. While this formulation has stimulated much valuable discussion, the 'feminization' thesis is troubling in that it rests on the increased participation of middle- and upper-class women in the waged labour force. Poor women have always performed subsistence work, often in waged contexts. Yet, they have historically been, and continue to be, disadvantaged by legal proscriptions that construct their identities as non-workers. Their struggles have not been valued, and they continue to be largely invisible in policy debates concerning work/family problems. Most labour law scholars, even those focusing on work/family issues from a feminist perspective, have not addressed the issues that intersect traditional labour law, low-waged work, subsistence work, poverty, and social welfare benefits.

But precisely for these reasons, the subsistence and caregiving work experiences of poor women can provide an important perspective within which to rethink the current discussions of work/family issues among the non-poor. Enlarging the category 'work' to encompass subsistence work outside waged work in the formal sector, as well as caregiving work, provides a critical lens through which to observe the multiple problems with which *all* women struggle in their effort to fulfil their caregiving responsibilities while providing for their families' subsistence.

This chapter attempts to build on and expand the current discussion of (waged) work and family tensions to engage more comprehensively with poor women's caregiving and subsistence work obligations, situated within an understanding of class and race differences. I first provide examples of ways in which poor mothers have historically experienced tensions between subsistence and caregiving work ('subsistence/ caregiving tensions'). Although I focus initially on the USA, I then draw connections to developing countries. Next, I discuss how legal rules, primarily in developed countries, have contributed to rendering invisible the subsistence/caregiving tensions of poor women by ignoring their subsistence work both in and outside the formal sector. Finally, I urge those engaged in exposing labour law's failure to appreciate work/ family tensions to expand their critical analysis to incorporate the experiences of poor mothers in broader family provision.

I THE CENTRALITY AND DEVALUATION OF BOTH CAREGIVING WORK AND SUBSISTENCE WORK IN POOR WOMEN'S LIVES

Whether in the informal economy, subsistence farming, in-kind bartering, or caregiving, the vast majority of 'work' performed in the world, particularly by poor women, is performed outside the formal sector. However, the role that poor women play both as subsistence workers and as caregivers historically has been and continues to be largely denigrated by the mainstream in most societies and by contemporary legal systems.

The US experience

In the USA, the role of women in both forms of family provision (subsistence and caregiving) has a long and somewhat schizophrenic history based primarily on class and race distinctions. Caregiving work has traditionally been valued as the appropriate forum for women's work if one was white and non-poor. The caregiving work of poor, slave, non-white, and immigrant women has been and continues to be deemed inconsequential and devalued by mainstream society. Here I set forth only a brief summary in order to provide a framework for situating the experiences of poor mothers within a discussion of the range of family provision.

Poor women, whether married or single, have always done subsistence work, either in traditional waged work, or, more commonly, in the informal economy. Given the absence of modern social welfare programmes in the past, subsistence work of some sort was the means by which women without other sufficient family support could provide for their families. But *single* mothers of all races faced particular difficulties. They could sacrifice earnings by limiting their hours of availability, leave their children unattended, or place them in institutions or foster care.

Race played a strong role in the production and maintenance of poverty, whether considering immigrant women (initially Irish, later Southern European and Eastern Europeans), or African-American women. During the slave era, slave women were forced to perform hard manual labour as field hands. Some who were not field hands were expected to serve as nannies, caring for their masters' children while their masters ignored the caregiving work of women slaves with their own children.

After the Civil War in the USA, women of colour were largely excluded from factory work. Although they were often the primary or sole support of their families, they were relegated to specific 'undesirable' jobs such as domestic, laundry, or agricultural work. They had little upward mobility, and few alternatives other than to care for middle-class, white families. The length of the working day for those jobs meant that their own children frequently had to fend for themselves.

Although a higher percentage of married African-American women performed subsistence work than both white married women and immigrant wives of the same socio-economic class, poor white women were not exempt from subsistence work. For example, poor white women in the rural South tended to be sharecroppers' wives who performed household tasks *and* field work.

The assumptions about what constitutes 'work' underlying these historical experiences continued to resonate after social welfare programmes were enacted. For example, note what constitutes 'work' in the testimony of a poor woman before the 1967 Mississippi Advisory Board of the Civil Rights Commission, which exposed the practice in a number of states (both in the North and South) of terminating 'welfare' or 'Aid to Families with Dependent Children' benefits (see discussion below) when the state administrating agency declared a given time period (invariably, the harvest season) to be one of 'full employment', ignoring an individual poor mother's actual employment status:

In the year 1965, I was receiving a welfare check. On the first of June, I came to Jackson for a demonstration. I got locked in jail and stayed locked in jail for eleven days, and when I returned home, the welfare lady...asked me where had I been. She came to my home, and where was I? I told her I was in Jackson at that time. And she asked me wasn't I in a demonstration? I told her, 'Yes, I was.' She said, 'Didn't you know that you didn't have any business to leave home, to leave your children?' She said, 'Where did you leave your children?' I said, 'I left my children. They were at home and they was in good care.' She said, *'You didn't have any business to go off and leave your children.'* And she said, *'You should have been here chopping cotton for $3.00 a day instead of going off on a demonstration.'* Then she said, 'If you will agree to chop cotton for $3.00 a day,' she said, 'you will get your check back in August'. This was in June. At this time, I belonged to a Freedom Labor Union in Indianola, Mississippi. This union was on strike. I refused to go back into the fields. I told her that this was a Freedom Labor Union, and this union was on strike and I refused to return to go back to the fields. She told me that if I refused to go back to the fields and chop cotton for $3.00 a day, then she would cut my check off, and she did cut it off. I didn't go back . . .[7]

The welfare administrator saw no threat to caregiving work in requiring women to leave their children in order to chop cotton for grossly substandard wages. But leaving them to participate in civil rights demonstrations, which aimed to establish a less racist society for their children to grow up in, constituted culpable deprivation.

In other words, the legal definition of 'work' is always embedded within political and social assumptions about economic structure, hierarchy, and racial domination. For the prosperous and growing middle class, the 'cult' or 'ideology' of domesticity[8] taught that a woman's role was to preserve the home as a haven for her children and a sanctuary to which her husband could escape the stresses of the impersonal, competitive world of the workplace. The 'domestic code' validated, indeed exalted, the role of woman as caregiver and homemaker, heralding 'womanhood' as the repository of the higher moral values and ethical concerns lost in the *laissez-faire* business world.

As applied to immigrants, African-Americans, widows, and single mothers, this same 'domestic code' isolated and denigrated 'deviants', and reinforced the patriarchal family. Married women who had to do subsistence work brought shame on their families because their action supposedly reflected their husbands' inability to provide for the family. Single mothers, who had to deal with *all* of their family obligations, providing for economic and emotional needs, were, at best, ignored, and often vilified.

Nor is this description of poor women's work in the USA only relevant historically. While policymakers talk as though social welfare programmes now provide for poor families in the USA, it is important to

[7] 113 Cong. Rec. 36,807 (1967) (quoting testimony of Mrs Ora D. Wilson, Miss. State Advisory Comm., US Comm'n on Civil Rights, Welfare in Mississippi, 30–1) (emphasis added).

[8] For a discussion of the domestic code (initially developed in the nineteenth century) historically and throughout the welfare debate in the twentieth century, see, Handler, J. F. and Hasenfeld, Y., *The Moral Construction of Poverty: Welfare Reform in America* (Newbury Park, CA: Sage, 1991).

note that large numbers of single mothers cycle between low-waged work and welfare programmes. Studies immediately preceding the 1996 'welfare reform' retrenchment in the USA document that welfare and waged work are inextricably intertwined, giving the lie to the widely held assumption that welfare recipients are a separate and distinct category from paid workers. A majority of women receiving welfare move in and out of low-waged work on a regular basis.[9]

According to the 2000 US census, millions of full-time, year-round workers in waged work in the formal economy live below the officially designated subsistence wage. Women predominate in the lowest-waged work positions. Of the twenty-five occupations with the lowest median earnings, nineteen are predominantly filled by women, in both the full-time and part-time categories. The percentage of workers in these occupations who are women is often in the 80–95 per cent range. For the average-sized family (a single mother with two children) receiving the current US social welfare programme for lone mothers—'Temporary Assistance to Needy Families', or 'TANF'—the *median* earnings of women working full-time, year-round in eighteen of these occupations is below the designated, and quite economically conservative, federal poverty level. Reflecting the legacy of poor women's history, these occupations fall into categories such as maids and housecleaning attendants (1.12 million), child-care workers (1.19 million), waitresses (1.04 million), cashiers (1.7 million), and a variety of food preparation and serving jobs (including fast food, cafeteria, and counter attendant jobs).[10]

A 2003 study that focused specifically on low-income, single-parent heads of household in the USA found that 78.2 per cent of those in waged work were concentrated in four typically low-income occupations: service, administrative support and clerical, sales, and operators, fabricators, and labourers. That figure rose to 81 per cent for single mothers. When broken down by industry classifications, 71 per cent of low-income single mothers worked in services or retail trade compared to 53.1 per cent of low-income single fathers. The percentage of all single parents participating in low-waged work rose from 60.4 per cent to 69 per cent

[9] For a fuller discussion, see Williams, L., 'Beyond Labour Law's Parochialism', in Conaghan et al., above, n. 6, 103, n. 9.
[10] Data compiled from Weinberg, D., *Evidence From Census 2000 About Earnings by Detailed Occupation for Men and Women*, Census 2000 Special Reports, CENSR-15 (Washington, DC: US Census Bureau, 2004), 9. Census 2000 PHC-T-33, *Earnings Distribution of U.S. Year-Round Full-Time Workers by Occupation: 1999, TABLE 1* (Washington, DC: US Census Bureau, 2000); Census 2000 PHC-T-33, *Earnings Distribution of U.S. Year-Round Full-Time Workers by Occupation: 1999, TABLE 3* (Washington, DC: US Census Bureau, 2000); *Earnings by Occupation and Education. TABLE 2. Earnings by Detailed Occupation: 1999 (United States; Both Sexes); Earnings by Occupation and Education. TABLE 2. Earnings by Detailed Occupation: 1999 (United States; Females)*. (Most data available online at www.census.gov.)

after the social protection reductions in 1996. However, the number of low-income single-mother household heads increased even more dramatically, from 58.5 per cent to 68.1 per cent. Only 7.3 per cent of all single-parent household heads were affiliated with unions, with an even smaller figure for women.[11]

On 19 December 2004, the *Boston Globe* newspaper gave these figures a graphic human face by juxtaposing articles of two strikingly different stories about women. One reported the story of a widowed mother working as a secretary who had been required to relinquish custody of her teenage son to the state so that he could receive needed state-funded social services.[12] The second article reported a 19 per cent increase in stay-at-home mothers over the past decade, concentrated in high-income families. Like nineteenth-century women who had the economic resources to observe the 'domestic code', these modern stay-at-home mothers represent 'a symbol of success akin to buying a new luxury car or a vacation home'.[13]

Developing countries

While many poor women in the affluent Western nations frequently move in and out of low-waged work in the formal economy, poor mothers in the rest of the world still largely work in subsistence agricultural and, to a lesser extent, domestic work. Of the 6.39 billion people in the world, only 0.9 billion live in the fifty developed countries, less than one-sixth of the world's population. Five billion live in developing countries. In 2003, 1.2 billion people lived on less that one dollar a day, the international poverty level, 900 million of whom lived in remote, rural regions where they survive primarily on subsistence agricultural work.[14]

Rural women produce one-half of the world's food output and between 60–80 per cent in most developing countries. They do so primarily through small-scale cultivation for household consumption.[15] After

---

[11] Institute for Women's Policy Research, *Before and After Welfare Reform: The Work and Well-Being of Low-Income Single Parent Families* (Washington, DC: Institute for Women's Policy Research, 2003), Tables 2.1, at 11, 2.5, at 15 and 19, 2.6, at 16. I am referring here to the data from Aug. 1999 to Feb. 2000.

[12] 'Cruel Bargain: Parents Lose Custody to Aid Teens', *The Boston Globe*, 1, A36 (19.12.2004).

[13] 'Stay-at-Home "Mommy Set" Seen as Latest Privileged Class', *The Boston Globe*, A36 (19.12.2004).

[14] 'Hunger Basics. World Hunger and Poverty: How They Fit Together', online at www.bread.org; 'Millennium Development Goals: A compact among nations to end human poverty', UNDP, Human Development Report 2003, online at www.undp.org; 'Rural Development is Key to Tackling Global Poverty', online at: www.choike.org.

[15] Food and Agriculture Organization of the UN, 'Gender and Food Security: Agriculture', online at www.fao.org.

harvest, poor women provide much of the labour for storage, handling, stocking, and processing. The number of poor female-headed households has significantly increased, largely because of the HIV/AIDS epidemic in a number of developing countries,[16] resulting in what some international organizations have termed a 'feminization of agriculture'.[17] Yet, because much of women's work in crop production consists of unpaid labour for family consumption rather than for market sale, it is unrecorded in labour statistics.

While waged work in the formal sector does provide a source of income for many poor families within developing countries, the vast majority of poor people, and especially poor women, provide for their families through small-scale production for sale (for example, fruits and vegetables, sewn goods), domestic work and other forms of subsistence work, and support from family and community networks, all of which is outside the formal economy. This strategy for family provision is not limited to rural areas; urban dwellers also engage in backyard farming and animal raising. A few vignettes provide a framework for understanding women's work:

- In Uganda, where subsistence farming is the main source of livelihood in rural communities, almost everyone capable of physical work is engaged in subsistence production. Women participate in petty trading and perform as much as 50 per cent of the work producing cassava, potato, and cotton crops.
- Informal work accounts for 40 per cent of Bulgaria's gross domestic product. Muslim families in particular produce large amounts of goods for their own consumption, including raising animals, growing food, and making textiles and garments. Only 27.6 per cent of female-headed households had a family member in permanent employment, as opposed to 74.6 per cent of male-headed households.
- In Latvia, people sell cosmetics and used clothes, as well as sort through rubbish for recyclable items. Women sell clothes that they have knitted, or work as domestics. Market-based activity, even in the informal sector, is decreasing, leading to a return to subsistence farming.

[16] A UN AIDS and UN Food and Agriculture Organization study found that, since 1985, AIDS has killed approximately 7 million agricultural workers, often a family's main provider, and will probably kill another 16 million by 2020. 'Addressing the Impact of HIV/AIDS on Ministries of Agriculture: Focus on Eastern and Southern Africa' (Rome: UNFAO/UNAIDS, 2003).

[17] UN Food and Agricultural Organization, 'The Feminization of Agriculture', online at www.fao.org; UNDP, 'Gender and Biodiversity Management: India', online at www.tcdc.undp.org.

- In Luanda, the capital of Angola, nearly three out of four households have a member working in the informal economy, usually women in commerce.
- In Indonesia, 70 per cent of all poor heads of household were self-employed, while only 28 per cent were waged workers in 1998.
- In South Korea, 50 per cent of all urban employment in 1993 was in the informal sector. Women are concentrated in agriculture and the services sector.[18]
- In a study of poor urban communities in the Philippines, Zambia, Hungary, and Ecuador facing economic crisis, women moved into the informal sector and girls took over their mother's domestic work, while boys went into paid work. Thus, girls' work, as previously with their mothers' caregiving work, is not documented, rendering it invisible.[19]
- In a number of countries, for example, Turkey, Georgia, Dominica, Kyrgyzstan, Republic of Moldova, Bangladesh, Pakistan, and Yemen, more than 50 per cent of the female labour force is engaged in agricultural work.[20]

This work is, of course, on top of caregiving work that is quite different from that experienced in developed countries, for example, collecting firewood and water for many hours each day, primarily women's tasks. In developing countries, women can spend up to two hours each day on these tasks, and several times longer in deforested areas.[21] In addition, households are responding to poverty caused by the loss of formal-sector jobs by increasing home-based production of goods previously purchased in the market. This burden predominantly falls on women.[22]

So, 'teaching a man [sic] to fish', that is, focusing on waged work in the formal sector, does not appear to be a panacea to poverty or, indeed,

[18] The above information and much more, as well as original sources, is compiled in González de la Rocha, M., *Private Adjustments: Household Responses to the Erosion of Work*: UNDP/SEPED Conference Paper Series (New York: UNDP, 2000).

[19] Moser, C., 'The Asset Vulnerability Framework: Reassessing Urban Poverty Reduction Strategies', *World Development* 26 (Jan. 1998), 1 and Moser, C., *Confronting Crisis: A Comparative Study of Household Responses to Poverty and Vulnerability in Four Poor Urban Communities* (Washington, DC: The World Bank (Environmentally Sustainable Development Series and Monograph Series No. 8), 1996), discussed in Cagatay, N., *Gender and Poverty*, UNDP Social Development and Poverty Elimination Division Working Paper Series (New York: UNDP, 1998), 9.

[20] UNDP, *Human Development Report 2004: Cultural Liberty in Today's Diverse World* (New York: UNDP, 2004), 229–32.

[21] Note, again, ways in which some activities cross-cut categorical lines. For example, collecting firewood for family cooking is caregiving, but it also can produce value (firewood can be sold).

[22] For example, in Bulgaria, the share of home-based production for own consumption in household income doubled from 14.1% in 1990 to 27.5% in 1995; González de la Rocha, above, n. 18, 25.

a useful model within which to explore ways in which to recognize, value, and incorporate *all* of women's work.

II THE LEGAL INVISIBILITY OF POOR WOMEN'S FAMILY PROVISION

Legal systems largely ignore and discount the work of poor women, both within and outside the home. Again, take the legal system in the USA as an example (which is replicated in many Western countries). The Social Security Act of 1935 (SSA) established, among other things, the Social Security and Unemployment Insurance Programs (social insurance schemes based on participation in formal-sector waged work and funded by employer/employee contributions), and Aid to Dependent Children (later Aid to Families with Dependent Children, or 'AFDC', now Temporary Assistance to Needy Families, or 'TANF') (a social assistance programme for single parents and their children funded from taxpayer dollars). Initially, note a gender distinction among the programmes. The recipients of Social Security and Unemployment Insurance, which pays higher benefits and has been politically sacrosanct, are formal-sector, waged workers, among whom white men have been historically over-represented. AFDC/TANF, which pays limited benefits and is politically disfavoured, provides benefits predominantly to single mothers who, in political rhetoric, are denigrated as 'unworthy'.

In addition, from its inception, the SSA allowed, and often mandated, the exclusion of African-Americans from social welfare programmes. This was done to get the votes of Southern Democrats by pandering to their desire not to disrupt the racially segregated economic structure of the South. As a result, certain categories of workers, specifically domestic and farm labourers, who were primarily African-American, were omitted from Social Security and Unemployment Insurance coverage.

The stated purpose of the AFDC programme, enacted as a discrete and modest portion of the SSA, was to 'release' mothers from the necessity of 'working', so that they could remain home to supervise their children rather than place them in institutions. The children to be cared for were those without a breadwinner or father. The dominant image was the white, chaste widow whose husband had been a productive member of the formal-sector labour market. The assumption was that the children needed a full-time maternal caretaker in the home so that they would grow up to be productive citizens themselves. As long as white widows stayed at home, it was proper to support them through AFDC.

Yet the vast majority of mothers raising their children alone, especially African-American women, were excluded from AFDC through a variety of mechanisms. Southern Congressmen ensured that states had significant discretion to determine eligibility. At the 1939 National Conference of Social Work, a welfare supervisor stated:

The number of Negro cases is few due to the unanimous feeling on the part of the staff and board that there are more work opportunities for Negro women and to their intense desire not to interfere with local labor conditions. The attitude that 'they have always gotten along', and that 'all they'll do is have more children' is definite...There is hesitancy on the part of lay boards to advance too rapidly over the thinking of their own communities, which see no reason why the employable Negro mother should not continue her usually sketchy seasonal labor or indefinite domestic service rather than receive a public assistance grant.[23]

However, the class distinction transcended race in important ways. Even if eligible for benefits, the amount provided was so low that poor women of all races had to develop other sources of income. Thus, poor mothers were faced with irreconcilable paradoxes: they were expected not to do subsistence work, but by necessity were required to obtain outside resources; they were expected to care for their children, yet many were forced to leave their children to provide for their families' survival.

As noted, however, African-American women had never been full-time caretakers for their own children. White mainstream society assumed that they should perform, and by necessity they had always performed, subsistence work, whether as single parents or in two-parent families. Thus, both practically and statutorily, women of colour were excluded by federal welfare policy from the vision of the virtuous widow with young children and thereby again denied the opportunity to perform full-time caregiving for their own children.

Such differential treatment based on racial image was in practice until the 1960s, when the image of a white female with a career became acceptable and often valued. Large numbers of white women entered the formal-sector labour market, at least on a part-time basis, because of both the opening of previously closed career paths and the real or perceived necessity for two incomes in white two-parent families. Thus, the image of a 'normal', 'productive', 'self-fulfilled' white woman expanded from homemaker to include career woman as well.

At the same time, law reform initiatives and civil rights activism finally succeeded in placing African-American women on the AFDC rolls.[24]

---

[23] Bell, W., *Aid to Dependent Children* (New York: Columbia University Press, 1965), 34–5 quoting Larabee, M. S., *Unmarried Parenthood Under the Social Security Act*, Proceedings of the Nat'l Conference of Social Work, 1939 (New York: Columbia University Press, 1939), 449.

[24] One of the major judicial victories that opened the AFDC programme to African-Americans is also indicative of how the symbols replicated through the expected roles also often contributed to judicial discourse, reinforcing the invisibility of poor women's experiences as *both* subsistence workers and caregiving workers in that realm as well. The named plaintiff in the first AFDC case to go to the US Supreme Court, *King v. Smith*, 392 US 309

Congress responded in 1967 by, for the first time, mandating a work requirement for single poor mothers receiving AFDC.

During the 1967 Congressional debates, race and class distinctions were evident in the discussion of caregiving work, with poor women's caregiving work being devalued, indeed ignored, while white married middle- and upper-class women's caregiving work was valued. When members of the National Welfare Rights Movement came to testify before the Senate Finance Committee, the chair of the Committee called them 'Black Brood Mares, Inc.', and stated:

One thing that somewhat disturbs me is this idea that all these mothers who are drawing welfare money to stay at home have to be provided with a top paid job... You know somebody has to do just the ordinary everyday work. Now, if they don't do it, we have to do it. Either I do the housework or [my wife] does the housework, or we get somebody to come in and help us, but someone has to do it, and it does seem to me that if we can qualify these people to accept any employment doing something constructive, that is better than *simply having them sitting at home* drawing welfare money...[25]

Likewise, he said:

We will do everything that the mind of man can conceive of to help put these people to constructive work—*for the first time in their lives for many of them and, for that matter, for the first time in the lives of the fathers and mothers of many of them*... [T]here are people right in this building who hire 15- and 16-year-old children as babysitters *to give their wives a much deserved evening out from time to time*. If these children, in that age bracket, can very constructively and usefully do work themselves, there is no reason why they should be seized upon as an excuse for their mothers to do nothing...[26]

Yet, while assuming that single mothers should participate in subsistence work, the US 'worthy' social welfare programmes, that is, Social Security and particularly the Unemployment Insurance (UI) programme, legally

(1968), was an African-American woman in low-waged work as a waitress, six days a week from 3:30 a.m. to noon, earning $16.00 a week. In addition, she was not an 'unwed' mother: her first husband and father of her first three children had died and her second husband and father of her last child had abandoned the family. Yet the state's (defendant's) brief argued: 'It is time for everyone to be rehabilitated and go to work. It does not appear that any of the major Congressional thrusts directed to solving poverty problems show any let-up in sight for persons who really want to remain dependent'. Brief for Appellants at 16–17, *King* v. *Smith*, 392 US 309 (1968). The lower court, never mentioning Mrs Smith's experiences, stated: 'Certain phenomena have become apparent and a matter of realistic concern to everyone is the continued procreation of illegitimate children by persons who seem economically unable to care for them and undoubtedly in some instances seem to lack initiative or the desire to properly care for them'. 277 F. Supp. 31, 40, n. 8 (M.D. Ala. 1967), *aff'd*, 392 US 309 (1968).

[25] *Social Security Amendments of 1967: Hearings on H.R. 12080 before the Senate Finance Committee*, 90th Cong., 1st Sess. 1127 (1967) (emphasis added).

[26] 113 Cong. Rec. 33,542 (1967) (statement of Sen. Long) (emphasis added).

define poor subsistence workers and even many waged workers as 'non-workers'. For example, through minimum earnings requirements and disqualifying reasons for termination, poor workers, including significant numbers of single mothers, are frequently excluded from the definition of 'employee', and are therefore ineligible for unemployment insurance.[27] Currently, in forty-one of the fifty states in the USA, men are more likely to receive UI than women.[28] As a result, when poor mothers become unemployed, they are forced to rely again on AFDC/TANF or 'welfare'. This legal definition, of course, constructs their identity as non-workers, that is, as social deviants who cause their own poverty by refusing to perform 'work'. They are then viewed as 'dependent' on the 'state', and the economic dependency that is a structural feature of low-waged labour markets is rendered invisible.

In symbolic terms, AFDC performed a shaming function by legitimating an assumption, partially constructed by legal definitions, that poor women do not perform 'work'. The legal structure does not respect poor mothers' subsistence work (it is considered non-existent) *or* caregiving work. It follows, for mainstream politicians and media pundits, that poor women must be forced to 'move into' waged work in the formal sector to gain dignity and self-respect.

Consistent with these images and assumptions, it is not surprising that the US Congress, in debating a reauthorization of the TANF programme in 2005, is considering mandating that single mothers participate in waged work for forty hours a week, all year round, as a condition of eligibility for benefits. This requirement is considered, by many policymakers, as reasonable for poor single mothers, in spite of the fact that the US Census classifies full-time year-round workers as individuals in waged work only fifty weeks a year and thirty-five hours a week, and that only 39 per cent of *all* women in waged work engage for forty hours a week.[29] Poor women's caregiving work is again considered inconsequential, while subsistence work outside the formal economy is rendered invisible.

---

[27] For example, two-fifths of high-wage unemployed receive UI, as compared to less than one-fifth of low-wage unemployed (note that 60% of low-wage workers are women). Lovell, V. and Hill, C., *Today's Women Workers: Shut out of Yesterday's Unemployment Insurance System* (Washington, DC: Institute for Women's Policy Research, May 2001). Women are four times more likely to be working part-time during their prime earning years than men, and twenty-five US states deny UI benefits to part-time workers. *Why Unemployment Insurance Matters to Working Women and Families* (New York: National Employment Law Project, 2004) online at www.nelp.org. Because only fifteen states allow individuals who must leave their employment because of compelling family circumstances to receive UI benefits, women who leave are 32% less likely than men to receive benefits. See more extensive discussion in Williams, above, n. 9, 104.   [28] National Employment Law Project, above, n. 27.
[29] Lovell, V., *Forty-Hour Work Proposal Significantly Raises Mothers' Employment Standard* (Washington, DC: Institute for Women's Policy Research, June 2003).

Unfortunately, Western legal systems are not alone in devaluing poor mothers' subsistence and caregiving work and assuming that instilling a 'work ethic' in poor people will provide the means for them to support their families in the formal sector. For example, South Africa is a country in which, depending on the definition of unemployment, 5.2 to 8.4 million persons are unemployed—between 31.2 per cent and 42.1 per cent of the working age population[30]—not because of lack of initiative, but rather because of the lack of jobs. Twenty-two million people live on less than R144 per month (approximately US$16), income primarily generated through the informal economy, including subsistence farming and domestic labour.

The government-appointed Committee of Inquiry (commonly known as the Taylor Report because of the name of its chair)[31] recommended the implementation of a universal Basic Income Grant (BIG) under which all South Africans (regardless of need) would be granted a monthly BIG of R100 per person, funded through a progressive income or wealth tax system. Even this *de minimis* amount (the equivalent of less than US$20) would 'nearly completely eliminate'[32] extreme poverty in South Africa. The Taylor Report's recommendation would not penalize people for earning additional income. Therefore, advocates argue that the BIG would give the poorest households the economic security for them to invest in finding waged work (when available), and educating their children.[33]

While, at least temporarily, sidelining the Taylor Report's recommendation, the South African government is funding a public works programme (Expanded Public Works Programme, or 'EPWP') intended to provide short-term (four- to six-month) employment for only approximately 200,000 individuals per year. The targeted populations are women (60 per cent of participants), youth (20 per cent) and the disabled (2 per cent). The jobs to be performed include ' "soft services" such [as] home-based care for the ill and the aged, early childhood development, school feeding, and feeding at clinics, as well as in more conventional programmes such as access roads in rural areas, fencing of national roads, removal of alien vegetation, and school cleaning and renovation'.[34] While these jobs are publicly funded, rather than being solely market driven, the underlying philosophy still relies on an assumption that waged work in the

---

[30] UNDP, *South Africa Human Development Report 2003: The Challenge of Sustainable Development* (New York: UNDP, 2003), 19–20.

[31] *Transforming the Present: Protecting the Future: Report of the Committee of Inquiry into a Comprehensive System of Social Security for South Africa* (Pretoria: Department of Social Development, 2002).   [32] Ibid., 62.

[33] 'BIG Coalition Leaders' Summit: Resolution', *South African Council of Churches*, 30 Nov. 2002, online at www.sacc-ct.org.za.

[34] 'Address by President Thabo Mbeki to the Growth and Development Summit', Johannesburg, 7 June 2003, online at www.nedlac.org.za.

'free market' is ultimately the means of reducing poverty, including that of poor mothers. In other words, long-term, poor, unemployed individuals will develop skills within four to six months that will translate into (currently non-existent) private-market jobs.

The government's reasons given for embracing the public works model are reminiscent of previously quoted US assumptions about waged work as the source of independence, and the ignoring of caregiving work:

The idea behind the programme is that temporary employment in public works programmes will give the unemployed an opportunity to develop some *work* experience and learn skills that will help them find permanent jobs or start their own businesses.[35]

On poverty alleviation, the government is likely to maintain its opposition to the introduction of a basic income grant—on the grounds that it will become unaffordable to the state in the long term and encourage *dependency* among South Africans, who they would prefer to see secure an income through entrepreneurship and other sustainable initiatives.[36]

[President Mbeki's] mission is essentially that of African *self-reliance*, of *dignity* and of equality (not only between races in South Africa but between Africa and the rest of the globe) and ultimately of magnitude.[37]

[A]s many people as possible should come out of *dependency* through measures that increase growth.[38]

If you give everybody a R100 a month it will not make a difference. The notion that one single intervention [read: give a fish] would help is wrong.[39]

The EPWP is a nation-wide programme that will draw significant numbers of the unemployed into *productive* employment, so that workers gain skills while they are gainfully employed, and increase their capacity to earn an income once they leave the programme.[40]

Public works programmes, properly implemented, can be an important tool in reducing poverty. But where is caregiving work, or an understanding of the dependent and subordinated status of low-waged formal-sector work in this picture? Who is going to care for women's children while they remove alien vegetation and build roads? Why should public funds go to pay women to provide caregiving for the ill, aged, and children outside one's family, but not to provide a BIG to allow a mother

[35] 'Getting Down to Business', *Mail and Guardian Online*, 16 Apr. 2004 (emphasis added), online in archives at www.archive.mg.co.za.   [36] Ibid. (emphasis added).
[37] 'Ideals of an African Utopia Hamper the BIG, Big Time', *Mail & Guardian Online*, 30 May 2003 (emphasis added), online in archives at www.archive.mg.co.za.
[38] Ibid. (emphasis added).
[39] 'Less Welfare, More Public Works', *Mail & Guardian Online*, 5 Aug. 2003 (statement by President Mbeki), online in archives at www.archive.mg.co.za.
[40] President Mbeki, Address to the National Council of Provinces, 11 Nov. 2003 (emphasis added), online at www.anc.org.za.

to provide those same services for family members within the home while also performing subsistence work? Much as the US legal system disregarded slave, agricultural, domestic, and caregiving work, South Africa's EPWP appears to embrace a perspective of productivity and valued 'work' which assumes that dignity is centred in waged work and which renders invisible both caregiving work and subsistence work outside of the formal sector.[41]

III 'FISHING' IN TRADITIONAL, CRITICAL, AND FEMINIST LABOUR LAW

Poor women's non-waged subsistence work has always been on the fringes of the legal treatment of work. Poor women's domestic and agricultural work, even when waged, is often excluded from social welfare and labour law protections. Formal-sector, waged jobs available for poor women, both historically and currently, do not provide enough for family support. Aside from minimal compensation, these jobs are commonly temporary, have no job security, and provide little or no non-wage benefits, such as health insurance, sick days, or vacation. Low-waged workers do not qualify for leave time for family illness or other caregiving responsibilities. Thus poor women in these waged-work settings frequently are required to resign or are fired from their jobs because of caregiving necessities. Yet, because of the legal definitions of 'worker' or 'employee' within the social security and unemployment insurance laws in Western, developed countries, low-waged, insecure workers are legally constructed as 'non-workers', and assumed by mainstream society to be 'lazy welfare recipients'.

Traditional labour law focused on a white male model of full-time, full-year, site-attached, long-term employment within the formal economy. Although that model served an important and progressive role, it was never sufficiently inclusive. Historically, it largely ignored the role of the poor, both male and female, in waged work, work in the informal economy, production for family consumption, and caregiving work.

In the last twenty years, the labour movement and critical labour law scholars have challenged this model, and attempted to expand it to focus on the waged labour of women, people of colour, and those in low-waged/contingent-waged work. However, most primarily continue to

---

[41] Note, also, the role of structural adjustment programmes and the dismantling of social programmes in developing countries, which has had a disproportionate impact on women. For example, state-supported childbearing and childrearing benefits in Mongolia were largely withdrawn in the early 1990s. As a result, publicly funded day care centres dropped from 441 in 1990 to 71 in 1996; González de la Rocha, above, n. 18, 17, 32.

assume that waged work within the formal economy is the key site of labour contestation, and that collective bargaining is the most important instrument for economic redistribution.

Much of the feminist scholarship which focuses on the failure of labour law to address work/family tensions also assumes waged work in the formal economy as the key site for women's economic position and opportunities. Feminist employment law scholarship primarily focuses on gender earnings gaps, sex discrimination, sexual harassment, and family and medical leave. Many feminist and critical scholars have called attention to labour law's bias in favour of the male, full-time worker with an at-home caregiver. This scholarship importantly argues for a waged-work environment that in practice, not just rhetoric, is friendly to women who perform a grossly disproportionate amount of caregiving.

But the work/family discussion must not be limited to the problems that developed-nation parents face in juggling tensions between formal-sector careers and caregiving. A much richer discourse is needed, one which incorporates the multiple experiences of poor women in family provision. Who provides the child-care for poor women's children while they till family gardens? Who cleans their homes while they are collecting water? Who is harvesting the coffee beans for the coffee that waged workers drink on their breaks?

So, place the opening fishing quotation in a different format: what if there are no jobs available in the formal economy (no fish)—certainly true in many developing countries? What if the available jobs pay such low wages that an employee cannot feed and house his/her family (lean fish)? What if those jobs provide no sick time for the employee, time to care for children, or health benefits (fish containing toxins)? What if a person is of limited intelligence that significantly reduces the jobs for which he/she could be hired (not adept at fishing)? What if you have a child with special needs for whom you must spend significant and quite unpredictable amounts of time, or your time to care for your family involves hours of gathering firewood and water? What if you live in a neighborhood where drugs are prominent (certainly not limited to poor neighbourhoods) or where the HIV/AIDS epidemic is ravaging the community and you want to be home to ensure your children's safety (competing needs to a traditional concept of fishing)?

More importantly, what is 'fishing'? 'Fishing' assumes an individualistic free-market structure within which any person in waged work can provide adequate income for one's family. Is 'teaching a person to fish' instructing a poor mother how to make nutritious meals on a sub-subsistence budget? Is it teaching literacy and the importance of reading to your child? Is it teaching empowerment, so that mothers become involved in political activity which can create a better life for their children?

As important as the current discussion of work/family problems is, it has largely ignored these questions. There is no distinct dichotomy between 'teaching to fish', and 'giving a fish'; indeed, to view the proverb as if there is one presupposes a dichotomy between dependence and independence instead of understanding the interconnection of these complex concepts. 'Fishing' is not a condition of independence; 'fishing' often does not provide for family economic necessities and can create counter-caregiving incentives. 'Being given a fish' is not necessarily a condition of dependence, but often is a valuation of caregiving work, and a recognition that for poor women, 'fishing', whether defined as waged work outside the home, or other subsistence work, is often not an option, or not the best option.

The invisibility of poor women within a discussion of work/family tensions is reminiscent of the welfare caseworker who articulated the view that a mother could leave her children to chop cotton, but not to attend a civil rights demonstration. Such a framing positions poor women as outside 'work' and as individually responsible for their economic and family caregiving condition. This supports a social welfare policy that focuses on personal fault and isolates much of the informal economy, production for family, and low-waged labour markets from the kind of structural critique that progressive thinkers have so rigorously applied to traditional waged-work settings. Labour law needs to rethink what is 'work', and who is a 'worker' from a blank slate. It must not only think outside the societal and legally reinforced distinction between paid (in the formal sector) and unpaid (in the home) work, that is, a dichotomy of waged work and family work. Rather, it must incorporate the extensive subsistence work performed by poor women that is not waged work, and view work from a global perspective, rather than largely within Western developed countries, in order to re-envision legal models through which to protect all workers.

Part III

'Family-friendly' Labour Law

10

Work, Family, and Parenthood: The European Union Agenda

CLARE McGLYNN

The European Union has long recognized that if it is to meet its own ambitious targets for economic growth and wealth creation, it needs to increase the participation of women in the labour market. Falling birth rates, an ageing population, and the challenges of globalization all demand measures to facilitate women's (re)entry into the paid workforce. The chosen solution is the promotion and promulgation of 'equal opportunities' laws and policies, creating a 'flexible' workforce, together with equality being 'mainstreamed' into all labour market policies. In particular, it has been acknowledged that difficulties in reconciling paid work and family life are a significant factor limiting women's labour market participation.[1]

While it may appear that the incorporation of equal opportunities language and concepts into mainstream economic policy, and labour law discourse, represents a success for feminists, there is in fact little to celebrate. While institutions of the EU such as the European Commission proclaim the need to resolve work and family conflicts for women *and* men, the reality is laws and policies premised on traditional concepts of family and the sexual division of labour. In other words, while lip service is now being paid to equality concerns, the fundamental changes required in how we allocate family time and resources are not taking place. Moreover, there is little consideration of how our traditional assumptions about the role and scope of labour law need to be re-examined and reimagined.

This is a cause for concern for three main reasons. First, in relation to a feminist agenda seeking to facilitate women's choices within the home and workplace, the reproduction of traditional family forms may entrench existing inequalities in the home and, where women are encouraged to (re)enter the labour market, it may in fact increase their dual burdens associated with paid work and family life. Secondly, while

---

[1] European Commission, *Report from the Commission on Equality between Women and Men 2005* (Brussels: European Commission, 2005), para. 1. The European Commission, together with the Council and the Court of Justice, is one of the three most important EU institutions. In relation to labour law, its function is to propose legislation, to review the implementation of existing legislation and to adopt and promote policies in relevant fields of activities.

these inequalities and disadvantages remain in place, the economic ambition of greater growth and productivity will not be achieved: many women will resist (re)entering the labour market and those that do may feel constrained to work at less than their full potential in order to ensure greater flexibility or reduced obligations. Finally, for so long as traditional norms of family life are left unchallenged, labour law's norms and assumptions about the unencumbered 'ideal' worker will continue, thus further entrenching women's disadvantaged status.

To develop these arguments, this chapter focuses on the concept of 'parenthood' employed in EU law and policy. It considers, first, the dominant ideologies of motherhood and fatherhood which are shaping current EU law and policy and sets out a preferable theoretical framework based on gender-neutral parenting. It then goes on to examine the EU's legislative initiatives which aim to facilitate the reconciliation of paid work and family life. The legislative approach is then contrasted with the jurisprudence of the European Court of Justice (ECJ).[2] It will be argued, in conclusion, that until a more progressive approach to parenthood, based on gender-neutral parenting, is adopted in practice as well as in the rhetoric, little change will be achieved in the participation of women in the workforce and few inroads will be made into our traditional conceptions of the role and purpose of labour law.

I IDEOLOGIES OF PARENTHOOD: TOWARDS GENDER-NEUTRAL PARENTING

The concept of parenthood and ideas and expectations about parenting vary over time, from society to society and are constantly changing.[3] Nevertheless, there appear to be certain constants, particularly the enduring desire of society generally to dichotomize sexual differences and to explain them as natural, not socially constructed. In the context of parenthood, this has led to the supremacy of the 'dominant ideology of the family'. Thus, the model of the caregiving mother/wife and breadwinner husband/father family has been a dominant presence in all European states, albeit that it has been more ingrained in some countries than others. Unfortunately, despite social and demographic changes, this normative vision of the family retains its purchase on law and policy-making within the EU.

[2] Judgments of the ECJ are binding on all member states and are supreme over contrary national law.

[3] See further Bainham, A., Day Sclater, S., and Richards, M., 'Introduction', in A. Bainham, S. Day Sclater, and M. Richards (eds.), *What is a Parent? A Socio-Legal Analysis* (Oxford: Hart Publishing, 1999), 1.

The concept of the 'dominant ideology of the family' views mothers as crucial to the emotional and physical well-being of any children, while the role of the father is to be the main/sole provider.[4] For women, these prescriptions on motherhood are based on an ideology of motherhood premised on the now discredited theories of mother–infant bonding which privileges the mother–child relationship. The consequences of an ineffective attachment or bond were said to have devastating pathological consequences for children, ranging from restricted development, to emotional immaturity, to juvenile delinquency.[5] Accordingly, it was claimed that full-time employment of a mother was on a par with 'death of a parent, imprisonment of a parent, war, famine' and so forth, as a cause of family breakdown.[6] Despite the scientific criticism of this research, and the changes in society and families since the research was published, there remains a 'direct continuation' of these ideas leading to prescriptions of 'what constitutes the right family and what provides for the needs of an infant and child in order for it to become a physically healthy adult'.[7] In this way, the mother–child dyad is not seen as based on choice, individualism, and equality, but on nature, self-sacrifice, and altruism.

Fatherhood is similarly constrained, this time by an exclusion from care work and an emphasis on paid work as being the primary role for fathers. Thus, the father–child relationship is not characterized by a 'natural' bond, but is based on social and legal reality, on proprietary rights, and is therefore more closely associated with concepts of rationality and rights. There is little scope for flexibility here. The father as breadwinner and provider, as authority figure and head of the family, remain dominant themes in discussions of fatherhood, even today: provision, protection, and authority, as described by Ruddick.[8] Thus, despite some acceptance of the changes taking place within families, there remains a continuing 'ideological emphasis on mother-as-carer and father-as-financial-provider that fixes the centrality of nuclear parenting, even where that is absent as a social reality'.[9] It goes without saying that this ideology of family is also heterosexist.

The aim here is not to disparage any need for parental 'bonding' with children. Indeed, as Sandra Fredman has cogently argued, there remains

---

[4] For a more detailed analysis of the dominant ideology of motherhood employed in the jurisprudence of the ECJ, see McGlynn, C., 'Ideologies of Motherhood in European Community Sex Equality Law', *European Law Journal*, 6 (2000), 39.

[5] Eyer, D., *Mother Infant Bonding: A Scientific Fiction* (Yale: Yale University Press, 1992), 47.

[6] Bowlby, J., *Maternal Care and Mental Health* (World Health Organization, 1951), 73, discussed in Eyer, above, n. 5, 50.

[7] Mitchell, J. and Goody, J., 'Family or Familiarity?' in Bainham et al., above, n. 3, 115.

[8] Ruddick, S., 'The Idea of Fatherhood', in H. Nelson (ed.), *Feminism and Families* (London: Routledge, 1997), 207, discussed in Diduck, A., *Law's Families* (London: Butterworths, 2003), 85.　　　　[9] Mitchell and Goody, above, n. 7, 115.

'insufficient recognition of the value of children and of active parenting' in European society.[10] The crucial point is the need to value *parenting*, not only mothering and not only parenting within the heterosexual nuclear family. An evolution in thinking is therefore required, away from the dominant ideologies of motherhood and fatherhood towards a gender-neutral approach to parenthood which seeks to free women and men to pursue the roles, both within families and in the public sphere, which suit them and their children best. Such an approach also acknowledges different forms of families as being equally viable and capable of fostering positive parenting. A 'gender-neutral' perspective therefore seeks an end to the heterosexual norm of parenting and to the defined roles of 'mother' and 'father'. This is akin to Susan Moller Okin's vision of a 'gender-free' society, which would result from a 'diminution and eventual disappearance of sex roles', enabling men and women to participate equally in all spheres of life, including infant care.[11]

In a two-parent household, same-sex or different-sex, this gender-neutral approach would be synonymous with 'equal parenting': the idea that parents share care work and paid work, a dual-breadwinner, dual-earner pattern.[12] Such an approach is to be preferred to the 'full-commodification' strategy of early second-wave feminism, based on facilitating women working full-time, with care work delegated to market or public services. This has proven to be largely a class- and race-bound strategy with care work delegated to other women, often immigrant or minority ethnic women.[13] Furthermore, fathers remain removed from childrearing and retain their primary role as financial providers.

What is required, therefore, are changes to workplace structures and the activities of fathers such that women *and* men, of all social classes and ethnicities, are able to enjoy time at home to care for their children. This is what Joan Williams means when she aims to 'democratize' access

[10] Fredman, S., *Women and the Law* (Oxford: OUP, 1997), 181.

[11] Moller Okin, S., 'Sexual Orientation and Gender: Dichotomizing Differences', in D. Estlund and M. Nussbaum (eds.), *Sex, Preference and Family: Essays on Law and Nature* (Oxford: OUP, 1997), 45.

[12] The discourse on 'equal parenting' generally proceeds on the basis of debating the negotiation of paid and care work between a heterosexual couple. This is not just due to the numerical significance of such families, but also because of the centrality of discussing heterosexual parenting to the gender contract. In addition, evidence suggests that in lesbian families, care work is already shared in a more egalitarian form: Dunne, G. (ed.), *Living 'Difference': Lesbian Perspectives on Work and Family Life* (New York: Harrington Park Press, 1998).

[13] For a discussion in the US context, see, Williams, J., *Unbending Gender: Why Family and Work Conflict and What To Do About It* (Oxford: OUP, 2000), 153; for a British perspective, see, Walby, S., *Gender Transformations* (London: Routledge, 1997), 23. For cross-national consideration of the legal regulation of paid live-in care workers, see Mundlak, in this volume.

to domesticity and care work.[14] Fundamental to this aim are radical changes in the structures of the workplace, to make it more flexible and amenable to workers with caring responsibilities, and in public services, particularly the provision of child-care and other caring services.[15] Feminist critiques of the structure and organization of paid work are long-standing and focus on the dominance of a masculine norm of work. This is the norm of the 'ideal worker'[16] who works full-time, is continuously employed until retirement, works long hours and who, therefore, has no family commitments. To a considerable extent, the workplace remains structured around this norm which excludes and/or places at a disadvantage all those who do not conform. Joan Williams argues that imbedded in the norm of the 'ideal worker' is a norm of 'mothercare', that is the assumption that care work is and should be carried out by women and that paid work can and should remain structured around this assumption. Williams convincingly argues that this norm of mothercare should become a norm of 'parental care', with the assumption that all parents have caring responsibilities, which limits their availability.[17] In time, this would encourage a move away from the norm of the 'ideal worker' and the assumption that the 'best' workers are those who work full-time, continuously, and who do not have parental responsibilities.[18] This would both facilitate time away from work, for those already in paid work, and encourage the further development of forms of work not based on the masculine norm of work, thus enabling others to enter the labour market.

Child-care support is also required, not least if lone parents are to be able to benefit from paid work. Child and other care services are widely available in some member states, but rare in others and can be a significant barrier to access to labour markets and facilitating time away from paid work, particularly for lone parents.[19] But facilitating equal parenting requires not only changes in the labour market and child-care services, but also in the behaviour and activities of men, particularly as fathers. Thus, change is required in the private sphere of the home and family. This is not a new argument. In 1978 Nancy Chodorow stated emphatically: 'It is politically and socially important to confront the

---

[14] Williams, above, n. 13, 174. For consideration of the relationship between the organization of working time and the gender division of labour, see Conaghan, J., 'Time to Dream: Flexibilities, Families and Working Time', in J. Fudge and R. Owens (eds.), *Precarious Work, Women and the New Economy: The Challenge to Legal Norms* (Oxford: Hart Publishing, 2005). See also Fudge, in this volume.   [15] See further, Fredman, above, n. 10, 206–44.
[16] Williams, above, n. 13, ch. 3.   [17] Ibid., 52.   [18] Ibid., 55.
[19] See further Millar, J. and Warman, A., *Family Obligations in Europe* (London: Family Policy Studies Centre, 1996); European Commission Childcare Network, *Leave Arrangements for Workers with Children* (Brussels: European Commission, 1994).

organization of parenting.'[20] Care of children, she continued, should
take place in 'group situations' and were this to happen, children 'could
be dependent from the outset on people of both genders'.[21] Chodorow's
thesis was that cultural assumptions about women and men, the reproduction of gender, was achieved through parenting by women only. In a
society in which both women and men cared for children, her hope was
that this would radically transform all aspects of society. Thus, her purpose was to eliminate gendered assumptions and roles in society through
changing parenting.

However, for many, a singular focus on sharing care within families
was and remains extremely problematic. Denise Riley has argued that
the principal problem with shared parenting is that it looks solely to
the private sphere of the family for change.[22] Emphasis shifts from the
public domain of the workplace and provision of child-care, to the private
realm of relationships and the negotiation of family roles. Shared child-
care, she argued, 'rests on private goodwill; but private goodwill cannot
be relied on to sustain a whole politics'.[23] In particular, her concern is that
shared parenting assumes an egalitarianism within families which is
generally absent. Parents may begin their parenting with unequal access
to work and money, and this is an imbalance which may be exploited in
any later collapse of the goodwill which sustained the original sharing,
or when the relationship breaks down. In either breakdown scenario, 'the
structures of public inegalitarianism emerge harshly'[24] in terms of access
to paid work, to public child-care and to financial and personal security
on divorce. Equally, the ideal of shared parenting has nothing to say
where there is no pair to share the care. That is, the single parent and
others 'whose lives do not encompass potential sharers in the upbringing of children' are excluded and ignored from this vision and their needs
forgotten.[25]

Increased public provision of child-care is clearly required to facilitate
the reconciliation of professional and family lives, not least because not
all parents can share care, but also because all parents need care support
services. However, the focus must not be on public services at the expense
of change in homes and families, as this could otherwise have the effect
of reinforcing women's role as primary child-carers. Jan Windebank has
demonstrated that although social policy measures designed to facilitate

[20] Chodorow, N., *The Reproduction of Mothering, Psychoanalysis and the Sociology of Gender*
(Berkeley: University of California Press, 1978), 214–17.
[21] Ibid. See also Firestone, S., *The Dialectic of Sex* (London: Paladin, 1972).
[22] Riley, D., ' "The Serious Burdens of Love?" Some Questions on Child-Care, Feminism
and Socialism', in L. Segal (ed.), *What is to be Done About the Family? Crisis in the Eighties*
(London: Penguin, 1983), reprinted in A. Phillips (ed.), *Feminism and Equality* (Oxford:
Blackwell, 1987).   [23] Riley, above, n. 22, 196.
[24] Ibid., 195.   [25] Ibid., 194.

paid work and family life can make some differences to some women's lives, this is generally in the form of a redistribution of work amongst women.[26] Changes are therefore required in families. It is only when change impacts on the private, as well as the public, that radical transformations may come about. And this is particularly the case in the context of the EU.

In EU law and policy there is an over-emphasis on the public, with little focus on the personal, private aspects of parenthood. Demands for changes in patterns of work are the meat and drink of EU discussions. Though to a lesser extent, even discussion regarding extending and developing child-care provision is a legitimate EU debate. The personal behaviour of men, and parents, however, is another matter. Though there are references to men's child-care patterns and responsibilities in EU law and policy, in effect, the private is eschewed in favour of debate regarding the public sphere. In the EU context, the private dimension of change has been lost; it must be reclaimed, albeit not at the expense of the debate regarding the need for reform in the public sphere. Equal parenting, with its emphasis on the private and familial, is therefore an essential part of seeking to ensure more gender-neutral parenting policies within the EU.

What must also be remembered in this discussion of the organization of parenting and the reconciliation of paid work and family life are the needs and desires of children. As Allison James has argued, there is a paucity of knowledge about what children think of parenting or family life in general, added to which there is an assumption that children are the passive recipients of 'parenting', a view which places parenting as essentially 'adult-centric'.[27] This view of parenting, as something which is 'done' to children, takes little account of children's own subjectivity and regards children as fundamentally vulnerable, dependent, and in need of protection.[28] Furthermore, the discourse on reconciliation of professional and family life tends to see children as objects and obstacles, rather than as subjects in their own right with their own needs and expectations.[29]

However, in the absence of knowledge about children's experiences, it is difficult to ensure that the analysis adopted and proposals made do not fall into this trap, though some attempts to consider the interests of children can be made. In this way, the gender-neutral parenting approach

[26] Windebank, J., 'To What Extent can Social Policy Challenge the Dominant Ideology of Mothering? A Cross-National Comparison of Sweden, France and Britain', *Journal of European Social Policy*, 6 (1996), 147, 160.

[27] James, A., 'Parents: A Children's Perspective', in Bainham, et al., above, n. 3, 181–3.

[28] Ibid.

[29] For a discussion of the adult-centric view of reconciliation, see Wintersberger, H., 'Work Viewed from a Childhood Perspective', *Family Observer* (Luxembourg: European Commission, 1999), 18–24.

advanced above, arguably may meet the interests of children in seeking to ensure that parents are able to spend time with their children, rather than being constrained by a workplace culture that affords them little time, and therefore energy, to care for their children.[30] Policies, therefore, which support equal parenting may, in some small way, be advanced on the basis that they support children's needs and expectations, as well as the wishes of parents.

In conclusion, therefore, the 'dominant ideology of the family', with its normative prescriptions for family life and familial roles, must be eradicated from EU law and policy. It must be replaced, in the context of parenthood, with a more modern, gender-neutral approach, based on equal parenting and respect for the needs and rights of children. Law's reproduction of the existing inequalities must be changed if steps are to be made towards a more progressive, egalitarian and gender-neutral rendering of parenthood. This is imperative if women are to be free to exercise choice in their lives, if men are to be released from their current strait-jackets of marketized automaton and principal breadwinner, and if children are to be allowed to enjoy time with their parents.

II RECONCILING PAID WORK AND FAMILY LIFE IN LAW AND POLICY

This section investigates the institutional and judicial approach of the EU to the reconciliation of paid work and family life. It is argued that there is a considerable disjuncture between the rhetoric employed at the institutional level regarding policies on reconciliation which express commitment to equal parenting and in the jurisprudence of the ECJ which reproduces traditional understandings of parenthood based on the dominant ideologies of motherhood and fatherhood.

The rhetoric of equal parenting: legislative and policy initiatives

Turning first to the positive aspects of the EU's policies on the reconciliation of paid work and family life, there is indeed much for an advocate of equal parenting to be pleased about.[31] As long ago as 1989, the EU

[30] Even though parenting, as experienced by children, is often not gender-neutral. Allison James discusses how, for children, the generalized concept of 'parent', or 'parenting' may have little meaning as for a child, his or her parents are regarded as gender-specific, 'my mum' or 'my dad'. See James, A., 'Parents: A Child's Perspective', in Bainham, et al., above, n. 3, 190.

[31] See further McGlynn, C., 'Reclaiming a Feminist Vision: The Reconciliation of Paid Work and Family Life in European Union Law and Policy', *Columbia Journal of European Law*, 7 (2001), 241; Caracciolo, E., 'The "Family-Friendly" Workplace: The EC Position', *International Journal of Comparative Labour Law and Industrial Relations*, 17 (2001), 325.

Social Charter included the non-binding commitment to enable 'men and women to reconcile their occupational and family obligations'. In 1992, a Recommendation on Childcare was adopted[32] which, although non-binding, was a symbolic achievement, the objective of which was to 'encourage initiatives to enable women and men to reconcile their occupational, family and upbringing responsibilities arising from the care of children'.[33] Peter Moss noted that this statement 'place[d] a clear commitment on member states to address the current unequal division of care and other family responsibilities' and was a 'formal recognition' at European level of the significance of the domestic division of labour.[34] In addition, successive equal opportunity action programmes have emphasized the importance of reconciliation and the need for change in families if that policy is to be effective.

The promotion of gender-neutral and equal parenting appeared, there-fore, to be firmly on the EU agenda. Indeed, the adoption of the Parental Leave Directive in 1996 seemed to set the seal on this approach.[35] The directive expressed the desire that 'men should be encouraged to assume an equal share of family responsibilities' and provided for a twelve-week period of leave for mothers and fathers. The directive was therefore gender-neutral in its treatment of parents.[36] Further, in 2000, the Council adopted a resolution on the balanced participation of women and men in family and working life, declaring that the 'de facto equality of men and women in the public and private domains' is a necessary condition for democracy.[37] Furthermore, the resolution stated that both 'men and women, without discrimination on the grounds of sex, have a right to reconcile family and working life'.[38]

The rhetoric seems clear: equal parenting and an equal sharing of family work is the ambition of EU law and policy. Ultimately, however, the reconciliation policy is a means to an end. The end is the increased

---

[32] Council Recommendation on Childcare 92/241/EEC, 31 Mar. 1992 OJ L 123/16.

[33] Council Recommendation on Childcare, art. 1.

[34] Moss, P., 'Reconciling Employment and Family Responsibilities: A European Perspective', in S. Lewis and J. Lewis (eds.), *The Work–Family Challenge* (London: Sage, 1996), 25.

[35] A directive is a binding instrument of EU law which member states are required to incorporate into national law. Council Directive 96/34/EC of 3 June 1996 on the Framework Agreement on Parental Leave Concluded by UNICE, CEEP and the ETUC, OJ L 145/9 1996, as extended to the UK by Council Directive 97/75/EC, OJ L 10/34 1998.

[36] At the time the directive was adopted, many member states had measures more extensive than the minimum provisions of the directive. Nonetheless, the adoption of this measure is symbolic in indicating the approach of the EU and in demonstrating an EU interest in reconciliation.

[37] The Council is the executive body of the EU and comprises representatives of the governments of the member states.

[38] Resolution of the Council and of the Ministers for Employment and Social Policy of 6 June 2000 on the Balanced Participation of Women and Men in Family and Working Life, Press Release no. 8980/00.

labour market participation of women, not equality in the home, more egalitarian family practices, or a reformulation of the norms of labour law. Thus, at the same time that the rhetoric considered above was proclaiming a commitment to equal parenting, the same policy documents also emphasize what might be said to be the real agenda, that of increasing the labour market participation of women. Thus, the European Commission has stated that reconciliation is necessary to 'reduce the barriers to access to and participation in the labour market by women'.[39] Increased women's employment would help to 'reflate' local economies by, among other things, generating 'new demands on transport' and 'consumption of child-care'. The Commission continued that the reconciliation policy was necessary to 'harness the economic potential of women' and meet their 'desire to enter or re-enter the labour market'.[40]

This emphasis on the labour market was confirmed with the inclusion of reconciliation as an essential element in the EU's employment policy: '[i]ncreasing female participation in the labour market, in view of impending demographic change, is an important objective of the European Employment Strategy.'[41] To this end, one of the original four pillars of the employment strategy was equal opportunities, an aspect of which was reconciliation.[42] All references to reconciliation include women and men, though the context is of the general overall objective of increasing the workforce participation of women. In other words, the *real* agenda is that the 'reconciliation of work and family life' is a *woman's* problem and one that inhibits their increased labour market participation. Thus, the 1999 and 2000 Employment Guidelines stated that '*women* still have particular problems in . . . reconciling professional and family life'.[43] The 2003 Guidelines emphasize the need to increase the labour market participation of women, with particular targets set, and stress that particular attention must be given to 'reconciling work and private life' including the 'encouraging of sharing family and professional responsibilities'.[44] The European Commission's explanatory document is even more

[39] Council Resolution on the Third Community Action Programme (1991–1995), OJ C 142, 31 May 1991. See also the Report from the Commission on the Third Community Action Programme, COM(95)246 final, 13 June 1995, at 38.

[40] Interim Report of the Commission on the Implementation of the Community Action Programme on Equal Opportunities for Men and Women (1996–2000), COM(98)770 final, at 20.

[41] A Concerted Strategy for Modernising Social Protection, COM (99) 347 final, at 10.

[42] COM (99)442 final.

[43] Draft Council Resolution of 16.12.1998, quoted in Annual Report from the Commission on Equal Opportunities 1998, COM(99) 106 final at 14; Proposal for Guidelines for Member States' Employment Policies 2000, COM(99) 441, 8 Sept. 1999, at 10.

[44] Council Decision of 22 July 2003 on guidelines for the employment policies of member states, OJ L 197/13, 5.8.2003, para. 6.

explicit, highlighting the need to facilitate the participation of 'mothers with small children'.[45]

Viewed from this perspective, the last thing that is recommended is the withdrawal of men from the labour market to care for children. This would not solve the 'problem' which is the anticipated reduction in the working population due to falling birth rates.[46] Equally, the limited role which many fathers currently play in family life is not considered problematic per se and in need of transformation. Accordingly, it seems that the suggested changes in workplace structures are focused on women, which is simply a false panacea, enabling more basic change in the relations between women and men to be avoided. The point, therefore, is that while the European Commission does state that more favourable conditions are required for women *and* men to enter, re-enter, and remain in the labour market, which include an 'equal share of care and household responsibilities' and an 'encouraged take-up of parental and other leave schemes by men', for so long as the focus is solely on the labour market participation of women, these suggestions are little more than cheap talk.[47]

While the increased participation of women in the labour force is important, serious concerns arise when the focus is primarily on women's entry into the workforce. Without concomitant changes in the structure of family and household work, an increase in women's labour market participation simply adds to women's existing responsibilities, creating and/or making worse women's 'double shift'. This situation has the likely effect of reproducing the very discrimination which an equal parenting policy might have originally tried to eliminate. In the short term, the increase in labour market participation will assist some women, facilitating their wish to participate in the labour market as well as continue their caring responsibilities. However, in the longer term it simply entrenches women's responsibilities within families, by confirming assumptions that such obligations are women's only, while doing little to change the marginalization of women's paid work.

Finally, although the Parental Leave Directive was highly symbolic in its grant of rights to mothers *and* fathers, it was ultimately a damp squib. There was no provision for paid leave and thus the directive only required changes in the laws of three member states. Similarly, the amended Equal Treatment Directive, while recognizing the importance

[45] Communication from the Commission to the Council, the European Parliament, the Economic and Social Committee and the Committee of the Regions, 'The future of the European Employment Strategy', COM (2003) 6 final, 14.1.2003, para. 2.2.9.

[46] See above n. 1.

[47] Communication from the Commission to the Council, the European Parliament, the Economic and Social Committee and the Committee of the Regions, 'The future of the European Employment Strategy', COM (2003) 6 final, 14.1.2003, para. 2.2.9.

of paternity leave, simply promotes it as an option for member states to consider.[48] In contrast, the Pregnancy and Maternity Leave Directive provides for a minimum of fourteen weeks' paid leave, together with significant protection from discrimination. While maternity leave is essential, if not complemented by changes in the role of men, it simply cements women's relationship to the home. And a directive which details considerable rights and entitlements for women on the birth of a child, but does not address men as fathers, is almost certainly likely to reproduce traditional approaches to parenthood. Although there is a need to be sex-specific when considering pregnancy, this should not extend to rights post-birth, which should be gender-neutral. Accordingly, although the directive brought an immediate improvement to the workplace rights of many women, its longer-term consequences are problematic. In this way, Patrizia Romito has argued that although such policies will seem to many women like the lifeline which keeps them afloat, they are in fact 'measures which rationalize the exploitation of the work mothers do both inside and outside the family'.[49]

Unfortunately, the EU Charter of Fundamental Rights simply reproduces the existing position, rather than attempts to map a more progressive approach to reconciliation and thereby to parenthood.[50] Article 33(2) of the Charter states that: 'To reconcile family and professional life, everyone shall have the right to protection from dismissal for a reason connected with maternity and the right to paid maternity leave and to parental leave following the birth or adoption of a child.' It can be seen that this carefully crafted provision simply restates existing entitlements under the Pregnancy and Maternity Directive and the Parental Leave Directive. In particular, the omission of a reference to 'paid' parental leave is most notable. This provision reinforces a hierarchical gendered preference for motherhood over fatherhood, via the provision of paid maternity leave, followed only by (unpaid) parental leave and no provision for paternity leave. Moreover, this 'right' is contained in the title on employment rights, not the title on equality. Its development, if there is to be any, will be bedevilled by the

[48] Directive 2002/73/EC of the European Parliament and of the Council of 23 Sept. 2002 amending Council Directive 76/207/EEC on the implementation of the principle of equal treatment for men and women as regards access to employment, vocational training and promotion and working conditions, OJ L 269, 5.10.2002, preamble, para. 13 and art. 2 (7).

[49] Romito, P., ' "Damned if You Do and Damned if You Don't": Psychological and Social Constraints on Motherhood in Contemporary Europe', in A. Oakley and J. Mitchell (eds.), *Who's Afraid of Feminism? Seeing Through the Backlash* (London: Hamish Hamilton, 1997), 183.

[50] The EU adopted a Charter of Fundamental Rights in 2000. While it is technically non-binding, it is being employed rhetorically in the promulgation of new legislation and is of persuasive authority in the European courts. If the proposed EU Constitution is adopted, the Charter will become binding.

same problems identified above in pursuing reconciliation through an employment policy.[51]

Generally, however, it is here, in the Charter, that the gap between the rhetoric and reality of Union policy is clearest. The Council adopted its forward-thinking resolution on the balanced participation of women and men in public and private lives in mid-2000, with its somewhat radical policy proposals and commitment to equal parenting and a right to reconciliation. Later that year, however, the Charter of Fundamental Rights was adopted which bears little resemblance to the resolution and which will effectively restrict future opportunities and reinforces the status quo. A resolution is cheap talk: whereas it appears to be too much of a risk to include progressive proposals and statements in a (non-binding) Charter of Fundamental Rights. Rhetoric and reality could not be further apart.

The European Court of Justice and the reproduction of traditional ideologies of parenthood

In the policy and legislative field, discussed above, measures which have been taken in the name of gender-neutral parenting are often merely exhortatory and generally require little or no action at member state level. Nonetheless, there are some moves towards gender-neutral parenting and the rhetoric, at least, is in the right direction. However, an analysis of the jurisprudence of the ECJ reveals that labour law's norm of the unencumbered 'ideal' worker remains largely intact via the reproduction and legitimation of traditional ideologies of motherhood and fatherhood.

The foundation of the Court's jurisprudence can be traced back to the *Commission* v. *Italy* and *Hofmann* cases of the mid-1980s.[52] The ECJ held in *Commission* v. *Italy* that Italian legislation which granted only women a right to leave on the adoption of a child was not contrary to the Equal Treatment Directive.[53] The Italian government, the ECJ held, had been motivated by a 'legitimate concern' which led it 'rightly' to introduce legislation attempting to assimilate the entry of adoptive and biological children into the family, especially during the 'very delicate initial period'.[54] Underpinning this judgment was a belief that different

---

[51] For a more optimistic approach, see Barbera, M., 'The Unsolved Conflict: Reshaping Family Work and Market Work in the EU Legal Order', in T. Hervey, and J. Kenner (eds.), *Economic and Social Rights under the EU Charter of Fundamental Rights: A Legal Perspective* (Oxford: Hart Publishing, 2003), 153.

[52] Case 163/82 *Commission* v. *Italian Republic* [1983] ECR 3273; Case 184/83 *Hofmann* v. *Barmer Ersatzkasse* [1984] ECR 3047.   [53] Directive 76/207.

[54] Case 163/82 *Commission* v. *Italian Republic* [1983] ECR 3273, para. 16.

treatment on account of motherhood (and not biological differences regarding the capacity to give birth) does not constitute unlawful discrimination. In so holding, the ECJ reinforced the sexual division of labour in which child-care is always the responsibility of mothers, ignoring any conception that the father may also have a legitimate need and/or desire for a period of leave. Fatherhood is thereby limited, by implication, to a breadwinning role, with the assumption that a father's primary commitment and identification should be with paid work, rather than child-care.

This approach was followed in *Hofmann*, which involved a challenge to German legislation which provided that only women were entitled to an optional period of maternity leave which took effect eight weeks after birth. Hofmann, the father of a newly born baby, argued that this leave was for child-care purposes and should therefore be available to mothers and fathers.[55] The German government justified the policy on the grounds that it had 'favourable repercussions in the sphere of family policy, inasmuch as it enables the mother to devote herself to her child', free from the 'constraints' of employment.[56] The ECJ agreed, holding that EU law was not designed to settle questions relating to the 'organisation of the family', or to 'alter the division of responsibility between parents'.[57] The ECJ suggested, therefore, that EU law stands outside the sexual division of labour in the home, thus absolving it from any responsibility for the 'social organisation' of family life.[58] However, in not intervening, the ECJ, and thereby EU law, effectively legitimated the status quo. The ECJ sanctioned legislation which helped ensure that women are, and should remain, primarily responsible for child-care.

In justifying the grant of leave to women only, the ECJ declared that it was 'legitimate to protect the special relationship between a woman and her child'.[59] This is the 'special protection' of a particular conception of motherhood, one that perpetuates the assumption, based on the bonding research, that because 'women bear children they are therefore

---

[55] This argument was strengthened by the fact that the second period of leave was withdrawn in the event of the death of the baby.

[56] Written observations to the Court at 3061, Case 184/83 *Hofmann* v. *Barmer Ersatzkasse* [1984] ECR 3047.

[57] Ibid., para. 24. A formula repeated in many subsequent cases: see, e.g. case C-345/89 *Stoeckel* [1991] ECR I-4047, para. 17.

[58] This apparent neutrality was echoed in Case 170/84 *Bilka-Kaufhaus* [1986] ECR 1607, para. 43, where the Court stated that employers, and EU law, did not have to take into account the 'difficulties faced by persons with family responsibilities' when establishing entitlement conditions for occupational pensions.

[59] Case 184/83 *Hofmann* v. *Barmer Ersatzkasse* [1984] ECR 3047, para. 26. The concept of the 'special relationship' has been reiterated in many subsequent cases, most recently in Case C-342/01 *Gomez* v. *Continental Industrias del Caucho SA*, judgment of 18 Mar. 2004.

automatically the sex that is responsible for rearing them'.[60] The ECJ conceived, normatively, of a workplace in which only women take time off to care for children and was effectively encouraging 'women to stay at home with their children during the early months at least, while men continue with their uninterrupted careers'.[61]

After much condemnation of *Hofmann* by feminist activists, scholars, and many others, it was thought that the ECJ's judgment in *Commission v. France* signalled a change of direction.[62] In this case, the ECJ rendered unlawful a range of rights granted to French women which included such matters as leave when a child is ill, the grant of an additional day's holiday in respect of each child, granting of time off work on Mother's Day and payments of allowances to mothers for child-care expenses.[63] The ECJ held that such entitlements breached the principle of equality as they granted women special rights in their capacity as parents, which is a category 'to which both men and women equally belong'.[64] Unfortunately, however, such optimism was misplaced and in *Abdoulaye*, *Hill and Stapleton*, *Lewen*, and *Lommers* the ECJ effectively reiterated its approach in *Hofmann*.

In *Abdoulaye* the ECJ rejected a claim that a payment granted to women 'when taking maternity leave' constituted discrimination against men.[65] The men had argued that this was a payment equivalent to a child allowance to which women and men should be equally entitled, as it was made on top of women's full salary and where a child was adopted, a payment was made to mothers or fathers. The ECJ justified its position by arguing that women taking maternity leave were in a unique position which made comparison between their rights and rights of women and men at work impossible.[66] However, the appropriate comparison should have been women and men becoming parents and, as the Court stated

---

[60] Bovis, C. and Cnossen, C., 'Stereotyped Assumptions *versus* Sex Equality: A Socio-Legal Analysis of the Equality Laws in the European Union', *International Journal of Comparative Labour Law and Industrial Relations*, 12 (1996), 7, 19.

[61] Fredman, S., 'European Community Discrimination Law: A Critique', *ILJ*, 21 (1992), 119, 127.

[62] Case 312/86 *Commission v. France* [1988] ECR 6315. For example, Cathryn Claussen suggested that if *Commission* v. *France* is to be taken as an indication of how the Court will decide similar issues in the future, it would 'represent a significant step forward': 'Incorporating Women's Reality into Legal Neutrality in the European Community: The Sex Segregation of Labor and the Work–Family Nexus', *Law & Policy in International Business*, 22 (1991), 787, 797.   [63] *Commission* v. *France*, above, n. 62, para. 8.

[64] Ibid., para. 14.

[65] Case C-218/98 *Abdoulaye and others* v. *Renault SA* [1999] IRLR 811 ECR 1-5723. See further McGlynn, C., 'Pregnancy, Parenthood and the Court of Justice in *Abdoulaye*', *European Law Review*, 25 (2000), 654.

[66] In particular, the ECJ held that women suffer 'several occupational disadvantages inherent in taking maternity leave', *Abdoulaye*, above, n. 65, para. 18, for which this payment is made in lawful compensation.

in *Commission* v. *France*, since this category applies to both women and men, they should both be entitled to equal rights.

The ECJ's ruling in *Abdoulaye* bears all the hallmarks of its earlier approach in *Hofmann* and its legitimation of the status quo. It sought to 'protect' women from having their existing rights diluted or removed. However, in doing so, it reinforced a traditional approach to women's responsibilities and capabilities. Although women may currently remain primarily responsible for child-care, the granting of rights to women to compensate therefore in fact entrenches their disadvantageous position. In effect, the ECJ's judgment reinforces the very discrimination that they are seeking to render unlawful. It is appropriate to ensure the continuation of women's employment rights whilst pregnant and giving birth, but such judicial enforcement should not extend beyond such biological and health requirements. Hence, the optional period of maternity leave in *Hofmann*, or the period of adoptive leave in *Commission* v. *Italy* and similarly the payment in *Abdoulaye*, should not come within this field of protection. To do so, as these judgments have done, is to perpetuate stereotypes about the roles of mothers and fathers. To exclude men from a societal recognition of the significance (and financial expense) of the birth of a child perpetuates traditional assumptions that the birth and care of a child is a woman's concern and responsibility. This not only does a disservice to women, ensuring the continuation of outdated assumptions about their familial and workplace roles, but it means that men are not encouraged and facilitated in taking up new and expanding opportunities to play a significant role in the care and upbringing of their children. The ECJ is reproducing the traditional ideologies of motherhood and fatherhood discussed above.

The judgment in *Abdoulaye* confirmed that the ECJ's earlier ruling in *Hill and Stapleton* was not as progressive as it might have first appeared.[67] In the context of considering potential justifications for indirectly discriminatory employment conditions, the ECJ had stated that it was EU policy to 'encourage, and if possible, adapt working conditions to family responsibilities'.[68] It continued that such a policy aims to ensure the '[p]rotection of women within family life and in the course of their professional activities', adding that this was also the case for men.[69] In many ways, this statement could be seen as progressive and a move away from the *Hofmann* approach. It does recognize a familial dimension to equality law and refers to the need for measures to facilitate a

---

[67] Case C-243/95 *Hill and Stapleton* v. *The Revenue Commissioners and the Department of Finance* [1998] IRLR 466 ECJ ECR 1-3739. See further McGlynn, C. and Farrelly, C., 'Equal Pay and the "Protection of Women in Family Life" ', *European Law Review*, 24 (1999), 202.
[68] *Hill and Stapleton*, above, n. 67, para. 42.   [69] Ibid.

reconciliation of paid work and family life.[70] However, the ECJ implies the need to adapt working conditions *to* family responsibilities, that is, to meet *existing* responsibilities: not that family responsibilities need to change in order to liberate women and men. Thus, the ECJ appears to assume a static position regarding family responsibilities and seeks to adapt working conditions to meet that reality. Although this does constitute a belated recognition of the need for some change, it is a limited vision.[71]

Such a limited approach was reinforced in the first case to consider the Parental Leave Directive. In *Lewen* the ECJ held that the payment of a Christmas bonus was not a 'right' protected by the Parental Leave Directive, despite the clause stating that 'rights acquired or in the process of being acquired' must be maintained. Accordingly, Lewen was not able to utilize the directive to challenge her employer's refusal to pay her the Christmas bonus while on parental leave. Although Lewen was granted a remedy in part, this was on the basis of indirect sex discrimination as 'female workers are likely . . . to be on parenting leave far more often than male workers'.[72] In this way, the potentially adverse impact of child-care responsibilities on employment opportunities is only recognized in the context of the existing sex equality laws, not the Parental Leave Directive, and only for women. This reinforces the assumption that such child-care commitments are the primary responsibility of women and it is only women whose employment rights require protection.[73] This ruling negates the purpose of the directive in that although men can take leave, their employment rights will not be protected to the same extent as those of women, as a man in a similar position to Lewen would not have been able to challenge the employer's actions. Moreover, as Lewen's rights were only protected by indirect discrimination, this means that as more men avail themselves of the right to parental leave, as is the explicit aim of the legislation, the rights of women will be reduced as they will be less able to claim indirect discrimination.

The implication of this line of case law is that women's rights are best protected by sex-specific, rather than sex-neutral, provisions. Thus, rather

---

[70] See also Case C-1/95 *Gerster* [1997] ECR I-5253, in which the ECJ, para. 38, stated that: 'The protection of women—and men—both in family life and in the workplace is a principle broadly accepted in the legal systems of the member states as the natural corollary of the fact that men and women are equal and is upheld by Community law.'

[71] It is also a principle which the Court did not apply in the later case of *Gruber* (Case C-249/97, [1999] ECR I-5295) in which the Court rejected the argument that resigning from employment because of the absence of adequate child-care arrangements was equivalent to the other 'important' reasons for leaving employment. The sex discrimination claim was therefore rejected.

[72] Case C-249/97 [1999] *Gruber v. Silhouette International Schmied GmbH & Co.* KG ECR 1-5295.

[73] See further Caracciolo di Torella, E., 'Childcare, Employment and Equality in the EC: First (False) Steps of the Court', *European Law Review*, 25 (2000), 310.

than supporting a move away from *maternity* rights, to *parenting* rights, the consequence of the ECJ's ruling may be to encourage the enactment of sex-specific rights. This is because where parenting rights are enacted in a gender-neutral fashion, it in effect reduces the rights and entitlements of women where those would have been characterized as maternity rights. In providing some protection for women, over and above rights for parents, the ECJ appears to be mimicking the approach to reconciliation considered in the section above. In other words, the reconciliation policy focuses attention on *women's* labour market position, rather than a more general approach to the parenting rights of women and men.

This approach has been confirmed in the extraordinary case of *Lommers*.[74] A branch of the Dutch civil service reserved nursery places for its women employees, except in cases of emergency when they could be offered to men. Unsurprisingly, a male employee challenged this policy as constituting unlawful sex discrimination. The ECJ held that the scheme does 'create a difference of treatment on grounds of sex'[75] and that the situations of a 'male employee and female employee, respectively father and mother of young children, are comparable as regards the possible need for them to use nursery facilities because they are in employment'.[76] However, the ECJ went on to state that the scheme was justified as a measure designed to 'eliminate or reduce actual instances of inequality which may exist in the reality of social life' and was intended to improve women's 'ability to compete in the labour market and to pursue a career on an equal footing with men'.[77] Of crucial importance was the existence of the potential exception in favour of men. The ECJ held that a scheme such as the one under consideration which did not grant access to men who 'take care of their children by themselves' would go beyond the permissible scope of EU law. The scheme, therefore, was held to be lawful for so long as men who take care of children by themselves have access to places on the same conditions as women.

Although the judgment of the ECJ suggests that this ruling is positive for women, in that it is a legitimate measure of positive discrimination in their favour, in practice it reproduces the dominant ideology of motherhood which hinders women's progress in the workplace and reaffirms the inferior status of fatherhood. Indeed, the ECJ referred to academic opinion which considers that 'measures such as those' under discussion are 'likely to perpetuate and legitimize the traditional division of roles between men and women'.[78] And this is indeed what such measures and this judgment will do. Legitimating the grant of child-care places to

---

[74] Case C-476/99 *Lommers* [2002] ECR I-2891.   [75] Ibid., para. 30.   [76] Ibid.

[77] In other words, it was a lawful measure of positive discrimination permitted under art. 2(4) of the Equal Treatment Directive: paras. 32 and 38.

[78] *Lommers*, above, n. 74, para. 22.

women only simply serves to reinforce the fact that they are primarily responsible for child-care. As with *Abdoulaye*, this judgment seeks to deal with the symptoms of discrimination, rather than treating the cause. It is the case that women remain largely responsible for child-care and that they are more likely than men to leave work if child-care is in short supply or is of poor quality. The remedy for this, however, is not to grant places only to women, but to ensure that women are not primarily responsible for child-care and that good quality child-care places are widely available. The judgment may assist some women in the short term, but in the longer term it reinforces disadvantageous assumptions.

Furthermore, the emphasis placed by the ECJ on the exception in favour of fathers 'who take care of their children by themselves'[79] is equally problematic. This formulation suggests that only single fathers would come within the exception, whereas there is no such proviso in favour of women.[80] This is precisely because of the underlying assumption that women, whether in partnerships or not, will take primary responsibility for child-care, whereas men will only do so where they are on their own. Thus, the exception for men simply reinforces the assumptions about women's roles and the dominant ideology of fatherhood. It suggests that in a partnership where child-care is shared, the father would not be eligible for a child-care place under this scheme. It is this result which ultimately demonstrates the adverse impact of this judgment.[81]

III CONCLUSION

Traditionally, labour law doctrine has presumed the existence of the sexual division of labour and traditional family forms. This has enabled the development of law and policy premised on the notion of the 'ideal' worker as being one unencumbered by familial obligations. While the EU has determined that it needs to increase the participation of women

---

[79] Ibid., para. 50.

[80] It seems that this is the interpretation placed on the judgment by the ECJ in its press release, which acclaims the judgment as representing 'progress for lone fathers' who are to be treated equally with lone mothers. *Agence Europe*, 21 Mar. 2002.

[81] Fortunately there are some limits as to how far the Court will expand the scope of justifications for discrimination. In *Griesmar* the ECJ held that a French government retirement scheme which granted credits to women with children, regardless of any time away from the workplace, constituted unlawful sex discrimination. Case C-366/99 *Griesmar*, judgment of 29 Nov. 2001. However, this simply demonstrates confusion in the ECJ's case law, described by Siofra O'Leary as being 'riddled with confusion and contradiction'. O'Leary, S., *Employment Law at the European Court of Justice* (Oxford: Hart Publishing, 2002), 220.

in the workplace, it has failed to address this traditional paradigm, within which European labour law operates. The rhetoric of EU law and policy recognizes the essential need for greater equality in relation to the reconciliation of paid work and family life but continues to emphasize only changes in women's responsibilities. The jurisprudence of the ECJ, again while paying lip service to the ideals of equality, effectively entrenches the existing situation. This situation is perpetuating the sexual division of labour, while at the same time increasing the demands on women. Accordingly, despite the EU's perceived economic need to ensure greater participation of women in the labour market, it fights shy of the real measures that would need to be taken if women were to feel able and willing to increase their paid work. A new paradigm needs to be developed where access to the workplace is facilitated, at the same time as distributing caring responsibilities equally among women and men.

11

Taking Leave: Work and Family in Australian Law and Policy

ROSEMARY J. OWENS

I INTRODUCTION

Australia is in the midst of intense national debate about the most appropriate way to accommodate work and family. At the centre of this debate is the issue of paid maternity leave. The urgency of the topic is a reflection of a complex set of changes at every level of society, including: the pressures imposed on businesses through the gradual incorporation of Australian industry into the new economy of the global era; the changing demographics of the workplace, especially the increased participation of women in paid employment; the declining fertility rate; and the ageing of the population. The popular characterizations of the work/ family interface make it clear that this arena is one where present tensions appear to be unsustainable and while the aspiration to harmonious interplay is reflected in metaphors of balance and reconciliation, the present reality is clearly one of collision and conflict.

While it can be acknowledged that a broad range of social, economic, and political factors constitute the institutions of workplace and family, the creation of the family-friendly workplace in Australia has, to date, been worked out primarily in the industrial arena. It is the province of labour law. There, a uniquely antipodean institution, the Industrial Relations Commission exercising powers of conciliation and arbitration, has sought to balance the interests of business, collective labour, and the wider community in the production of award standards governing work relations. Commencing in the late 1970s the Australian Council of Trade Unions (the ACTU) initiated a series of test cases before the federal Commission, leading to the establishment of the basic rules aimed at enabling workers to accommodate their family responsibilities. However, the period of most intense concern with the problem of constructing family-friendly workplaces has coincided with the demise of the Commission's role in establishing fixed standards through the arbitral process. There is now an increased emphasis on flexible standards and agreements through which the immediate parties at the workplace take a more direct responsibility for the governance of their own relations.

In the lengthy engagement of Australian labour law with work/ family issues, taking leave, that is the exclusion of the worker from paid work, has been the model solution adopted. This reflects an institutional acceptance of the separation of work and family, of the public and private sphere, and a denial of the dependence of the market on reproductive labour. Further, the costs of all forms of leave taking have been, with rare exception, absorbed by individual workers, indicating both an abnegation by the state of responsibility for the cost of social reproduction and a continuing exploitation of family and care work by the market. So inadequate has been the legal provision for leave that, when coupled with a degree of resilience in the model worker as a full-time 'harvester man', there has evolved an acquiescence in entrenched abstentionism as women's employment has become structured as part-time and casual. In its treatment of work/family issues, labour law has come to compromise itself through failing to protect those who are most vulnerable and in reality has achieved only a very limited success in transforming the Australian workplace into something that might be described as 'family-friendly'.[1]

In this context the proposal by the Sex Discrimination Commissioner of the Human Rights and Equal Opportunity Commission (HREOC) for a scheme of paid maternity leave based upon equality principles promised a productive encounter with labour law.[2] Equality law to date has played only a limited role in securing a family-friendly workplace in Australia. While in most Australian states there is now some specific protection against discrimination on the basis of family or care responsibilities, at the federal level such protection is restricted to cases involving termination of employment and only where there has been direct, but not indirect, discrimination.[3] Individuals have, in a few instances, successfully used anti-discrimination legislation to require employers to take account of workers' family responsibilities in the arrangements of shifts and rosters and to secure part-time work or flexible working arrangements that will enable them to collect children from school

[1] Cf. Department of Family and Community Services and the Department of Employment and Workplace Relations, *OECD Review of Family Friendly Policies: The Reconciliation of Work and Family Life, Australia's Background Report* (Canberra: Commonwealth of Australia, 2002).

[2] See HREOC, *A Time to Value: Proposal for a National Paid Maternity Leave Scheme* (Sydney: HREOC, 2002).

[3] The Anti-discrimination Amendment (Carer's Responsibilities) Act 2000 (NSW) provides the most extensive legislative protection of all the states. One state, South Australia, provides no specific protection against discrimination on the basis of family or care responsibilities. The relevant federal legislation is the Sex Discrimination Act (Cth), s. 7A. However, it can be noted that federal industrial legislation prohibiting dismissal on the basis of family responsibilities could provide protection against indirect discrimination; see Workplace Relations Act 1996 (Cth), s. 170CK(2)(f).

and take them to childcare.[4] But these individual battles have often been drawn out and not always successful.[5] While the inadequacies of anti-discrimination law have long been exposed,[6] in the work/family debate over paid maternity leave, anti-discrimination or equality law offered a means of transcending some of the limitations inherent in labour law and thereby opening a space for further positive reform or transformative developments.

However, after the publication of HREOC's proposal, the issue of paid maternity leave in Australia continued to be deeply contested. In the months that followed, the proposal's failure to gain formal support at the political level reflected the degree to which gendered assumptions about paid (or productive) and unpaid (or reproductive) work remained enmeshed in understandings about the nature of the family, the state's interest in and responsibility for social reproduction, the function of the state and the role of regulation, and the relations of all those things to the market. The eventual concession by both major political parties, prior to the 2004 federal election, that the state should provide a maternity payment to all women at the time of the birth of a child, represented less a radical intervention to resolve an issue of work and family conflict and more a pragmatic acceptance that in the current context the issue could no longer be totally ignored. The meaning of this maternity payment, in particular whether it can be viewed as offering a real scheme of paid maternity leave, will continue to be matter of vigorous contestation.

II THE EVOLUTION OF A FAMILY-FRIENDLY AUSTRALIAN LABOUR LAW

From maternity to carer's leave

Since the late 1970s, award standards aimed at facilitating the resolution of work/family conflict have steadily evolved in Australian law through a series of test cases conducted before the federal Industrial Relations Commission. These standards enable workers to take leave from their

---

[4] See e.g. *Mayer* v. *ANTSO* (2003) EOC 93-285; *Escobar* v. *Rainbow Printing Pty Ltd (No 2)* (2002) 120 IR 84; *Song* v. *Ainsworth Game Technology Pty Ltd* (2002) EOC 93-194.

[5] See e.g. the *Schou* litigation: *Schou* v. *State of Victoria* [1999] VCAT 631; [1999] VCAT 632; [2000] VCAT 1453; [2002] VCAT 375; *State of Victoria* v. *Schou* (2001) 3 VR 655; [2001] VSC 382; *Schou* v. *State of Victoria* [2002] VCAT 375; and *State of Victoria* v. *Schou* (2004) 8 VR 120.

[6] These have been extensively documented by feminist scholars: see e.g., in Australia, Thornton, M., *The Liberal Promise: Anti Discrimination Legislation in Australia* (Melbourne: OUP, 1990), and in the UK, Fredman, S., *Women and the Law* (Oxford: OUP, 1998), esp. ch. 7.

employment for family and care purposes without risking the security of their labour market participation.

In the first of these cases, the *Maternity Leave Test Case*, there was established a standard of up to twelve months' unpaid maternity leave for the private sector.[7] The reasoning of the decision centred on the special industrial requirements of women who give birth; the biological needs of the mother to recover her health and to bond with and breast-feed her new child were relied upon to found a new standard of twelve months' unpaid leave, six weeks of which was compulsory both imme-diately before and after the birth in recognition respectively of her special needs and the possibility of her impaired performance in those periods. While the period of leave was not to interrupt the mother's continuity of employment for the purposes of access to other entitlements and seniority, nor was it allowed to count positively towards them. However, most importantly, the decision acknowledged that motherhood and participation in the paid workforce could be combined and it established an entitlement for the mother to return to her former position, or an equivalent position, at the end of the period of maternity leave.

Although this right to maternity leave was articulated very much in terms of women's biological uniqueness, within a short period of time the extension to adoptive mothers of a like entitlement for leave neces-sarily admitted the social and cultural aspects of her bonding with and caring for her children.[8] From there, it was not a very big step to acknow-ledge the social importance of all parental care for children new to a family, and in 1990 the ACTU instituted before the Commission a further claim for leave for new fathers. The *Parental Leave Case*[9] set a new standard for the private sector. It allowed new fathers a period of 'short' unpaid paternity leave, a week at the time of birth or three weeks at the time of adoption[10] of their child, granted specifically so that they could support the mother and play a parental role to any of their other children at this time. However, this was only one part of a larger package of leave provisions settled in this decision: the total period of 'long' leave now granted to both parents was fifty-one weeks, with any period of maternity or paternity leave to be reduced by the amount of leave taken

---

[7] *Re: Electrical Trades Union of Australia—application to vary Metal Industry Award 1971 re: maternity leave* (1979) 218 CAR 120. Prior to this test case, provision for private-sector mater-nity leave in federal awards was extremely limited. In the provision of maternity leave the public sector had led the way; see e.g. Maternity Leave (Commonwealth Employees) Act 1973 (Cth).

[8] *The Clothing and Allied Trades Union of Australia v. Australian Confederation of Apparel Manufacturers of New South Wales (the Adoption Leave Test Case)* (1985) 298 CAR 321.

[9] (1990) 36 IR 1.

[10] This extended period of time recognized that many adoptive parents needed to travel overseas to take custody of the child.

by the other spouse, and with only the first week after the birth allowed to be taken concurrently. These standards have since been replicated in federal legislation.

In the *Parental Leave Case* the ACTU had also made a second claim for a period of five days' unpaid 'special family leave' to accommodate parents' absences from work as a result of their responsibilities in relation to the educational or medical needs of their children. The claim was not pursued at that time but reactivated in what became known as the *Family Leave Test Case—November 1994*.[11] The ACTU was galvanized into action at this time as a result of the incorporation of provisions in the Industrial Relations Act 1988 (Cth), which sought to ensure the implementation in Australia of the ILO Convention concerning Equal Opportunities for Men and Women Workers with Family Responsibilities (Convention (C156) (1981)) by requiring the Commission itself to instigate an inquiry if a test case were not initiated.

The focus of the *Family Leave Test Case—November 1994* was an examination of the legal conditions upon which employees were entitled to use their own leave entitlements in circumstances requiring them to care for family members. The case was conducted in two stages, with the Commission addressing outstanding matters in the *Personal/Carer's Leave Test Case—Stage 2—November 1995*.[12] First, the Commission accepted employees' right to access five days of their own sick leave to care for ill members of their 'immediate family', a decision that to a large extent formalized existing social practice. In the second stage, the Commission decided to aggregate employees' current year's entitlement to sick leave and bereavement leave, in effect allowing them to access more of their paid leave entitlements for the purposes of providing care. To address employer concerns with cost, it was decided to cap every component of the leave: there was to be a maximum of five days' leave for care purposes, which could be taken in periods of less than a single day, and the entitlement to leave in cases of illness or bereavement was also capped at the existing award entitlement, usually eight and three days respectively, giving eleven days' personal leave in total, with any available accumulated sick leave still able to be accessed in the case of the worker's illness. With very minor adjustments the federal safety net award standards for parental leave and personal leave remain today as established in the 1990 and 1994–5 test cases respectively.[13]

---

[11] (1994) 57 IR 121.   [12] (1995) 62 IR 48.

[13] e.g. *The Award Simplification Decision* (1997) 75 IR 272 removed the compulsory requirement for women to take 6 weeks' leave prior to the birth of the child on the basis that it was discriminatory. The federal standards have in most cases been adopted at state level; see e.g. *Family Leave Test Case NSW* (1995) 59 IR 1 and *Re: Application for Adoption of Provisions for Family Leave* (1995) 62 IR 403 (SA).

These test cases marked, in social terms, a broadening in labour law's understanding of workers' responsibilities for family care work. While the standard for 'short' maternity and paternity leave was stated to be related to the distinct roles of men and women workers at the time of the birth of their child and therefore not interchangeable, the acknowledgement that either parent might become the primary caregiver in the first year of the child's life and that both should be provided with the same job protection was the first departure in Australian labour law from the view that family care work was solely the responsibility of women. Personal/carer's leave expressed a social aspiration for an even broader shouldering of the responsibilities for unpaid work. In 1995, the Commission had noted the resilience of the gendered division of care labour despite demographic shifts in the composition of the paid workforce. It determined because of this to expand access to carer's leave in the hope of facilitating a more equal sharing among workers of care work, observing that at the time there was a strong and expanding economy which would cushion the impact on employers of any resultant additional costs.

The test case standards also expanded the concept of family responsibilities, encompassing not only care responsibilities for young children but also for ageing parents and relatives, partners, and others with whom there are close and loving relations within a household. While parental leave in Australian labour law still assumes a nuclear family formed by a heterosexual couple, either married or *de facto*, the personal leave standard is more inclusive. In the *Family Leave Test Case* (1994), the submissions of parties regarding the meaning that should be assigned to 'immediate family' covered a broad range of alternatives. Some confined themselves to a focus on the traditional nuclear family centring on a heterosexual couple, either in a married or *de facto* relationship, and including their children and step-children, grandchildren, older parents, grandparents, and siblings. Single-parent families were also usually included here. More controversially, others advocated that the definition be expanded to include the families of same-sex partners, and still others sought an extension to include the much wider range of relations incorporated in the conception of the family as understood in some minority cultures including indigenous communities. Finally in the second stage of the decision, and after a more expansive approach to the same question in one of the states, the federal Commission accepted the need for a non-discriminatory provision that would extend to same-sex relations. In the interests of protecting the privacy of employees from having to disclose their sexuality to their employer it framed the clause in terms of care for 'immediate family' and 'a member of the household'. Regrettably, the more contentious issue of wider kinship relations was sidestepped and left to be determined on a specific case-by-case basis. Nonetheless, the decision was significant in acknowledging the needs of workers in a greater diversity of family types, and the change in name from family to carer's leave reflected a growing acceptance that where a person with close affective ties was genuinely in need of care of another who was in paid work then that care should be able to be provided without a detrimental impact on the worker's employment position.

From uniform standards to facilitative clauses and enterprise agreements

The initial regulatory response to work and family matters was to facilitate the worker's exit from the workplace for discrete periods, on a temporary basis, thus erasing for a short time but not really resolving the inevitable and ongoing conflict between the two. From the mid-1990s a secondary emphasis on flexible work relations was presented as offering a more enduring resolution.

In the *Family Leave Test Case* (1994) the Commission also introduced 'facilitative provisions' to provide greater flexibility in the way in which employees could arrange their hours of work or take annual leave or unpaid leave. As the Commission described it:

A 'facilitative provision' is that part of an award clause which enables agreement at enterprise level to determine the manner in which that clause is applied at the enterprise. A facilitative provision normally provides that the standard approach in an award provision may be departed from by agreement between an individual employer and an employee or the majority of employees in the enterprise or part of the enterprise concerned. Where an award clause contains a facilitative provision it establishes both the standard award condition and the framework within which agreement can be reached as to how the particular clause should be applied in practice.[14]

Industry-wide leave standards thus became flexible, able to be varied through collective, and even individual, workplace agreements. The new facilitative provisions enabled the taking of up to a week of annual leave in single days, time off in lieu of payment for overtime, and agreements for the provision of additional unpaid leave for the care of an ill family member.

The use of facilitative provisions presaged the movement away from rigid standard setting to a more 'contractualist' approach in the regulation of workplace relations. Since the mid-1990s federal awards have been restricted to minimum conditions, and statutory agreements have become the mechanism through which better work conditions, including

---

[14] *Family Leave Test Case* (1994), above, n. 11, at 147.

improved family-friendly protections, must be established. However, nearly a decade on, agreements seem to have produced few innovations in this arena. From the latest evidence it can be seen that the most common family-friendly provisions in federal collective (or certified) agreements are little different from those established by the test case standards:[15] family or carer's leave is included in 27 per cent of federal collective agreements, most often comprising the right to access other leave for caring purposes (in 19 per cent of agreements), or unpaid family leave (in 9 per cent of agreements), but only rarely paid family leave (in 3 per cent of agreements). In only a small number of federal collective agreements is there provision for paid maternity leave (7 per cent of agreements) and in fewer still is paid paternity leave to be found (4 per cent of agreements). The second most common feature identified as a family-friendly measure, and now found in about a quarter of federal collective agreements, is the provision for part-time work and this, along with access to single days of annual leave (found in 13 per cent of agreements), appears to be the fastest growing of the family-friendly provisions. The number of other family-friendly measures in collective agreements, such as employer-provided childcare, is negligible and there is also minimal provision for alternative employment options, such as home-based work or job-sharing arrangements.

Family-friendly flexibility?

Apart from those provisions in collective agreements described above and specifically acknowledged as 'family-friendly', it is common to point to the benefits that flexibility can offer workers with family and care responsibilities. 'Hours flexibility', in particular, is claimed as having a family-friendly character. In recent years, there has been a stronger emphasis in agreements on such flexibility, including annualized hours, the ability to negotiate the hours of start and finish of work, the capacity to take time off in lieu of overtime worked either on penalty or ordinary rates, the removal of restrictions on days to perform ordinary hours, and the ability to bank or vary rostered days off by mutual agreement. In addition, the use of facilitative provisions, through which individual workers can agree with their employer their own work arrangements, are continuing to be used to facilitate the balancing of work and family life. These can enable, for example, leave agreements, whereby employers

---

[15] See Department of Employment and Workplace Relations and the Office of the Employment Advocate, *Agreement Making in Australia under the Workplace Relations Act 2000–2001* (Canberra: Commonwealth of Australia, 2002), 80–4. All statistical information regarding federal agreements in this chapter is derived from this source. This evidence relating to federal agreements is significant because they are generally now regarded as at the forefront of improved industrial standards.

offer employees with family responsibilities the option of purchasing additional leave, usually in amounts up to two months, to cover periods such as school holidays. Such arrangements, however, are usually restricted to those employees who have worked for the employer for at least a year, and are also subject to the employer's approval as to timing, thereby ensuring that the interests of the enterprise are balanced with business requirements in respect of the job.

In the main then, the so-called 'new and innovative family-friendly clauses'[16] emphasize the incompatibility of care responsibilities and paid work and continue to deal with this conflict through the provision of extra or extended leave, the facility to use other leave entitlements for family care purposes, and sometimes the creation of new leave entitlements such as pressing emergency domestic leave of one day per each occasion but always subject to managerial approval. Far less frequently do they mandate some reorganization of the workplace, such as the taking into account of family responsibilities in the arrangement of shifts, and ensuring equal access to training and promotional opportunities for part-time workers.

While it has been widely argued that flexibility provisions are central to making it possible for workers to accommodate their paid work and their family and care responsibilities, the primary impetus for them has been, and continues to be, the needs of the enterprise.[17] Indeed, demands imposed by the flexible workplace of the new economy are inflicting, in Australia as elsewhere, yet another set of pressures upon families, and exacerbate the difficulties of those who would seek to avoid a work/family collision.[18] The issue of long working hours is particularly problematic. This was confirmed in *The Reasonable Working Hours Test Case*, where evidence was presented of longer working hours and a substantial reduction in the number of employees who worked standard hours. This was coupled with information on employee preferences for a change in hours with many full-time workers wanting fewer hours and many of the part-timers wanting more hours. However, despite strong indications of the negative effect of long hours on family life, the case resulted in only a weak amelioration of the problem. Rather than curtailing the

---

[16] See ACIIRT, *Agreements Database And Monitor (ADAM) Reports*, nos. 1–39, 1993–2003, University of Sydney, available at www.acirrt.com, for examples of innovative clauses in agreements. A database of family-friendly clauses in agreements is also available at www.workplace.gov.au. [17] See above, n. 15, 78–80.
[18] See Pocock, B., *The Work/Life Collision* (Sydney: The Federation Press, 2003), ch. 6; Watson, I., Buchanan, J., Campbell, I., and Briggs, C., *Fragmented Futures: New Challenges in Working Life* (Sydney: The Federation Press, 2003), chs. 7 and 9; Cass, B., 'Employment Time and Family Time: The Intersection of Labour Market Transformation and Family Responsibilities in Australia', and Davis, E. and Morehead, A., 'Commentaries', in R. Callus and R. D. Lansbury (eds.), *Working Futures: The Changing Nature of Work and Employment Relations in Australia* (Sydney: The Federation Press, 2002).

explosion in working hours by providing a definitive statement as to their limit, and perhaps be seen as interfering with management's right to the efficient organization of its business, the Commission established a standard which allows employees to refuse a request for working overtime where it is unreasonable, having regard to the employee's personal circumstances, including their family responsibilities, as well as other, more conventional, industrial indicators, such as occupational health and safety, the needs of the workplace, and the notice period given. This determination depended, in part, on the Commission's reasoning that the relationship between hours and family life was complex and not always harmful, as the opportunity to work longer hours often meant increased household income and a consequent reduction in economic stress for families.[19]

In 2003, another attempt to restrain, through the award safety net the deleterious impact of flexibility on employees seeking to balance work and family, was initiated by the ACTU. After a period of conciliation, the hearings to arbitrate this *Family Provisions Test Case* commenced in August 2004.[20] The ACTU's initial claims included the extension of unpaid parental leave from twelve to twenty-four months, incorporating eight weeks' simultaneous leave for both parents, provided an employee satisfies the qualifying criterion of twelve months' continuous service with the employer; the right to be consulted about significant changes to the job while on parental leave; the provision of a genuine right to return to part-time work on return from parental leave and up until the child reaches school age, by removing the employer's right to veto this; the provision of five days' paid carer's leave, in addition to the prospect of using five days' personal leave for care purposes; the provision of flexibility in hours through a right for employees to request a variation in hours worked, the arrangement of the hours worked, and the place of work, which the employer cannot reasonably refuse; the provision of the capacity to take up to six weeks' unpaid leave and average wages over a period of time as requested by the employee; and the provision of a right to a reasonable period of unpaid emergency leave for family emergencies and care purposes.

At its strongest, in respect of the claims in relation to part-time work, the case amounts to a demand for workplace *rights* to accommodate work and family. In relation to many of the other claims, the case seeks to impose on employers a duty to act positively by flexibly organizing the workplace in ways that will enable employees to accommodate their work with family responsibilities: that is, employers must not

---

[19] (2002) 114 IR 390 at para. 169.
[20] For details, see ACTU website at www.actu.asn.au.

'unreasonably refuse' employees' requests for flexibility, must explore alternative options, and can only refuse a worker's request on the ground of necessity when there are no other options available to meet the needs of the enterprise. It is unlikely, given the present regulatory reluctance to impose constraints upon employers' control of their businesses, and thus upon their ability to respond to the demands of the market, that all these claims will be granted. But it is very likely that the Commission will impose a greater responsibility on business to establish procedures that recognize at least a duty to consider the needs of workers with family responsibilities seriously and fairly.[21]

An inability to recognize family-friendly measures as a matter of substantive right is symptomatic of a wider problem in labour law's capacity to deal with the work/family interface. In Australia, there are two critical issues here. First is the breadth of coverage offered by the industrial system. Although the framework legislative instruments establishing both federal and state industrial systems proclaim their family-friendly purposes,[22] there is no comprehensive general system of protections in place for workers with family and care responsibilities. Australian labour law is to be found in a complex of instruments at both Commonwealth and state level, which include legislation, industrial awards, as well as statutory agreements that may be either collective or individual. Minimum entitlements are to be found mainly in industrial awards, yet a significant number of workers are not covered at all by awards, or are excluded from many of their benefits. Legislative minimum standards also exclude many workers. In any event they are rare with respect to work/family matters and nationally offer only a right to twelve months' unpaid maternity, paternity, and parental leave with a right for the worker to return to their previous position at the end of that period.[23] Only for some public-sector workers is there more comprehensive legislative provision.[24] There is no national legislative right to a wider family or carer's leave.

---

[21] Cf. the recent legislative developments in the UK establishing a process for employers to deal with the requests of parents of young children for part-time work, considered by Collins, in this volume.

[22] e.g. one of the main objects of the Workplace Relations Act 1996 (Cth) is: 'assisting employees to balance their work and family responsibilities effectively through the development of mutually beneficial work practices with employees' (s. 3(i)). This legislation also includes minimum entitlements to parental leave, and prohibits the termination of employment on the basis of family responsibilities.

[23] See Workplace Relations Act 1996 (Cth), Sch. 14; and at state level, see e.g. Industrial Relations Act 1999 (NSW), Part 4, Parental Leave and Industrial Relations Amendment Act 1986 (Vic), Part VIIA, Maternity Leave.

[24] See e.g. Maternity Leave (Commonwealth Employees) Act 1973 (Cth), which includes, by regulation, a period of paid leave.

The problems of coverage have also been exacerbated by the greater industrial emphasis on agreements. Most agreements, certainly in the federal sphere, are to be found in male-dominated industries, such as construction, manufacturing, and transport and storage, whereas there are comparatively few in retail, finance, and insurance, and only slightly more in health and community services and education, all of which are female-dominated industries. Thus, most women who bear the primary responsibility for family and care work are dependent upon the protections available in the award or legislative safety net. Not surprisingly too, patterns of sex segregation in workplaces influence the inclusion of family-friendly measures in agreements. In industry sectors where women predominate, such as finance and insurance, retail trade and accommodation, cafes and restaurants, nearly three-quarters of federal agreements have parental and carer's leave clauses, whereas in transport and storage these are included in less than one-third of agreements and in the construction industry in not even a tenth of agreements. Part-time work provisions are common in female industries, and are included in as many as four-fifths of communication services and retail trade agreements, but appear in only a tiny proportion of agreements in male industries, ranging from only 4 per cent of construction agreements and 25 per cent of manufacturing agreements. Paid parental leave occurs in 51 per cent of education agreements but only 1 per cent of construction agreements. Access to leave for caring reasons is provided for in 63 per cent of retail agreements and 53 per cent of finance and insurance agreements, but only in 19 per cent of all agreements. Job-sharing and home-based work arrangements are concentrated in finance and insurance and, to a lesser extent, government or public-sector jobs. In this way agreements at the enterprise level operate to reinforce and construct the responsibility for unpaid care work as gendered, and thus counteract the broader scope of some of the earlier test case standards. Simultaneously, workplace agreement-making has delivered fewer real improvements to women workers in the paid workplace; women and part-time workers are more likely to be covered by agreements with paid leave and equity provisions, while men do much better with consultative provisions, work organization matters, and performance indicators, all of which focus on their development within the workplace. The present system of workplace bargaining has thus served to emphasize that success in the paid workplace is incompatible with family responsibilities and thereby to exacerbate women's inequality.

Secondly, within the industrial system, only family-friendly provisions that have been relatively cost neutral to business in the marketplace have ever been introduced. The view of business, and especially small business, that the imposition of additional costs on it would be unfair, and therefore unacceptable, has usually been persuasive in the Commission hearings. Additional costs to business have been imposed only where they have been explained as inevitable or negligible and, in any event, able to be supported by an expanding economy, or to be balanced by additional gains to the enterprise, such as the retention of skilled workers.

Thus, in the industrial system, the cost of the resolution of family/ work conflict has been borne overwhelmingly by carers themselves, and those carers are predominantly women. Leave for parental (maternity and paternity) purposes is unpaid; that is, parents (usually mothers) pay for it. Payment for carer's leave is also made by the worker through the surrender of workplace entitlements, ordinarily intended to be accessed for their own personal and health needs. This sacrifice, built upon an ethic of selflessness assumed as characteristic in carers and natural in women, has been incorporated not only into the award safety net standard, but also has become the norm in collective agreement making. Bargaining in the workplace involves a trade of items that have value in the market- place, more efficiency and increased production in exchange for a benefit, but in service industries where women predominate there is usually little in the way of extra efficiencies available to trade, so cannibalizing their existing entitlements continues to be the only available option. In any event, when the costs of care have always been absorbed by the carer and kept separate in the private sphere, there is little apparent economic incentive for the marketplace to assume responsibility for them.

Finally, the accommodation of family and care responsibilities often means only a partial involvement in the paid workforce for carers and the cost of this exit is paid for by them. In effect, the carer becomes a non-standard worker. This may come about indirectly, with agreements to buy additional leave that can be characterized as little more than arrangements to take leave without pay. Alternatively, because the price of the leave, usually equivalent to the amount the employee would have earned for the period, is deducted from the employee's pay in equal instalments over the entire year, another way of characterizing such arrangements is to say that these workers now work part-time, although with an annualized salary. However, arrangements for non-standard work are usually more direct. Part-time work and casual work have become the most common way of securing the resolution of work and family conflict in Australia, through a *de facto* exclusion of women from the paid workforce, which simultaneously ensures that the costs of care work are borne by them. The corollary of all of this is that the dependency of the market on unpaid care work is not acknowledged and carers do the double shift and with fewer protections.[25]

[25] For a more extensive analysis of this issue, see Rittich, K., 'Feminization and Contingency: Regulating the Stakes for Work for Women', in J. Conaghan, R. M. Fischl, and K. Klare (eds.), *Labour Law in an Era of Globalization: Transformative Practices and Possibilities* (Oxford: OUP, 2002).

Non-standard work: a family-friendly alternative?

Non-standard employment, that is, employment deviating from the traditional model of a 'harvester man' working full-time in an ongoing employment relation, has been specifically promoted by Australian labour law as a way to accommodate family and care responsibilities. Until the early 1990s many awards imposed quite severe restrictions on part-time employment, either prohibiting it altogether, or confining it to a limited percentage of employees who worked defined minimum and maximum hours. Following ACTU arguments, that owing to the paucity of childcare for very young children it would be useful for workers to be able to access part-time work up to their child's second birthday, the 1990 *Parental Leave Case* also opened up flexible options for part-time employment for up to two years when it was associated with the birth or adoption of a child. As well as being available to women for the period before the birth where this was medically necessary, where a parent employee did move to part-time work at the end of a period of parental leave there was a right, exercisable only once, to return to their former full-time position. However, parents did not acquire a *right* to transfer to part-time work in the first instance. Rather, part-time work was only to be permitted where the individual employer and employee *agreed* about it, again reflecting a reluctance on the Commission's part to interfere directly in the managerial control of the organization of the workplace.

In the first instance, part-time work was thus constructed specifically as something to enable workers to accommodate childcare responsibilities, independently of the more general restrictions on such work in existing awards. By the time of the *Personal/Carer's Leave Test Case Stage 2* (1995), the Commission, noting that a significant way of managing care responsibilities in many families was through women's part-time work, set about making wider provision for part-time work by announcing a review of awards and the adequacy of existing provisions for part-time work in particular industries and enterprises. At this stage, the Commission was anxious to stress that it considered part-time work to be an appropriate means of enabling workers to accommodate their family and care responsibilities, providing that the pro-rata enjoyment of benefits and a minimum number of regular hours were guaranteed to the worker. Quality part-time employment, not the provision of mere casual jobs, was envisaged. Such part-time work was seen as balancing the twin purposes of ensuring that there was no unfairness to workers and that the flexibility of the business was not impeded. But this became unsustainable with the further 'deregulation' of non-standard work as labour law prohibited the Commission from placing any limits on part-time work.

Now, the main way in which women workers accommodate the pressures of paid and care work is through non-standard employment. In Australia, this trend is far more intense than in other industrialized market economies.[26] The rate of growth in non-standard work in Australia is surpassed only by the Netherlands amongst other OECD countries.[27] While all sectors of the paid workforce have seen an increase in this kind of work, in Australia women are disproportionately represented in part-time work. While most men are still employed on a full-time basis, only a little more than half of women are so employed. For women, part-time employment is a characteristic of their entire working life; at least a third of every age group of women workers is employed on a part-time basis.

The most striking feature of this part-time employment now is that it is overwhelmingly casual; that is, this part-time work is in jobs with little access to workplace entitlements or security. In the vast majority of cases casuals are excluded from the enjoyment of workplace protections and benefits, including family-friendly provisions. This exclusion is sometimes direct. In other instances, it follows either from the inability of casual workers to access other entitlements,[28] or because they cannot satisfy a requisite period of continuity of employment with their employer.[29] These casual workers are the most vulnerable of all workers, and labour law has been slow to extend its benefits and protections to them. However, more recently, in the *Parental Leave (Casuals) Test Case*, the Commission, with the support of all the major industrial players except the federal Liberal coalition government, extended to those award workers who are labelled 'casual' but are in reality long-term employees, the right to twelve months' unpaid parental leave and a return to their previous position.[30] Thus, many casuals who have at least twelve months' *de facto* continuous service and who also have a reasonable expectation of ongoing employment can now access this entitlement.

---

[26] OECD, *Babies and Bosses: Reconciling Work and Family Life, vol I, Australia, Denmark and the Netherlands* (Paris: OECD, 2002).

[27] See OECD, *Employment Outlook* (Geneva: OECD, 2002). For the latest statistics on the Australian labour force, see the Australian Bureau of Statistics, *Year Book Australia 2004, Labour*, available online at: http://www.abs.gov.au. All labour force statistical information in this chapter is drawn from this source.

[28] See e.g. Maternity Leave (Commonwealth Employees) Act 1973 (Cth), s. 3(e), which excludes all those who are not entitled to paid sick leave; that is, casuals and other non-standard workers, such as those working through an agency, many of whom also work as casuals.

[29] See the definition of 'continuity of service' in Workplace Relations Act 1996 (Cth), s. 2, Sch. 14, governing maternity, paternity, and parental leave.

[30] (2002) 110 IR 487. This standard was quickly replicated in some of the states through incorporation either into awards; see e.g. *Parental Leave (Casual Employees) Award Case* [2002] SAIRComm. 2, or into legislation, see e.g. Industrial Relations Act 1999 (Qld), ss. 15A and 16(1), and the stricter provisions in the Industrial Relations Act 1996 (NSW), as amended, ss. 53(2) and 57(3).

But while some casuals may now be able to access unpaid parental leave, other family-friendly standards, such as the ability to use other workplace entitlements such as sick leave or annual leave for care purposes, are, by definition, unavailable to them because they do not have the base entitlements to trade in the first place. Rather, casual employment remains a means of accommodating family and care responsibilities at the cost of the worker. The main reason women give for taking on part-time and casual work is to accommodate work and family responsibilities, and therefore the growth in this type of work is often justified using the rhetoric of choice. But the reality is there are few alternative work arrangements available to them. In effect, they have been forced to take at least some leave of paid employment.

III CREATING A FAMILY-FRIENDLY LAW OF WORK: A CONTRIBUTION FROM EQUALITY LAW?

Paid maternity leave in Australia

In recent years, the national work/family debate has been focused on the issue of paid maternity leave, the inadequacies of the system highlighted by the fact that at the commencement of the twenty-first century Australia stood, along with the USA, as one of the only two OECD countries not to have a national system of paid maternity leave. Only a very few women, some of those employed in the public sector, enjoy a legislated entitlement to paid maternity leave.[31] For the remainder, including all of those who work in the private sector, the only avenue to secure such a right is through the processes of workplace bargaining. Where paid maternity leave is provided for in agreements, the rate of maternity pay is frequently equivalent to full replacement salary, but the average period of entitlement is only for seven weeks. In those few agreements where maternity pay is for a longer period, the quantum provided for drops significantly as a proportion of usual earnings. While there have been some successes, for the vast majority of women working in the marketplace, bargaining processes have not been able to deliver paid maternity leave.[32] Fewer than 40 per cent of all women employees have any access to paid maternity leave; of these, the main beneficiaries are those who are in full-time employment, 51 per cent of whom have

[31] See e.g. Maternity Leave (Commonwealth Employees) Act 1973 (Cth).

[32] See HREOC, *A Time to Value*, above, n. 2, 29ff. Indeed, only 3% of large enterprises, those with more than 100 employees, report providing for paid maternity leave for a period of 14 weeks, the standard set by the ILO in the *Convention concerning Maternity Protection* (No 183) (2000); see Equal Opportunity for Women in the Workplace Agency, *Work-Life Survey*, 11 Dec. 2003.

some paid maternity leave, whereas only 21 per cent of women in part-time employment receive any payment for maternity leave and a staggeringly small 0.4 per cent of those engaged as casuals have access to paid maternity leave. The higher the skill and the pay levels of women workers, then the greater is the likelihood that they will have some access to paid maternity leave through agreements. Thus, labour law has produced an outcome that amongst women in the paid workforce is inequitable, ad hoc, and disadvantages the most vulnerable of women workers, those who are in low-skilled, low-paid and non-standard jobs.

The issue of paid maternity leave came to the forefront of national political debate with the conclusion of a report of inquiry by HREOC into discrimination against women in the workplace on the grounds of pregnancy and potential pregnancy.[33] It flagged the issue of paid maternity leave as a significant one impacting on the decision of women when and whether to have children. When its recommendation, that government undertake investigation and economic modelling of the various ways in which such a scheme might be introduced to Australia, was ignored, HREOC pursued the matter itself. After consulting widely, it produced a preliminary paper outlining a number of options for such a scheme,[34] and following further broad-ranging community discussion and consultations with representatives of women, employers, trade unions, and other community groups, HREOC finally presented a proposal for a scheme of nationally paid maternity leave.[35]

A Time to Value: a proposal for paid maternity leave

The philosophical and legal underpinning of HREOC's proposal was to be found in the conception of the equality of women and their special needs in the workplace as enunciated in the Convention on the Elimination of Discrimination against Women and the ILO Convention concerning Maternity Protection.[36] The essence of HREOC's recommended scheme for paid maternity leave was for a payment, capped at a rate equivalent to the minimum wage set in federal awards, to be made by the federal government for 14 weeks to all eligible women in the paid workforce. If implemented, the proposal would have brought Australia broadly in line with the standard set down in the ILO Convention.

---

[33] See HREOC, *Pregnant and Productive: It's a Right not a Privilege to Work while Pregnant* (Sydney: HREOC, 1999).
[34] See HREOC, *Valuing Parenthood: Options for Paid Maternity Leave: Interim Paper* (Sydney: HREOC, 2002).   [35] See *A Time to Value*, above, n. 2.
[36] Convention on the Elimination of All Forms of Discrimination Against Women, GA res. 180 (XXXIV 1970) 19 ILM 33 (1980), and ILO Convention concerning Maternity Protection (No. 183) (2000).

When compared with a labour law model infused with a neo-liberal ideology, there were certain advantages evident in the specific detail of the proposal to using an equality or human rights approach to create a family-friendly law of work. In particular, for those women in paid work who were most vulnerable, it offered distinct advantages in the proposed rules for access, and hence the coverage of the benefit, and in the philosophy and mechanism for payment.

Access and eligibility

Presented as a social justice initiative based on a human rights imperative, the proposal for paid maternity leave was not restricted to women in any particular paid work relation. Rather, it extended to all women in paid work in the marketplace, be they employees, agency workers, contract labourers, partners, or directors. It was an approach that necessarily moved 'beyond employment',[37] mandating an inclusiveness that has been lacking in traditional labour law.

Given that women, and especially young women, are in casual work in disproportionate numbers, HREOC considered it important to ensure that any system of paid maternity leave did not disadvantage, even more, those who are already disadvantaged in accessing family-friendly measures. In addition, if the scheme were to have any success in implementing its goal of enhancing labour attachment it had to extend to non-standard and especially casual workers, because young women especially are over-represented there. Thus *A Time to Value* contained an important statement of principle:

HREOC considers that the form of a woman's employment should not affect her eligibility for paid maternity leave. This would mean that women in casual work, on contract and the self employed should have access to a government funded system of paid maternity leave. The relevant point is that the woman has been required to forgo regular income due to the birth of a child. This applies equally to women in paid work regardless of their form of employment.[38]

Taking account of the nature of women's work relations, the eligibility criteria differed in some significant ways from those imposed by labour law for unpaid maternity leave. As a right attached to paid work, a woman needed to show that she had regular income. But HREOC rejected labour law's usual qualifying period of twelve months' continuous service, reasoning that it is premised upon a:

. . . balancing of obligations and benefits for employers and employee. The obligation on an employer to hold the position open for an employee is balanced by an established relationship with the employee. The benefits to the employer

---

[37] Cf. Supiot, A., *Beyond Employment: Changes in Work and the Future of Labour Law in Europe* (Oxford: OUP, 2001).   [38] Above, n. 2, 175.

of retaining a staff member with 12 months employment history in the organization are also much more direct. In contrast, a paid maternity leave scheme funded
by Government and without a right to return to the same position imposes minimal
to no cost on employers and hence does not require the same level of balancing
of the interests of employers and employees.[39]

As a payment from government, maternity benefit could be set free of
the usual limitations of labour law. A twelve-month eligibility criterion
poses a dual problem for non-standard workers in both the length and
the continuity of service required. This was avoided in the proposal's
criterion that pregnant women be eligible for the payment, where they
have been in paid work for a period of at least forty out of the previous
fifty-two weeks. Most significantly, portability across different employers
or different modes of work also satisfied the eligibility criterion, thus
emphasizing labour force attachment rather than employment with a
single employer.

Thus, in the context of women's over-representation in non-standard
work, including that they often held several jobs simultaneously, and
experienced frequent transitions between jobs, the loosening of the
eligibility criteria from the employment relation, and its positioning
with respect to paid work, was significant. The proposed requirements
were drawn in a way that would ensure access to the entitlement by
many of the most vulnerable of women workers. Thus, as with anti-
discrimination legislation more generally, the proposal was set to play a
part in creating a new law of work, because it responded better to the
reality of the nature and patterns of women's paid work relations in the
new economy.

Income replacement

The payment in HREOC's proposal was primarily conceived of as income
replacement, access to which would provide women with some income
security at the time of birth, as well as the secondary benefits of lessen-
ing the inequity which childbirth has on women's lifetime capacity to
earn, and providing some additional support to the initial cost of raising
a child. Most importantly, it was a workplace right compensating women
for the losses that they incur when they have a child, and, as such, it was
important in validating a woman's independent right to an income in a
way that does not discriminate against any women by virtue of her
family relationships.

With a government-funded 'income replacement' scheme, HREOC
reasoned, it was appropriate for the federal minimum wage to be used
to set the upper level of payment, because the community understood

---

[39] Ibid., 173.

this as fairly calculated through the Industrial Commission's public processes. HREOC's recommendation was thus that payment be at the rate of the federal minimum wage or the woman's previous weekly earnings from all jobs, whichever was the lesser amount. The calculation of previous earnings was to be based either on the weekly average the woman had earned over the previous twelve months or her earnings immediately prior to leave, whichever was the greatest, and included all sources of income from the different jobs the woman may have held.

The proposed level of maternity pay did not, therefore, represent the full income replacement that ILO Maternity Protection Recommendation 191 identifies as the standard to which nations should aspire. However, given the existing levels of income earned by Australian women the proposed level of payment would have represented true income replacement for about one-third of women in the workplace and for at least another third it was equivalent to two-thirds of their income, the level established in the ILO's Maternity Protection Convention. As indicative of the low level of women's earnings this was not particularly a cause for celebration, but it was a great improvement over the existing system that benefits only the minority of women in high-paid and high-skilled employment.

Mimicking paid maternity leave: the maternity payment

HREOC's proposed scheme for paid maternity leave had many benefits. Most significantly, it demonstrated the potential for the productive intersection of labour law and anti-discrimination law to play an important strategic role in forging a more family-friendly law of work. It promised, through the terms of its coverage, to close some of the gaps in the existing labour law system, and the proposed level of payment was at an internationally acceptable standard for paid maternity leave for the majority of women workers including those who were most vulnerable. Above all, it underscored women's equality in the labour market. In acknowledging that taking leave for childbirth has economic consequences for women and that women's equality in the paid workforce demands income replacement during this period of leave, the HREOC proposal had a strong symbolic value.

The proposal was not, however, without fault. Indeed, it acknowledged that paid maternity leave was no panacea to the problem of assisting workers to accommodate their family and care responsibilities. Other public measures, such as the provision of adequate childcare, were also desperately required. The proposal could also be criticized strongly on its own terms, primarily because it did not go far enough. For more than a decade, Australian labour law, through the provision of parental leave has formally recognized the equal role of parents in responsibility for the care of a new child, and a proposal extending payment to either parent, or indeed to any person with the primary responsibility for the care of the newborn or newly adopted child, would have had a greater potential to transform gender relations for this care work.[40]

More significantly, by confining its focus to women in paid employment, the proposal, like labour law, also incorporated the public/private distinction and did not avert adequately to the implications of this. The removal of any period of service as a criterion of eligibility would have been more in accordance with the ILO Maternity Protection Convention, but HREOC reasoned that it was necessary to have some eligibility criterion regarding length of service, because the proposed benefit was to be earned from work in the paid workforce; the eligibility criterion 'establishes a standard for what constitutes paid work', justifying the different treatment of women in paid and those in unpaid work.[41] But this was more than a little specious and the exercise of line drawing there was clearly arbitrary. While the disadvantage that women experience in the paid workforce as a consequence of maternity does need to be addressed, the distinction between women according to their participation in the paid workforce was not argued as cogently as it might have been. From this perspective, the relation of the proposed maternity pay to other welfare payments available to women who have given birth was critical. But it remained largely unaddressed in HREOC's proposal, except to the extent that it was suggested that any woman could opt for welfare payments where they were greater than the maternity pay. Conceptualizing maternity pay as income replacement was vital in valuing women's paid or market work. But that was a limited tool for recognizing the value of women's reproductive work, which the proposal also sought to emphasize, because it did so only in a way that unpaid work was parasitic upon paid work in the marketplace. Thus, it could be interpreted as simultaneously devaluing unpaid care work and entrenching existing negative concepts of dependence on the state.[42] At the same time, the criticism could be made that in placing the responsibility for maternity payment with the state rather than the market, the proposal ignored the dependency of the market on, and therefore the market's responsibility for, reproductive labour. These public/private issues

[40] Jill Murray makes a similar criticism of the revamping by the ILO of the Maternity Protection Convention in 2000. See Murray, J., 'The International Regulation of Maternity: Still Waiting for the Reconciliation of Work and Family Life', *International Journal of Comparative Labour Law and Industrial Relations*, 17 (2001), 25.

[41] *A Time to Value*, above, n. 2, 181.

[42] See Williams, L., 'Beyond Labour Law's Parochialism: A Revisioning of the Discourse of Redistribution', in Conaghan et al., above, n. 25, for a more extensive discussion of these themes.

remained very much an unspoken subtext in the proposal, but they
became pivotal in the political responses to it.

The regulation of work and family raises, as Jill Murray has noted,
'notoriously complex issues which are difficult [indeed, I would say,
impossible] to disentangle from ideological concerns'.[43] The Australian
response to HREOC's proposal exemplified this. In the aftermath of its
publication, the political contest over whether Australia should have a
national paid maternity leave scheme and if so, which form it should
take, became even more acute and seemingly paralysing. In the months
that followed, there were some isolated initiatives at state level attempting to use public fiscal measures to encourage greater take-up of paid
maternity and adoption leave through industrial processes,[44] but at the
federal level there was little action.

Conservatives, concerned less with enhancing women's equality
and participation in the paid workforce and more with the demise of the
traditional family life and the declining fertility rate, judged HREOC's
proposal for a national system of paid maternity leave of scant value.
Although those pushing the proposal's reform agenda had attempted to
gain some traction for it from concern about 'the fertility crisis', the
conservative Liberal coalition government was influenced more by the
view that it would have little impact on the work/life 'choices' that
women make.[45] Adhering to neo-liberal values, the government also
emphasized the need to respect the 'choices' women did make. Its
existing taxation and welfare law rewarded women who exited the
workforce after childbirth, thus supporting those 'choosing' a traditional
model of the family,[46] and conservative 'think tanks' argued for the
reinforcement of these purposes in any maternity payment scheme,
advocating that mothers should be paid to stay at home and care for their
children.[47] However, this also posed another set of policy dilemmas in an
era of 'small government'. The interest of the state in social reproduction
and the preservation of the family did not sit easily alongside the
government's neo-liberal desire to preside over a diminishing welfare
state. In the deregulated state, neo-liberal ideology was much more at
ease insisting that maternity payments needed to be negotiated through

[43] Murray, J., *International Legal Trends in the Reconciliation of Work and Family Life*, a report
prepared for the ACTU's Work and Family Test Case, Apr. 2004, 52.

[44] The Victoria state government enacted the Pay-roll Tax (Maternity and Adoption Leave
Exemption) Act 2003 (Vic), exempting from tax, wage payments made to women on maternity or adoption leave.

[45] Hakim, C., *Work-Lifestyle Choices in the 21st Century* (Oxford: OUP, 2000). Hakim's work
was particularly influential, especially after her visit to Australia shortly after the release of
HREOC's proposal.

[46] These policies and law are discussed in *A Time to Value*, above, n. 2, ch. 21.

[47] See Sullivan, L., *The Influence of Income Equity and the Total Fertility Rate* (Barton, ACT:
The Menzies Research Centre, 2003).

workplace bargaining or resolved through relations of economic dependency in the privacy of the family.

The policy paralysis was broken when, in the lead-up to federal elections in 2004, the Australian Labor Party announced its policy of a 'Baby Care Payment', which it stated satisfied its existing commitment to paid maternity leave.[48] A short time later, in May 2004, in its pre-election Budget, the Liberal coalition government also announced its support for a 'maternity payment'.[49] After the Liberal coalition victory Australia thus introduced a payment of $3,000 to every woman upon the birth of a child. The quantum of this payment is significantly lower than the federal minimum wage, which was used as the basis of HREOC's calculations (this is so, even given its tax-free status; however, the government has promised to increase the payment, over the next three to five years, to $5,000, thus closer to the federal minimum wage). While Labor policy was always to means-test women on the basis of their family income at the time of the birth and deliver the payment over a fourteen-week period, the government now offers the payment to all women and it is available to be taken either as a lump sum at the time of the birth or over regular intervals during a three-month period following the birth.

While some elements of the maternity payment may faintly mimic a system of paid maternity leave, it is in essence a welfare payment providing some minimal financial assistance to women at the time they give birth. In so far as it is some recognition of the social value of reproductive labour, and because it will mean more to economically disadvantaged women than others, it may be applauded. But in terms of the advancement of women's workplace rights it is, if not a retrograde step, more a marching on the spot than a step forward; it places no emphasis on the rights of women to participate equally in paid (productive) labour, and it certainly does nothing to challenge the existing gendered approach to unpaid (reproductive) labour. As such it offers no really meaningful contribution to the resolution of problems at the work/family interface, problems which will continue to be a matter of political and legal contest.

---

[48] Australian Labor Party, *Balancing Work and Family: Baby Care Payment* (Policy Document, 31 Mar. 2004).

[49] Appropriation Bill (No. 1) 2004–2005, Second Reading speech, House of Representatives, Parliament of Australia, Hansard, 11 May 2004. The Treasurer's speech referred to the maternity payment as one element of the government's new policy, *More Help for Families*.

12

A New Gender Contract? Work/Life Balance and Working-Time Flexibility

JUDY FUDGE*

The story of work-life balance cannot be told without mentioning the growing involvement of women in the labour force and the concomitant shift toward the dual earner family.[1]

I INTRODUCTION

Work/life conflict grew dramatically during the 1990s, fuelled by growing numbers of employed women, dual-earner, and single-parent families, and the increasing proportion of the population who are elderly and in need of care as well as employment restructuring, job insecurity, increased hours of employment, and technologies that blur the boundary between work and family. By the beginning of the twenty-first century, developing and implementing policies designed to help Canadians to achieve a better work/life balance moved to the top of the labour policy agenda.[2] The emergence of work/life balance as a key issue for labour law and policy reveals the breakdown of the post-war 'gender contract' for resolving the tension that has always plagued advanced market economies—how to co-ordinate the competing demands of raising children and caring for and maintaining a healthy and cohesive population, on the one hand, and producing the goods and services necessary for a prosperous society, on the other. This gender contract was based upon a male breadwinner and female housewife model in which men worked full-time for a wage that was sufficient to provide

* This chapter was presented as the Women's Studies Lecture, University of Alberta, 27 Jan. 2004. I would like to thank Joanne Conaghan and Leah Vosko for their helpful comments on an earlier draft.

[1] Duxbury, L. and Higgins, C., *Work-Life Balance in the New Millennium: Where Are We? Where Do We Need To Go?* (Ottawa: CPRN Discussion Paper No. w/12, Oct. 2001), 6.

[2] Ad Hoc Committee on Work-Life Balance, Canadian Association of Administrators of Labour Legislation, *Work-Life Balance: A Report to Ministers Responsible for Labour in Canada*, 2002, 4, available online at www.labour-travail.hrdc-drhc.gc.ca; Johnson, K., Lero, D., and Rooney, J., *Work-Life Compendium 2000: 139 Canadian Statistics on Work, Family & Well-Being* (Guelph, Ontario: Centre for Families, Work & Well-Being, 2001); Duxbury, L., Higgins, C., and Coghill, D., *Voices of Canadians: Seeking Work-Life Balance* (Hull: Human Resources Development Canada, 2003); Duxbury and Higgins, above, n. 1.

for a dependent spouse and children, and women, once they married, confined themselves to performing unpaid domestic labour.[3] Work/life balance policies are part of an attempt to forge a new gender contract— a set of norms, practices, and policies that govern how men and women allocate their time when it comes to performing the wide variety of labour necessary to maintain a society—to respond to the new economic and social context.

In this chapter I shall focus on a specific set of work/life balance policies that provide employed parents, especially mothers, with the flexibility to take leave from paid work in order to care for family members. But instead of examining these policies in isolation, I shall place them in the wider context of the regulation of paid working time and the trend towards more 'flexible' working hours. The question I am interested in is whether this new gender contract, which is composed of work/life balance and flexible working-time policies, promotes women's equality. How men and women allocate their time between paid and unpaid labour is a good test of equality.[4]

I begin by providing a theoretical framework and broader context for the case study that I will use to explore the emerging gender contract. The first part defines key concepts and then uses them to illustrate how changes in the labour market and household composition have rendered the old gender contract outmoded. It ends with a description of how work/life balance policies were developed as a response to the intensified time demands on men and women. The second part presents the case study, which is from Ontario, where, in 2000, the Conservative government made major changes to the basic labour protection statute in order to give employers and workers more flexibility to control paid working time, especially flexibility regarding limits on hours of work and entitlement to overtime pay, and to provide family-friendly leave. These changes are important not only because Ontario is the province that has the largest workforce in Canada, but because they set a precedent

---

[3] Appelbaum, E., Bailey, T., Berg, P., and Kalleberg, A., 'Shared Work/Valued Care: New Norms for Organizing Market Work and Unpaid Care Work', *Economic and Industrial Democracy*, 23 (2002), 125; Esping-Anderson, G., 'Towards a Post-industrial Gender Contract', in P. Auer and B. Gazier (eds.), *The Future of Work, Employment and Social Protection: The Dynamics of Change and the Protection of Workers* (Geneva: ILO, 2002), 109; Fraser, N., *Justice Interruptus: Critical Reflections on the 'Postsocialist' Condition* (New York: Routledge, 1997), 41–66.

[4] Laufer, J., 'Public Sphere, Private Sphere: The Issue of Women's Rights', in J. Jenson, J. Laufer, and M. Maruni (eds.), *The Gendering of Inequalities* (Aldershot: Ashgate, 2000), 231, 236; Rubery, J., Smith, M., and Fagan, C., 'National Working-Time Regimes and Equal Opportunities', *Feminist Economics*, 4 (1998), 71; Figart, D. and Mutari, E., 'Work Time Regimes in Europe: Can Flexibility and Gender Equity Coexist?', *Journal of Economic Issues*, 34 (2000), 847; Mutari, E. and Figart, D., 'Europe at a Crossroads: Harmonization, Liberalization, and the Gender of Work Time', *Social Politics*, 8 (2001), 36.

for other provinces.[5] The political process that led to the legislation and the justifications offered by the Conservative government, as well as the changes that were introduced, are described, as is the response of the Liberal government, which was elected in 2003, to the Tory legislation. How these laws are likely to influence men's and women's allocation of time between paid and unpaid work is also assessed. My goal is to discover what this specific combination of family-friendly and flexible working-time policies reveals about the new gender contract and what this contract means for gender equity.

II CONCEPTS AND CONTEXT

Social reproduction, gender contracts, and working-time regimes

The concept social reproduction refers to the social processes and labour that go into the daily and generational maintenance of the working population. Like every social system, capitalism imposes a specific relationship between the production of goods and services and the process of social reproduction of the population. The transition from home to market production, and the accompanying specialization of labour, was a long and gradual process. Over two centuries ago Adam Smith pointed out the gains from the division of labour, and since then technological developments have led to incredible economies of scale and huge productivity gains. Service providers have taken over tasks formerly performed in the home, and specialization and streamlining have led to more efficient production.[6]

There is, however, a social anomaly in how production and services are organized in modern industrial market economies. Production technologies, which have resulted in great material wealth, have evolved in such a way as to be increasingly incompatible with childrearing and caregiving. Specialization and technology have meant that many of the tasks of modern employment require concentration and undivided attention. Caring for children, especially young ones, is labour-intensive and is only compatible with work that can be performed intermittently.[7]

---

[5] According to the 2001 census, over 11.4 million inhabitants or about 38% of Canada's population lives in Ontario (www.statscan.ca). British Columbia followed Ontario's lead of injecting more flexibility into its hours of work rules by, among other things, amending its legislation to permit individual overtime averaging agreements. See Ministry of Skills Development and Labour, *Fair and Effective: A Review of Employment Standards in British Columbia (Discussion Paper)* (Victoria: Ministry of Labour, Nov. 2001); Employment Standards Amendment Act, 2002, S.B.C. 2002, c. 42.

[6] Leete, L., 'History and Housework: Implications for Work Hours and Family Policy in Market Economies', in L. Golden and D. Figart (eds.), *Working Time: International Trends, Theory and Policy Perspectives* (New York: Routledge, 2000), 250, 252.   [7] Ibid., 254.

There is a mismatch between how productive activity and social reproduction, caring for and sustaining life on a daily and generational basis, are organized in advanced market societies. The tendency towards the separation of the site of procreation and daily and generational maintenance (the household) from productive relations (waged work) means that social reproduction is not directly organized by employers, but is typically organized in households and predominantly performed by women.[8]

In general, economics has traditionally paid little attention to social reproduction or the gender division of labour. According to the neoclassical model of the labour market, the work women perform in the household is simply a matter of personal consumption, rather than a social requirement of production. But this view of domestic (or reproductive labour) is mistaken. Domestic work is *productive* activity; in fact, it produces the key component in the labour process—labour power, which is essential for the production of other commodities. Waged work is the *exchange* of labour and is functionally dependent upon labour's production. But, while the household is linked to the process of production through the wage, both in influencing the cost of labour power and by providing access to the means of subsistence, it is not subject to the same logic or discipline as the production process. This separation of production from reproduction gives rise to an essential contradiction in capitalist social formations—the conflict between the standard of living of the workers, and the drive for accumulation. The state's role is crucial in mediating this contradiction and organizing social reproduction.[9]

A key component of the state's role is to stabilize a specific gender order.[10] Social reproduction has predominantly been organized in households through normative families and kin relations, characterized by a gendered division of labour.[11] Gendering is a process in which social significance is attached to sexual difference which, in turn, 'structures

[8] Fudge, J. and Cossman, B., 'Introduction', in B. Cossman and J. Fudge (eds.), *Privatization, Law, and the Challenge to Feminism* (Toronto: University of Toronto Press, 2002), 3.
[9] Picchio, A., *Social Reproduction: The Political Economy of the Labour Market* (Cambridge: Cambridge University Press, 1992).
[10] Connell, R. W., *Gender and Power* (Cambridge: Polity Press, 1987). Connell, at 87, describes a gender order as a 'structural inventory of an entire society' and it refers 'to the way that power relations, and definitions of femininity and masculinity, have been historically constructed in societies through three interrelated structures of gender relations' (Fagan, C. and O'Reilly, J., 'Conceptualizing Part-Time Work: The Value of an Integrated Comparative Perspective', in J. O'Reilly and C. Fagan (eds.), *Part-Time Prospects: An International Comparison of Part-time Work in Europe, North America and the Pacific Rim* (London: Routledge, 1998), 1, 14). These structures are the division of labour, power relations (authority, control, and coercion), and cathexis (emotionally charged social relationships with other people), and they may have effects that contradict with one another.
[11] Acker, J., 'Class, Gender, and the Relation of Distribution', *Signs*, 13 (1988), 473; Seccombe, W. A., *Millennium of Family Change* (London: Verso, 1992).

organizations, affects social and political relationships, and becomes intrinsic to the construction of significant social categories and political identities'.[12] The gender order is stable to the extent that it has been institutionalized. According to Connell, 'the state of play in gender relations in a given institution is its "gender regime" '.[13] The gender regimes of interacting institutions are rarely completely harmonious; however, there must be some fit, however temporary, fragile, and incomplete, between the processes of reproduction and production.

This fit is achieved if a gender contract—a set of normative understandings, practices, and policies about the appropriate roles and expectations of, and rewards for, men and women—is institutionalized in key sites like families, firms, schools, state policies, and the market. The gender contract consists of the 'unspoken rules, mutual obligations and rights which define the relationship between women and men, between gender and generations, and finally between the areas of production and reproduction'.[14] The gender contract is normative rather than descriptive, and it develops historically and is supported by welfare, taxation, and family laws and policies as well as cultural and religious practices. It is the basis of how men and women negotiate the tension between reproductive and productive labour, and it influences the ways in which women and men engage in the labour market and organize their labour within the household.[15] Gender contracts are riven with tensions and subject to renegotiation, which, as Colette Fagan and Jacqueline O'Reilly explain, has 'more to do with changes in social

[12] Frader, L. L. and Rose, S. O., 'Introduction: Gender and the Reconstruction of European Working-Class History', in L. L. Frader and S. O. Rose (eds.), *Gender and Class in Modern Europe* (Ithaca: Cornell University Press, 1996), 1, 22.

[13] Connell, above, n. 10, 120.

[14] Fagan and O'Reilly, above, n. 10, 15, quoting Rantalaihio, L., 'The Gender Contract', in H. Vasa (ed.), *Shaping Structural Change in Finland: The Role of Women* (Helsinki: Ministry of Social Affairs and Health, 1993), 2.

[15] Fagan, C., O'Reilly, J., and Rubery, J., 'Part-Time Work: Challenging the "Breadwinner" Gender Contract', in Jensen et al., above, n. 4, 174, 175, and Hirdman, Y., 'State Policy and Gender Contracts: The Swedish Experience', in E. Drew, R. Emerek, and E. Mahon (eds.), *Women, Work and the Family in Europe* (London: Routledge, 1998), 36. The problem with calling this arrangement a contract is that it implies that its terms are explicitly negotiated by individuals on the basis of rational calculation. But a gender contract is not like an individual commercial contract; it is more akin to a social contract. Catherine Hakim, in *Work-Lifestyle Choices in the 21st Century: Preference Theory* (Oxford: OUP, 2000), 32–3, offers a two-fold criticism of the concept gender contract; it falsely assumes 'that every society has a single model of the family and sex-roles, which is promulgated in a consistent, co-ordinated, systematic, and hegemonic manner', and it falsely assumes that 'social and political systems are successful in persuading all citizens to accept and aspire to the dominant model of the family.' However, Hakim's criticisms are overstated; the concept gender contract does not assume either that everyone endorses it, or that the norms it embodies are promulgated consistently. All it assumes is that key institutions embody normative understandings about the appropriate roles and expectations of, and rewards for, men and women.

practices and particular institutional reform rather than explicit and open political negotiation'.[16]

The gender contract embodies norms about how men and women should allocate their time between productive and reproductive labour. Differences between how women and men allocate their time to the home and to paid work are linked to differences between men's and women's paid work and to inequality in the labour market. In their study of the relationship between time allocation and women's paid employment, Jill Rubery, Mark Smith, and Colette Fagan found that although women performed the bulk of the domestic labour across Europe, the extent and degree of the inequality in women's paid work varied between countries, and depended upon the national working-time regime.[17] Working-time regimes include the set of legal, voluntary, and customary regulations which influence working-time practices, which include daily and weekly working hours, shifts, overtime premia, vacation leaves, and public paid holidays.[18] Each working-time regime has two key components: the model or norm of standard working time and a series of carefully crafted provisions for formal variation from this norm.[19]

The breakdown of the male breadwinner and female housewife gender contract

The male breadwinner and female housewife model was the basis of the post-war gender contract in advanced industrialized and liberal capitalist economies. The standard employment relationship, consisting of full-time, full-year, continuous employment, was the lynchpin of the model, providing both a family wage and a range of social entitlements.[20] It also stabilized the working-time regime by establishing the male-breadwinner employment model as the norm for allocating paid work and leisure. A working-time regime based on a standard of forty to forty-eight hours a week, distributed in equal daily segments over five days, and joined with annual leave and public holidays was generalized in most OECD countries after World War II.[21] The working-time regime ignored reproductive labour because it was developed for an employment model that was based on a gender contract that assumed that

[16] Fagan and O'Reilly, above, n. 10, 16.   [17] Rubery et al., above, n. 4, 72.
[18] Ibid., 74.
[19] Campbell, I., 'Working-Time: Comparing Australia and Germany', in R. James, W. F. Veit, and S. Wright (eds.), *Work of the Future: Global Perspectives* (St Leonard, NSW: Allen & Unwin, 1997), 119, 201.
[20] Fudge, J. and Vosko, L., 'Gender Segmentation and the Standard Employment Relationship in Canadian Law, Legislation and Policy', *Economic and Industrial Democracy*, 22 (2001), 271; Supiot, A., *Beyond Employment: Changes in Work and the Future of Labour Law in Europe* (Oxford: OUP, 2001), 59.   [21] Campbell, above, n. 19, 201.

women, and not men, would perform the bulk of the reproductive work. However, beginning in the early 1980s, the Canadian labour market went through a period of profound restructuring driven by freer international trade, common-market agreements, information technologies, and neo-liberal fiscal and monetarist policies. The manufacturing sector shrank and the service sector massively increased. The standard employment relationship, the family wage, and the working-time regime were under pressure. The changes in the labour market combined with demographic changes, especially in household composition, to undermine the post-war gender contract.

By the 1990s, women's and men's labour participation and employment histories had begun to converge. Although women enjoyed significant improvements in labour market outcomes (earnings and employment), these gains were offset by the general deterioration for men. The type of jobs created in Canada in the 1980s and 1990s shifted away from full-time, full-year employment with a single employer on an indefinite basis to non-standard, contingent, precarious, or feminized forms of employment. The standard male employment relationship declined and forms of employment historically associated with women such as part-time and temporary work increased. The real earnings of labour market entrants (particularly young men and male immigrants) dropped, despite the increase in the human capital (skills and experience) of these workers. For the first time since the early 1930s, in the 1980s there was a fall in men's average annual wages as they lost relatively good unionized jobs in the primary labour market. The decline in men's wages and the increase in women's labour force participation meant that dual-earner families were the norm; by the mid-1990s, they comprised seven out of ten families. The male breadwinner employment model was no longer viable.[22]

Just as the restructuring of the labour market undermined the material base of the male-breadwinner family-wage norm, second-wave

[22] Armstrong, P., 'The Feminization of the Labour Force: Harmonizing Down in a Global Economy', in I. Bakker (ed.), *Rethinking Restructuring: Gender and Change in Canada* (Toronto: University of Toronto Press, 1996); Fudge, J., 'Precarious Work and Families', *Working Paper for the Centre for Research on Work and Society* (Toronto, Ontario: Centre for Research on Work and Society, 1997); Gunderson, M., *Women and the Canadian Labour Market: Transitions Towards the Future* (Toronto: Nelson, 1998); Lipsett, B. and Reesor, M., *Flexible Work Arrangements: Evidence from the 1991 and 1995 Survey of Work Arrangements* (Ottawa: Human Resources and Development Canada, 1997); Picot, G. and Heisz, A., 'The Performance of the 1990s Canadian Labour Market', Research Paper Series, Analytic Studies Branch, No. 148, Statistics Canada, Apr. 2000; Rashid, A., 'Seven Decades of Wage Changes', *Perspectives on Labour and Income*, 5 (1993), 9; Scott, K. and Lochhead, C., 'Are Women Catching Up in the Earnings Race?', Social Research Series, Paper No. 3 (Ottawa: Canadian Council on Social Development, 1997); Vanier Institute of the Family, *Profiling Canada's Families II* (Ottawa: Vanier Institute of the Family, 2000).

feminism's struggle for equality challenged the normative basis of women's dependency. Women's demands for equal rights rejected men's claim to superiority and contested the patriarchal basis of men's authority. Women won greater legal and political independence from men and made some strides towards gender equality. Improved access to the labour market and social welfare programmes, especially for lone mothers, provided a material base for women's independence. So, too, did more effective and reliable mechanisms for reproductive control. Women began to have fewer children (in 2001 the fertility rate was only 1.5), and wait until they were older to have them. Divorce laws were liberalized and marriage breakdown increased. The numbers of women who gave birth to and raised children alone rose dramatically. In 2001, 24 per cent of all families with children at home were headed by a female lone parent, up from 13.2 per cent in 1971.[23]

However, women's greater independence was not matched by greater economic equality. Lone mothers and their children are among the most economically disadvantaged group in Canada. Divorce is more likely than unemployment to throw women and children into poverty. Almost half of all families headed by women parenting alone were well below the low-income cut-offs established by Statistics Canada. In part, this was because only about half of these women were employed, well below the proportion for other families. Another important factor is that many of the female lone parents who worked had low-paying jobs. Women in Canada are much more likely than men to work in low-paid employment.[24] The continued gender division of labour within the family is linked with women's paid employment. Women with children are still less likely to be employed than women without children and women who are lone parents are less likely than mothers in two-parent families to be employed. The proportion of women working part-time is twice as high as men, and part-time jobs tend to be lower paid, have fewer benefits, and less opportunity for promotion than full-time jobs. Many women take up part-time work and solo self-employment, which is also low-paid and with few benefits, because they need the flexibility to accommodate

[23] Jenson, J., *Catching Up to Reality: Building the Case for a New Social Model*, CPRN Social Architecture Papers, Research Papers F/35 (Ottawa: CPRN, 2004), 6.

[24] In 1994–5, 34.5% of women as compared to 16.1% of men worked in low-paying jobs, which the OECD defines as work that pays two-thirds or less than the median income of full-time employment; Baker, M., *Families: Labour and Love* (Vancouver: University of British Columbia Press, 2001), 157. Jenson, above, n. 23, 18, 37; Devereaux, M. S. and Lindsay, C., 'Female Lone Parents in the Labour Market', *Perspectives on Labour and Income*, 5 (1993), 9; Eichler, M., *Family Shifts: Families, Policies and Gender Equality* (Don Mills, Ontario: OUP, 1997), 37–8; Lochhead, C. and Scott, K., *The Dynamics of Women's Poverty in Canada* (Ottawa: Status of Women Canada, 2000). It is important to note that overall there are still more dual-parent families with children than lone-parent families.

family responsibilities.[25] Thus, although the majority of women are no longer entirely financially dependent on a male breadwinner, the majority of them are not financially independent either. The nature of women's employment—fewer hours and lower pay—means that women continue *partially* to rely on a partner's income. And when this income is removed at separation or divorce, women continue to be at high risk of falling into poverty, notwithstanding that they are employed.[26]

The dual-earner household, working time, and work/life balance

Two elements in labour market restructuring since the 1980s—the increased labour force participation rate of women, especially those with young children, and the growing diversity in patterns of working time—have led some analysts to question whether the post-war male bread-winner and female housewife gender contract is being supplanted by one in which gender is differentiated by time rather than participation and non-participation in the market.[27] The Canadian data indicates that there is some truth to this observation. Most women in Canada engage in paid work, and there is a clear emphasis in social policy on employment over welfare even for women who are lone parents.[28] Staying out of the labour force is simply not an option for the vast majority of women.

At the same time as women's labour market participation has increased, patterns of working time have polarized and the prevalence of the standard working week has declined. By the mid-1960s, the standard working week levelled off and stabilized at thirty-seven to forty hours of work over five days by the mid-1960s.[29] Between 1976 and 1998, the proportion of employees working thirty-five to forty hours declined from 65 per cent of all workers to 54 per cent, while the proportion working more or less increased. Women are (and historically have been) far more likely than men to work short hours of employment. In 1998, 50 per cent of women and just 28 per cent of men worked less than thirty-five hours per week, in part because women's absence rate is almost twice that of

[25] Comfort, D., Johnson, K., and Wallace, D., *Part-Time Work and Family Friendly Practices in Canadian Workplaces*, Statistics Canada, HRDC (Ottawa: Ministry of Industry, 2003), 18–22 Cooke-Reynolds, M. and Zukewich, N., 'The Feminization of Work', *Canadian Social Trends*, (2004), 24 (Statistics Canada Catalogue No. 11–008).

[26] Lochhead and Scott, above, n. 24.

[27] Jenson, J., 'A Comparative Perspective on Work and Gender', in Jenson et al., above, n. 4, 3; Mutari and Figart, above, n. 4, 38.

[28] The labour force participation rate in 2001 for women over 15 was 59.7%, compared to 72.5% for men; Jenson, above, n. 23, 6; Bashevkin, S., *Welfare Hot Buttons: Women, Work, and Social Policy Reform* (Toronto: University of Toronto Press, 2002).

[29] Ontario Task Force on Hours of Work and Overtime, *Working Times: The Report of the Ontario Task Force on Hours of Work and Overtime* (Toronto: Ministry of Labour, 1987), 13.

men. Men outnumber women at the long hours end of the distribution. At least twice as many men as women worked between forty-one and forty-nine hours a week (15 per cent compared with 7 per cent). However, polarization in working hours is occurring among women as well as among men.

Polarization in working-time patterns is also evident by industry; long hours are still more common in goods-producing sectors, where men predominate, and short hours more common in service-producing industries, where women are more likely to be employed. Similarly, the number of hours worked is highly dependent on the type of work performed. Male-dominated occupations in manufacturing and the trades are associated with long hours, while sales and service occupations where women are crowded are increasingly likely to be below the standard work week. Occupations are differentiated by working time, and this reinforces sex segregation in employment, which remains very stubborn in Canada.[30]

The polarization in hours of work contributed to the increasingly unequal distribution of earnings since the early 1980s.[31] Younger workers have experienced a deterioration in wages relative to older workers. The gap in male earnings has widened considerably as high earners captured the largest share of wage increases while median male wages have stagnated and low-wage earners have lost. The gradual deregulation of the Canadian labour market beginning in the 1980s fuelled the polarization in earnings, and, in turn, deregulation and wage inequality exacerbates the polarization in working time.[32]

Despite the huge increase in women's labour force participation since the 1960s, their total share of unpaid work has remained the same, at about two-thirds of the total.[33] This domestic work includes caring for children and other family members (such as elders), housework, and emotional labour. In 2001, women were twice as likely as men to spend at least thirty hours a week on cooking and cleaning or on childcare, and twice as many men as women say they do no domestic work at all. Women also spend more time caring for elderly parents than do men, and they are more likely than men to reduce their hours of paid work to accommodate caring responsibilities.[34] Unpaid labour is distributed unequally even when both men and women are working full-time.

[30] Sheridan, M., Sunter, D., and Divery, B., *The Changing Workweek: Trends in Weekly Hours of Work in Canada* (Ottawa: Statistics Canada, Catalogue No. 71-001-XPB, 1996); Hall, K., 'Hours Polarization at the End of the 1990s', *Perspectives in Labour and Income*, 11 (1999), 28.
[31] Ibid.
[32] Jenson, above, n. 23, 34–5; Bosch, G., 'Working Time Tendencies and Emerging Issues', *International Labour Review*, 138 (1999), 131, 135.
[33] *Statistics Canada, Women in Canada 2000: A Gender-based Statistical Report* (Ottawa: Statistics Canada, 2000), 111.   [34] Jenson, above, n. 23, 14.

Women work, on average, two more weeks a year than men do when both paid and unpaid work are combined.[35] Even when employed full-time, women are responsible for the bulk of the work of looking after their families and households. Housework is still considered to be women's work and women's responsibility. The only women who have succeeded in reducing their share of domestic work are women who perform long hours of paid work and earn more than the men they live with.[36]

The increase in hours of work and the decline in the standard working week has had some measurable negative individual and social consequences. Although relatively little research has been devoted to the health implications of working long hours, preliminary research has revealed that an increase in working hours is associated with increased cigarette and alcohol consumption, weight gain, and depression.[37] Studies have shown that time stress is on the increase for every age group of Canadians, especially those who have the most responsibilities. The 'struggle to juggle' in 1998 was most difficult for those aged twenty-five to forty-four who were married parents and employed full-time. Men in this group averaged 48.6 hours and women averaged 38.8 hours per week of paid work and work-related activities, an increase of two hours per week since 1992 for both men and women. This same group of men spent 23.1 hours a week on unpaid work (including volunteer work) compared to the 34.3 hours spent by the same category of women. Levels of severe time stress are the highest for employed married mothers.[38]

The recent focus in labour policy on work/life issues is a response to a labour market in which women are stretched to meet the combined demands on their time of paid and unpaid work, and men are working longer hours at their jobs.[39] These policies build upon the work/family and family-friendly policies that began to be popular in the 1980s. However, in the late 1990s the term 'work/life' replaced 'work/family' to signal that conflicts between work and life can potentially affect all workers, not just caregivers and family members.[40] In part, this change of name and broadening of focus is explained by the backlash against working mothers of young children; there is a perception that employees who have made the personal choice to have children or care for others are getting away with less work than other employees. However, increased attention to the social, medical, and work consequences of the

[35] Freeze, C., 'Women outwork men by two weeks every year', *The Globe and Mail*, 13 Mar. 2001, A1, 9, reporting on Statistics Canada General Social Survey: Time Use (Nov. 1999), available online at www.statscan.ca.　　　[36] Baker, above, n. 24, 171.
[37] Shields, M., 'Long Working Hours and Health', *Perspectives on Labour and Income*, 12 (2000), 49.　　　[38] Statistics Canada General Social Survey, above n. 35.
[39] Duxbury and Higgins, above, n. 1.　　[40] Johnson et al., above, n. 2, 3.

stress resulting from work/life conflict also helps to explain the broader focus.[41]

Underlying the arguments for work/life balance policies is 'a recognition that "standard" full-time employment is not easily compatible with responsible parenting, that the majority of mothers as well as fathers of dependent children are employed in paid work, and that the role conflicts generated by such patterns may be socially and personally dysfunctional'.[42] Work/life balance policies are designed to achieve a new accommodation between the processes of production and requirements of social reproduction in light of the breakdown of the post-war gender contract. Their goal is to institutionalize a form of family-friendly flexibility that enables workers to allocate their time between paid and unpaid work in order to meet their individual needs and domestic responsibilities. Family-friendly flexibility makes it easier for individuals and households to combine family life and working life by providing employees with the right to change their working hours to accommodate changes in family composition and to adjust to sudden changes in the family timetable. Key components of policies for a work/life balance are leave for family responsibilities and flexible working-time arrangement that allow employees to reduce the hours that they work either by having the right to refuse to work overtime or being able to move into part-time employment easily.[43]

III *TIME FOR CHANGE* IN ONTARIO: WORK/LIFE BALANCE OR WORKING-TIME FLEXIBILITY?

How do Canadian laws, policies, and practices measure up when it comes to a work/life balance? What do they indicate about the main features of the new gender contract? I will address these questions in the context of the revisions to basic labour standards legislation by the Ontario government in the second half of the 1990s. When the

---

[41] Duxbury and Higgins, above, n. 1, 4–5. At work, the conflict is linked to productivity decreases, increased absenteeism, higher turnover, lower commitment, and poorer morale. This conflict manifests in the family in the form of marital problems, reduced family and life satisfaction (especially for women), and increased burnout and stress-related illnesses. Long hours of paid work are associated with fatigue, work-related accidents, and repetitive strain injuries. Employees with high work/life stress place higher demands on the health system (ibid.).

[42] Purcell, K., 'Flexible Employment and Equal Opportunities: Compatible or Contradictory?', in 11th World Congress of the International Industrial Relations Association: Conference Proceedings, *Developing Competitiveness and Social Justice: The Interplay between Institutions and Social Partners*, 22–5 Sep. 1998, Bologna, Italy, 249, 250.

[43] Duxbury and Higgins, above, n. 1; Purcell, above, n. 42; Gonas, L., 'Balancing Family and Work: To Create a New Social Order', *Economic and Industrial Democracy*, 23 (2002), 59.

Conservative government was elected in 1995, it depicted the Employment Standards Act, which provided basic standards and rights for working people in Ontario, as outdated and cumbersome.[44] But instead of attacking the standards directly, it proposed to introduce a bit more flexibility. While the government emphasized that flexibility was necessary for the province's workforce to remain competitive, it also stressed the needs of individuals and families for flexibility in order to achieve a better work/life balance. But, as the case study demonstrates, family-friendly flexibility was clearly subordinate to flexibility for competitiveness. The need to help families, especially mothers, was used by the government to avoid public debate over the implications of the new working-time flexibility.

Flexible and family-friendly employment standards

In January 1997, the Red Tape Review Commission, which was composed of Conservative members of the provincial legislature appointed by the government to identify regulation that made Ontario uncompetitive, took aim at the hours of work rules contained in the Employment Standards Act. It recommended increasing the length of the maximum working week from forty-eight to fifty hours (or 200 hours averaged over a four-week period) and abolishing the requirement that employers obtain government approval for workers to be allowed to work up to 100 hours of overtime annually. The next year, the Ministry of Labour released a consultation document called *The Future of Work*, which identified some key labour market trends and asked a series of general questions about employment labour standards. The document emphasized the flexibility that firms need in order to respond to competitive pressures, although it asked specific questions about hours of work and balancing family responsibilities.[45] On the eve of the 1999 election, the government released its *Blueprint for Change*, which promised greater flexibility for employers and employees in designing working-time arrangements and family-crisis leave.

In July 2000, after the Conservative government was re-elected, the Minister of Labour, Chris Stockwell, released a consultation paper, *Time for Change*, which proclaimed the need to update the Employment Standards Act to meet the challenges of the twenty-first century.[46] The

[44] This case study is based in part on Fudge, J., 'Flexibility and Feminization: The New Ontario Employment Standards Act', *Journal of Law and Social Policy*, 16 (2001), 1.

[45] Ontario Ministry of Labour, *The Future of Work in Ontario*, 1999, available online at www.gov.on.ca.

[46] Ontario Ministry of Labour, *Time for Change: Ontario's Employment Standards Legislation*, July 2000, available online at www.gov.on.ca.

document targeted the working-time rules, claiming that they 'do not always accommodate the needs of employers to run their businesses in a way that meets market pressures, new manufacturing processes or the intensive requirements of high technology industries. The hours of work standards also do not accommodate the needs of workers to vary working hours according to individual preference or to balance work and family responsibilities'.[47] Flexible hours of work would be achieved by reducing the role of government regulation and allowing individuals to opt out of standards. Moreover, the document proposed ten days of unpaid family leave 'to recognize the various demands Ontario employees face today and to promote a better work-family balance'.[48] According to the government, flexibility is good for businesses *and* families.

Despite the promise of family leave, the family-friendly component of the government's reform package was politically vulnerable because it did not contain any proposals for extending the length of job-protected parental leave beyond eighteen weeks. As part of its work/family balance policy, the federal government announced that starting on 31 December 2000, it would extend the period of entitlement for parental benefits provided through the employment insurance system from eighteen to thirty-five weeks.[49] Unless the Ontario government extended the period of job protection for an employee on parental leave to thirty-five weeks to match the period of benefits, employees in the province would not be entitled to return to their jobs if they decided to stay away from work longer than eighteen weeks.

Public consultations were conducted in five cities in Ontario over two weeks in the late summer. Although 240 groups and individuals attended, the consultation hearings attracted little media or public

[47] Ibid.   [48] Ibid.

[49] Speech from the Throne to Open the Second Session, Thirty-Sixth Parliament of Canada, 12 Oct. 1999 available online at www.pco-bcp.gc.ca. The federal government already provided 17 weeks of maternity benefits as well as 18 weeks of parental benefits. The provinces and territories have jurisdiction over employment standards that do not pertain to federal undertakings and are responsible for providing job-protected maternity and parental leaves in their labour protection statutes. On 27 Jan. 2004, the Quebec Court of Appeal ruled that the federal government's parental and maternity benefits programme is unconstitutional on the ground that the federal government cannot use the Employment Insurance Act to offer social benefit programmes that are exclusively a provincial jurisdiction. The Court ruled that employment insurance exists only to replace wages for people who lose their jobs for economic reasons not for the interruption of employment for reasons related to personal conditions. Quebec offers a more generous parental and maternity benefits programme and has long sought to control this aspect of the employment insurance programme. The federal government has appealed the decision to the Supreme Court of Canada. Deguin, R., 'Quebec court rejects federal aid for parent', *Globe and Mail*, 28 Jan. 2004, A1. However, it also announced that it had negotiated a deal with Quebec whereby it will contribute to the financing of Quebec's comprehensive parental-leave programme (effective 1 Jan. 2006). Seguin, R., 'Quebec to assume control of parental-leave programme', *Globe and Mail*, 20 May 2004, A12.

attention. The public process came to an end in late September and all was quiet on the employment standards front until the beginning of November 2000, when, in response to a reporter's question, Premier Mike Harris stated that his government had no plans to extend the length of parental leave. He said he had not received any significant pressure from women to change the leave provision.[50] The next day, an opposition member of the provincial parliament introduced a private member's bill to extend parental leave to thirty-five weeks.[51] Later that day, the Minister of Labour stated that the government might reconsider and lengthen the leave.[52]

On 23 November 2000, during the National Week of the Child, the Minister of Labour introduced a brand new Employment Standards Act. Despite the fact that the legislation had been completely rewritten, and neither the public nor the opposition had been given an opportunity to study the 150-page bill, Minister Stockwell insisted that it be passed immediately. He claimed that since there were only three weeks remaining in the legislative sitting, if the government did not act quickly, new parents would not be entitled to the length of job-protected leave needed for them to enjoy the extended employment insurance benefits that would become available to them in the New Year. After the government used its majority to limit legislative review, on 20 December 2000, a slightly revised bill received third reading.[53] While the changes extending the length of parental leave came into effect on 1 January 2001, the rest of the Employment Standards Act, 2000 only became law seven months later, on Labour Day, 4 September 2001. The timing of the bill and the lengthy delay before it was given effect suggests that the parental and family leave provisions were used to sugar coat what was otherwise a bitter pill for most Ontario workers—the changes relating to working hours.

The new working-time regime: competitive flexibility

The working-time regime provided in the Employment Standards Act before the 2000 changes was extremely complex, comprising maximum hours of work and minimum periods of rest on a daily and weekly basis, entitlements to overtime pay, daily meal periods, statutory holiday, and paid vacations. The standard working day was eight hours and the

[50] Brennan, R. and Mallan, C., 'Ontario won't extend parental to full year', *Toronto Star*, 1 Nov. 2000.

[51] Bill 138, Fair Parental Leave Act, 2000, introduced by Shelley Martel, 2 Nov. 2000.

[52] Mallan, C., 'Small firms fear longer baby leave', *Toronto Star*, 2 Nov. 2000.

[53] Perkins, C., 'Critics predict sweatshops' *Globe and Mail*, 25 Nov. 2000; Mackie, R., 'Contentious changes to labour bill passed', *Toronto Star*, 21 Dec. 2000; Employment Standards Act, 2000, S.O. 2000, c. 41.

standard working week was forty-eight hours, with entitlement to overtime pay (a premium of one and a half times the regular rate of pay) after forty-four hours of work. Exemptions and exceptions as well as specific provisions for certain industries and occupations were contained in a large number of regulations. In addition, flexibility was injected into the maximum hours of work standards through an elaborate permit system that allowed the agency authorized to administer the legislation to exempt employers from daily and weekly limits on hours of work. The hours of work (and other employment) standards applied to employees regardless of whether or not they were covered by a collective agreement and represented by a union, although the legislation accommodated collective bargaining by permitting trade unions to enter into agreements that bound the individual employees they represented. But, in practice the working-time regime was breaking down. Permits were easily obtained by employers and functioned simply as a rubber stamp for long hours of work. Moreover, the failure of the Ministry of Labour to enforce the legislation meant that the standard working week functioned more as an exception than the rule.[54] But instead of reinforcing the working-time regime by reducing the length of the working week and tightening the exemptions, which was recommended by the Task Force on Hours of Work and Overtime that was appointed in the mid-1980s,[55] the Conservative government moved in the opposite direction, increasing the length of the working week and abolishing the permit system. The government also changed the overtime pay rules to make it easier for employers to reduce the cost of overtime. While on its face the Employment Standards Act, 2000 retained the previous standards for

[54] For descriptions of the working-time regime provided in the Employment Standards Act, R.S.O. 1990, E.14 see Ontario Task Force on Hours of Work and Overtime, above, n. 29 and Parry, R. M., *A Practical Guide to Employment Standards in Ontario* (Toronto: Carswell, 1996). The Director of the Employment Standards Branch of the Ministry of Labour had the authority under the Employment Standards Act to issue a variety of different permits: annual permits allowing 100 excess hours of work for each worker in a year, industry permits, and special permits for extraordinary situations. Employers were not required to offer an explanation in order to obtain a 100 excess hours permit, as they were issued automatically upon an employer's request. By the mid-1960s, these permits allowed for an additional 1.2 million overtime hours. Under the industry permits, which covered 26 industries including retail stores, hotels, logging, and taxis, in the mid-1980s, 865,000 workers had their maximum working day extended from 8 to 10 hours. The special permits were available once the overtime provided in a 100 excess hours permit was exhausted in order to give employers increased flexibility. Employers in the automotive sector were the heaviest users of these permits. For compelling criticisms of the permit system, see the Ontario Task Force on Hours of Work and Overtime, above, n. 29, 27–40.

[55] The Task Force recommended that an employer could ask each employee to work a total of 250 hours a year over the 40 hours per week, and that for hours of work in excess of that amount a revised permit system be retained. Ontario Task Force on Hours of Work and Overtime, above, n. 29. Both the Liberal, and subsequent New Democratic governments, ignored the Task Force's recommendations and left the working-time rules alone.

hours of work (eight in a day and forty-eight in a week) and overtime pay (forty-four hours a week), it granted employers a great deal more flexibility to ask employees to work long hours. This flexibility was achieved in two principal ways; first, and most controversially, by allowing individual employees to opt out of the standards without any kind of administrative check and, secondly, by providing for even longer hours through regulations that receive little legislative oversight and scant opportunity for public input. The Employment Standards Act, 2000 allowed employees to agree to work more than eight hours a day and up to sixty hours in a week, and only retained the requirement to obtain administrative approval for working weeks in excess of sixty hours.[56]

Not only did the Employment Standards Act, 2000 make the standard working week more flexible, it also made the practice of long hours less costly to employers by changing the entitlements to overtime pay. From 1975 to 2000, the law in Ontario provided that employees who were not excluded from the employment standards legislation in general or the overtime provisions in particular were entitled to be paid time and a half their regular rate for all hours worked in excess of forty-four hours in a week. It also permitted agreements to average entitlement to overtime over a longer period, on condition that the agreement was approved by the Director.[57] While the Employment Standards Act, 2000 maintained forty-four hours as the general standard for overtime pay, it permitted an employer and an employee to agree that this entitlement to the time and a half overtime rate will be averaged over a period of up to four weeks. These averaging agreements no longer required approval by the Director and the legislation makes it very difficult for employees to revoke them; in fact, once employees agreed to average overtime they cannot revoke the agreement until it expires, which can be for up to two years, unless the employer agrees to the revocation. The potential savings to employers in overtime costs of this flexibility in averaging overtime are enormous.[58]

[56] Employment Standards Act, 2000, S.O. 2000, c. 41, s. 17, 18; O. Reg. 285/01, ss. 31, 32, and 32.1. For a detailed discussion of the Employment Standards Act, 2000, and comparison with its predecessor statute, see Fudge, above, n. 44, and Mitchell, E., 'The Employment Standards Act, 2000: Ontario Opts for Efficiency over Right', *Canadian Labour & Employment Law Journal*, 10 (2003), 269. In addition, this legislation relaxed the provisions that permit an employer to require employees to exceed the limits on maximum hours of work in the event of an emergency situation (s. 19). It also extended the list of employees exempted from the limits on hours of work and overtime pay to include massage therapists, chiropractic practitioners, and information technology professionals (O. Reg. 285/01, s. 2).

[57] Employment Standards Act, R.S.O. 1990, E.14, s. 24, O. Reg. 325, s. 2(2).

[58] Employment Standards Act, 2000, S.O. 2000, s. 22(6). Under the Employment Standards Act, 2000, if an employee agrees to have his or her overtime entitlement averaged over four weeks and to work up to 60 hours in a week, it is possible that the employee could work 60 hours in a week and not be entitled to any overtime pay. Indeed, in the worst-case

While Ontario is not alone in recognizing some form of agreement between employees and employers to vary statutory standards, 'in no other jurisdiction in Canada does the legislation contemplate such a wide range of employer/employee agreements, permit them to govern the parties' rights in core areas, or leave employees so isolated in negotiations with employers'.[59] The government justified the use of individual agreements by employees to opt out of employment standards on the ground that it was good for business and for employees. While the benefits for employers of this increased flexibility in working time are obvious, the case for employees is harder to make. The government claimed that the new flexibility would give employees the opportunity to design their own work/life balance. But how individual agreements will increase an employee's ability to bargain a better work schedule is hard to fathom. The majority of employees who are neither highly skilled nor union members have little bargaining power. Individual agreements to work long hours and average overtime, especially when entered into at the time of hire, are as likely a reflection of an employee's lack of alternatives as they are of an employee's choice. It is because individual employees are vulnerable to exploitation by employers who typically have more bargaining power that there are employment standards. Instead of correcting the deficiencies of the permit system, the Employment Standards Act, 2000 reverted to individual contracting.[60]

The changes to the working-time regime embodied in the Employment Standards Act, 2000 introduced a form of flexibility designed to increase competitiveness. Combined with broader trends towards labour market deregulation, these changes 'lead to greater pressure on men to work all hours that are required of them by employers, often without compensation in terms of overtime or unsocial hours premia'.[61] By contrast, work/life balance approaches emphasize the need to counter the culture of overwork by giving employees the right to work overtime. The individual opt-out from the forty-eight hour week made a nonsense of any attempt to combat the long-hours culture.[62]

---

scenario, this employee could work 60 hours in week one, 60 hours in week two, 56 hours in week three, and 0 hours in week four, and not be entitled to any overtime pay because the employee did not work more than 176 hours over the four-week period. Under the law as it existed from 1975 to 2000, this same employee would have received time and a half for 16 hours in week one, 16 hours in week two and 12 hours in week three.

[59] Mitchell, above, n. 56, 284. Some jurisdictions impose a requirement that the majority of the employees at the workplace support the agreement or that the agreement receive administrative approval. There is very limited provision for individual agreements without some sort of check.   [60] Ibid., 283.

[61] Rubery et al., above, n. 4 at 72.

[62] Conaghan, J., 'Women, Work, and Family: A British Revolution', in J. Conaghan, M. Fischl, and K. Klare (eds.) *Labour Law in an Era of Globalization: Transformative Practices and Possibilities* (Oxford: OUP, 2002), 53, 66.

Moreover, the competitive flexibility provided in the Employment Standards Act, 2000 was neither family- nor women-friendly. A policy of increasing limits on maximum hours of work and reducing the overtime premium through averaging agreements is likely to drive up employer demand for average overtime hours per employee (due to the reduced short run marginal cost of overtime) and make working weeks and schedules more unpredictable.[63] Thus, a policy of overtime deregulation 'runs the risk of actually making workplaces more family unfriendly than friendly, thus harming worker "utility" on the balance'.[64] As well, women's need to have flexible working hours and to be able to take care of family members makes them 'vulnerable in relation to employer-driven flexibility and changing work hours'.[65] Combined with the unequal gender division of labour in the household and family, competitive flexibility in working time will likely reinforce gendered and unequal patterns of working time, which, in turn, will reinforce occupational segregation and labour market segmentation.[66]

Family-friendly policies and women's work

The family-friendly component of the Employment Standards Act, 2000 was confined to the extension of the parental leave from eighteen to thirty-five weeks and the introduction of ten days of family-crisis leave. These changes introduced a form of family-friendly flexibility that enabled employees more easily to balance the demands of work and family. However, they also tended to reinforce the unequal and gendered division of unpaid labour. Moreover, they are least likely to be used by women with low income.

While extended parental leave, especially when combined with parental benefits, helps to ease the competing demands of work and family at a time when the contradiction is most profound—when there is an infant to care for—it does not do much to challenge the unequal division of reproductive labour. Although there was a substantial increase across Canada in the number of women and men taking parental leave after the length of benefits was extended, in 2002, women received 93 per cent of the parental benefits. In 2001, 10 per cent of male parents claimed parental benefits, up from 3 per cent before the duration of the benefits was extended.[67] In part, the low participation rate of men is explained

---

[63] Golden, L., 'Better Timing? Work Schedule Flexibility among US Workers and Policy Directions', in L. Golden and D. Figart (eds.), *Working Time: International Trends, Theory and Policy Perspectives* (London: Routledge, 2000), 212, 228.   [64] Ibid.

[65] Gonas, above, n. 43, 63.   [66] Ibid., and Rubery et al., above, n. 4, 72.

[67] In 2002, an average of 108,7000 mothers collected parental benefits each month, four times as many as in 2000. The average number of fathers receiving parental benefits each month rose to 7,900 in 2002, five times more than in 2000. In part, the increase in women's

by social norms about the roles of men and women when it comes to parenting young children. But it also makes economic sense for women to take parental leave given the way that parental employment insurance benefits are structured. The low ceiling on the maximum amount of insurable earnings (which was Can$413 a week in 2002) combined with benefits levels pegged at only 55 per cent of average weekly earnings, and the requirement that the parental benefits be shared between the parents creates an incentive for the lower-income earner in a dual-earner household, typically the woman, to take parental leave.[68] Few employers supplement the income that employees receive while on maternity or parental leaves, and those that do, do so only for a short period of time.[69] Thus, in their current form, the leaves institutionalize a norm of temporary homemaking for women, who, in turn, face potentially negative consequences for their earnings and long-term employment trajectories.[70]

Moreover, the low-income replacement rate of the benefits not only reinforces the gendered and unequal division of unpaid labour, it also means that low-income women are more likely to take a shorter leave than women who earn more or live in households with greater income. Lower individual earnings and lower household income are associated with a quicker return to work from parental leave because low-income workers cannot afford to absorb the lost income that low benefit levels entail.[71] Higher parental benefit levels would not only create an incentive for low-income workers to take longer periods of leave, they would likely increase men's uptake rate.[72]

take-up rate of parental benefits is attributable to the reduction of the qualifying requirement from 700 to 600 hours of paid employment. The increased take-up rate of men is likely attributable to the fact that fathers are no longer required to fulfil the two-week waiting period if they are sharing parental benefits with the child's mother. Perusse, D., 'New Maternity and Parental Leave Benefits', *Perspectives on Labour and Income*, 15 (2003), 1. For a discussion of the federal government's decision to extend parental benefits, see Calder, G., 'Recent Changes to the Maternity and Parental Leave Regime as a Case Study: The Impact of Globalization on the Delivery of Social Programs in Canada', *Canadian Journal of Women and the Law*, 15 (2003), 342–66.

[68] Evans, P. and Pupo, N., 'Parental Leave: Assessing Women's Interests', *Canadian Journal of Women and the Law*, 6 (1993), 402; Iyer, I., 'Some Mothers are Better than Others: A Re-examination of Maternity Benefits', in S. Boyd (ed.), *Challenging the Public/Private Divide* (Toronto: University of Toronto Press, 1997), 168; Madsen, L., 'Citizen, Worker, Mother: Canadian Women's Claims to Parental Leave and Childcare', *Canadian Journal of Family Law*, 19 (2002), 11; Marshall, K., 'Benefiting from Extended Parental Leave', *Perspectives on Labour and Income*, 15 (2003), 5.

[69] Harding, K., 'Few employers are topping up parental benefits', *The Globe and Mail*, 23 Apr. 2003. Only 20% of employees who took parental leave in 2001 received any kind of employer top-up.

[70] Morgan, K. M. and Zippel, K., 'Paid to Care: The Origins and Effects of Care Leave Policies in Western Europe', *Social Politics*, 10 (2002), 40.   [71] Marshall, above, n. 68.

[72] If the goal of work/life policy is not simply to enable women to accommodate the dual demands on their time but to increase gender equity in the division of unpaid labour, parental leaves and benefits should not be shared between the parents. Instead fathers

The family-crisis leave in the Employment Standards Act, 2000 provides workers with more flexibility to adjust to the immediate demands of family life. It entitles an employee who is employed in a workplace that regularly employs at least fifty employees to ten days of unpaid leave for absences caused by a personal illness, injury or medical emergency, the death or illness, injury or medical emergency of, or urgent matter concerning, a family member.[73] Although it is gender-neutral, more women than men are likely to take advantage of emergency leave. In 1999 women employees across Canada missed an average of seven days due to personal illness or family commitments, while employed men missed only one day.[74] Although the leave will allow some women to accommodate better the conflicting demands of employment and family, it is likely to reinforce the perception that women are primarily caregivers. This perception, as well as the different hours that men and women work, tends to reinforce the persistent gender segregation in occupations.[75]

Moreover, the fact that the family leave does not extend to workplaces that regularly employ fewer than fifty employees means that the emergency leave provision is least likely to be available to those workers who need it most; women workers in small firms who do not have the benefit of a collective agreement.[76] While the government has justified the fifty employee requirement as necessary to protect small business, it is unlikely that many small businesses would be made uncompetitive simply because they were not allowed to dismiss employees who took off a few days on account of a personal illness or a family emergency. The small business exemption to the family leave exemplifies the extent to which the government regards family-friendly flexibility as incompatible with, and subordinate to, flexibility for competitiveness.

A liberal dose of flexibility

In 2003, a Liberal government 'committed to ending the 60-hour work week brought in by the previous government' was elected in Ontario, and it promised to introduce legislation to bring back the forty-eight hour

should be given specific entitlements to parental leave and benefits that cannot be transferred to mothers. Esping-Anderson, above, n. 3, 124–5.

[73] Employment Standards Act, 2000, s. 50.   [74] Statistics Canada, above, n. 35, 103.

[75] Gonas, above, n. 43, 63; Rubery et al., above, n. 4, 72.

[76] In the early 1990s, almost 31% of all women employees, in contrast to 25% of all men employees, were employed by firms that employed fewer than 20 employees; White, J., *Sisters and Solidarity: Women and Unions in Canada* (Toronto: Thompson Educational Press, 1993), 1992. In 2002, 96% of Ontario businesses had fewer than 50 employees; Ontario Ministry of Labour, Backgrounder, 'McGuinty Government taking Steps to help Employees When Family Members Gravely Ill', 13 Apr. 2004, available online at www.gov.on.ca.

working week.[77] In January 2004, the Ministry of Labour released a discussion paper that sketched two models for changing the working-time regime contained in the Employment Standards Act, 2000; the first model provided for standard block permits for up to 120, 240, or 360 extra hours in a calendar year, and the second model allowed for customized permits, based on agreements between employers and employees for hours beyond forty-eight in a week. The discussion paper also proposed that under either of the models random checks would be conducted to ensure that any agreements by employees to work long hours were voluntary. It was also careful to emphasize both that the models it proposed were simply examples and that there was a need to provide flexibility for business while at that same time protecting employees.[78] The discussion paper criticized the old permit system as overly complex and the Conservative government's new working-time regime for failing to protect employees.

But the Liberal government's promise to reinstate the standard forty-eight hour working week ultimately amounted to very little. The legislation, which came into effect on 1 March 2005, simply inserted a requirement for employers to obtain approvals (an expedited type of permit) in addition to an individual employee's agreement to opt out of the standard working week or to average entitlement to overtime premia over a four-week period.[79] While the Liberal amendments reinstated the requirement for employers to obtain approvals for long working hours from a government department, it did not reinstate the right of individual employees to refuse to work long hours on any specific occasion, nor did it get rid of the incentive (provided through overtime averaging) for employers to demand long working hours. Like its Conservative counterpart, the Liberal government was willing to sacrifice employee protection for greater flexibility for employers.

However, in contrast to its predecessor, the Liberal government reacted favourably, and immediately, to the federal government's use of employment insurance benefits to force the provinces to provide job-protected leave. In 2004 the federal government began to provide compassionate care benefits through the employment insurance system. Employees who had accumulated 600 insured hours in the qualifying period (typically the fifty-two week period immediately before the claim

[77] Ontario Ministry of Labour, 'Ending the 60-hour Work Week: A Discussion Paper', Jan. 2004, available online at www.gov.on.ca.   [78] Ibid., 2.

[79] An Act to Amend the Employment Standards Act, 2000 with respect to hours of work and certain other matters, S.O. 2004, c. 21. In addition to requiring Director approvals for agreements to work hours in excess of 48 in a week and average overtime entitlements, the legislature requires employers to provide employees with an official notice of their employment standards rights regarding working hours.

for benefits) and experienced a 40 per cent decrease in regular weekly earnings were entitled to six weeks of employment insurance benefits to compensate for absences from work in order to care or support a gravely ill family member with a significant risk of death within twenty-six weeks.[80] The Minister of Labour, Chris Bentley, quickly introduced and enacted legislation to amend the Employment Standards Act, 2000, to provide eight weeks of family medical leave to dovetail with the federal compassionate care benefits (six weeks of benefits after a two-week waiting period).[81]

While the compassionate care leave and benefits will enable employees to balance the care for a dying family member with continued employment, and some replacement income, they are likely to reinforce the gendered nature of unpaid care work. Although framed in gender-neutral terms, the structure of the benefits (which is identical to that of the parental and maternity benefits) will likely reinforce the existing pattern of care for the elderly; women are more likely than men to reduce the amount of paid work in order to care for elderly people.[82] The Liberal revisions the Employment Standards Act, 2000 will likely do little to reverse the erosion of the standard working week and the unequal allocation of unpaid labour, although they are likely to ease the burden on employees of caring for dying family members.

Entrenching inequality

The Conservative government justified the changes to employment standards by asserting the need to be more competitive in order to improve the quality of life for working people in the province. For the most part, flexibility was equated with deregulation and employers will benefit from it. Employers have greater flexibility to ask employees to work longer hours for less money. Some employees will be willing to work longer hours, in part to compensate for stagnant and declining real wages. A few employees may want to compress their working week in order to accommodate other commitments. And others will feel pressured to agree to employers' requests. The likely impact of this change to employment standards is to reinforce deleterious trends in the labour

---

[80] Available online at www.hrdc.drhc.gc.ca. The compassionate care benefits can be shared with other family members (who must apply and be eligible for the benefits).

[81] An Act to amend the Employment Standards Act, 2000, in respect of family medical leave and other matters, S.O. 2004, c. 15. The legislation also provides that the leave is to be shared between two or more employees who apply with respect to the same person. The compassionate care leave is in addition to the family responsibility leave, but unlike the family responsibility leave it does not require that the employee's employer employ a minimum of 50 employees in order for the employee to be eligible for the leave.

[82] Jenson, above, n. 23, 14.

market. More people will work long hours that are injurious to their health. The struggle to juggle family responsibilities will get harder and combined with a growth in part-time jobs, longer hours for some will contribute to deepening polarization in the labour market. Moreover, according to Rubery, Smith, and Fagan, 'flexible, unpredictable and unsocial working hours have the potential to undermine the division between work and private life, to increase the problems of combining work and family life, and to reinforce gender pay divisions in the labour market'.[83]

Both the Conservative and Liberal governments interpreted employees' need for flexibility in a highly gendered fashion; women's responsibilities for providing care for others was clearly the target of the family-friendly component of its labour standards policy. Some mild obligations were placed on employers to accommodate employees' domestic duties, although women continue to bear a disproportionate share of the economic cost of performing this labour.[84] Leave provisions provide women with the employment flexibility to accommodate better the demands of unpaid work, they do not lead to a more equitable division of unpaid labour. In fact, they are likely to reinforce the gendered and unequal division of unpaid work in the family. Differences with respect to time will continue to provide employers with an opportunity to use gender to segment the labour market. Moreover, poorly paid and non-standard forms of employment do not provide women with the economic independence required to bargain for a better division of household labour.[85]

Flexible working-time policies like those introduced in Ontario are the antithesis of policies that are designed to achieve a more equitable or healthy work/life balance. Competitive flexibility in working time will likely lead to an increase in paid work and a deterioration in the standard working week. The family-friendly leave policies enacted by the government provide women with greater flexibility to accommodate the dual demands on their time, but they do not challenge the unequal gender division of unpaid labour. Combined, these policies are likely to exacerbate, rather than ameliorate, gendered inequality in the allocation of time both within and between paid and unpaid work.

A new gender contract?

The new dual-earner gender contract at the heart of the Ontario government's employment standards policy is unsustainable.[86] It does

---

[83] Rubery et al., above, n. 4, 99.   [84] Esping-Anderson, above, n. 3, 122–3.

[85] Baker, above, n. 24, 170–2.

[86] 'Public policy in 2002 imposes conflicting logics. First, everyone should work, but, second, families are still expected to carry the lion's share of the care giving for children, frail elders, and other dependents. As the baby boomers enter their late 70s and their health

not challenge either the male norm of full-time employment or the female norm of primary caregiver. In the American context, researchers have called this gender contract 'the ideal worker/marginalized caregiver model', which 'allows women and men to work, as long as they maintain the ideal of the male employee with no domestic obligations'.[87] Competitive flexibility supplements a deteriorating standard (male) employment relationship, which is no longer capable of supporting a family's customary standard of living, with feminized forms of employment that do not provide the workers with the economic resources to live independently of another wage earner. Instead of changing the male employment norm to make it accommodate better the demands of caregiving, it provides supplementary forms of employment that are adaptable to the demands of domestic work. The problem with this gender contract is that it assumes that women's capacity to labour is completely elastic and that both men and women will continue to accept increasing demands on their time in order to maintain their standard of living. It also condemns the growing numbers of women who are sole support parents—and their children—to poverty.

Moreover, this gender contract would lead to greater inequality between men and women and among women since differences with respect to time will continue to provide employers with an opportunity to use gender to segment the labour market and segregate men's and women's jobs. Men will continue to work long hours of paid work, and women will be expected to be employed, but their employment will have to accommodate the socially necessary unpaid labour that they perform. Some women will choose either not to have children or, if they are highly educated and willing to work very long hours at their jobs, they will purchase domestic labour. However, most women are likely to choose to work fewer hours and in non-standard forms of employment in order to accommodate the demands of domestic labour. Since men's share of the domestic labour in a household increases as the income of their female partner increases, poorly paid and non-standard jobs do not provide women with the economic independence required to bargain a better division of household labour.[88] Nor do non-standard jobs provide women with economic security. Dependence upon a male earner is not a substitute for an independent source of income that can sustain an autonomous life.

becomes more frail, this tension between work and care-giving could become intolerable for many Canadians.' Maxwell, J., 'The Great Social Transformation: Implications for the Social Role of Government in Ontario', paper prepared for the Panel on the Role of Government, 2003, 12, available online at www.cprn.org.

[87] Appelbaum et al., above, n. 3, and Gonas, above, n. 43, 65.
[88] Baker, above, n. 24, 171.

The policy debate 'does not yet start from the explicit premise that both men and women should be expected to contribute actively to work and family life. The dominant discourse remains ambivalent about women's role and relies on a framework of promoting choice for women'.[89] Women should be free to choose the balance between employment and domestic life that is good for them. But policy discourse has barely begun to register ideas about men's greater involvement in domestic life. The problem is that so long as men can choose not to do domestic labour women will have no choice but to do it. The choices of individual women are shaped by the opportunities open to them and the cultural norms that prevail. Choice is not simply the endogenous property of free will but is a socially embedded activity. Perhaps this explains why, in the late 1990s, only 1 per cent of the couples composed of men and women had switched traditional male and female roles, so that the woman worked for pay, and the man kept the house and minded the children.[90]

It is important to increase the incentives for men to take on a greater share of unpaid labour, and to challenge cultural norms that associate women with certain kinds of domestic labour if women are to be given a real choice about how they spend their time. What is needed is an equal opportunities policy when it comes to men and domestic labour. But instead of imposing quotas and setting targets for men's domestic work, we should examine the policies that we now have and eliminate the gender bias in them. Shortening the standard working week and giving employees the right to refuse overtime would counter the culture of long hours of work, as would higher marginal tax rates for individuals. While such policies would limit the choices of men to work long hours and the choices of high-income earners, who also tend to be men, to purchase services on the market, these policies would also increase the choices of women to work in a variety of jobs and to use publicly provided services instead of performing domestic labour themselves. Whose choice is being maximized is a crucial question of social policy.

But in order to increase women's choices it is necessary to go beyond the structure of economic incentives and look at cultural norms.[91] In an ideal world, the gender and employment contract would value caregiving and cultivate 'new modes of life beyond male and female roles',[92] as well as permit 'more diverse employment and working-time patterns without

[89] Probert, B., 'Gender and Choice: The Structure of Opportunity', in P. James, W. F. Veit, and S. Wright (eds.), *Work of the Future: Global Perspectives* (St Leonards, NSW: Allen & Unwin, 1997), 181.   [90] Baker, above, n. 24, 171.

[91] Olson, K., 'Recognizing Gender, Redistributing Labor', *Social Politics*, 9 (2002), 380.

[92] Gonas, above, n. 43, 64, quoting Beck, U., *The Risk Society: Towards a New Modernity* (London: Sage, 1992).

any loss of rights or marginalization'.[93] However, in *this* world, maintaining a standard working week and reducing long hours of work is essential for achieving a work/life balance.[94] In order to be sustainable, the dual-earner gender contract must challenge the male norm of employment, and place limits upon the extent to which waged work dominates our lives.[95] It is only possible to move to equality of opportunity in the labour market through a more balanced allocation of time in paid and unpaid work.

[93] Rubery et al., above, n. 4, 99.

[94] This project also entails addressing the growing inequality in earnings and the increasing deregulation of the labour market because both of these processes are incompatible with strategies designed to reduce hours of work; Bosch, above, n. 32, 147.

[95] Appelbaum et al., above, n. 3, advocate a new model called 'shared work and valued care'; see, also, Esping-Anderson, above, n. 3, and Fraser, above, n. 3.

13

Work and Family Issues in the Transitional Countries of Central and Eastern Europe: The Case of Hungary

CSILLA KOLLONAY LEHOCZKY

I INTRODUCTION

The euphoria over the fall of the communist regimes and the economic and political shift from an authoritarian party-state and centralized economy to parliamentary democracy and a privatized market economy in the Central and East European (CEE) countries (including the Eastern states of the reunified Germany) very soon gave way to disillusionment and a bitter soberness amongst the many who felt themselves to be losers in the changes. Although the overall gains have never been questioned and a reversal of the transformation has never seriously been raised, the sweep of the 'new freedoms' desired and celebrated so much on the eve of the shift raised the question of the balance of the gains and losses brought about by privatization and the various economic freedoms, particularly in the field of labour and social law.

The previous high labour market activity of women has decreased in most of the transition countries;[1] however, it remains close to that of men, and in some countries women have even fared better than men in escaping unemployment. The quality and conditions of female employment as well as the overall quality of life of women, have also deteriorated. Moreover, the treatment of family issues as 'women's' issues has not changed much. Even more questionable is the balance of the changes in the field of women's equality in the family and in the workplace. Here, questions arise from the controversial way in which the communist regimes tried to 'liberate' or, as it was called, 'emancipate' women from their former and historically subordinate role.

---

[1] This is true practically everywhere, with the exception of Hungary, Estonia, and Lithuania. See Paci, P., 'Women in Transition', World Bank Report on Eastern Europe and Central Asia Region, 24617, 21 May 2002, online at: www.wds.worldbank.org, 40, Table 2.2; Lourdelle, H., 'Central and Eastern European Countries: The Transition from a *Planned* to a *Market* Economy', in H. Sarfati and G. Bonoli (eds.), *Labour Market and Social Protection: Reforms in International Perspectives* (Geneva: International Social Security Association (ISSA), 2002), 231ff.

This chapter gives an overview of the development of work and family issues in the post-socialist countries, many of which are already members of the European Union, and indicates where they still show special characteristics in respect of these issues in comparison to the older, Western industrial democracies. This overview will be presented in three steps, and will attempt to show the common features in the developments affecting female workers, as well as those affecting the labour force in general.

The first step will be to summarize the ambiguous character of 'socialist emancipation', underlining its traps and harms but also presenting its achievements. Although the communist regimes achieved outstanding records in female employment, this was, to a large extent, a result of state coercion. As a result, the transition era was welcomed as introducing 'the freedom to choose' for women between occupation and family. However, although favourable treatment in employment to facilitate women's 'second shift' had an adverse effect on women, both in the family and the workplace, its 'market style' correction also raises questions and problems.

The second step considers the backlash against the past that, coupled with the impact of the political and economic shift, resulted in a special combination of economic liberalism with conservative social values. This part will look at the consequences of the decline of the previous large-scale and generous provision of child-care and family services available primarily through the workplace, but also through the subsidized, state-controlled 'market' which effectively operated as a form of central distribution and rationing rather than a real market.

The final step is to look into the changes that seem to promise favourable developments in respect of the elimination of the differences based on gender roles, the only way to true labour market equality. It will present the positive changes in the position of women initiated at the beginning of this century as a result of the stabilization of the new regime and the European accession process, which have started to change the approach to issues of female labour in new, progressive ways.

II THE CONTROVERSIAL 'SOCIALIST EMANCIPATION'

The right and duty to work

Economic independence has been regarded, from the beginning of women's movements everywhere in the world, as an indispensable precondition of the equality of women. Since economic independence requires independent sources of income, engaging in paid work outside the family home has always been considered the principal way to equality. 'Socialist emancipation' not only built on these historic ideas, but also narrowed down the equality objective to equal access to employment.

'Socialist emancipation' put a very strong emphasis on labour market participation but it was distinctly silent about 'equal rights'. In practical terms, 'emancipation' was identified with equal access to the labour market *in abstracto* without the intention of the qualitative equalization of job opportunities. Fuelled by exaggerated industrialization,[2] the labour market needed women in large numbers, especially once other reserves of human resources (in particular the agricultural population) were already drawn into industrial production. The regime not only guaranteed the right to work to everyone but made work a duty. 'Participation in the building of socialism'—the most frequently sounded slogan—usually at a state-owned company, was enforced primarily through the so-called 'two wage-earner' family model devised by the centrally set wage system. Wages were intentionally set so low that two incomes were needed for the subsistence of a family, while income resources other than waged work were abolished and prohibited. This economic coercion was coupled with heavy propaganda in favour of female labour and was supported by legal means too.[3]

Furthermore, the predominant pattern of female employment was, in contrast to the Western model, full-time work in open-ended employment with guaranteed job security. The female working life track had become practically identical with that of male workers; working from the end of studies up to retirement was the only socially acceptable pattern. Staying at home and working only in the household was considered a departure from the normal standard.[4] It was surrounded by political suspicion and condemned as a 'bourgeois remnant' unless it was justified by the presence of a large number of children, a disability in the family, or similar reasons. Consequently, for a considerable part of the society, opposing the regime by staying at home as a housewife and mother became a positive attitude, even a form of 'civil courage', because it represented an opting-out of the ruling system and the

---

[2] In order to 'win' over capitalism in terms of production figures, tons of steel and metal produced, metres of textile woven, etc., the countries of the communist bloc engaged in extensive and exaggerated increases in industrial production which generated an increased appetite for labour.

[3] This was achieved through formerly tough, then gradually softening, rules prosecuting 'idling' and 'parasitism' by administrative and criminal measures. The articles of the Criminal Code on 'publicly dangerous idling' were abrogated only after the political shift in Hungary.

[4] In Hungary child-care leave was available from the late 1960s for serious demographic reasons, but only for working mothers with children under three. Similar leave provisions were enacted later in the other socialist countries which confirmed this pattern.

preservation of 'true family values' that had been devastated by communist power.

Facilitation of women's 'second shift'

All CEE countries belonging to the socialist zone, including Hungary, had (and still have) societies with conservative cultural traditions regarding the role of and relationship between the sexes. The state socialist regimes did not make any effort to reconstruct either these relationships or family obligations. Instead, parallel with forcing women to enter the labour market and follow a full-time career, women were charged with the responsibility of reproducing society by delivering and bringing up new generations, sometimes without the right to any birth control. In order to diminish the tension between the two roles, the governments made steps 'to facilitate the second shift of women'. While this frequently used motto is in itself revealing, the various measures that were adopted under this label obviously relieved the burden of child-care and household duties on women, although not without side effects.

Household assistance: outside and inside employment

The measures aimed at such facilitation, in spite of the questionable motives and slogans behind it, were actually helpful. They ranged from household and child-care goods and services such as cleaning, repair services, and catering, and included a large system of child-care institutions where care was available at a nominal or very low price. Similarly, there were also care centres available for the elderly, the disabled, or children whose parents were either unable to perform or had abandoned their duties. This system of family-related goods and services was complemented by the large scale of goods and services available at the workplace, like workplace canteens with subsidized prices and 'take-home' food, company nurseries and kindergartens, leisure time opportunities such as sporting facilities and vacation houses, and workers' hostels for domestic migrants provided by the workplace free of charge or at a heavily subsidized price. Although these benefits were labelled as part of the fulfilment of the 'social role' of the socialist state-owned companies and were also featured as 'pro-women' provisions, the real reason behind them was the competition between employers who were attempting to cope with labour shortages. Providing more and better benefits was a way of competing for workers in a centrally regulated wage system.[5]

---

[5] The self-increasing mechanism of the shortages in the socialist economy is described in János Kornai's seminal work, *Economics of Shortage* (Amsterdam: North-Holland, 1980); on labour scarcity and the reaction of employers, see, in particular, 306–9.

Employment privileges and benefits

This system of goods and services to facilitate family care was accompanied by a number of extra benefits and protective provisions in labour law granted to working mothers. Benefits predominantly meant various kinds of extra time off and leaves of absence,[6] whereas privileges meant the prohibition of certain kinds of work assignments for mothers. They included prohibitions on overtime, night shifts and working out of town; the duty to place pregnant women in a suitable job or, in the absence of such jobs, to exempt them from work with full pay; and enhanced protection of their employment through preferential hiring and prohibitions on dismissal.

The popular explanation for these measures was that since women in society (read 'in the family') were *de facto* unequal, their position had to be equalized by *de jure* inequality.[7] This justification fitted well with the overall approach of the communist regimes to equality, which was to be sharply critical of the formal equality of civil democracies and supportive of positive measures and entitlements provided on a merit basis to various groups in society.

The impact of socialist emancipation on the position of women

The generous system of benefits and social services made female labour a burdensome, expensive resource and, in spite of the wide range of protective regulations coupled with intense propaganda about the equality of women, discrimination remained unchanged both at the workplace and in the family. Instead of something positive, the system became associated with the so-called 'working mother syndrome':[8] a stressful life for women with double responsibility (frequently triple, as 'political activity'—participating at meetings, seminars, and attending 'communist Saturdays'—was *equally* required from women) which confined them to careers on the lower rungs of the hierarchical ladder. On the other hand, the extensive system of maternity benefits reinforced the traditional concept held by the society about family roles. By granting

[6] By the end of the 1980s, mothers were entitled to nine different kinds of shorter or longer leaves, most of them paid, in order to be able to tend to their maternal and household duties: maternity leave, child-care leave, nursing breaks, nursing leave, child supplement to annual vacation leave, large-family mothers' extra leave, a monthly household day, and spousal non-paid leave when the spouse works abroad.

[7] See Nagy, L. and Weltner, A., *Magyar Munkajog: Egységes jegyzet a jogi karok számára. Bpl. 1976 (Hungarian Labour Law: Uniform Textbook for the University Law Faculties)* (Budapest: Tankönyvkiadó, 1976), 46.

[8] Einhorn, B., 'Right or Duty? Women and the Economy' (Part 4) in *Cinderella Goes to Market: Citizenship, Gender, and Women's Movements in East Central Europe* (London: Verso, 1993), esp. 114–17.

the benefits only to women, the law itself reinforced the idea that household work and child-care were the duties of the mother in the family. The fact that certain privileges were granted to *single* fathers, too, confirmed and emphasized the legislators' understanding that family obligations shifted to the father only in the absence of the mother.

On the one hand, it was true that communist societies offered women 'full citizen' status by drawing them into wage-earning work, and thereby avoided the division of society into 'workers' and 'carers' in which only wage-earners are labelled as 'workers'. On the other hand, the impressive labour market participation of women was coupled with the clear exclusion of 'family care' from the status of 'work'. Not only was family care excluded from the concept of 'work', as moral and legal sanctions were incurred if this was the main activity of a person: its 'leisure time' label was also confirmed by the fact that it was expected to be done *in addition* to attending to the duties associated with full-time employment.[9]

In summary, state socialism achieved in each country a very high rate of labour market participation by women, one never even dreamed about by Western women's movements. Notwithstanding its favourable effect on the position of women, female work and family careers remained both questioned and questionable throughout the socialist era due to their mandatory character, and the autocratic nature of the detested political power that imposed them upon women and families. 'Socialist emancipation' became associated with inefficient and expensive labour and, as a consequence, with embedded and shrewd practices of discrimination in the labour market. On the other hand, consistent references to child-care and household work as the 'second shift' or 'double shift' of women prevented any redefinition of the conventional family roles and confirmed their traditional distribution between men and women. In addition, the low wages that effectively required two wage-earners in a family left women unable to establish economic independence. In the final analysis, the system deprived women of their classic status as caregivers but did not qualify them as real workers either.

III THE BACKLASH AGAINST COMMUNISM AFTER ITS FALL

The backlash against 'socialist emancipation'

Analysing the transition, one cannot avoid being confronted with the contradictions of its framework and content. The contradictory character is a result of the special historic circumstances that include the lack of an

[9] A recent and very clear criticism of this 'leisure time' argument as a justification for the discriminatory conditions of flexible forms of work under British law is made by Sandra Fredman in 'Women at Work: The Broken Promise of Flexicurity', *ILJ*, 33/4 (2004), 299–319.

overall theoretical framework for the changes—the fall of communism swept Eastern Europe almost unexpectedly—and the consequent experimental character of the transition. In part, this is behind the disparity between the constitutional-political changes on the one hand and the social developments on the other. Social developments lagged behind, due to a legal and political attitude that was the combined result of confusion about values and the repercussions of the past.[10]

These repercussions were a distorted eruption of the silent, massive opposition to the hypocritical ideology that already existed during the communist era. In the wake of the fall of the regime, this opposition manifested itself openly and in an extreme way: social values which were supported by or associated with the fallen regimes were seen as evil, obviously negative, and only worthy of the rubbish dump of history, while anything which was rejected or prohibited by the communist regime appeared now as a positive value that was, in principle, worthy of respect.[11] Since the so-called 'emancipation of women'[12] was a central part of communist ideology and politics, the backlash hit hard. One result was that the glory of high levels of female labour market participation was in danger of being disparaged as one of the evils of the communist regime that dissolved traditional families and family values.

Repercussion 1: live for your 'real profession'!

Without open questioning of the progressive value of high labour market participation for women, a reverse trend appeared in society in the 1990s. If work was a duty in the past, now not to work appeared as an achievement, a new freedom. If in the past, not working outside the home was officially condemned as a form of deviation from social standards, now it received official praise as a virtue in accordance with the values of the new post- (anti-?) communist regimes.

Among the repercussions of the political affiliation of high female employment with the former regimes was that 'full-time mothering' became featured as an important value that had been unjustly oppressed in the past. The new political regimes intended to 'liberate' women for their 'true profession', that is, motherhood. The new slogan 'free to

---

[10] I have dealt with the effect of the lack of a theoretical framework and the exposure to the 'repercussionary' effect in labour and social matters in more detail elsewhere. See 'Nouvelles méthodes de gouvernance et politiques sociales et d'emploi: À propos de l'expérience d'un nouvel État membre de l'Union européenne post-socialiste', *Bulletin de Droit Comparé du Travail et de la Sécurité Sociale* (forthcoming, English manuscript available with the author).

[11] See Kollonay Lehoczky, C., 'European Enlargement: A Comparative View of Hungarian Labour Law', in G. A. Berman and K. Pistor (eds.), *Law and Governance in an Enlarged European Union* (Oxford: Hart Publishing, 2004), 210–11.

[12] The official phraseology of the fallen socialist regime preferred 'emancipation' over 'equal treatment' or 'equal opportunity'.

choose' emphasized the opportunity to 'choose' between occupation and family as a new freedom, a gain of the democratic transition.[13] While the freedom to choose is better than the lack of choice coupled with coercion, it seemed to be forgotten that the real freedom lies in whether one can 'choose' both: having a profession *and* a family, a freedom that is naturally and obviously granted to men.

The elevation of 'motherhood as a profession' certainly resulted in positive changes in the form of giving modest acknowledgement to certain forms of socially useful but previously not credited work. In 1993, a law on various forms of social assistance[14] made it possible for women with three or more children to undertake 'full-time mothership' (as it was jubilantly named, even by women's rights advocates) by providing them not only with social income but also social security credits.

Although the reasons are certainly complex, the fact is that the willingness of women to undertake employment has shrunk in the wake of the revolution. For the good portion of women who were engaged in strenuous and frequently monotonous jobs, exposed to bad working conditions, and arbitrary or abusive management, the opportunity *not* to engage in work was viewed as an achievement. As a result of the deteriorating ethos and conditions surrounding female employment, the number of people who supported female employment fell considerably, from 81 per cent in 1986 to 66 per cent in 1995 among both female and male respondents.[15]

Repercussion 2: if you choose working life: be equal on equal terms!

If numerous employment benefits were a part of the previous regime, a logical step was to abolish them so that everything turned into its opposite. The legislature removed a number of previous benefits and privileges considered incompatible with a privatized market regime. The primary justification behind the reforms was to reduce labour costs and attract private investors. However, while the impact on the position of female labour may be to create a balancing effect for women in the long run, it is certainly one that is painful for individual women in the short run.

---

[13] Mixed feelings were raised when the World Bank Report (see above, n. 1) simply stated in a subtitle: 'The transition has permitted women to opt out of the labour market', without inverted commas or question marks, ch. 2, 33, s. 2.14.
[14] Act III of 1993 on Social Administration and Social Assistance. Later, norms on 'full-time mothering' were transposed from this law to Act LXXXIV of 1998 on the Support to Families. See '*Kodexpress*', Official Bulletin of the Ministry of Justice, 661/3, vol. XIV, no. 1/3, 7 Jan. 2005, 977–1019, and 1959–65, respectively.
[15] Frey, M., 'A nők helyzete a munkahelyen és a háztartásban' ('The position of women in the labour market and in the household'), in *Employment, Income Relations, Labour Conditions* (Budapest: Struktúra-Munkaügy Publishers, 1996), 11–85.

Entitlements to time off have been cut, preferential hiring has been abolished, while the pension age of women has started to rise to that of men.[16] These steps were painful for individual working women suddenly confronted with conditions 'equal to men', especially given that in their private lives their burdens have not decreased but rather increased. Yet these measures, although experienced as a deprivation for individual women, may be the price for the long-term advantage for the class as a whole for the following reason. The abolition of a good part of the benefits and privileges could contribute to the slow rehabilitation of the reputation of female workers in the labour market and thereby assist in achieving equal (or at least more equal) opportunities for female workers. Needless to say, such liberalization and formally equal treatment, if not coupled with the rearrangement of family chores and the creation of equally situated groups, will only preserve past inequalities.

Repercussion 3: the discrediting of gender equality regulation

The fact that protective legislation resulted in additional economic and managerial burdens on establishments, while creating no significant change in the relationship of the sexes, discredited equal opportunity legislation in the eyes of both employers and society. Management regarded equality norms as an imposition accompanied by periodic political vexation; consequently, women could not expect much more than results 'for show'. On the whole, the controversial character of the norms of emancipation had built up an attitude of suspicion and scepticism in society toward any state measure aimed at promoting equal opportunities. For these reasons, the identification of backlash effects is highly important to understanding the social atmosphere surrounding equality legislation on the one hand, and to the search for measures that are adequate to the reconstruction of trust within society and in statutory and governmental instruments on the other.

The impact of market liberalization on the living and working conditions of women

The impact of transition on women was not only due to the changing assessment of the family and the changes to the laws just described; it also came about through the impact of the market on women's lives.

---

[16] Through a gradual rise from 55 for women and 60 for men, the pension age in Hungary will be 62 for both sexes from 1 Jan. 2009. In other CEE countries, the equalization is more moderate: in the Czech Republic, by 2007, women's retirement age will be 61, one year less than that of men, or less, up to a maximum of four years if they have children; in Poland, the former difference of five years between men and women remains. See Fultz-Markus Ruck, E. and Steinhilber, S. (eds.), *The Gender Dimension of Social Security Reforms in Central and Eastern Europe: Case Studies of the Czech Republic, Hungary and Poland* (ILO Subregional Office for Central and Eastern Europe, 2003), 33.

Economic background: rising prices—stagnating wages

One of the very first measures implemented during the transformation into a market economy was the abolition of centralized wage- and price-setting.[17] But whereas price liberalization immediately pushed prices up, wage liberalization had no such impact on wage levels.[18] Industrial wages remained the same, as they were set by the 'owner-state', who, as an employer, paid only nominal, artificially low wages, although it had also provided its citizens (or 'subjects') with a wide range of goods and services free or at nominal prices, even if the quality was low and even if the provision served political goals. The price rises were particularly painful for families with children who were deprived of formerly subsidized basic goods and services, such as food, energy, transportation, rent and housing, children's clothing, in addition to household-facilitating goods and services such as cleaners, repair services, cheap 'kitchen-ready' food, etc. Child-care institutions, which had been generally available at nominal or no fees, disappeared, and most parents who retained access at all had to pay considerable fees.

This opposite movement of wages and prices had a double impact on household operations. Since a lot of traditional, manual work was done at home because of the lack of financial resources to buy goods and services, the time needed for household activity increased; however, the time spent outside the home to earn money also increased in order to obtain the additional income that was needed for maintaining the family living standard.[19] So, while one adult (generally, the male) had to withdraw from his work at home, the other (generally, the female) had to cope alone with the increased chores, something that limited considerably the chances of women to compete with men under equal conditions in the labour market, if they were even able to undertake external jobs at all.

One of the characteristic symptoms of the 'repercussion' of communism and the confusion of values was the ambivalent attitude towards the

---

[17] With the narrow exceptions of salaries in public employment and the price of a few fundamental goods and services (energy, petrol, medicines, social rents, etc.) which remained centrally regulated.

[18] The changes in consumer prices and net earnings between 1990 and 2000 (both expressed in the percentage of the previous year) show the strong divergence (source: Labour Market Mirror, 2002, MTA-OFA, 280):

	1990	1991	1992	1993	1994	1995	1996	1997	1998	1999	2000
prices	117.2	128.9	135.0	123.0	122.5	128.2	123.6	118.3	114.3	110.0	109.8
net earnings	94.3	93.0	98.6	96.1	107.2	87.8	95.0	104.9	103.6	102.5	101.5

[19] According to the official statements of the Hungarian government to CEDAW, child-care is shared by parents in 27% of families, while nursing sick children is a shared task in only one-fifth of families; nursing other sick relatives is shared in 22% of families.

employee–employer relationship. The past ideology labelled private property, and market transactions, as a source of, or even identical with, exploitation. Now, when private property and the market became glorified, exploitation (that is, the excessive use of hired labour up to or beyond the limits set by law) logically, if hesitantly, began to appear as an 'efficient' use of labour, although perhaps one that seemed unusual to the 'spoiled' socialist worker. The exploitative habits that quickly spread among new private employers, such as requiring a high level of 'flexibility' from their employees in performing work beyond scheduled hours without extra pay and being available at irregular times, aggravated the situation of women both within the family and the workplace. Thus, both economic pressures, and the disappearance of cheap household support services, pushed families back to a traditional distribution of gender roles and widened the gap between female and male roles.

The withdrawal of the state from the provision of services

The provision of social security and social welfare benefits on a large scale by the state was part of the heritage of state socialism and its paternalist relationship to its citizens. The employer-state did not pay fair wages; instead, the provider-state provided workers with the necessary means of subsistence at a low, equalized level. The elimination of this paternalist relationship by allowing citizens to provide for themselves in an autonomous way through the withdrawal of the state was a primary demand of the political shift.

One of the naïve expectations of transition, and a symptom of the lack of an elaborate theoretical framework for the process, was the serious error of supposing that the simple abolition of social provisions and entitlements alone would automatically produce the necessary social and economic capacities of citizens to care for themselves. Similar to a number of other processes of transition, the demolition of past institutions was easier and went faster than the construction of replacements or corresponding market economy institutions. The removal of social care, coupled with the overall glorification of private property and private entrepreneurship, left the weak unaided and prevented the wages set by the socialist state from catching up with market economy prices.

The increased burden described above was aggravated by the multiple effects of the reduction of personnel in public services. First, discharged employees were predominantly women. Secondly, the remaining employees had to carry an increased workload while, as they were mainly women themselves, coping with increased duties at home. As a result, an absent woman in the public service might result in another woman absent from work elsewhere. The deteriorating working conditions of women in the public service (mainly in health, education, and personal services) has had a direct impact on the quality of life, and on the labour market chances, of a whole class of women who have to make up for the missing or deficient services themselves, often at the cost of their rest time, dedicated work, or studying opportunities. For this reason, the conspicuous wage rise in the public sector in 2002 of 50 per cent should be seen as an example of *de facto* 'affirmative action' for all those, mainly women, who are in need of public services.

The disappearance of company services

Not surprisingly, the attractive benefit systems provided by the employers were quickly demolished after 1989. The various facilities such as nurseries, kindergartens, workers' hostels, holiday houses, sports and other recreation opportunities were, in the case of most employers, sold or transformed into other businesses or factory buildings. The justification for their destruction was the indisputable profit and efficiency require-ments under market relations, a justification that was confirmed by a social attitude that considered all these 'socialist' services to run counter to the effectiveness of the market.

The ambivalent social attitude towards female employment has been further tainted by the obvious pressure on families in the wake of privatization and the withdrawal of the state from the social field. Social networks and services have collapsed as privatization washed away company nurseries and holiday centres. The necessary cuts to public expenditures, together with the changing perception of the role and function of the state, have resulted in a radical reduction of state-financed facilities too.

A combined effect of the changes to the social and economic environ-ment of female labour is that the labour market activity of women has fallen radically, from over 80 per cent in 1989,[20] a rate far above that of the industrialized countries as a whole, to around 50 per cent. Although, from a rate of 52.6 per cent in 1997, there has been a slow increase in the rate of female labour participation, it was still below 57 per cent in 2003, forecasting a long way to and slow process of recovery.[21]

The overall state of the labour market: 'feminized' terms and conditions, 'masculinized' requirements

The first phase of the post-transition period (roughly, the first half of the 1990s) brought about an extreme and rapid liberalization of the labour

[20] The labour market participation rate of women aged 15–59 was 83.6% in 1989. Frey, M., 'The Position of Women on the Labour Market after the Change of Political System', in *Women in the World of Work: Women Workers' Rights in Hungary* (Budapest: ILO-CEET, 1998).
[21] *Labour Market Mirror, 2004* (MTA-OFA, Budapest, 2004), 229.

market in general, not only for women. The new Labour Code[22] removed several former labour standards and safeguards that were considered incompatible with a privatized market economy, although it still preserved more than was regarded as convenient by the new private employers. Consequently, they tried to broaden the space for contractual opt-outs from the existing and already loosened statutory limitations. The number of atypical contracts such as fixed term, casual work, and home-work increased. Temporary agency work, something that was previously unheard of, started to spread quickly, circumventing or blatantly infringing existing legal barriers as, for example, where people were engaged without any contract and not reported for taxation and social security purposes.[23] Tasting their new 'freedom', employers converted their employees *en masse* into contractors or self-employed workers by simply contracting out to their employees the same jobs that they had previously filled. These 'forced entrepreneurs' accepted the disadvantageous changes rather than opting for dismissal, the second alternative 'offered'.

This pervasive recontractualization process was strongly enhanced by the backlash effect that glorified (almost) everything that was declared 'evil' and 'the enemy' by the former regime. It had a large role in the rapid transformation of the labour market from one characterized by full employment and full-time work to one in which there is a low activity rate and a good part of the working population is engaged in short-term, insecure, semi-legal jobs such as seasonal, project-based, agency, free-lance, out- or self-employed work. Or they may be employed in 'show partnerships' or as companies, or simply work on the black market without being reported for taxation and social security purposes. Needless to say, working conditions have deteriorated along with the decreased level of security of such jobs.

In summary, the society of previous 'core' workers that was typical of male employment, but under socialism had been extended to both genders, has now been converted into a society of 'peripheral' workers more typical of female employment (and that of other disadvantaged groups such as disabled and racial or ethnic minority workers in market

---

[22] Act XXII of 1992, *Törvények és rendeletek Hivatalos Gyujteménye* [*Official Bulletin of Laws and Decrees*] (Budapest: Közgazdasági és Jogi Kiadó, 1993), 52–73.

[23] One employer trick typical of the time was to hire and dismiss workers at will, without any procedure and without even paying for their work, through the promise of 'proba-tionary work', making workers work without a contract and without agreed wages, with the promise that where they satisfied the requirements of the prospective employer, they would be hired for a probationary period of three months that might then be followed by a permanent contract. In such cases, the employer's defence before the court was that the several days of work without pay was just a 'usual testing method' before concluding a contract with an employee even for a probationary period (Case 608 of 1995 published by Bírósági Határozatok Tára [*Bulletin of Court Decisions*], 1995).

societies). However, in the wake of the transition it has been extended to both genders.

Similar tendencies towards 'flexibilization' or 'escape from labour law' have become widespread in the developed industrial countries since the last quarter of the twentieth century, especially where statutory labour standards have reached a high level. However, workers in the post-communist countries who were suddenly exposed to the tremendous uncertainties accompanying the first wave of privatization were particularly helpless due to their lack of market experience and lack of skill in negotiating for themselves. As a result, the effects of the process, in terms of deteriorating conditions, decreasing wages, weakening rights enforcement and declining collective representation among intimidated workers, have been much more sweeping and devastating. This gives the process often called the 'feminization of work' a new meaning,[24] as the extension of all the negative features of female labour conditions to male workers has had a more aggressive 'downward harmonization' effect on the terms and conditions of work for both sexes in the CEE region than elsewhere. However, this phenomenon also underlines one of the overall lessons for global labour processes: uncorrected injustices of 'female employment' (or those of weaker groups of workers in any sense) sooner or later reach 'male employment' (or stronger groups of workers) through the downward harmonizing effect of global competition, unless conscious and concerted national and international measures prevent the detrimental spillover of the weaker groups' conditions. In the final analysis, all unfair practices in employment which may be considered gender-specific are potentially and ultimately gender-neutral, in the sense of detrimentally affecting both sexes. Therefore, the response also has to be the elimination of the gender-specificity of the source of the problem, that is, the 'gender-neutralization' of both family *and* employment roles.

IV DEVELOPMENTS IN RECONCILING PRIVATE LIFE AND WORKPLACE DUTIES

Legislative changes: transposition of the *acquis communautaire*

The late 1990s, and the turn to the 2000s, witnessed the emergence of a counterbalancing trend to the downward liberalizing race. This was a result of two intertwined factors: social-economic consolidation and

---

[24] For an early analysis of this phenomenon, see Standing, G., 'Global Feminization Through Flexible Labor', *World Development*, 17/7 (1989), 1077–95, and a more recent follow-up from the same author: 'Global Feminization Through Flexible Labor: A Theme Revisited', *World Development*, 27/3 (1999), 583–602.

European accession. The completion of the privatization process, economic stabilization, and the experiences of the first decade of transition obviously involved a clarifying and learning process. Still, the second factor, 'Europeanization', was an indispensable element of the favourable changes, as well as a support to the process of consolidation itself.

The accession process was to a great extent a one-way communication, even a dictate, whereby the candidate countries had to transpose the *acquis communautaire* of the European Community into their national legal regimes. This process, through a fortunate coincidence of developments, was carried out in major part at a time when the social dimension of European integration came quite forcefully to the forefront within the governing institutions of the European Union.[25] One of the most significant motivations was the realization that the lack of social integration might undermine the completion of political and economic integration,[26] as well as an acknowledgement of the importance of social cohesion and the inclusion on an equal footing of different groups and members of society to all-important spheres of social life. In 1993 when the so-called 'Copenhagen criteria' of accession were designed, no social criteria had yet been included.[27] By the end of the decade and into the early 2000s, motivated both by processes within the EU itself and by the fear of the possible effects of social dumping, the candidate countries were confronted in their country reports with the social standards of the European Union and their adjustment to the social *acquis* was regularly evaluated.

This process proved quite successful; the motivating factor of the strong desire to join the EU coupled with competition among the candidate countries (itself boosted by the long uncertainty about the countries of the first accession round) proved powerful enough to overcome the hidden barriers deriving from the conservative attitude of the accession societies. This was true for the protection of social rights of workers in general, and particularly true with respect to gender equality. By the end of 2002, when the Copenhagen Summit finally decided on the

---

[25] For an overall analysis, see Trubek, D. M. and Mosher, J. S., 'New Governance, EU Employment Policy, and the European Social Model', in J. Zeitlin and D. M. Trubek (eds.), *Governing Work and Welfare in a New Economy: European and American Experiments* (Oxford: OUP, 2003); Betten, L., 'The Democratic Deficit of Participatory Democracy in Community Social Policy', *European Law Review*, 23 (1998), 20.

[26] Leibfried, S., 'Towards a European Welfare State?', in Z. Ferge and J. E. Koberg (eds.), *Social Policy in a Changing Europe* (Boulder, Colorado: Westview Press, 1992), 247 ff., and 261; for a summary of the deficits in the social area, see Bercusson, B., Deakin, S., Koistinen, P., Karavaritou, Y., Mückenberger, U., Supiot, A., and Veneziani, B., *Manifesto for Social Europe* (Brussels: ETUI, 1995).

[27] The three criteria, set for the candidate countries at the 1993 June Copenhagen Council meeting, were: (1) a functioning market economy; (2) stability of the institutions guaranteeing the rule of law and the protection of human rights including minority rights; and (3) the ability to take on obligations deriving from the economic, monetary, and political union.

Csilla Kollonay Lehoczky

date of accession (1 May 2004), the mandatory transposition assignments had been completed at the legislative level to the extent necessary for accession.[28]

Among the provisions on equal pay and equal employment opportunity, the most important adjustment from the standpoint of the current discussion was the elimination of differences in the entitlement of men and women to family and child-care-related benefits. The strategic value of such provisions goes far beyond the significance attributed in general to these roles, as the achievement of labour market equality cannot be completed without the full merger and equalization of the roles of the caregiver and the worker.

Equalization of the Hungarian benefits system

The two main areas where differences had to be removed concerned pension rights and various leaves of absence, supplemented by minor differences regarding work assignment privileges.

The 'gender-neutralization' of family-related benefits in labour and social law had been nearly completed by 2002. This meant that Hungarian legislation, not unlike most of the CEE accession countries, extended all former maternity or caring benefits and privileges to male employees[29] with the narrow exception of benefits closely connected to the biological functions of pregnancy, childbirth and breastfeeding. The benefits are of two kinds: first, entitlements to be absent from the workplace with the right to return to the same job and secondly, entitlements to be paid for those times not spent in work and to have those periods credited for pension and employment seniority purposes.

While on the one hand, the legal norms reflected serious efforts to 'gender-neutralize' the various benefits, social prejudice and practices around these issues have not significantly changed. With respect to the last, intense efforts to comply with the EU gender and employment *acquis* led the Hungarian government to enact a couple of norms which represent unequivocal efforts effectively to change gender-specific family

[28] See ch. 13, and the final conclusions of the last, fairly uniform, comprehensive monitoring reports on the accession countries published at the end of 2003; available online at www.europa.eu.int. Also, *Legal Issues in Gender Equality, Bulletin of the Commission's Network of Legal Experts on the Application of Community Law on Equal Treatment between Women and Men*, No. 1/2004, produced by Sacha Prechal and Annick Masselot (Theme CE-V/2-01-004-EN-C, European Commission Directorate-General for Employment and Social Affairs Unit EMPL/G/1), 7.
[29] Some minor differences remain that could be called merely matters of 'cosmetic' significance; however, as a matter of principle they need modification. Two such provisions (one in the Labour Code and one in the Law on Employment and the Assistance for the Unemployed) are where the employee has a right not to work beyond an acceptable distance, such a distance being defined in terms of the duration of travel, and that duration is shorter for women or single fathers raising a young child.

TABLE 13.1 *The Hungarian benefits system*

Type of leave	Beneficiary	Time and length of absence	Compensation	Source of compensation
1. Maternity leave	mother (father if the mother dies or abandons the child)	24 weeks (4 weeks before and 20 weeks after delivery)	70 per cent of gross salary	health insurance fund
2. Paternity days off	father	5 days within 2 months from childbirth	full salary	health insurance fund
3. Nursing time off	mother	2 hours/day for 6 months, 1 hour/day up to the 9th month of the child	full salary	employer
4. Additional holiday	any parent	2–5 additional days (dependent on the number of chidren)	full salary	employer
5. Child-care leave	any parent	up to the 3rd (in case of medical reasons, the 14th) birthday of the child	70 per cent of salary in the first 2 years, afterwards a lump sum equal to the national minimal pension	0–2 years: health insurance fund 2–3 (14) years: nat. budget
6. Child-raising benefit (only cash benefit, right to workplace beyond deadlines above in item 5)	any parent	in case of 3 or more minor children, until the youngest reaches 8	lump sum allowance, equal to minimal pension	nat. budget

TABLE 13.1 *Continued*

Type of leave	Beneficiary	Time and length of absence	Compensation	Source of compensation
7. Sick child nursing leave	any parent	period of sickness of the child up to the 12th birthday of the child	70 per cent of salary	health insurance fund
8. Sick relative nursing leave	any person	max. 2 years absence from employement with the same relative	around national minimal pension (means tested) might be paid longer than absence from employment	nat. budget
9. Housing leave	any person	max. 1 year absence for building, reconstruction, or renovating own home	non-paid	

and employment patterns. Three relatively recent measures should be mentioned.

One of these measures is a provision for days off for young fathers, introduced in December 2002,[30] which wisely allocated the burden of compensation to the health insurance fund rather than the employer. The second is financial support for the education, postgraduate education or retraining of those on longer child-care leave[31] which had already been enacted in 2001. Since such parents, if they meet admission requirements, have an enforceable right to have their (sometimes expensive) university tuition fees waived, this opportunity may have a double effect. It might maintain or improve the labour market chances of women during parental leave, and it might also motivate fathers to undertake child-care for a period of time, especially given that admission to tuition-paying higher education is more readily available than admission to its state-subsidized forms. The third and most recent provision is a subsidy granted from January 2005 to employers who hire persons returning from any longer form of child-care leave and who do not have a job. The subsidy is the reimbursement of half of the social security contribution paid by the employer above the wages of the employee for a maximum of nine months, provided that the employer undertakes to provide an additional three-month period of employment.

Any measure that improves the labour market chances of women who withdraw from work due to child-care is a significant step to promote gender equality. However, the long-term significance of measures which stimulate men to take some leave and stay at home and take care of children are greatly superior, due to the beneficial impact they have on the mental attitudes of members of both sexes and not least because of their effect upon employers.

Concepts of sex and gender

Measures to gender-neutralize legislation are frequently painful under current conditions and are often regarded as unjustly favouring men; hence the heavy criticism from feminist organizations of the resolution of the Constitutional Court which declared discriminatory and therefore unconstitutional what was then a provision of the Social Security Act.[32] While the gradual equalization of retirement ages had already started (and will be completed by 2009), a provision concerning the pre-conditions for early retirement was found unconstitutional in as much as it gave a 'premium' year for raising children only to women or to single

---

[30] No. 2 in Table 13.1.   [31] Items 1, 5, 6 in Table 13.1.
[32] Act no. II. of 1975 on Social Security, replaced by Act LXXXI of 1997, in force from 1 Jan. 1998. *Kodexpress*, Official Bulletin of the Ministry of Justice, no. 661/5, vol. XIV, 1/5, 7 Jan. 2005, 1659–76.

fathers. Based on its earlier declaration that providing equal rights for men and women 'is only (and only then) reasonable if we recognize the natural difference between man and woman and equality is realized with this in mind',[33] the Constitutional Court concluded that with regard to the regulation in dispute, the 'natural differences between genders' were irrelevant factors. Therefore, treating men and women differently in relation to child-care is unjust and amounts to unconstitutional discrimination. What is historic in the resolution is the declaration that 'the two genders have equal rights and obligations from the point of view of child-care as a regulatory concept'.[34]

The importance of this decision was that the Constitutional Court, even if with some uncertainty,[35] seemed to accept the distinction between the concepts of 'sex' and 'gender', a conceptual step that has to be made in the post-socialist countries, including Hungary. The reception of this distinction is difficult because the conceptual gap is aggravated by a language gap (obviously there is a correlation): the word 'gender' is missing from the Hungarian and other CEE languages.[36]

The lack of knowledge and awareness of this distinction is reflected by the text of the Act on Equal Treatment and Equal Opportunity,[37] adopted as the completion of the adjustment of Hungarian law to the equality legislation of the European Union with special regard to its recent developments.[38] The Law sets up a long (nineteen-item) list of prohibited grounds of discrimination, in which 'sex' is a prime ground and 'maternity (pregnancy) or paternity' is listed as a separate ground. While pregnancy is clearly connected to the biological sex of the person, 'maternity' and 'paternity' might not be, as parenthood is a social role that has no necessary connection to either of the sexes.

Social policy and company developments

The transition period processes have shown a double trend; even though on the one hand entrepreneurial arbitrariness and the abuse of new

[33] 14/1995 (III.13.) Constitutional Court Decision. ABH, 1995, 84.

[34] 32/1997(V.16.) Constitutional Court Decision. ABH, 1997, 161–5.

[35] In other decisions, the court referred to the 'biological and *psychological* dimensions of motherhood, and also to the physiological attributes of women that might be a ground for differential treatment' (which the court called 'positive discrimination'); 7/1998 (III.18.) (emphasis added).

[36] As the literature on gender uses the expression 'socially constructed sexes' for gender, it is hoped that the word 'gender' will simply be naturalized from English.

[37] Act CXXV of 2003.

[38] That is, Council Directives nos. 2000/43/EC on racial and ethnic discrimination, 2000/78/EC on equality in employment ('Framework Directive'), and Council Directive 76/207/EEC on equal treatment of men and women in employment (modified by Council Directive 2002/73/EC), as well as 97/80/EC on the burden of proof. Other directives—especially those on social security, parental leave and self-employed persons—had been transposed to Hungarian law earlier.

freedoms emerged as a new norm in employer behaviour, another, opposite tendency also appeared. Companies with long-term thinking and a high level of personnel management have started to provide their employees with fringe benefits on a broad scale. The composition of benefits might be different now than those previously provided, having been adjusted to the contemporary needs of employees and also to the financial constraints on employers, where the taxes on wages and other benefits have replaced the centralized wage system. While child-care institutions have been mostly closed, company canteens and cafeterias have been maintained, although with limited financial support mainly due to the rigorous watch of tax authorities. No longer does the 'socialist brigade movement' bring people and families together for weekends and holidays; however, 'personnel cohesion development' and 'team-building' sometimes does similar things, often with a considerable contribution by the employer.

Again, the resemblance to the past—lots of propagandistic, inefficient, or manipulative measures, wasteful state enterprises, efforts of the party-state to rule its citizens' private life through the state-owned workplace—might invite the 'backlash' effect of painting black everything that was a part of the communist past. However, as the above-mentioned recent developments suggest, even if the shadow of the past can cause managerial reluctance and employee scepticism, and might be a hindrance to the development of institutions, the 'Western' origin and new vocabulary can also have an impact, speeding up the process of conceptual and institutional development. Of course, the 'credibility stamp' can only be effective if the process is coupled with genuine efforts to improve work and family life together and is free of any of the manipulative and direct production-efficiency intent.

The Family Friendly Workplace programme

The 'Family Friendly Workplace' programme (FFW) was launched by the Ministry of Labour and Social Affairs in the year 2000, with the intention of raising consciousness among employers, in particular, human resource managers, of the importance of appropriate attention to and support for employees with family responsibilities. Looking at its goals and at the achievements of the awardees, it is difficult to avoid a sense of scepticism once one becomes familiar with the background, content, and achievements of the 'movement'.

There seems to be no difference in the standard appraisal of such initiatives in Hungary and abroad. The optimistic forecasts try to convince employers and readers that a workplace that observes family obligations is attractive for employees with families as well as increasing the competitiveness of the company. The argument is that where the reconciliation of family and work is a goal for management, employees are more motivated, their work performance is more efficient, and stress, absenteeism, and labour turnover decreases. In the final analysis, a committed labour force brings more profit in the long run. Behind these optimistic appraisals, however, one finds little in the way of tangible results, and even less evidence of changes to the rights and duties of the parties to the employment relationship that would adjust the terms and conditions of work so as to relieve the double burden experienced by employees with family duties.

The questionnaire for applications for the 2004 award under the FFW programme contained the following items: (1) working time, guaranteeing the opportunity to choose from patterns of working time; (2) continuous education in correspondence with the individual phase of life of the employee; (3) prevention, information and consciousness-raising programmes in order to preserve health, prevent diseases, and avoid the consumption of drugs and the harmful consumption of alcoholic drinks; (4) dealing with employees on leave for child-care purposes by (a) facilitating their return to work, (b) providing them with training and professional information, (c) keeping contact with them, and (d) offering them part- time work, telework, or project work. Other listed considerations include (5) workplace events and the provision of holiday vacation with a view to the interest and possibilities of employees with family duties, as well as (6) child-care facilities, their preservation, maintenance, development, and modernization.

On their face, the questions obviously offer a series of advantages to employees, although not all of them relate directly to the reconciliation of family and workplace duties. Indeed, only the first, fifth, and sixth questions directly address caregivers' problems. The rest of the services and opportunities that are offered are useful for the career development of all employees, although not all of them are useful all the time and they do not directly address the workplace problems of parents with children. As to 4(d), this raises the suspicion that flexible working arrangements might serve the interests of employers as well as, and maybe more than, employees.[39]

The impact of Family Friendly Workplace programmes on gender equality in a post-socialist social environment

It has been conspicuous that, apart from enthusiastic rhetoric, no evidence is available on the costs and benefits of investments designed to obtain the FFW title. What is more, the FFW programmes seem to run parallel with the downsizing of the existing labour force, the result of which is that the same (or more) tasks have to be attended to by fewer

---

[39] See Sandra Fredman's evaluation on such arrangements, above, n. 9.

people. For example, one of the flagships of the FFW project, the main Hungarian telecommunication company, MATAV, stepped up publicly as a powerful promoter of gender equality and a family-friendly work environment nearly at the same time as it announced the reduction of its labour force by three thousand people, citing the demands of global competition and the need to reduce costs in the field of telecommunications.

For the moment, rather than an adjustment of workplaces to the caregiver role, facts show the adjustment and subordination of the caregiver to the requirements of the workplace. As recent sociological research in Budapest has shown, the main option available to young women with small children is to drop out of the labour market. Other groups of women working in corporate life compete with men, are employed almost exclusively full-time, and have an almost continuous working-life cycle with short career breaks; in short, these women adjust themselves to the male norm of employment.[40]

It seems important here to remember that all conspicuous managerial movements that on their face appear to be an effort to humanize the workplace, and make them worthwhile places for employees, lose momentum among employees if it turns out that they are merely new techniques to increase profits. This is what occurred in efforts to 'humanize work' through involving employees in decisions relating to their jobs in the first half and middle of the twentieth century and to the movement to create 'autonomous groups', that is to grant *quasi*-entrepreneurial autonomy to smaller groups, in the late 1970s and 1980s. When workers realize that the only, or the main, purpose is to enhance profits, interest in the new methods dissipates and the methods fade away.

V CONCLUSION

Gender equality is still far from the norm in Hungarian workplaces, even if company managers are sincerely convinced that they follow equality policy because they treat women equally if they are able to compete with men according to male norms. These male norms, especially in the transition economies that are permeated by neo-liberal ideology and that consider the owner to be the absolute monarch, require employees to be flexible and ready to accept excessive workloads, two attributes that are very difficult to achieve for someone with family responsibilities.

The only solution towards equality is the removal of the male norm and the redesigning of the employment relationship in a gender-neutral

[40] Nagy, B., *Equal Opportunity Policy of Hungarian Companies* (Budapest: Institute of Economics, Hungarian Academy of Sciences, 2003). The final research paper can be found at www.policy.hu.

way. A gender-neutral construction of employment would break with the classic conception, which, in spite of all declarations of equality, constructs workers as male and without family duties and presumes a female in the background who takes care of the family and all of the household needs of the worker.[41]

Family-friendly practices as they are performed in Hungary today (and perhaps elsewhere, too) do not seem to solve the problem for a number of reasons. First, in the case of some Hungarian FFW prize-winners, benevolent efforts include continuing to address 'family' problems through attention to women by putting the emphasis on the availability of special arrangements for young mothers who return to work or those still on leave. Secondly, the various initiatives do not really rearrange the content of employment. Instead, they involve a lot of new activities, such as designating coordinators and launching training programmes for the coordinators or for the parents on health, family, and other issues; however, these activities do not resolve the problem of child-care or elder care. Last but not least, family-friendly initiatives, if they are more than mere lip service or 'eye wash', cost money. Amidst sharpening competition with competitors who do not even observe mandatory employment regulations, it is naïve to think that employers can absorb the costs of such measures over the long term. The state can give acknowledgement and some support; however, such support cannot maintain these projects indefinitely. This difficulty is evident in the stagnation and even regression of the number of applications for the FFW prize in Hungary. In summary, family-friendly workplace initiatives can provide exemplary models in some respects and give encouragement to both employees and human resource management, but as Bob Hepple summarized in respect of voluntary efforts to provide decent work, they are 'doing good but doing little'.[42] They are doing little not only because of the scarcity of such examples, but also because most such initiatives or programmes do not address the real problems of the reconciliation of duties from the two spheres of human life.

While it may sound radical, only the legislative rewriting of the content of employment can degenderize the roles of 'worker' and 'caregiver' by inserting duties into employment that, regardless of the sex of

---

[41] The gender division of workplace and family roles has been explored in the earliest writings of feminist legal theory; perhaps the most articulate early presentation of this division is Olsen, F. E., 'The Family and the Market: A Study of Ideology and Legal Reform', *Harvard L. Rev.*, 96 (1983), 1497. Although this work has been followed by a series of similarly eloquent papers on the issue of the construction of gender in the market, they seem to have avoided the attention of law-makers when it comes to reshaping the content of the employment relationship.

[42] Hepple, B., 'Equality and Empowerment for Decent Work', *International Labour Review*, 140(1) (2001), 15 ff.

the worker, would provide a right for anyone with children (or, perhaps with elderly family members), to things such as the provision of working-time allowances, extra leave, and some flexibility in working-time schedules. Child-care institutions or the provision of child-care in other ways also belong to the benefits to which employees must be entitled. What is of vital importance is that the benefits are provided to *both* parents and even require that both of them either take the leave or benefit.

While it is easy to forecast the arguments against such proposals—that they would harm business interests and further impair competitiveness under globalized competition—it is also easy to imagine the response to such concerns. The problem of the downward effects of competition on working conditions goes beyond the scope of this chapter and must be addressed elsewhere. However, it is important to mention that the 'increased price' of labour in this context would only be the *fair* price of labour. It is a commonplace of economics that the price of labour should include not only the daily reproduction of the capacities of the individual worker, but also the costs of producing new generations of workers. In the past, these costs were compensated to some extent by the family wage. The communist regimes abolished family wages, and they were not restored after the fall of the party state. Consequently, at the current moment the price for the use of human labour is not fairly paid. The present situation saves costs for the user (the employer) and transfers these costs to society, primarily to those who do the work of reproduction 'freely', that is without compensation: the women (and those fathers who do their share).

In the nineteenth century, it was unthinkable to provide workers with a minimum of four weeks' holiday with pay, and the idea of such a provision would have raised apocalyptic fears of the collapse of business life; there would have been similar reactions to the idea of paid lunch breaks, paid sick leave, or other benefits. Once it becomes widely realized and acknowledged that the concept of worker has no gender and that the worker is rather a person who, as a human being, has a family to care for, not only a body to feed and restore, it will be obvious that these needs have to be met. This is the basis of the hope that in some years or some decades from now, the provision of benefits and services for the worker-parent will seem as natural as the provisions for the worker as a biological being.

14

Issues of Work and Family in Japan

HIROKO HAYASHI

I INTRODUCTION: THE FUTURE OF WOMEN'S LABOUR[1]

The implications of *OUT*[2] by Natsuo Kirino

I travelled to Hawaii at the end of May 2003 to be one of the lecturers for the Freeman Foundation 2003 Summer Research Training on Japanese Studies. There I met Gay Satsuma, a researcher on Japanese literature in the Centre for Japanese Studies at the University of Hawaii. It was a year since we had last met. She asked me about recent popular female writers, and I replied with titles by Banana Yoshimoto, Yuko Tsushima, Eimi Yamada, Kaori Ekuni, as well as *OUT* by Natsuo Kirino. Although *OUT* is not properly characterized as 'high' literature, it is a Japanese bestseller, winning the fifty-first *Nihon Suiri Sakka Kyokai Chohen* (Japanese Crime Fiction Novelists' Association Prize).

In *OUT*, a unique crime novel, the main characters are four house-wives who work part-time. The women work in a boxed-lunch, or *sozai* factory in the suburbs of Tokyo, working strenuously from midnight to dawn on an endless factory line. The novel depicts well the emotional and physical impasse encountered by Japanese housewives who also have to work part-time during late night hours. The main character is forty-three-year-old Masako Katori. She has a husband and a son but their home is a desolate place where nobody talks to each other. Masako used to work for a trust bank and liked working in the financial sector. She continued to work after her marriage until her son went to high school at which point she asked for equal treatment with the male employees. Her request was rejected and, eventually, she was forced into retirement.

What made Masako angry more than anything else was that even though she had worked hard for many years, she had never been given a management post. Instead, she had to do the same clerical work in the loan section, the work she had been doing since she started working for

---

[1] Hayashi, H., 'The Future of Women's Labour', *Rodo Horitsu Junpo*, 1554 (2003), 4.

[2] Kirino, N., *OUT* (Tokyo: Kodansha International, 1997). *OUT* was translated into English by Stephen Snyder and published in 2003. Ms Kirino was nominated for the Edgar Awards 2004 by the Mystery Writers of America.

the bank. Even though she started work as early as eight in the morning and often worked late, until nine at night, the work she had been assigned had not changed in all those years. However hard she worked, only the men were permitted to do the important jobs like taking decisions on loan applications. Her role was to assist them. Moreover, all the men employed in the same year as she was had gone through training and become managers in about ten years, moving ahead of her. Men who started working after her had already become supervisors.

One day, she saw the salary details of a male colleague who was as old as she was and her blood boiled. His annual income was close to two million yen more than hers. After twenty years of working, her annual salary was only 4.6 million yen. After agonizing over this for a while, Masako went directly to her manager, who started working at the same time as she did. She said: 'I want to do the same kind of work as the men are doing. I will work hard, so could I be considered a candidate for management positions?'

The fury Masako felt upon refusal reflects the kind of discrimination experienced by women who are pursuing actions against wage and promotion discrimination in courts all over Japan. This kind of discrimination is institutionalized and universal. Masako's reasonable request was met from the following day onwards with blatant harassment and bullying. Even the female employees started avoiding her after rumours went around that she had tried to go behind their backs to get more favourable treatment. She became isolated in the bank.

Later, after the bank's merger, she was ordered to transfer to another branch. To do so, she would have had to relocate alone, leaving behind her son who was preparing for high school exams. When she refused, she was asked to leave her job. Hearing that she was leaving, applause went around her office. As Masako could not find a new full-time job, she began working at night at the boxed-lunch factory in which context she became involved by chance in a horrific crime.

The rapid growth in the *sozai* industry and increasing shift work at night

On 30 September 1991, a shocking crime occurred in Fukuoka City. Two part-time housewives, working in a bakery factory from 10:00 p.m. to 5:00 a.m., were stabbed by a stranger while riding home together on a bicycle. One was killed and the other was seriously wounded. The incident happened around 4:50 a.m. As it was considered to fall within the scope of a commuting accident, the victim and families eventually received workers' compensation.

As a result of the incident, the issue of housewives working part-time and late at night attracted public attention.[3] Like the fictional character in *OUT*, the Fukuoka housewives worked in a bakery factory. The consumption of *sozai* in Japan has increased more than twofold since 1985 compared with a 140 per cent increase in frozen processed food in the same period. *Sozai* originally meant side dishes to be eaten with rice. However the term now refers to rice, bread, and noodles sold in the form of box-lunches and sandwiches. The industry which calls all of these take-out foods '*sozai*' is currently a sixty billion dollar business.

During preparations for my lecture in Hawaii, I learned that *sozai* was now a word commonly used in English.[4] *Sozai* is also an important keyword in the context of examining shifts in Japanese society, evoking and denoting *inter alia* the increase in dual-income families, eating at home alone, changes in housework and in the family, the rise in women working part-time at night, the impact of recession on household food expenditures, and class differences, all of which are somehow captured in the banality of packed lunches sold at a convenience store or in the basement of a long-established department store.

It is useful to consider the employment of *sozai* workers, and the increasing importance of the work in which they were engaged, against a background of wider economic and legal change. As a matter of general law, the *sozai* industry can employ women workers over eighteen years of age in shifts from 10:00 p.m. to 5:00 a.m., as long as these do not exceed six hours. This is because the Labour Standards Law Amendment, which was introduced with the enactment of the Equal Employment Opportunity Law (EEOL) in 1985, relaxed the pre-existing limitations on women's working hours considerably, while the 1997 Amendment to the Labour Standards Law (LSL) removed the late-night limitations on their working hours entirely.

At the same time, legal changes alone do not account for the surge of women engaged in this work. The unemployment rate in Japan has been high due to an economic downturn and the part-time labour market is also experiencing decreased demand. However, cashier positions at supermarkets are dominated by people who can work during the day and younger men and women. Housewives who have children or elderly people to take care of cannot easily get these kinds of jobs. Consequently, some are compelled to work night shifts at *sozai* factories to earn a living. The pressure to engage in such work is intensified by

[3] *The Nishinihon Shinbun* (evening edition), 30 Sept. 1991; *The Nishinihon Shinbun* (morning edition), 13 Nov. 1991.
[4] Kakuchi, S., 'Japan: Take-out Food Edging out Home-Cooked Meals in New Trend', *Global Information Network* (New York, 21 Mar. 2002).

the fact that despite their prohibition in the EEOL and in the amendment to the LSL, dismissals due to pregnancy and childbirth are increasing in conjunction with the recession; dismissals because of requests for maternity or child-care leave are also rising. In any case, half the women working today are in non-regular positions and are not entitled to either child-care or elder-care leave.

A right to be exempted from night work was introduced by an amendment to the Child Care Leave and Family Care Law for both women and men. However, due in part to changes driven by globalization, including increasing pressure from employers for greater flexibility on the part of their workers, more women are working night hours. Moreover, most night workers in *sozai* factories do not even come within the scope of the exemption in the first place. Even those employees who do come within its scope may find that their employers attempt to circumvent the requirements or discourage employees from attempting to assert their entitlement to exemptions. For example, in February 2003, Japan Airlines International, a major airline company, announced that from April, they would limit the number of employees exempted from working night shifts on grounds of child-care or care for other family members to seventy-five applicants, selected by lottery. (Previously, the company had granted exemptions to all applicants who fulfilled certain conditions.) Following advice from the Tokyo Equal Employment Office, the company later changed the selection method to one based on workers' needs. In August, they removed the limitation on the number of applicants, but sharply cut applicants' working days per month. On 23 June 2004, two female flight attendants who applied for the night shift exemption sued Japan Airlines International, claiming damages. Because of the drastic cut in working days, their monthly income had decreased from 700,000–900,000 yen to 40,000–200,000 yen.[5] Later two more female attendants joined this litigation. The case is still pending at Tokyo District Court.

Hardships in night work and the future of women's labour

OUT is a realistic depiction of the situation of part-time housewives working the night shift at a boxed-lunch factory. The author, who actually went to see such a factory in 1996 before writing the novel, uses the term 'slave labour' to explain the hardships of the women working there.[6] Since her visit seven years ago, the processing line has grown faster and far more complicated. Workers are required to stand continuously in

[5] *Japan Airlines International Case; A Petition to the Tokyo District Court*, 23 June 2004.
[6] Kirino, N., 'Women Working in "Slave Labour" during Night Hours at Boxed Lunch Factories', *Economist*, 18 Feb. 2003, 66–8.

front of the conveyor belt from midnight to 5:30 in the morning. They have no breaks, and are not allowed to move away from the line once they start the processing. Going to the bathroom requires first obtaining permission and then waiting in turn. The male manager then comes and calls the workers when it is time to change shifts. When they get to the bathroom, workers have to totally re-disinfect themselves from head to foot. To avoid bothering their colleagues, workers generally try to avoid going to the bathroom as much as possible.

The factory itself is kept cool like a refrigerator, and the cold rising from the concrete floor makes it a very difficult place for women to work. The room where they take a rest is a large hall with *tatami* mats. There are no separate dressing rooms for men and women (raising potential human rights issues). The part-time housewives are generally middle-aged or older, most of them probably in their forties or fifties. What the author found surprising was the presence of Brazilian workers; half of the workers in the factory were from Brazil and lived in dormitories nearby. Their wages were less those that of the Japanese part-time house-wives.[7] In addition, none of the workers had any prospect of a pay rise. If they managed to continue working under these harsh conditions for three years, in theory they had an opportunity to become 'semi-regular' employees, although even these positions had age limits.

The author explains that *OUT* describes the plight of 'middle-class' part-time housewives and foreign workers who work as 'slave labour' in present day Japan. She is concerned that young women who have lost employment opportunities will one day also become part of this new 'slave labour'. The very demands for convenience food which women's greater employment participation is generating are simultaneously spawning new forms of gender-based discrimination and exploitation in a paid work context.

II WORKING WOMEN AND THE JAPANESE LABOUR MARKET

Historically, the Japanese female labour participation rate has been relatively high—with more than half of Japanese women in paid employment in 1960 (54.5 per cent). Of these, 15.8 per cent were self-employed,

---

[7] Kirino, N., 'Women Working in "Slave Labour" during Night Hours at Boxed Lunch Factories', *Economist*, 18 Feb. 2003, 66–8. There is further evidence of the use and possible exploitation of foreign workers. Recently, five foreign workers of the Salad Club Co. were arrested for suspected violation of the Immigration Control Law. Salad Club Co., a subsidiary of Kewpie Co., the largest mayonnaise manufacturing company in Japan, employed 26 Chinese and Mongolian workers without working visas. The factory runs 24 hours and almost all midnight shift workers have been foreigners. At this company, 18% of the 328 employees are foreigners. It is estimated that about 220,000 illegal foreign workers are employed in Japan; *The Asahi Shinbun* (evening edition), 8 June 2004.

Hiroko Hayashi

43.4 per cent were engaged in family businesses, and 40.8 per cent were employed by other employers. However, since the 1960s, a drastic change in the nature of female labour force participation has occurred. By 1985, the percentage of women engaged in family businesses had decreased to 20 per cent and the rate of employed female workers had increased to 67.2 per cent. Since then, the number of employed female workers has continued to increase steadily. In 2003, they represented 83.8 per cent of the total female workforce. At the same time, 9.2 per cent were engaged in family businesses and 6.6 per cent were self-employed. In 2003, Japanese women made up 41 per cent of the labour force, and women over 15 had a labour force participation rate of 48.3 per cent. The changed industrial structure has forced Japanese women to become employed workers, as in the USA and the EU.[8]

Increase in part-timers

In the 1960s female part-timers began to increase. In 2003, 40.7 per cent of employed women worked part-time. Over 70 per cent of all Japanese workers are regular employees (85 per cent of whom are male workers) with a long-term employment relationship with their employers. Rapid globalization and a long-term recession after the collapse of the Japanese bubble economy has led to an escalation in the number of workers in atypical or non-regular employment according to the employment portfolio by *Nikkeiren* (the Japanese Federation of Employers' Organizations).

In 1995 *Nikkeiren* published a famous report: *Shin Jidai no Nihonteki Keiei* (Japanese Management in the New Era) which described the future of Japanese personnel management after the bubble economy. The report classified workers into three categories: (1) long-term regular workers who expand their capabilities; (2) fixed-term contract workers or dispatch workers with highly professional abilities; and (3) flexible contract employees—casual, part-time, and temporary workers. Workers in the third category were predominantly female. In 2002, almost half of working women (49.3 per cent compared with 15 per cent of working men) were non-regular. In particular, part-time workers comprised 39.8 per cent of female workers and 8.0 per cent of male workers, and dispatch workers included 1.6 per cent of female and 0.3 per cent of male workers.[9]

Non-regular workers in Japan frequently work part-time. They are paid considerably less and have fewer training and promotion opportunities

[8] Equal Employment, Children and Families Bureau, Ministry of Health, Labour, and Welfare (ed.), *White Paper on Womens' Labour* (2003 edition), 21 *Seiki Shokugyozaidan* (Tokyo, 2004), Appendix 16.
[9] ibid., Appendix 7. In 2002 the percentage of non-regular workers reached 50.7% of women and 14.8% of men (Ministry of Health, Labour, and Welfare, *Basic Survey on the Employment Structure* (2002)).

than regular workers. Women constitute around 70 per cent of part-time workers (those working less than 35 hours per week), and around 40 per cent of employed women work part-time. The salaries of such workers are lower than those of full-time workers. Female part-time wages were 65.7 per cent of female full-time wages in 2003. In 2001, the average hourly wage of part-time workers was 893 yen; regular female workers' average hourly wage was 1,359 yen.[10]

Equal employment legislation

Article 14 of the Japanese Constitution declares that 'All people are equal under the law and there shall be no discrimination in political, economic or social relations because of race, creed, sex, social status or family origin'. The Article prohibits sex discrimination as a basic human right. However, Article 3 of the Labour Standards Law 1947 provides only that 'An employer shall not engage in discriminatory treatment with respect to wages, working hours, or other working conditions by reason of nationality, creed, or social status' and Article 4 only prohibits wage discrimination against women. ('The employer shall not discriminate concerning wages by reason of the worker being a woman.') Thus, the LSL prohibits wage discrimination by sex but does not clearly prohibit sex discrimination in the context of recruitment, hiring, job assignments, or promotions. Except for Article 4 of the LSL, there is no explicit legislation prohibiting sex discrimination by employers in the private sector.

The Equal Employment Opportunity Law[11] was enacted in 1985 in connection with Japan's ratification of the 1979 United Nations Convention on the Elimination of All Forms of Discrimination Against Women (CEDAW). Prior to the enactment of the EEOL, the LSL was the principal law in Japan protecting women in the private sector. Although the Japanese Constitution prohibits sex discrimination, the LSL and the EEOL only prohibit discrimination against women and are not gender-neutral. In Japan, even today there is no legal definition of sex discrimination in the private sector. Moreover, even after the enactment of EEOL, most court decisions relied on the Civil Code, not on the EEOL. The Japanese Civil Code, amended after the Constitution in 1947, is

---

[10] Above, n. 8, 31.

[11] Equal Employment Opportunity Law, Law No. 45 of 1985. The long Japanese title may be translated as 'Law to Promote the Welfare of Female Workers by Providing for Equality of Opportunity and Treatment in Employment for Women'. See Hayashi, H., 'Sexual Harassment in the Workplace and Equal Employment Legislation', *St John's Law Review*, 69 (1995), 37–60.

gender-neutral in principle. Article 1-2 of the Civil Code provides that the Civil Code should be interpreted according to the principle of individual dignity and essential equality between sexes.

In 1967, Japan ratified ILO Convention No. 100 concerning Equal Remuneration for Men and Women Workers for Work of Equal Value. However, except for Article 4 of the LSL, there is no legislation which defines the concept of equal pay for equal work in Japanese labour law. Moreover, there are disputes about whether Article 4 of the LSL means equal pay for equal work, or equal pay for work of equal value for both men and women. In Japan, neither the court nor the government has approved the principle of equal pay for work of equal value. In the *Maruko Keihoki Case* described below, the district court ruled that there is no legislation in Japan which describes the principle of equal pay for work of equal value. In 2002, the Research Committee on the Wage Differential between Men and Women proposed the application of the principle of equal pay for work of equal value to improve the wage gap, but this proposal was not accepted by the government.[12]

As earnings of regular workers in Japan are not set by the type of job, it is difficult to translate the concept of equal pay for equal work between regular and non-regular workers into practice. To assist part-time workers, the Part-Time Work Law ('Law Concerning the Improvement of Employment Management, etc. of Part-Time Work Law') was enacted in 1993. However, the law only requires employers to ensure the balanced and fair treatment of full-time and part-time employees; after ten years of enforcement, the wage differential between part-time and full-time workers has expanded.[13]

The *Maruko Keihoki Case* proved to be a landmark case in practical terms.[14] The case was brought by twenty-eight married women who had worked for the Maruko Keihoki company from six to twenty-seven years on renewable two-month contracts. Their jobs were the same as those

---

[12] Equal Employment, Children and Families Bureau, Ministry of Health, Labour, and Welfare, *Report of the Research Committee on the Wage Differential between Men and Women* (Tokyo, 2002). Following proposals by the Committee, the Prefecture Labour Standards Office issued guidelines in 2003 (*Guidelines on Wage and Employment Management Improvement to Dissolve Wage Differential between Men and Women*). However, these guidelines do not refer to the principle of equal pay for equal value at all.

[13] The Minister of Health, Labour, and Welfare is required to publish guidelines on Art. 10 of the Part-Time Work Law (Law Concerning the Improvement of Employment Management, etc. of Part-Time Workers, Law No. 76, 1993). Based on the Part-time Workers Research Committee Report issued in July 2002, the amendment of the Part-Time Work Law was discussed. However, at the Labour Policy Board, employers and workers could not reach agreement on the equal treatment of full-time and part-time workers and the government only revised the guidelines on 25 Aug. 2003.

[14] *Maruko Keihoki Case*, Ueda Branch, Nagano District Court, 15 Mar. 1996, 690 *Rodo Hanrei* (1996), 32.

of the regular female employees, but their wages were only 50 to 60 per cent of the regular employees' salaries. The plaintiffs claimed that the wage gap with regular employees contravened the equal pay for equal work legislation as well as the principle of equal treatment. The Ueda Branch of the Nagano District Court ruled that if plaintiffs' wages were less than 80 per cent of female regular employees with the same length of service, the wage differential clearly exceeded the acceptable level. The Court consequently ruled that the employer had violated Article 90 of the Civil Code (public order and morals) and ordered the employer to reduce the wage differential to 80 per cent. A wage gap of 20 per cent for equal work was considered acceptable by the Court, presumably based on the result of a closed conference of judges arranged by the Supreme Court.[15] Nevertheless, this illustrates that unexplained pay discrepancies between regular and non-regular workers are the norm, not the exception.

The *Sumitomo Cement Case*,[16] the first Japanese female employment discrimination case, concerned marriage retirement. In 1966, the Tokyo District Court ruled in favour of the plaintiff and declared that the system of forced retirement upon marriage was against good public order as defined by Article 90 of the Civil Code.[17] Consequently, the marriage retirement system was declared null and void. Since then, women have sued successfully regarding sex discrimination in the workplace.[18]

To catch up with the international gender mainstreaming policy promoted through United Nations leadership, the Basic Law for a Gender Equal Society was enacted in 1999.[19] Moreover, in June 2004, the Report of the Research Committee on the Equal Employment Opportunity Policies between Men and Women was submitted. The Committee recommended: (1) amendment of the EEOL to prohibit discrimination not only against women but also against men; (2) implementation of an indirect

---

[15] General Affairs Bureau, Supreme Court, *The Outline of the Conference of the Judges taking charge of the Labour Relations Cases and Administration Litigation*, 27 Oct. 1998, 171.

[16] Tokyo District Court, 20 Dec. 1966, 467 *Hanrei Jiho* (1967) 26.

[17] As the Constitution does not apply directly to private contractual arrangements, Art. 90 and Arts. 1 and 2 of the Civil Code have been the main sources of private causes of action.

[18] See *Mitsui Shipbuilding Case* (Osaka District Ct., 10 Dec. 1971), declaring forced retirement at childbirth illegal (645 *Hanrei Jiho* (1972) 29); *Tokyu Kikan Kogyo Case* (Tokyo District Ct., 1 July 1969), holding the forced retirement of women at 30 illegal (560 *Hanrei Jiho* (1969) 23); *Nagoya Broadcasting Case* (Nagoya High Ct., 30 Sept. 1974), holding the forced retirement of women at 30 illegal (756 *Hanrei Jiho* (1979) 56); *Nissan Motor Case* (Supreme Ct., 24 Mar. 1981), holding the forced retirement of woman at 55 and men at 60 illegal (360 *Rodo Hanrei* (1981) 23); *Koparu Case* (Tokyo District Ct., 12 Sept. 1975), declaring layoffs focusing on female employees with children illegal (789 *Hanrei Jiho* (1975) 18).

[19] Hayashi, H., 'Gender Mainstreaming and Sex Discrimination Law: International Trends and the Present Situation in Japan', *Jurist*, 1237 (2003), 77.

discrimination prohibition according to CEDAW Recommendations;[20] and (3) effective realization of gender equality through positive action.[21]

The original EEOL introduced in 1986 prohibited employers from imposing mandatory retirement at marriage, childbirth, or upon reaching a certain age. In actuality, the EEOL only encouraged firms to provide equal opportunities to men and women in recruitment, hiring, job assignment, and promotion. The EEOL was amended in 1997 to prohibit discrimination against women with regard to recruitment, hiring, job assignment, promotion, and the provision of education and training. Upon the enactment of EEOL in 1985 and its amendment in 1997, the LSL was amended to relax or abolish the protective provisions except for those concerning maternity protection and menstrual leave. Now, Japanese women over the age of eighteen may work overtime and on the night shift.

Although, the LSL and the EEOL both prohibit discrimination against women, despite longer terms of service and higher educational levels, Japanese women are often still in low-status employment. It is also difficult to find them in managerial positions. According to a 2003 survey, female workers held only 9.4 per cent of managerial positions[22] and earned only 66.8 per cent of average male earnings.[23] Thus, even highly educated women workers seldom have the same career opportunities as their male counterparts. This in turn contributes to women's labour force withdrawal. The better-educated married women are more likely to quit work on childbirth than those with a lower level of education. Only 27 per cent of those with a university diploma continued working compared to 44 per cent of those with a junior high school diploma.

The two-track personnel management system

Much of the wage disparity between men and women in Japan has resulted from the 'two-track' personnel administration system. Since the 1960s, especially after enactment of the EEOL, a two-track employment system has been instituted by a number of Japanese employers, particularly large companies. The managerial track is available to employees destined for management positions and the general track is open to all other

---

[20] CEDAW considered the fourth and fifth periodic reports of Japan on 8 July 2003 (CEDAW/C/2003/II/CRP.3/Add.1/Rev.1). CEDAW recommends that a definition of discrimination against women encompassing both direct and indirect discrimination, in line with Art. 1 of the Convention, be included in domestic legislation.

[21] Positive action provision is included in the EEOL through the amendment in 1997 but is left up to employers' 'voluntary implementation' (Art. 9). The government will only give employers advice (Art. 20).

[22] Managers: 3.1%; section chiefs: 4.6%; subsection chiefs: 9.4%, See above, n. 8, 97.

[23] ibid., 18.

employees. Under this system, newly-hired workers are placed into one of two categories: (1) the managerial track (*Sogo Shoku*), in which those engaged in planning and decision-making jobs have the potential to become top executives; or (2) the general track (*Ippan Shoku*), in which employees are engaged in general office work under different wage scales with limited promotion.[24] The two-track system facilitates a sophisticated form of discrimination against women.

In 2000, an average of 7.1 per cent of companies had introduced the two-track system. However, the introduction rate was much higher in large-scale companies—51.9 per cent in companies with more than 5,000 employees and 39.9 per cent in companies with 1,000–4,999 employees.[25] A Ministry of Labour survey in 2000 found that 52.9 per cent of companies with a two-track personnel system did not have women in managerial track positions. Moreover, according to recent research by the Ministry of Health, Labour, and Welfare, only 3 per cent of employees on the management track in 2003 were women. Only 10 per cent of women were hired on the managerial track, but 90 per cent were hired on the general track. About 80 per cent of companies later introduced a transfer system between tracks, but 75.6 per cent of those required a supervisor's recommendation for transfer.[26]

The Ministry of Labour (since 2001, the Ministry of Health, Labour, and Welfare) issued guidelines on the two-track system, *inter alia* warning against its sexually discriminatory effects.[27] However, the Ministry asserts that the two-track system in itself is not discriminatory and does not violate the EEOL provisions. This is because selection, the Ministry understands, for entry into either career track is based upon the employee's willingness to accept sex-neutral working conditions, such as long working hours and numerous potential job transfers.

The EEOL does not create a private cause of action; instead it allows for advice, guidance, and recommendations provided by the Director of Women and Young Workers' Office (later amended to the Director of Prefecture Labour Standards Bureau) and mediation by the Equal

[24] US Department of State, *Japan, Country Reports on Human Rights Practices 2002*, released by the Bureau of Democracy, Human Rights, and Labour, 31 Mar. 2003.

[25] Above, n. 12, 13.

[26] In July 2004, the Equal Employment, Children, and Families Bureau of the Ministry of Health, Labour, and Welfare published *Introduction of Two-track Personnel Management System and Advice* (2004). They reported that 44.9% of 236 companies adopted the two-track system; 26.3% adopted the managerial track, general track, specialist track, and manual labour track, and 8.9% adopted the managerial track, general track, quasi-managerial track, and middle track. Some 92.8% of companies decide employees' track at recruitment and hiring.

[27] The Ministry of Labour issued guidelines on the two-track personnel management system, *Preferable Way of the Two-track System*, in 1989 (later abolished in 2000) and *Consideration Matters for Personnel Administration divided by the Track* (2000). These guidelines show examples of legal and illegal track systems for employers for their guidance.

Opportunity Mediation Committee in each prefecture. Since enforcement of the EEOL began, mediation has not served as a viable option because the EEOL requires both parties' consent for mediation and consent is often not forthcoming. For example, female employees of Sumitomo Life Insurance, Sumitomo Electric Industry, Sumitomo Chemical, and Sumitomo Metal requested mediation, but the Director rejected their requests except with regard to the *Sumitomo Metal Case* in which mediation was conducted with the employer's consent. The proposed recommendation by the Mediation Committee was rejected by female employees in March 1995 because it included no concrete remedies. Female employees of Sumitomo Life Insurance and the Sumitomo Electric Industry claimed damages against the state for denial of mediation by the Director of Women and Young Workers' Office. They also sued their employers for sex discrimination and claimed damages.[28] Catherine Hakim has pointed out that 'in Europe, legislation prohibiting sex discrimination and promoting equal treatment of men and women in the labour force is the main tool of social engineering'. In Japan, by contrast, the EEOL has prohibited sex discrimination only indirectly and the main tool of social engineering has been litigation pursued by working women.[29]

After ten years of enforcement, many female workers have realized the limitations of the remedies offered under the EEOL and the mediation by the Equal Opportunity Mediation Committees. In the 1990s, the second boom in Japanese litigation concerning sex discrimination in employment started. Most of this litigation was concerned with promotion and wage discrimination under the two-track personnel management system.[30] The first employment discrimination case concerning two-track personnel administration was the *Nihon Tekko Renmei Case* in 1986.[31] In this case, female employees suffered wage and promotion discrimination, but the company asserted that the men's jobs were managerial and the women's jobs were non-managerial. In other words, they engaged in different jobs. Therefore, there was no sex discrimination.

The Tokyo District Court ruled that two-track personnel administration by sex is against the intention of Article 14 of the Japanese Constitution,

---

[28] The *Sumitomo Life Insurance Co. Case* and the *Sumitomo Electric Co. Case* were the first cases in which the plaintiffs sued the state for the illegal discrimination by the Director of Women and Young Workers Office. The *Sumitomo Life Insurance Co. Case* concerned discrimination in wage and promotion between married and unmarried women.

[29] Hakim, C., *Key Issues in Women's Work: Female Heterogeneity and the Polarisation of Women's Employment* (London: Athlone Press, 1996), 187 and see Hayashi, above n. 19, 87.

[30] *Nomura Security Case* (Tokyo District Court, 1993); *Okaya Koki Case* (Nagoya District Court, 1995); *Sumitomo Electric Industry Case* (Osaka District Court, 1995); *Sumitomo Chemical Case* (Osaka District Court, 1995); *Sumitomo Metal Case* (Osaka District Court, 1995); *Kanematsu Case* (Tokyo District Court, 1995).

[31] Tokyo District Court, 4 Dec. 1986, 486 *Rodo Hanrei* (1987) 28.

but does not violate good public order under Article 90 of the Civil Code. The reasoning of the court was that when the plaintiffs were employed, between 1969 to 1974, employment-at-will was the governing legal principle and there was no legislation to make the two-track employment system illegal. Since then five claims based on two-track system discrimination[32] have been decided by the district courts, but in all these cases the plaintiff lost on almost the same reasoning as in the *Nihon Tekko Renmei Case*. In the *Sumitomo Electric Industry Case* in 2000, the court ruled that the two-track personnel administration is against the intention of Article 14 of the Japanese Constitution, but when the plaintiffs were employed, women were expected to retire at marriage or childbirth. Until the enforcement of the amended EEOL in 1999, treating female workers differently from male workers did not violate good public order under Article 90 of the Civil Code. This decision effectively rationalized the two-track system via statistical discrimination, totally neglecting Article 1-2 of the Civil Code.[33]

In all of the cases, the female plaintiffs were employed in the 1960s before the enactment of the EEOL and continued to work after the amendment of the EEOL in 1997. The EEOL has no retroactivity clause, and cannot be applied to cases before its enforcement.

III GENDER, WORK, AND FAMILY

Since paid female employment has increased, work and family have become prominent social issues. In addition to discrimination, the traditional male and female division of labour at home places a disproportionate burden on working women, who are still responsible for almost all child-care and household duties. In 2001, the wife and husband of a dual-income couple spent 3.83 and 0.6 hours per day respectively on housekeeping.[34] The pressure which a highly gendered division of labour within the spheres of paid and unpaid work in combination with radically increased rates of female employment participation places on social

---

[32] *Sumitomo Electric Industry Case* (Osaka District Ct., 31 July 2000), 792 *Rodo Hanrei* (2001) 48; *Sumitomo Chemical Case* (Osaka District Ct., 18 Mar. 2001), 807 *Rodo Hanrei* (2001) 10; *Nomura Security Case* (Tokyo District Ct., 20 Feb. 2002) 822 *Rodo Hanrei* (2002) 13; and *Kanematsu Case* (Tokyo District Ct., 5 Nov. 2003) 867 *Rodo Hanrei* (2004) 19, *Okaya Koki Case* (Nagoya District Ct., 22 Dec. 2004, 888 *Rodo Hanrei* (2005) 28). The *Sumitomo Electric Industry Case*, the *Sumitomo Chemical Case* and the *Nomura Security Case* ended in a settlement on 24 Dec. 2003, 29 June 2004, and 15 Oct. 2004 respectively.

[33] See, Hayashi, H., *Amicus curiae brief* on the Sumitomo Electric Industry Osaka District Ct. decision to Osaka High Court (2002), 1528 *Rodo Horitsu Junpo* (2002) 49.

[34] Ministry of Public Management, Home Affairs, Posts, and Telecommunications, *Basic Survey on Social Lifestyles* (2002).

reproduction has, inevitably, generated legal and policy measures to effect a proper 'balance' between work and family considerations.

Family-friendly measures

Maternity leave and child-care leave

Maternity leave for all women was introduced as part of the LSL in 1947. During maternity leave, 60 per cent of the average wage is paid by National Health insurance. The employer and economic organizations, however, have been negative about the enactment of child-care leave, mainly because of the increased cost. Nevertheless, since 1991 when the total fertility rate went down to 1.57 (the '1.57 Shock'), the low birth rate has become recognized as a crucial social issue. At the same time, there has been anxiety about the shortage of future labour in Japan.[35] As a consequence, the 1991 Child Care Leave Law was enacted to provide the right to a maximum of one year's child-care leave. This new legislation stemmed from the EEOL which requests employers to endeavour to provide child-care leave for their female employees. The Act was passed in May 1991, coming into effect for firms with 30 or more employees in April 1992 and in April 1995 for firms with under 30 employees. It also provides for shorter working hours for employees with pre-school age children. Under the Act's gender-neutral provisions, men as well as women can take child-care leave.

Sixty-four per cent of Japanese women who had babies took child-care leave in 2002. However, only 0.33 per cent of men did. The women's percentage varies, depending on the size of companies with 77.2 per cent in companies of 500 and over employees, 75.9 per cent in companies of 100–499 employees, 64.2 per cent in companies with 30–99 employees, and 55.6 per cent in companies of 5–29 employees.[36]

At the time the Child Care Leave Law was enacted, there was no income security during leave. As a result of a subsequent amendment in 2001, 40 per cent of prior income is now provided by employment security insurance. Upon application, social insurance premiums for medical insurance and pension may be suspended. These are premium contributions which are otherwise paid to the government by the employer (50 per cent) and the employee (50 per cent).

---

[35] In the 1990s late marriage and childbirth promoted the low fertility rate which had already become a social issue in the 1980s. In 1950, just after World War Two, the Japanese total fertility rate was 3.65. In 1980, it fell to 1.75, decreasing further to 1.29 in 2003, the lowest in Japanese history. It is estimated that in 2006 the population will reach its peak—126 million. After 50 years, the Japanese population will decrease to 64 million.

[36] Equal Employment, Children, and Families Bureau, Ministry of Health, Labour, and Welfare, *Female Employment Management Basic Survey* (2002).

With regard to the reconciliation of work and family life, not only child-care but also family, mainly elder, care has become an important issue. The Family Care Leave Law was enacted in 1995[37] and was enforced as the Child Care and Family Care Leave Act from 1999. Coverage was extended to all companies. The term of family care leave[38] is limited to three months for each family member; as with the child-care leave, 40 per cent of prior income is now provided by employment security insurance.

Night-shift and overtime work exemptions

Night work and overtime for women and men who have babies or elder family members to care for have been regulated by the Child Care and Family Care Leave Law 1997 and 2001 respectively. As a result of the 2001 amendment, after one year of child-care leave, parents are entitled to work shorter hours until their children reach three years of age. This law also encourages employers to permit employees to take five days' leave of absence a year in order to care for sick children.

Pension premiums during child-care leave

Under the Pension Reform Act of 2004, the exemption from payment of pension premiums will be extended from one year to three years from 1 April 2005. If workers apply for shorter working hours for child-care and their income is decreased, their pension premium will be calculated on the decreased income. However, the amount of pension accrual for a maximum of three years will be based on their ordinary salary. These amendments would be more valuable to workers if they were permitted to take child-care leave for more than one year, the current legal maximum. However, 86.1 per cent of workers were only able to take less than one year of child-care leave in 2002, as the amount of child-care leave that workers are able to take depends on the size of the company and the work rules that govern them.

Problems with the scope and operation of family-friendly initiatives

Despite government initiatives purporting to facilitate the combination of work and family responsibilities, there are a number of problems with the scope and operation of the current legal framework.

[37] Law Concerning the Welfare of Workers who Take Care of Children or Other Family Members Including Child Care and Family Care Leave (Law No. 76 of 1991 and Law No. 107 of 1995).

[38] Family care leave means leave which a worker takes in order to take care of 'a subject family member in need of care' (Art. 2(2)). 'In need of care' means conditions requiring constant care for a period as provided by Ministry of Labour Ordinance due to injury, sickness, or mental disability (Art. 2(3)). 'Subject family member' means spouse, parents, children, and parents of spouse (Art. 2(4)).

Exclusion of non-regular workers

About half of Japanese working women are not full-time workers. Consequently, they are excluded from the scope of child-care and elder-care leave provision. The law excludes fixed-term workers as well; most fixed-term contract workers have renewed their contracts several times, but they are not permitted to request child-care leave and elder-care leave. However, on 31 October 2003, the Tokyo District Court ruled for the first time on the availability of child-care leave for a fixed-term female worker. In the *Nichio Sangyo Kyoryoku Centre Case*,[39] the English plaintiff was employed by an unincorporated association in Japan from 1 July 1996. Her one-year contract had been automatically renewed six times without any problem. During those six years she gave birth three times and for every child, she took maternity leave and her wages were paid. During the maternity leave for the third child, she requested child-care leave. The director of the association dismissed her because her employment contract was fixed and thus was not covered by the Child Care and Family Care Law. The court ruled that this dismissal was an abuse of the employer's right to dismiss and ordered payment of damages. According to the guidelines for the Child Care and Family Care Law, since this plaintiff had renewed her employment contract several times, she would be covered by the provisions. The revised Child Care and Family Care Leave Law prohibits disadvantageous treatment of employees taking child-care or family-care leave.

The Bill on the Amendment of the Child Care and Family Care Leave Law was submitted to the Diet in 2004.[40] Present law excludes workers with daily and fixed-term contracts. This Bill will extend the coverage to workers with fixed-term contracts employed for more than one year by the same employer. At the same time, before the baby becomes one year old there will be no contract renewal. However, the scope of application is limited by several conditions so that the estimated number of employees within the scope of the application of this amendment is only 10,000. In special cases, child-care leave will be extended for a maximum of one and a half years. Five days of sick leave a year will also be required by the law.

Changes in employment status before and after childbirth

Among industrialized countries, only Japanese women have still kept the 'M curve' labour market participation pattern, which means that most female workers tend to retire from the labour market before or after their first child and return once their children are grown. This is notwithstanding increased levels of education and skills among women. The percentage of women who went to universities (not including junior

---

[39] 862 *Rodo Hanrei* (2004) 24.   [40] The amendment is in force from 1 Apr. 2005.

colleges) increased from 13.7 per cent (38.6 per cent for men) in 1985 to 33.8 per cent (47.0 per cent for men) in 2002.[41] In Japan, young women are now better educated than men, but the participation rate in the labour market of female university graduates was only 68 per cent in 2001, compared to 90 per cent in Sweden, 87 per cent in England, 84 per cent in France, and 81 per cent in the USA.[42] So many unemployed well-educated women reflects a considerable waste of investment in human capital.[43]

About 90 per cent of Japanese women are finished with childbirth before the age of 35.[44] A recent survey reveals, however, that three-quarters of women workers retired before or after their first childbirth. On 17 March 2004, the Ministry of Health, Labour, and Welfare released statistics on changes of employment status before and after childbirth.[45] Table 14.1 shows that about 60 per cent of working women retire before and immediately after the birth of their first child, leaving the paid labour force. (The total includes unidentified cases.)

The Ministry surveyed the change in employment status of 21,879 women who had babies from 10 to 17 January 2001, at four different times: one year before childbirth; at childbirth; six months later; and one year later. A total of 54.4 per cent of them had a job one year before their

TABLE 14.1 *Change of employment status of Japanese mothers (2001)*

	Employment status of mother					
	Total (%)	Employed (%)	Out of work (%)	Total	Employed	Out of work
One year before childbirth	100.0	54.4	44.5	21,879	11,897	9,741
Childbirth	100.0	23.0	77.0	21,879	5,022	16,857
Six months later	100.0	25.1	73.6	21,879	5,483	16,099
One year later	100.0	31.1	68.1	21,879	6,808	14,890

[41] Ministry of Education, Culture, Sports, and Technology, *Basic Survey on Schools* (issued each year at the end of March).

[42] OECD, *Education at a Glance 2003*, Labour Force Participation Rate by level of educational attainment and gender, 25–64-year-olds.

[43] OECD, *Babies and Bosses: Reconciling Work and Family Life*, vol. 2 (Austria, Ireland and Japan), 39.　　　[44] Ministry of Health, Labour, and Welfare, *Vital Statistics* (2001).

[45] The Statistical Information Department, Minister's Secretariat, Ministry of Labour, Health, and Welfare, *Statistics on the Change of Employment Status before and after Childbirth: Special Report on Population Dynamics* (2003).

childbirth; 61 per cent retired before or after their childbirth; and 53 per cent retired before childbirth and stayed out of work. Only 23 per cent did not retire, took child-care leave and then returned to work. Thirteen per cent of those who resigned because of childbirth later returned to their former job or found a new job. Thirty-six per cent of women who had their second childbirth had jobs and 44 per cent of them continued to work after childbirth. Twenty-six per cent of them resigned but later returned to their former workplace or found new jobs. Twenty-six per cent retired after childbirth and stayed out of paid employment. This research indicates that working women are more likely to retire after the birth of the first child than after the second.

Of those women who continued to work before and after childbirth, 57 per cent of them relied on nurses and 23 per cent relied on grandmothers for weekday child-care. Only 18 per cent cared for their babies by themselves. Ninety-eight per cent of women who retired before or after childbirth cared for their babies by themselves during the week. About 30 per cent of re-employed women who were employed as full-timers before childbirth later found full-time jobs; on the other hand, 60 per cent were re-employed as part-time workers. Most women who continued to work before and after childbirth and later were re-employed live in small cities or towns rather than big cities. They are members of three-generation families rather than nuclear families.

Seventeen per cent of husbands whose wives continued to work after childbirth shared child-care responsibilities with their wives, and 33 per cent took their children to play outside. However, only seven per cent of husbands whose wives retired shared child-care and only 14 per cent took their children to play outside.

Inter-relationship between issues of fertility and gender inequality

There has been a marked change in the relationship between fertility and female employment during the last thirty years or so. Only recently, however, has the Japanese government started to consider the low rate of reproduction to be not just a woman's issue but a more general concern, as declining fertility becomes a serious social problem. In this context, policy considerations regarding gender inequality are increasingly becoming entangled in a wider agenda addressing the implications of the low birth rate in Japan.

New legislation for the next generation

In 2003, the Law on Support for the Next Generation (Law No. 120 of 2003) and the Basic Law against Decrease in the Rate of Childbirth (Law No. 133 of 2003) were enacted. The Law on Support for the Next

Generation requires prefectures and municipal offices and private companies with 300 or more employees to set up action plans to promote child-care leave.

This law is the first piece of legislation in Japan to encourage society in general to co-operate in producing the future generation. In September 2002, the government adopted the 'Plus One' strategy as a counter-measure against the low birth rate. The government has adopted several plans to cope with the falling fertility rate since 1999. However, they have not been effective. 'Plus One' means that the government has added more effective strategies to the present ones. One of the strategies aims for 80 per cent of female workers who give birth, and 10 per cent of men whose spouses have babies, respectively, to take child-care leave. In 2003, the 'Measure Plan on Support for the Next Generation' was set up with the aim of further improving the well-being of children and the working conditions of potential parents.

Economic factors pushing younger women's re-entry into the labour market

Since 1986, the EEOL has prohibited gender-biased employment practices forcing women to retire after marriage or childbirth and stay at home as housewives. Nevertheless, three-quarters of working women today still leave their jobs after their first child. The total Japanese fertility rate, however, has continued to decline. In Japan, not only weak legislation and public services to support working mothers, but also strong gender bias on the part of employers partially explains why Japanese women's labour market participation rate still adheres to the M curve. However, the period out of work after childbirth is becoming shorter, mainly for economic reasons. Likewise, the average age of re-entry into the labour market is falling.[46] This suggests that the economic need of individual women to return to work soon after childbirth operates in a cultural and political environment which remains insufficiently supportive of working women's needs.

Illegal dismissal and forced retirement

In this regard it is striking to note that the rate of illegal dismissals and forced retirements because of pregnancy or childbirth has recently been rising. The Equal Employment Office received 122 consultations in 2002, 77 of which were related to pregnancy and childbirth.[47] Because of the economic recession and the consequent decrease in household income,

---

[46] The female labour participation rate at the age of 30–4 increased from 52.7% in 1993 to 60.3% in 2003. The Ministry of Health, Labour, and Welfare, *Labour Force Survey* (1993 and 2003).

[47] *Assistance for the Individual: Disputes Solution by the Equal Employment Office* (2002); and above, n. 8, 111.

334 Hiroko Hayashi

younger women increasingly have to work. However, for companies, accommodating maternity and childbirth remains costly.

In the *Ken Wood Case*,[48] a female plaintiff with a three-year-old child was transferred from the main office to a remote office. She refused, and did not go to the remote office for thirty-six days. The company suspended the plaintiff and then dismissed her. She claimed that the longer commuting hours and shortage of nursery schools made it difficult for her to reconcile work and child-care. On 28 January 2000, the Supreme Court approved the company's business necessity for this transfer and ruled that the plaintiff's disadvantage was permissible. In the *Tohogakuen Case* in 2003,[49] the Supreme Court ruled that the 90 per cent clause, which requires more than 90 per cent attendance to receive a bonus, is against good public order in so far as it discourages parents from taking maternity leave or short working hours for child-care reasons. Moreover, some employers use it to try to control workers' ability to use legal rights or discriminate against workers who take leave to which they are legally entitled.

Inter-relationship between the total fertility rate and female labour participation

In general, the total fertility rate in industrialized countries is decreasing, but in countries with a high female labour market participation rate, the rate is decreasing more slowly; in some of these countries, the fertility rate has actually increased. If Japanese companies adhere to the policy of forcing women to leave their jobs after marriage or childbirth, it will be difficult to stop the decreasing fertility rate. *Time for Equality at Work*,[50] a global report by the ILO on the state of equality at work, classifies the gender policy for industrialized countries according to four groups: the formal egalitarian model; the substantive egalitarian family-centred model; the traditional family-centred model; and the economy-centred model. The report forecasts that the traditional family-centred model is less likely to remain viable in the long run because of both economic pressures and the growing pervasiveness of gender egalitarian ideals. Japan is still classified as a traditional family-centred model with few or no formal legal commitments and no substantive services for working women.

In 2003, CEDAW recommended to the Japanese government that measures allowing for the reconciliation of family and professional

---

[48] 774 *Rodo Hanrei* (2000) 7.   [49] 862 *Rodo Hanrei* (2004) 14.
[50] ILO, *Time for Equality at Work: Global Report under the Follow-up to the ILO Declaration on Fundamental Principles and Rights at Work 2003* (Geneva: ILO, 2003), 44; Chang, M. L., 'The Evolution of Sex Segregation Regimes', *American Journal of Sociology*, 105 (2000), 1658.

responsibilities be intensified, that equal sharing of domestic and family tasks between women and men be promoted, and that changes to the stereotypical expectations of women's role in the family and labour market be encouraged.[51] If Japan promotes a more effective gender equality policy with accompanying legislation in accordance with this recommendation, it will also provide a stable basis for raising the next generation.

IV CONCLUSION

When the Equal Employment Opportunity Law was amended in 1997, Japanese women expected discrimination against them to end and their working conditions to improve. In reality, however, the working conditions of women workers have deteriorated except for a limited number of full-time regular female employees.

In January 2005, Ms Kirino, the author of *OUT*, was interviewed by a journalist from *Asahi Shinbun*, the leading Japanese newspaper, as part of a series entitled '60 Years Since the End of World War II: Where We Are Now?'[52] The English version of *OUT* had attracted the attention of many readers and critics because it depicted poverty in the otherwise affluent Japanese society. In the interview, Ms Kirino disclosed that she had received many questions from readers in foreign countries, asking, for example: 'why in Japan do housewives work in blue-collar employment although their husbands are in white-collar work?'

Ms Kirino visited the boxed-lunch factories in 1996, just after the collapse of the Japanese bubble economy. There, she alleged, part-time housewives worked like 'slaves'. She defined slaves as people who could not be what they wished to be, no matter how hard they worked. Part-time housewives worked either to support their families economically or to earn their own spending money. Ms Kirino wondered whether the husbands knew their wives were engaged in slave labour. It seems that not only their husbands but also the wider Japanese society did not realize the existence of a class disparity within so-called middle-class Japanese families. When their husbands' companies employed more part-time workers to cut down personnel costs, the wives were pushed into even more contingent work.

If a 'full-time housewife family' was the model for the middle class in Japan, then the existence of housewives engaged in slave labour symbolizes a new, tragic, social structure of the middle class. However,

[51] See above, n. 20.
[52] *The Asahi Shinbun* (morning edition), 4 Jan. 2005.

when Ms Kirino looks back at the late 1990s, she believes that today's economic situation is even worse than it was in those horrible years. She points out that two poor classes were bred in these years, both of which are still present: one class is non-regular female workers, especially dispatch workers; the other class is young workers of both sexes who cannot find well-paid regular jobs.

After World War Two, the bubble economy in the 1980s seemed to herald for the first time in Japanese history an age in which women and men could work equally. During the bubble economy, the status of women was improved and companies could afford to spend money on corporate philanthropic projects. In 1985 the Equal Employment Opportunity Law was enacted, and the Japanese Government ratified CEDAW. However, the EEOL's by-product was the two-track personnel administration system. Discrimination has become more indirect and more complicated as a result. It has not been erased. The wage disparity between men and women has not narrowed as expected.

Ms Kirino, who before becoming a novelist was a university-educated office worker, believes that if the bubble economy had continued for 100 years, Japanese society's treatment of women would have matured to the point where it could not have been turned back. However, in the after-effects of the short bubble economy, Japan has faced drastic down-sizing, a high unemployment rate, and increases in the numbers of non-regular female workers and jobless youth. Now those people who had enjoyed the affluent bubble economy have had their dreams and desires popped—like a bubble. Women in their forties and fifties in particular, like Masako and her colleagues in *OUT*, have reached a hopeless impasse.

The long-standing family model comprising a regular worker husband and a full-time housewife has played out its historical role. To realize equal working conditions for men and women and a reconciliation of work and family life, we need not only legislation prohibiting sex discrimination, but also a new family relationship free from stereotypical expectations about women, that is based on the co-equal roles of both partners.

Part IV

Conclusion: A Cautionary Tale

15

A Woman's World: What if Care Work were Socialized and Police/Fire Protection Left to Individual Families?

RICHARD MICHAEL FISCHL*

I LOST IN TRANSLATION

A couple of summers ago, I was living in London and teaching a course on comparative labour and employment law to visiting American students. I was also finishing work on the first volume of INTELL essays—*Labour Law in an Era of Globalization*[1]—and decided to take the 'nigh completed manuscript for a test run, assigning it as a principal reading for the course. Judging from the quality of the final examinations, the students gained much from the book, and the experience of teaching my way through it benefited the editing process enormously. But my effort to mix scholarship and pedagogy had a difficult start.

A number of essays in the earlier collection presaged the themes of this book, emphasizing the division of work into the dichotomous realms of unpaid labour (intrafamilial 'care work' such as raising children, caring for elders, nursing the sick, and maintaining a household) and paid labour (more or less everything else, including care work done for families other than one's own); the role of law in creating and maintaining those dichotomous realms; and the untoward consequences for the increasing number of women (and not a few men) who struggle to straddle the divide and thus to square the demands of life in the paid labour market with the responsibilities of care work.[2]

* Earlier versions of this chapter were presented at the Sixth INTELL Conference in Catania, June 2002, and at the Annual Meeting of the Law & Society Association (Chicago, 2004); many thanks to the participants in those sessions for their thoughtful reactions. Special thanks to Rachel Arnow-Richman, Tom Baker, Mario Barnes, Susan Bisom-Rapp, Karl Klare, Tom Morawetz, Jeremy Paul, Susan Silbey, and Bert Westbrook for particularly insightful criticisms; to Joanne Conaghan, Pam Fischl, and Kerry Rittich for inspiration and encouragement; and of course to my students from whose engagement and scepticism the ideas presented here have benefited enormously.
[1] Conaghan, J., Fischl, R. M., and Klare, K. (eds.), *Labour Law in an Era of Globalization: Transformative Practices and Possibilities* (Oxford: OUP, 2002).
[2] See Conaghan, J., 'Women, Work, and Family: A British Revolution?'; Williams, L. A., 'Beyond Labour Law's Parochialism: A Re-envisioning of the Discourse of Redistribution'; Rittich, K., 'Feminization and Contingency: Regulating the Stakes of Work for Women'; and

As we explored the essays, a growing undercurrent of hostility emerged in class discussion. At the time, the reaction surprised me. In my experience, contemporary American law students are for the most part quite receptive to discrimination claims and to gender-equity claims in particular. I would therefore have expected the care-work material—focusing, as much of it did, on barriers to labour market participation faced primarily by women—to be uncontroversial among all but the most conservative participants.

In retrospect, however, perhaps I ought to have anticipated the disquiet the material in fact produced. Like many contemporary Americans, my students seem to value individual autonomy and free 'choice'—from the bedroom to the marketplace—at least as much as they oppose discrimination. And when discussion turned to the problems faced by working women, true to form many students in the summer class saw 'choice'— exercised in *both* the bedroom and the marketplace—as the simple and straightforward solution.[3]

Of course labour market participation and care work pull Americans in different directions, they acknowledged, but what is wrong with simply leaving it to individual couples to work out a division of paid and unpaid labour to suit their particular needs, talents, and preferences? The possibilities, the argument continued, are endless: a couple can choose to have (or not to have) children (as well as when to have them, how many, etc.); they can 'contract out' care work (to nannies, housekeepers, etc.) so that they can focus on their paid work careers—indeed, with the help of new reproductive technologies, they can even contract out gestation and birthing; alternatively, they can sacrifice a second income in order to secure the benefits of stay-at-home child-care; or they can 'have it all', with both partners participating in the paid labour market and adjusting outside work, child-care, and housework duties and schedules as they see fit.

The questionable assumptions undergirding this tidy little matrix did not go unremarked. In response to objections from a handful of students—and to a bit of Socratic prompting from the front of the room— the class considered some of the more salient choice-resistant constraints

Kraamwinkel, M., 'The Imagined European Community: Are Housewives European Citizens?'; in Conaghan et al., above, n. 1, chs. 3, 5, 6, 16.

[3] Despite the obvious tension between a celebration of choice and opposition to discrimination (see e.g. Epstein, R. A., *Forbidden Grounds: The Case Against Employment Discrimination Laws* (Cambridge, Mass.: Harvard University Press, 1995)), it's my sense that many Americans see anti-discrimination law as facilitating the market and lifestyle choices of would-be victims—rather than as restricting the choices of would-be discriminators—and accordingly experience their positions as quite consistent with one another. This would certainly help explain the way we embrace anti-discrimination norms even as we domesticate and commodify them. See Frank, T., *The Conquest of Cool* (Chicago: University of Chicago Press, 1997). But the underlying tension may also create opportunities for critical insight, a point to which I will briefly return at the close of the chapter.

that might come into play in the course of parenting: biology (despite precautions babies have an uncanny knack for showing up on their own schedule, and whether you want them or not); religious beliefs and philosophical commitments (the choice to terminate a pregnancy may be no choice at all for many couples); single parenthood (which is sometimes a 'chosen' condition but is frequently instead the product of death, divorce, or abandonment); reliable child-care (a constant challenge even in the best of circumstances); and, of course, financial wherewithal (with the decline of the 'family wage', an increasing number of middle-class families find that two incomes are a necessity, not a luxury, to say nothing of the plight of families living at or near poverty level).

But I could tell from the tenor of the discussion that I was preaching mostly to the faithful and getting nowhere fast with the majority of the class. A number of students expressed the view that we were subjecting an arena of personal choice and intimate relations to wholly inappropriate political analysis, and the prevailing reaction to my efforts to explore the various limits on parental choice was bluntly summed up by a particularly outspoken sceptic: 'Well, those constraints aren't likely to constrain *me*'.

'Just wait until you have kids of your own' is a line I long ago promised I would never use in public, lest my gradual transformation into the image and likeness of my parents be complete. Obviously, I needed a more convincing way to make the point and briefly considered a frontal attack on the ideology of choice itself.[4] But that seemed unwise in light of a second discomfiting development in the class dynamic. By this point, my students were provoked enough to read the assigned material in advance of class discussion—a positive development indeed, especially given the distractions of study abroad. But in doing so, they

---

[4] A substantial body of critical scholarship challenges that ideology by revealing that what we think of as 'choice' is the product of a complex interplay between freedom and coercion (see e.g. Hale, R., 'Coercion and Distribution in a Supposedly Non-coercive State', *Political Science Quarterly*, 38 (1923), 470); is frequently 'determined' rather than autonomous (see e.g. Kelman, M., *A Guide to Critical Legal Studies* (Cambridge, Mass.: Harvard University Press 1988), 126–41); and is sometimes simply not good for you (see e.g. Kennedy, D., 'Distributive and Paternalist Motives in Contract and Tort Law, with Special Reference to Compulsory Terms and Unequal Bargaining Power', *Maryland L. Review*, 41 (1982), 563). Some of the most trenchant recent critiques—focusing on a wide variety of ways in which real-world 'choosing' departs from our idealized images—have been developed by behavioural and second-generation law-and-economics scholars. See e.g. Sunstein, C. R., 'Human Behavior and the Law of Work', *Virginia L. Review*, 87 (2001), 205 (collecting sources and discussing the literature). The ideology of choice has a more ambiguous relationship with contemporary American feminism. On the one hand, political activists have frequently cast their arguments favouring such causes as reproductive rights and labour market participation in the rhetoric of 'freedom of choice'. At the same time, this strategy has been subject to critical scrutiny by feminist scholars who have explored the role of choice discourse in replicating and reinforcing patriarchy. See e.g. Schultz, V., 'Telling Stories About Women and Work: Judicial Interpretations of Sex Segregation in the Workplace in Title VII Cases Raising the Lack of Interest Argument', *Harvard L. Review*, 103 (1990), 1749.

encountered material they liked even less than they did all the talk about care work and unpaid labour.

In the best tradition of American critical legal studies, a number of the essays in *Labour Law in an Era of Globalization* forthrightly take what Duncan Kennedy has described as a 'distributive' approach to the study of law and legal institutions,[5] and it may well be that the principal ideological success of the Reagan-Gingrich-Bush rightward lurch in US politics has been to move any talk of 'distribution'—and particularly talk of *re*-distribution—outside the boundaries of legitimate discourse. Judging from my own classroom experience, deploying the D-word (let alone the R-word) seems naively 'retro' (a mortal sin among students who are plainly tired of hearing about the good old days) and in any event flies in the face of the now conventional wisdom that redistribution kills the goose that lays the golden egg of economic prosperity.

Ironically, the provocation for what I now think of as 'the July rebellion'—oh, the perils of exposing Americans to British rule during the summer months—was an essay that offered a thoughtful defence of free trade while arguing forcefully for a trade regime that would reduce the incentives for individual nations to seek comparative advantage by lowering domestic labour standards.[6] The essay unabashedly favoured a modest redistribution of wealth from developed to developing countries, but the students who could no longer contain their rage at the Red Flag of Redistribution may have missed the point that this was offered by the author as a potential benefit of trade *de*regulation, not as a policy to be pursued via the visible hand of some utopian global government. Yet it was too late for such nuances, and the class would suffer in surly silence no longer. 'All this talk about redistribution,' one student angrily proclaimed. 'Are you and all your labour law friends communists or what?'

I was eventually able to clarify the point about the supposed virtues of free trade for developing nations, but the outburst left me on perilous ground in my efforts to challenge the role of 'choice' as we continued our discussion of the problem of unpaid labour. So I reached into my pedagogical bag of tricks in search of that handy rhetorical device that, when properly deployed, can at once change the subject and make a point effectively: the analogy. What I wanted was an illustration that could

---

[5] For examples of the offending materials, see Klare, K., 'The Horizons of Transformative Labour and Employment Law', and Williams, L., 'Beyond Labour Law's Parochialism: A Re-envisioning of the Discourse of Redistribution', in Conaghan et al., above, n. 1, chs. 1, 5. On the 'distributive' approach to the study of law more generally, see Kennedy, D., *A Critique of Adjudication (fin de siècle)* (Cambridge, Mass.: Harvard University Press 1997), 65–9.

[6] See Langille, B., 'Seeking Post-Seattle Clarity—and Inspiration', in Conaghan et al., above, n. 1, ch. 7.

reframe the debate to bring into view the decidedly *un*chosen dimension of care work; to highlight the public/social (as opposed to merely private/individual) costs and benefits of such work; and to shift the debate back to the safer terrain of anti-discrimination norms by exploring the distributive implications of the fact that care work is gendered as well as unpaid.

Nice work if you can get it—paid or not, I suppose—but my first effort along those lines was not exactly a success. Long ago, I learned that there is nothing more dangerous in the classroom context than an analogy you haven't thought through carefully, and for me that means writing it out (or at least outlining it) in order to figure out whether and how well it works. No analogy is perfect, of course, and half the fun is poking holes, but I prefer going into class already knowing where to find most of the holes, and I would rather not find myself surprised by a complete unravelling in mid-presentation. I should therefore have thought long and hard about the analogy I selected, especially given that open warfare had quite nearly broken out in my class.

Instead, I rashly cited the first analogy that came to mind: national defence. To highlight the social benefits of care work, I wanted an example of a 'public good'—some uncontroversially important public service that the usual market mechanisms are unlikely to provide—and national defence is a tried and true classic of the genre. As I began to spin out a point I had made many times in other contexts (if you protect your house from nuclear attack, the chances are the house next door will be protected too, etc.), it occurred to me that the question of how to pay for the *labour* costs of national defence offered an intriguing parallel to the care work problem. I played with that notion a bit, exploring the distributive implications of providing military labour via the draft (where the human and financial costs are spread throughout the society via universal conscription) versus the volunteer army (where financial costs are shared by the society as a whole but the human costs are paid largely by the working class and the poor). I was about to draw some explicit contrasts and comparisons with care work when I realized that most of the class had stopped listening, utterly outraged by my seemingly casual support for conscription over voluntary service and now convinced that their worst suspicions about my politics had been confirmed. My effort to change the subject had thus fuelled the fires of controversy rather than providing critical distance; indeed, for this audience, my analogy hadn't changed the subject all.[7]

---

[7] As it happens, the July rebellion took place two months before Sept. 11, in the aftermath of which the funding of national defence—and the prospect of a revived draft—have become more familiar topics in American politics. It is possible that the 'war on terrorism' has made those of a certain age more receptive to the possibility of a draft, though at the time of writing it is equally possible that the multiplying disasters associated with the

Rioting students do have a way of concentrating the professorial mind, and that night I sought refuge in the Last Resort of Desperate Legal Academics: a hypothetical ('when reality just won't do the job'). A soul-searching and enormously enlightening conversation with my wife Pam produced the thought experiment—a world in which care work is social-ized and protective services (carried out against attack, robbery, fire, etc.) are not—that comprises the remainder of this chapter.

I call it 'A Woman's World', and the title refers to the eponymous television advertising campaign mounted a while back by a world-famous athletic shoe manufacturer and featuring a series of vignettes that present ostensibly humorous gender-role reversals. In one spot, a group of apparently close female friends are gathered in a living room watching a sporting event on television, utterly oblivious to both the noise and the mess they are making, as a beleaguered house-husband replenishes their drinks and cleans up after them. In another—this one set in a bar, the prominently displayed name of which is an obvious phallic reference—rowdy female patrons leer and grope at scantily clad male waiters. In yet another, extremely fit women doing strenuous workouts in a health club strike poses of amused superiority as a lone male arrives and clumsily drops his water bottle, falls off a treadmill, etc.

Not to put too fine a point on it, the vignettes were more plausibly understood as apology than as critique. Although the parodied male practices were not exactly glorified, the suggestion that 'a woman's world' would look an awful lot like the present one was difficult to ignore. Indeed, that message reflects an understanding of American feminism—that is, as interest group pleading in the context of a zero-sum contest between genders—which is evident in many popular treatments and not a few scholarly ones. I appreciate that I run the risk of reinforcing that understanding by my use of the quoted title, but I trust it will be clear from the rest of the chapter that the target of this critique is the game itself and not merely its current distributive consequences.

II A WOMAN'S WORLD

What if life in the USA were reversed in the following way: what if 'care work' (child-care, elder-care, care of the infirm, etc.) were provided by the state, and individuals and families were left to fend for themselves

second Iraq war will produce the opposite effect. Indeed, the unwillingness of either major-party candidate in the American Presidential election in 2004 to acknowledge even the pos-sibility that a renewed draft might be necessary to satisfy existing (let alone potential) military commitments—particularly with both candidates eager to portray themselves as unwavering proponents of American military strength—would seem to confirm that the political 'third rail' I touched in the summer class retains its charge.

with respect to police and fire protection? Here is one version of what life in such a world might be like.

Caring centres: the nanny state reconceived

In the place of police and fire stations, imagine 'caring centres' in every town—and, in larger cities, in every neighbourhood—where working parents leave their pre-school children and their ageing and/or infirm relatives for state-funded care during the course of the workday. The caring centres are a source of long-term relatively stable employment; staffing them is 'blue-collar' work, but high-status blue-collar work and decently paid as well. Indeed, in most jurisdictions, care staff are unionized and also enjoy civil service protection.

Naturally, there is a long tradition of gender segregation in these jobs; even today, most caring centre workers are women, a tradition reinforced by a common practice of daughters following their mothers into this occupation, sometimes dutifully but often with a fierce sense of family pride. Historically, men did not even apply for these positions; indeed, in the world of our thought experiment, historically men refrained from engaging in most kinds of paid work, but more on that in a moment.

As part of a gender-equity revolution that began in the 1960s, men did begin seeking care staff positions, but they were typically turned away by managers who held firm to the view that men were just 'not suited' to this line of work. Referring in particular to child-care, a frequently heard joke was that 'men have a role to play in reproduction, but it's not *this*.'

The brave few men who gained early entry into caring centre work were commonly subjected to a variety of forms of harassment at the hands of their female colleagues. Thus, male workers would find dirty diapers in their lockers; they would find themselves relegated to the most difficult and distasteful tasks (like pushing strollers and staffing the changing tables); and they were frequently the target of crude and suggestive comments from co-workers—as well as anonymous notes and postings on centre bulletin boards—slyly referring to or even graphically depicting their 'proper' role in reproduction.

What's more, women workers in caring centres—like other female civil servants—have long enjoyed a 'pregnancy preference', enabling those who have lost time in the workforce due to childbearing to jump the seniority queue and bump the childless from their jobs in the event of reductions in force. Between baby booms, men—even those who have served on care staff for some time—have almost invariably been the first to go with each round of layoffs. An infamous Supreme Court decision from the late 1970s upheld this practice against a sex discrimination claim on the ground that the challenged preference was 'by its very terms based on pregnancy, not sex'.[8]

Men's work

Quite apart from suffering the indignity of the occasional 'clueless' judicial decision, men in the world of our thought experiment live lives largely consumed by providing protective services for their families—the modern equivalent of (the classic American film star), John Wayne, leading the wagon train through the Wild West. For men of virtually every class and station, much of the day is spent ensuring the safety of their families and homes.

Informal networks of men form neighbourhood watch groups that protect against assaults, burglaries, and home invasions, and fires are frequently fought by men working bucket brigades. As part of the daily routine, most men escort their wives to the office and their children to school or caring centres. Typically, their presence is enough to deter attacks, but occasionally men are called upon to repel would-be attackers with physical force. Although the beneficiaries make a fuss on Father's Day or after a particularly difficult encounter, this work is for the most part taken for granted by family members in a hurry to get on with their daily activities. Political consultants in the 1990s paid homage to the electoral importance of these mostly upper-middle-class suburban men when they coined the term 'sock-him dads' to describe the demographic and the all-too-frequent occasions in which fisticuffs (or worse) were required to secure safe passage.

Historically, of course, this work was so consuming that it was immensely difficult for men to venture into the market for paid work, and women were accordingly the primary breadwinners for many families. To be sure, working-class and poor families who needed a second income to make ends meet did not have the luxury of a full-time 'stay-at-home dad', but decently paid jobs for men were scarce, and substitutes for the protective care of absent fathers could be awfully hard to come by.

The plight of the urban poor was especially dire. Facing the dual challenge of gender and racial discrimination in the paid labour market, the best that many inner city men of colour could do was to find work providing full-time protective services for middle- and upper-class white families, earning marginal pay and virtually no benefits. On the other hand, certain cultural practices gave extended African-American and Hispanic families and other close-knit inner city communities some advantages

---

[8] Cf. *General Electric Co.* v. *Gilbert*, 429 US 125 (1976).

in dealing with their plight; in some cases, for example, grandfathers were able to take on the protective role for their children's families, and in some neighbourhoods enterprising fathers would charge for taking other families under their protective wing even as they took care of their own. But in working poor families of all ethnicities, wives and children all too frequently had to fend for themselves.

A brief history of the gender equity revolution

In a now familiar story, the barriers that rich and poor men alike faced in entering the market for paid work broke down in three stages in the latter half of the twentieth century.

Stage One: confronting overt and intentional gender discrimination

In the 1950s and 1960s, for a host of economic and social reasons, men increasingly sought entry into the paid workforce, but found themselves confronted by gender stereotypes that made employers reluctant to hire them for many jobs, especially those on the professional or managerial track. The prevailing view among employers—largely a reflection of the dominant views in the society as a whole—was that men were simply 'designed', by nature or by Providence, for the protection of their families and not for employment outside the home. Indeed, the very characteristics that made men successful in performing their protective duties—their physical strength, their fierce protective instincts and quick temper—rendered them unsuitable for most paid work. All those fights just made them too competitive and aggressive for most employment settings, the dominant view went, and they would not perform well in contexts where teamwork and a high value on relationships were the keys to success.

The equality revolution of the 1960s and 1970s eventually broke down the formal barriers, and in this the men were unwitting beneficiaries of a last-minute effort to defeat the Civil Rights Act of 1964 by adding 'sex' to the list of prohibited bases for discrimination, a gambit that opponents of racial equality wrongly thought would be utterly unpalatable ('surely they'll draw the line at being forced to work shoulder to shoulder with *men*').

Stage Two: structural barriers and wealth disparities

Armed with the legal right to equal opportunity in the workplace, men entered the paid workforce in unprecedented numbers in the 1970s and 1980s, but faced many obstacles that were all but invisible to their female colleagues. Because it still fell mostly to men to keep their homes secure and to get children and spouses safely to and from their daily destinations, men frequently arrived late to work and departed early, prompting employers to conclude that they were 'just not serious about their jobs' and engendering hostility in female colleagues on whom it fell to handle the neglected tasks. Likewise, men would be called away from the office unexpectedly during the day to tend to various emergencies, and more than occasionally they would show up for work in the morning utterly exhausted from a night of fighting a hostile gang or a nearby fire.

Predictably, these burdens fell more heavily on men from families of more modest means because wealthier families were able to 'contract out' their protective services and relieve men of those responsibilities—usually, as suggested earlier, by hiring men of colour from inner cities. In a related development, many families in wealthy suburbs and highbrow urban neighborhoods recruited handsome young European men to provide protective services, sowing the seeds of marital discord when some wives suddenly began to demonstrate an intense but previously undisclosed interest in what was going on at home.

As more men undertook paid work, the market responded to the resulting need for protective services, and private protection firms began popping up, particularly in large urban areas. Long queues to engage the services of such firms were not unusual, nor were exorbitant prices for those who succeeded in retaining them. A series of scandals involving protection firm employees with criminal histories—as well as firms too understaffed to respond effectively to calls for assistance—produced a public outcry for regulation, resulting in a flood of legislation (and not a few criminal prosecutions) in the late 1980s and early 1990s.

Somewhat surprisingly, working-class men—whose families were almost invariably priced out of the private protection firm market—were at first unable to persuade their labour unions to take their plight seriously. Female union officials patiently explained that 'the size of the paycheck is what our members care the most about' (as if 'our members' referred exclusively to people who didn't have families to protect) and that the union could not afford to take on 'luxury' issues like the provision of family-protective services for working men (as if protecting a family from fire and other physical danger were a 'luxury'). Likewise, unions and employers alike were slow to see the need for health insurance policies that covered injuries sustained by employees in the course of their protective endeavours. 'The employees who receive these injuries do so on their own time, and—as much as we sympathize with their plight—there is simply no connection to their work for us', went the conventional wisdom; analogies to pregnancy benefits for women, long covered by virtually all employers, went unheeded.

By the latter part of this period, though, the demographics of organized labour in the USA had changed in significant ways. A sharp decline in both employment and union density in traditionally female occupations was accompanied by a substantial increase in union representation among men in various pink-collar and lower-level blue-collar jobs. Accordingly, the politics of organized labour began to change as well, and by the early 1990s, 'protective services for working families' was high on the list of demands at every bargaining table.

Stage Three: the decline of career employment and changing social mores

In the late 1990s, men continued their accelerating entry into the paid labour market, but the decline of 'career' employment and the emergence of 'new work forms' created special problems for them. 'Flexibility'—the rage among corporate consultants and human resource management specialists—was fine for many women (especially younger ones without families) who could move easily from job to job, focusing like a laser beam on 'upgrading their human capital'. But high-velocity labour markets provided enormous practical challenges for men who had substantial protective responsibilities and for whom predictability and stability in the paid workplace were at a premium.

At the same time, sociologists began to note the sizeable (albeit mostly middle- and upper-class) population of men who chose to 'stay at home' rather than entering the paid labour market. When surveyed, many of the men reported that they found protective work extremely fulfilling and had little interest in the 'rat race' of paid employment. Others stated the belief that there was no higher calling than 'protecting one's family' and were content to put off paid careers, at least until the children were grown and able to attend to such matters on their own.

Indeed, many men were proud of the sacrifices they made and deeply resented the suggestion that protecting one's family was somehow less important than an office job. It was an all too common experience for such men to encounter a raised eyebrow or a thoughtless remark when they revealed to others—and especially to ambitious young professionals of either gender—that they were staying at home. More than one highly educated man—who might easily have succeeded in a well-paying career but who chose instead to focus on his family's protection—was heard to respond, 'But I thought that choice was what the whole gender-equity movement was about! Why aren't *my* choices valued?' (The social slights and resulting defensiveness were a two-way street, of course, and men who worked outside the home—either by choice or by force of circumstance—frequently found themselves the target of insensitive and even snide remarks about the peril their absence created for their families.)

Non-traditional families—single parents, gay and lesbian couples, communes of various sizes and configurations—were usually ignored (when they were lucky) or demonized (when they weren't) during family protection debates, just as they were ignored or demonized during arguments about other 'family' issues. Yet in the wake of the Supreme Court decision famously striking down American anti-sodomy laws, the movement in support of same-sex marriage gained a great deal of attention and some legal ground as well. News stories about the lives of and challenges faced by same-sex couples abounded, and a survey reported by the *New York Times* in early 2004 revealed that lesbian couples with children were more likely than their heterosexual and gay male counterparts to have 'traditional' parenting relationships, with one parent serving in the 'breadwinner' role and the other providing stay-at-home protection.[9] There was a lively debate about whether that trend was the result of choices born of economic advantage (even by this time, women still earned considerably more than their male counterparts in the paid workforce), of the fact that lesbian couples were already more accustomed to living lives outside the boundaries established by traditional gender stereotypes, or of some combination of those and other factors.

But in most families, gay or straight—and in virtually all working-class and poor families—two incomes were a necessity, not a luxury, and accordingly in a substantial majority of families two spouses did paid work, with the result that protective work was handled by some combination of 'contracting out' and making do. And in most families, it was the man who did the making do.

To be sure, this development was offset somewhat by the assistance that some men were beginning to receive at home from their spouses. Although the trend—the subject of frequent human interest stories in various lifestyle publications—always looked better on paper than it did in practice, survey data confirmed that women were indeed beginning to take on a share of protective work. Corporate America took notice of the trend as well, from elite companies that began developing 'family friendly' workplace policies (such as subsidizing the costs of hiring private protection firms and providing time off for women as well as men with protective work responsibilities) to national fast-food chains that began installing gun-cleaning 'stations' in women's restrooms. The extent of the share was always a bone of contention, though, and nothing would send a gathering of men into paroxysms of laughter more quickly than someone's spot-on imitation of a clueless wife: 'Honey, where do we keep that fire hose again?'

Protective services, politics, and public policy

In the world of our thought experiment, it isn't difficult to imagine the eventual emergence of a political movement among men (and of

---

[9] Cf. Bellafante, G., 'Two Fathers, with One Happy to Stay at Home,' *New York Times*, 12 Jan. 2004, A1.

course some women) in support of turning a significant share of protective services over to the state; or of subsidizing such services via a system of employer and/or publicly funded insurance; or of reorganizing paid work in ways that eased the burdens on protective care providers; or of proceeding on multiple fronts at once.

Nor is it difficult to imagine the arguments that would likely emerge in opposition to such measures: it is not fair to saddle either employers or the state (that is, taxpayers) with the cost of providing a public subsidy for those whose needs are entirely a product of their own private and personal choices; indeed, no one forces men to have families and, if they have them, no one forces them to take on the resulting protective work by themselves. Nor is the fact that so many parents choose to provide their own protection a reason for regret, for no one can do so better than a caring father—or, with increasing frequency, a caring couple—and the notion that police and fire protection might be effectively provided by the faceless bureaucratic state is fanciful at best.

III AFTERWORD

Back to the real world for a moment, where the notion of socialized police and fire service doesn't seem so fanciful at all. To be sure, in the USA and elsewhere, a host of troubles attend the state provision of police services, among them the same sort of wealth disparities in the availability of such services imagined in the thought experiment. Although fire services fare somewhat better in this respect, I do not for a moment mean to suggest (as some readers of an earlier draft surmised) that we ought to follow the police/fire model for care work and thus immediately begin the construction of state-run 'caring centres' in every neighbourhood; indeed, my point is not to suggest any particular solution to the problem of unpaid care work at all. A growing body of thoughtful and promising scholarship is already taking on that task; witness the other contributions in this volume, as well as recent symposia on the topic appearing in US law journals.[10] By contrast, the point of this contribution is not so much to solve the problem of unpaid care work as it is to help us see it as a problem in the first place.

If the thought experiment succeeds in this quest, it does so by bringing to the foreground the social and structural dimensions of work that we tend to think of as either natural (we'll call that 'the traditionalist view') or personal and chosen (we'll call that 'the modernist view'). As the

[10] See 'Symposium: Law, Labor, and Gender', *Maine L. Review*, 55 (2003), 1–333; 'Symposium on the Structures of Care Work', *Chicago-Kent L. Review*, 76 (2001), 1389–992.

thought experiment reminds us, providing protective services through the state—and care work through individuals and families—is no more the 'natural' product of a world in which women alone have the physical capacity to gestate than the reversal of fortunes imagined in our thought experiment would be the 'natural' product of a world in which men may have a greater physical capacity than women to do some of the more familiar kinds of protective work. The current provision of care work, like the current provision of police and fire protection, is a matter of social convention—a product of history, politics, and culture rather than biology.

To be sure, that doesn't make it easy to change; deeply rooted social structures may be quite nearly as immutable as 'natural' ones. Nor does that mean that our current social practices are wrong. One cannot study American law, even labour law, and fail to develop a healthy appreciation for the 'collective wisdom and experience' sometimes embodied in social structures and institutions. But it does mean that we cannot pin our current predicament on nature, and—in the face of gender and economic inequities of the sort highlighted by the thought experiment—we ought therefore to take the call for re-examination and critique quite seriously.

If the traditionalist view seems unfashionably essentialist, the modernist view clearly has some force: care work *is* intensely personal and frequently 'chosen'. Yet as the thought experiment suggests, our choices are shaped and constrained in countless ways by social, political, and economic structures that we take utterly for granted—structures that are, in day-to-day life, virtually invisible—and those structures are all but impervious to individual choice. At the same time, care work provides a 'public good'—one no less vital than police and fire protection—on which not only immediate family members but also employers, communities, and society as a whole 'free ride'. The question therefore is not whether care work ought to be 'subsidized'; like the protective work in the thought experiment, it is already subsidized by the unpaid labour of those who provide it. The question, rather, is *how* it ought to be subsidized, and accordingly questions of gender as well economic equity—questions put into stark relief by the thought experiment—are fair game for consideration and inquiry.

The power of the thought experiment, of course, depends in no small measure on whether the reversal of protective work and care work seems plausible, and not for the first time a law professor can summon a bit of reality to support a classroom hypothetical. In a world of 'gated communities', for-profit prisons, private security guards, and—to cite the latest contribution of US foreign policy to world peace and humane governance—for-hire interrogation services, it isn't difficult to imagine a privatization of protective work along the lines sketched out in the thought experiment. Likewise, in the USA we already socialize care work for children aged five and above—and are doing so increasingly for younger children as well—through our system of public education. (That schools are both learning *and* caring centres will be clear to any over-committed parent who has forgotten until late Sunday night that Monday is a school holiday; facing that predicament, a parent's first thought is decidedly not, 'Oh, my, what can we do to make sure that Molly learns something tomorrow?') Semi-socialized care for the elderly and infirm, in the form of state or church-supported convalescent homes and, more recently, 'day care' centres, is not uncommon either. In other words, then, the world of privatized protection and socialized care work described in the thought experiment is not unimaginably different from the world in which we already find ourselves.

Less plausible, perhaps, is the notion that a reversal of traditional gender roles would lead to 'a woman's world' rather than simply a different sort of patriarchy. A world in which men stayed home to do protective work might, after all, be a world in which protective work rather than paid labour was treated as the centrepiece of civil society. This point is chillingly suggested in a short story by Margaret Atwood in which men have taken over the kitchen, banishing women to the office and factory.[11] As Atwood observes of her imagined world: 'A man's status in the community was now displayed by the length of his carving knives, by how many of them he had and how sharp he kept them, and by whether they were plain or ornamented with gold and precious jewels'.[12]

Substitute 'hunting' for 'carving' and it isn't difficult to fathom the relevance of that passage to the world of our thought experiment as well. Perhaps we should not be so quick to dismiss the traditionalist view that nature has a not-so-invisible hand in all of this, although before succumbing to the temptations of that sort of essentialism we ought to recall the sharp retort offered by Katherine Hepburn's Rose Thayer to Humphrey Bogart's Charlie Allnut in *The African Queen*: 'Nature, Mr Allnut, is what we are put in this world to rise above'.[13] Indeed, the possibility that patriarchy runs deeper than the social, economic, and cultural structures of care work seems to me to confirm rather than undermine the pressing need to change the way we think about work and gender alike.

Which brings us back to the classroom where our story began and where the thought experiment received its first public hearing. Truth be

[11] See, Atwood, M., 'Simmering', in S. Thomas (ed.), *Wild Women: Contemporary Short Stories by Women Celebrating Women* (Woodstock, NY: The Overlook Press 1994), 59–61. I am extremely grateful to Rachel Arnow-Richman for bringing this story to my attention.
[12] Ibid., at 60.   [13] *The African Queen* (United Artists, 1951).

told, I don't think it had much effect on the leaders of the July rebellion, though they liked the funny parts and seemed impressed by the fact I had gone to so much trouble to address their arguments. (For the record, I was likewise impressed by their efforts to engage mine and am happy to report that they received some of the highest marks that summer on the anonymously graded final.) At the other end of the spectrum, the handful of students who were already receptive to the critique of unpaid care work responded enthusiastically—some of them literally bouncing in their seats as I spun out the thought experiment—though I'm not sure I opened any minds there either.

But for the rest of the class—a substantial group in the middle—the thought experiment seemed from the ensuing discussions to have had its intended effect. The strategy of 'putting the shoe on the other foot' enabled many to see a problem of gender equity where they had previously seen only an arena of personal and individual choice, confirming for me the utility of deploying one widely shared contemporary norm against another in an effort to prompt students to think more critically about both.

Index

ACTU, *see* Australian Council of Trade Unions
AFDC, *see* Aid to Families with Dependent Children
AWA, *see* Australian Workplace Agreement
Aid to Families with Dependent Children 200, 206–9
Amsterdam Treaty 99
annualized hours 109, 118, 119
anti-discrimination law
  Act on Equal Treatment and Equal Opportunity (Hungary) 308
  Australia 92–7, 238–9, 255–6
  Japan 184, 186, 191–2, 317–18, 321, 323–7, 333, 334–6
  UK 31, 105, 121
  see also gender-based discrimination
arbitration 81–2, 85, 237
Atwood, Margaret 353
atypical workers 90–1, 177, 301, 320
  see also casual workers; contingent workers; non-regular work/workers; non-standard work/workers; peripheral workers
Australian Council of Trade Unions 237, 240, 246, 250
Australian Workplace Agreement 93

BIG, *see* Basic Income Grant (South Africa)
bargaining power 72, 116–17, 150, 158, 166–8
Basic Income Grant (South Africa) 210–11
Berns, Sandra 81, 85–7, 94
breadwinner 195
  see also breadwinner/homemaker model; harvester man; male breadwinner
breadwinner/homemaker model 80–1, 82–6, 88, 92, 96–7, 218–20, 350
  see also breadwinner; harvester man; male breadwinner
British Workplace Employee Relations Survey 118

CEDAW, *see* Convention on the Elimination of All Forms of Discrimination Against Women
CEE, *see* Central and East European Countries
Canadian Supreme Court 174
capitalism 263
care/caregiving work 26, 30, 40, 55, 56, 74, 139–40, 197–205, 209–12, 312–13, 339–40, 344–6, 352–3
  see also child-care; childrearing; parental leave
casual workers 90–1, 102, 104, 108, 251–2, 254, 301, 320–1
  Parental Leave (Casuals) Test Case 251
  see also atypical workers; contingent workers; non-regular work/workers; non-standard work/workers; peripheral workers
Central and East European countries 289, 292, 302, 304
  see also Labour Code (CEE)
child-care 57, 70, 113–14, 152–3, 160, 161, 174, 197, 213, 221–2, 226, 230, 235, 238–9, 290, 291, 292–3, 298, 307, 309, 312–13, 318, 327, 340
  see also care/caregiving work; childrearing; parental leave
childrearing 263
  see also care/caregiving work; child-care; parental leave
Chodorow, Nancy 221–2
citizenship 27, 41, 148
Civil War (USA) 200
collective agreements 93, 94, 118, 125, 134, 244, 249
  see also collective bargaining; workplace bargaining
collective bargaining 94, 102, 103, 104, 118, 213
  see also collective agreements; workplace bargaining
collective *laissez-faire* 21
commodification/recommodification 55, 60, 71, 127, 145, 147, 149–51, 152, 155–6, 220
  see also decommodification